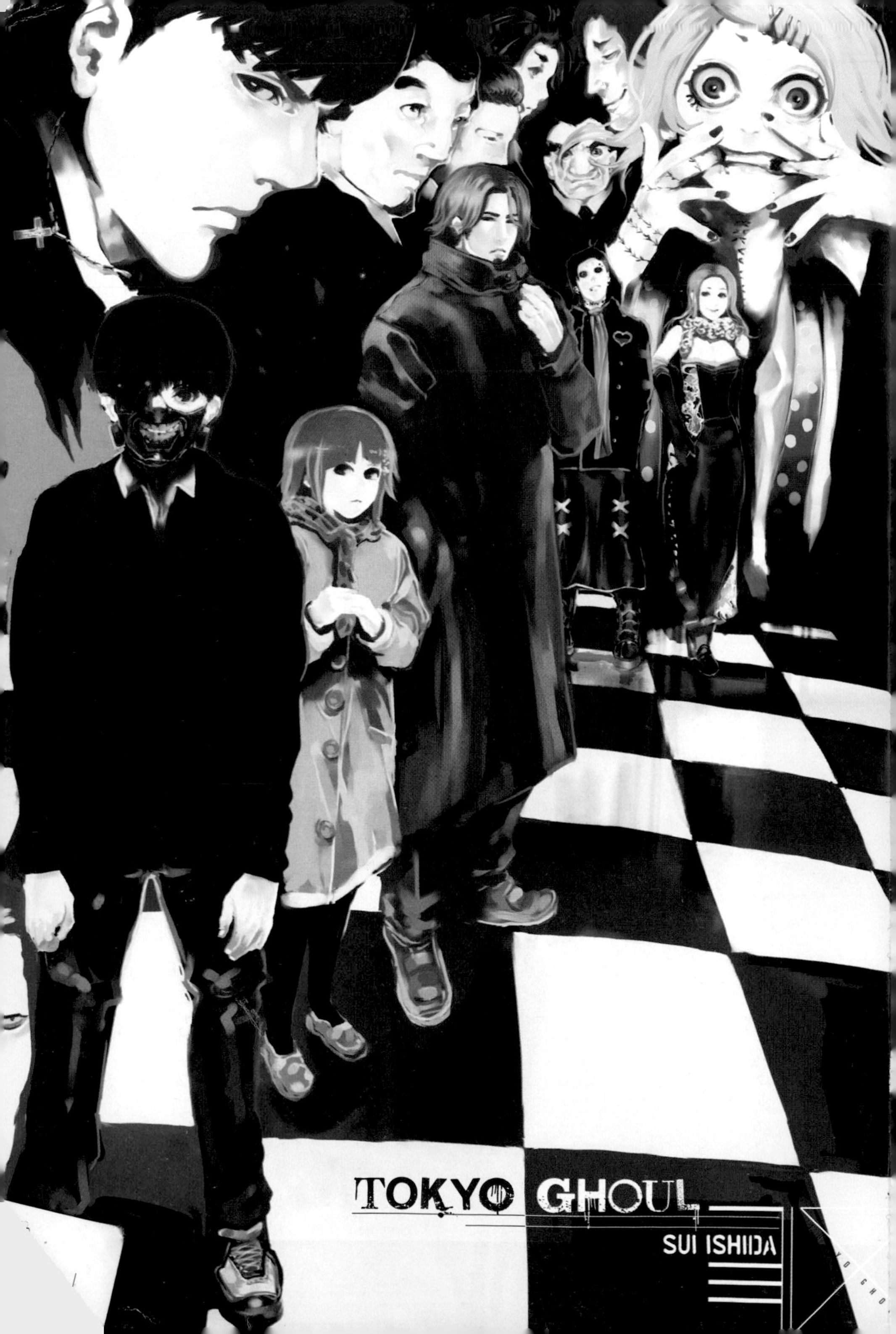
TOKYO GHOUL
SUI ISHIDA

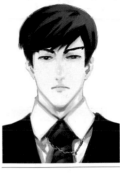

**KOTARO AMON**

亜門鋼太朗（アモン コウタロウ）

**BORN** April 7th Aries

Graduated Ghoul Investigator Training Academy (Head of the Class)
CCG Main Office Rank 1 Investigator

**BLOOD-TYPE:** A

**Size:** 191 cm 94 kg FEET 28.0 CM

**Likes:** Working out, investigating, sweets (donuts, etc.)

**Interests:** Rabbit, Eye-patch Ghoul

**Quinque:** Dojima ½: Kokaku
A heavy, club-shaped Quinque. A memento of a friend and Academy classmate. Destroyed by Kaneki and currently under repair.

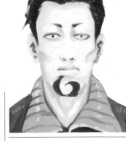

**KAZUICHI BANJO**

万丈数壱（バンジョウ カズイチ）

**BORN** October 11th Libra

Former 11th Ward leader

**BLOOD-TYPE:** A B

**Size:** 187 cm 92 kg FEET 28.5 cm

**Likes:** Rize, his Ghoul subordinates, strength

**Weaknesses:** Life-or-death situations, reading and writing, bu

**Rc Type:** ?

**SUI ISHIDA** was born in Fukuoka, Japan. He is the author of ***Tokyo Ghoul*** and several ***Tokyo Ghoul*** one-shots, including one that won him second place in the *Weekly Young Jump* 113th Grand Prix award in 2010. ***Tokyo Ghoul*** began serialization in *Weekly Young Jump* in 2011 and was adapted into an anime series in 2014.

東京喰種

TOKYO GHOUL

TOKYO GHOUL

SUI ISHIDA

TOKYO GHOUL

sui ishida

TOKYO GHOUL

TOKYO GHOUL

6

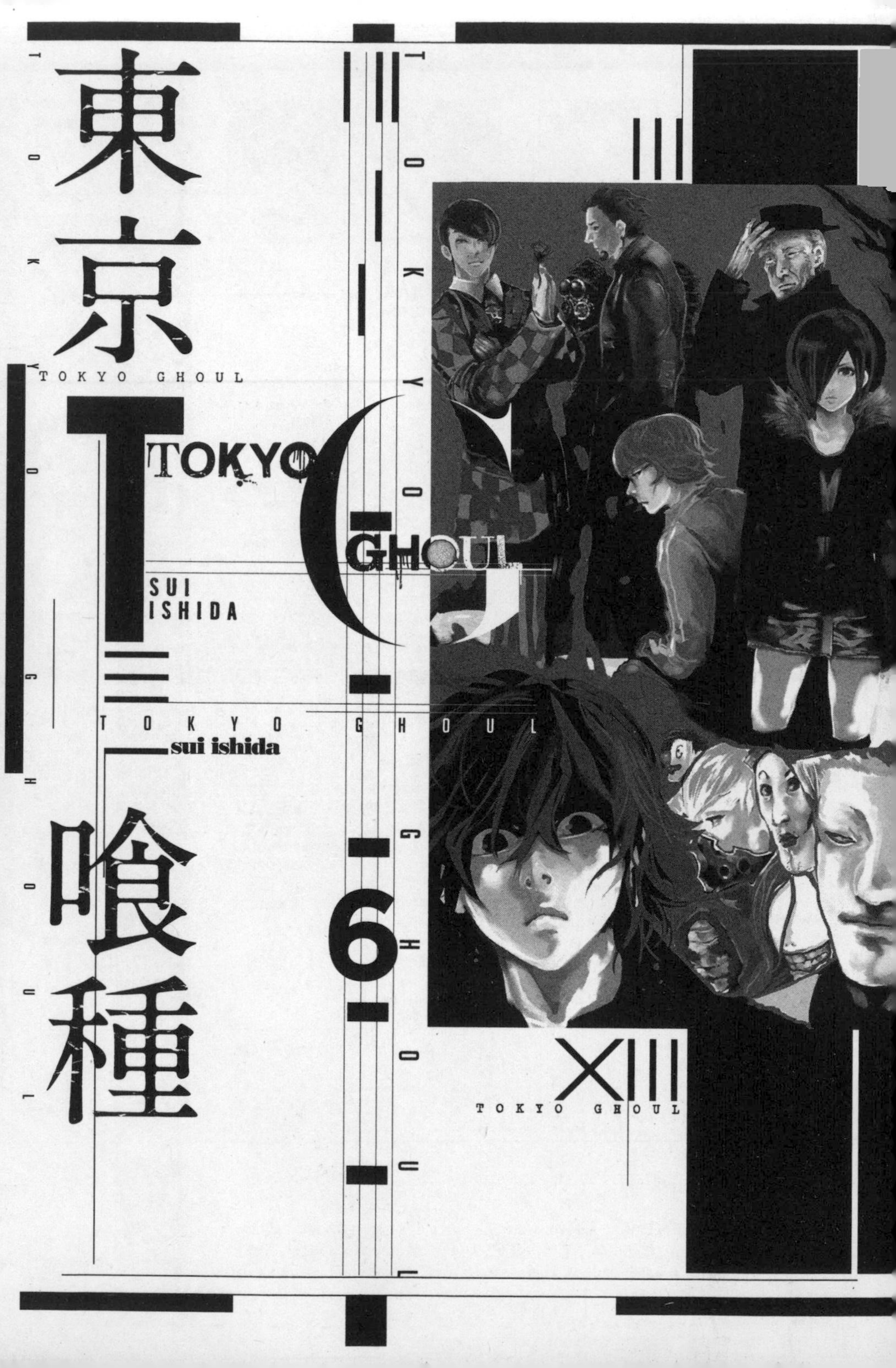

XIII

TOKYO GHOUL

# TOKYO GHOUL SO FAR

## ANTEIKU

The café where Ghouls gather. Known for their slow-brewed coffee. Has many human fans as well. Helping each other is the Ghouls motto.

20TH WARD

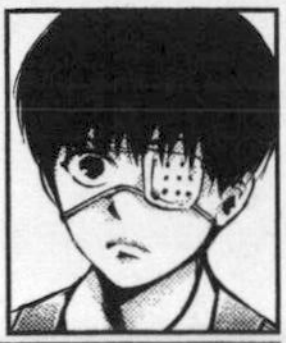

**KEN KANEKI (KANEKI)**

An ordinary young man with a fondness for literature who meets with an accident and has Rize's organs transplanted into him. Becomes a half-Ghoul. Struggling to find his place in the world.

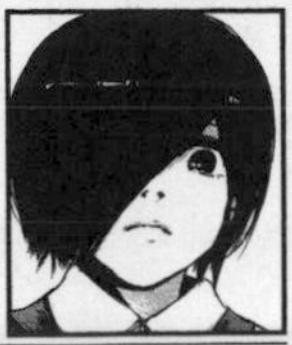

**TOUKA KIRISHIMA (TOUKA)**

A conflicted heroine with two sides, rage and kindness. Longs to become human. Hates Investigators…?

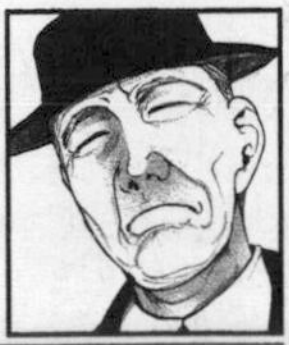

**YOSHIMURA (MANAGER)**

The owner of Anteiku. Guides Kaneki so he can live as a Ghoul. Often works with Yomo. Shrouded by mystery.

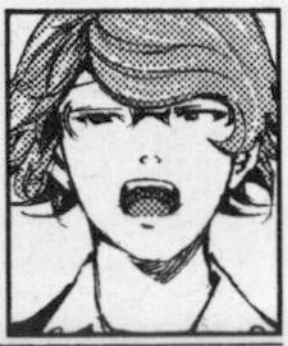

**NISHIKI NISHIO (NISHIKI)**

A 2nd-year at Kaneki's university. Adept at blending into human society. Eats *taiyaki* with no difficulty.

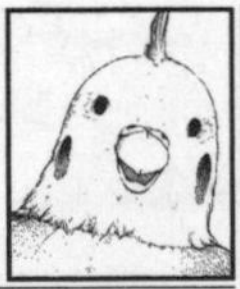

**HETARE**

A parakeet Hinami found. Basically only says "Hetare."

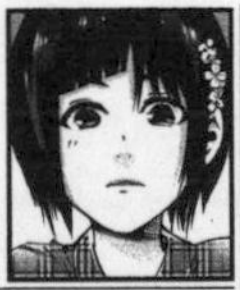

**HINAMI FUEGUCHI (HINAMI)**

An orphan whose parents were killed by the CCG. Displays tremendous power when she is awakened. Living with Touka.

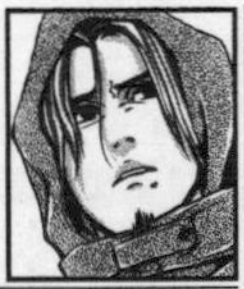

**RENJI YOMO (YOMO)**

Does not appear out in the open that often. Frequently works with Yoshimura. Concerned about Kaneki's condition.

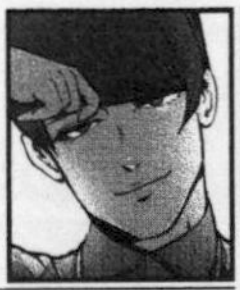

**SHU TSUKIYAMA**

A Gourmet who seeks the taste of the unknown. Obsessed with Kaneki, who is a half-Ghoul.

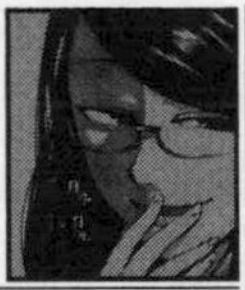

**RIZE KAMISHIRO DECEASED (RIZE)**

A freewheeling Binge Eater who despised boredom. Previously lived in the 11th Ward. Meets Kaneki in the 20th Ward and then has an accident. There are rumors she used an alias to hide her true identity.

## [GHOUL]

A creature that appears human yet consumes humans. The top of the food chain. Finds anything other than humans and coffee unpleasant. Releases a highly lethal weapon unique to Ghouls known as Kagune from their body to prey on humans. Can be cannibalistic. Only sustains damage from Kagune or Quinques that are made from Kagune.

人 HUMANS 間

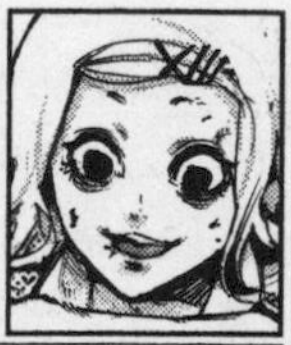

**JUZO SUZUYA**
**(RANK 3 INVESTIGATOR) (JUZO)**

An eccentric who joined the CCG under special dispensation. Enjoys killing and longs for exceptionally lethal Quinques.

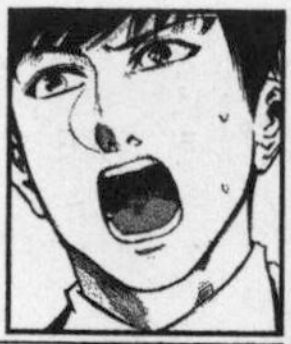

**KOTARO AMON**
**(RANK 1 INVESTIGATOR)**

An Investigator with a very strong sense of justice. Determined to eradicate Ghouls. Dedicated to avenging Mado's loss through his ongoing battle with Kaneki.

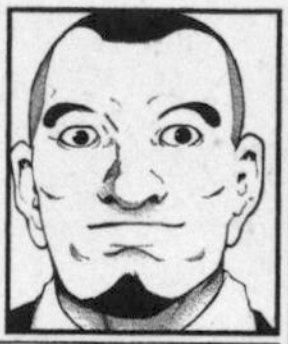

**YUKINORI SHINOHARA**
**(SPECIAL INVESTIGATOR)**

Ex-Academy instructor. A one-time colleague of Mado and Amon's drill instructor. Appears easygoing, but…

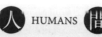

## CCG
### GHOUL INVESTI-GATORS

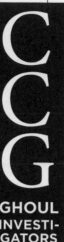

A government agency founded by the Washu family. Develops Ghoul extermination specialists at the Academy to maintain peace in the wards. Its principal functions are the development and evolution of Quinques, which can kill Ghouls, and the eradication of Ghouls from Tokyo. Their headquarters is based in the 1st Ward.

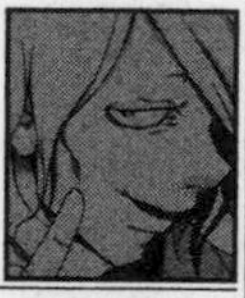

**KUREO MADO**
DECEASED

An Investigator with an unusual obsession with Quinques. Loathed the Ghouls who killed his family. Eventually lost his life.

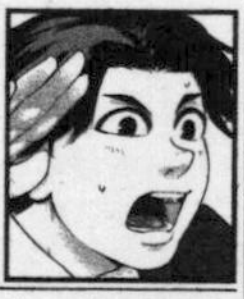

**SEIDO TAKIZAWA**
**(RANK 2 INVESTIGATOR)**

Joined the CCG the same year as Juzo. Admires Amon.

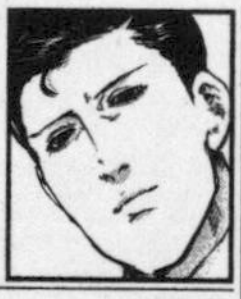

**KOSUKE HOJI**
**(ASSISTANT SPECIAL INVESTIGATOR)**

Mado's ex-partner.

## 11TH WARD GHOULS

Where Rize used to reside. Their origin is still a mystery.

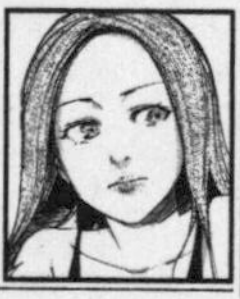

**ITORI**

Owner of Helter Skelter, a bar in the 14th Ward that is frequented by humans as well. Places the utmost value on information.

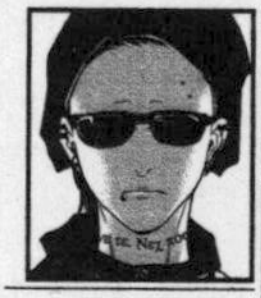

**UTA**

Owner of HySy Artmask Studio, a mask shop in the 4th Ward. Has a troubled history with Yomo.

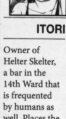

*Summary*

When he's turned into a Ghoul by Rize, Ken Kaneki struggles on a very personal level with the existence of creatures that take human lives to survive. Now, news has reached Kaneki that numerous Ghoul Investigators are being dispatched to designated wards, their intentions unknown. And in the midst of it, an old enemy with a new face resurfaces.

東京喰種

TOKYO GHOUL

TOKYO GHOUL

SUI ISHIDA

TOKYO GHOUL

# C O N T E N T S



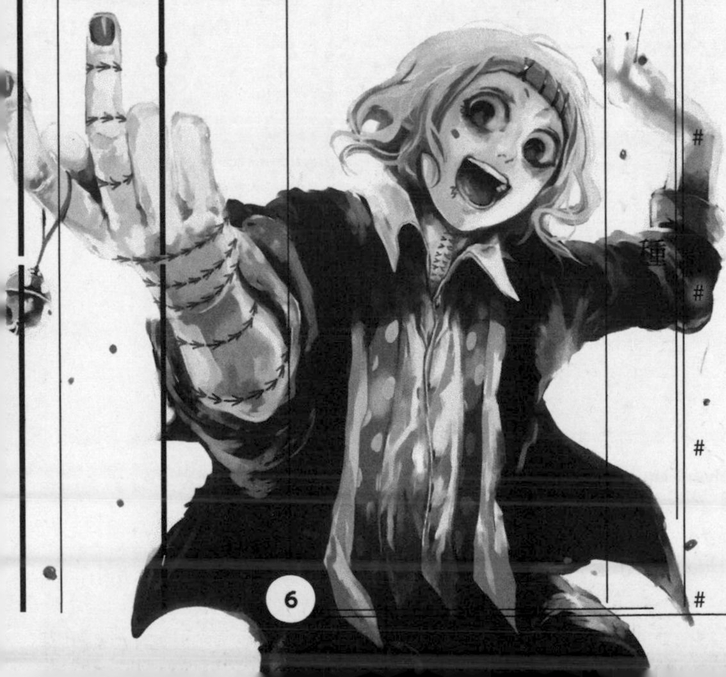

6

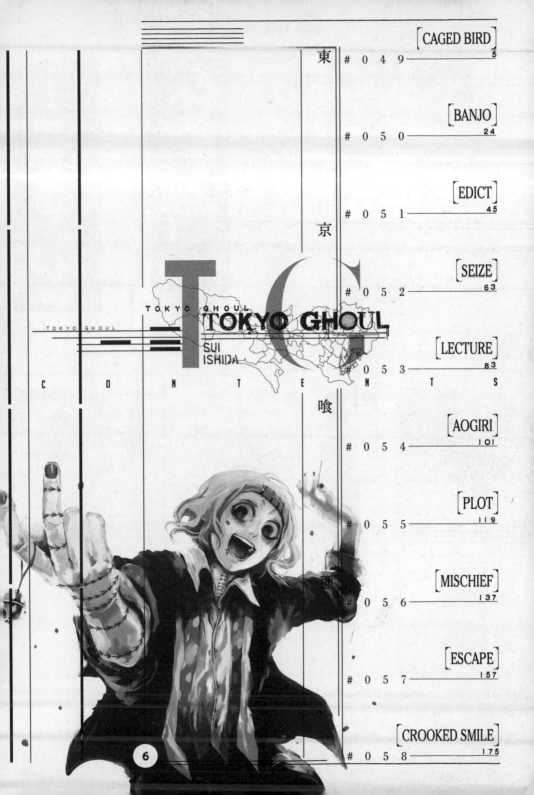

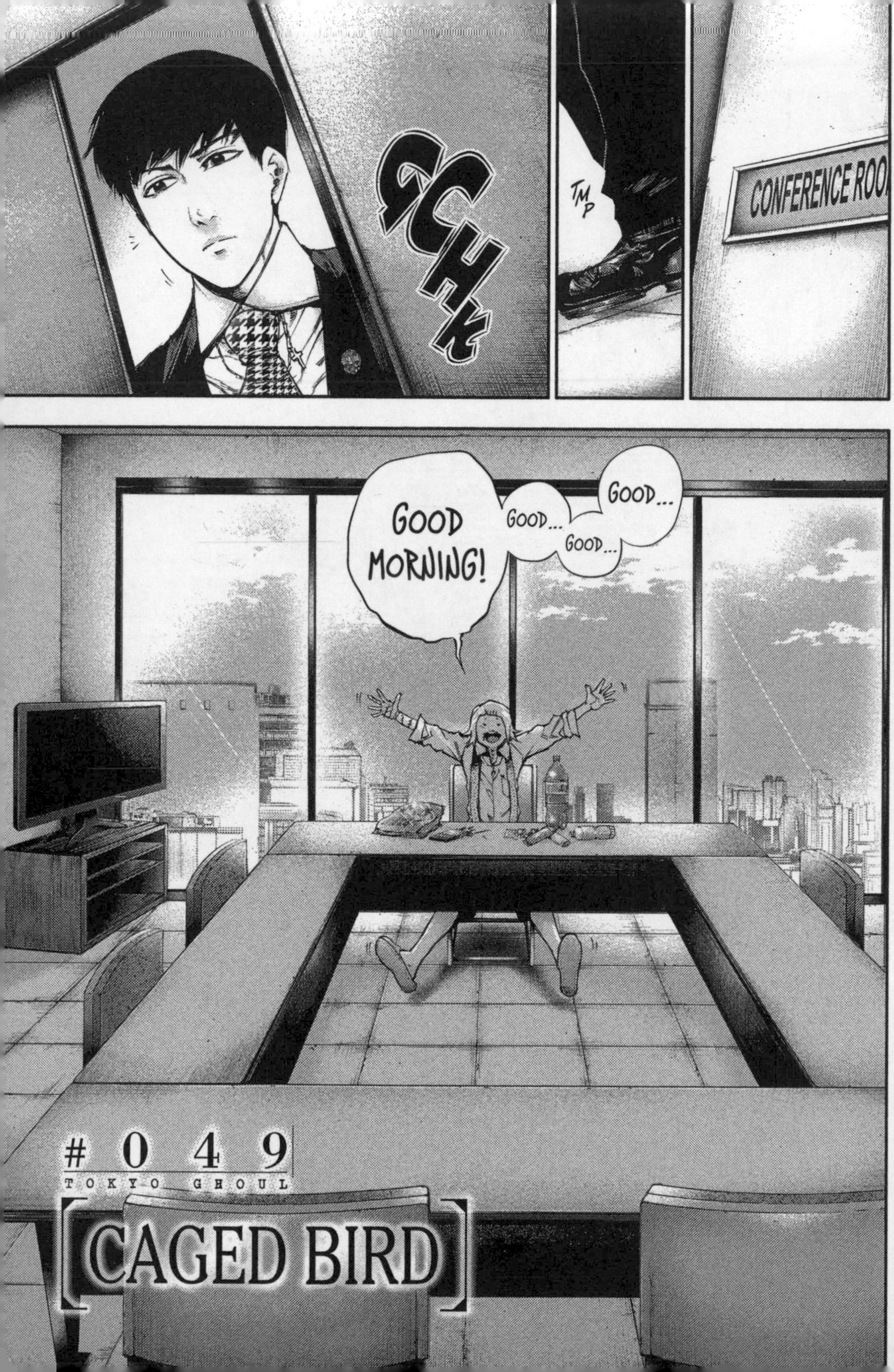

CONFERENCE ROO
TMP
GCHK
GOOD MORNING!
GOOD...
GOOD...
GOOD...
#049
TOKYO GHOUL
CAGED BIRD

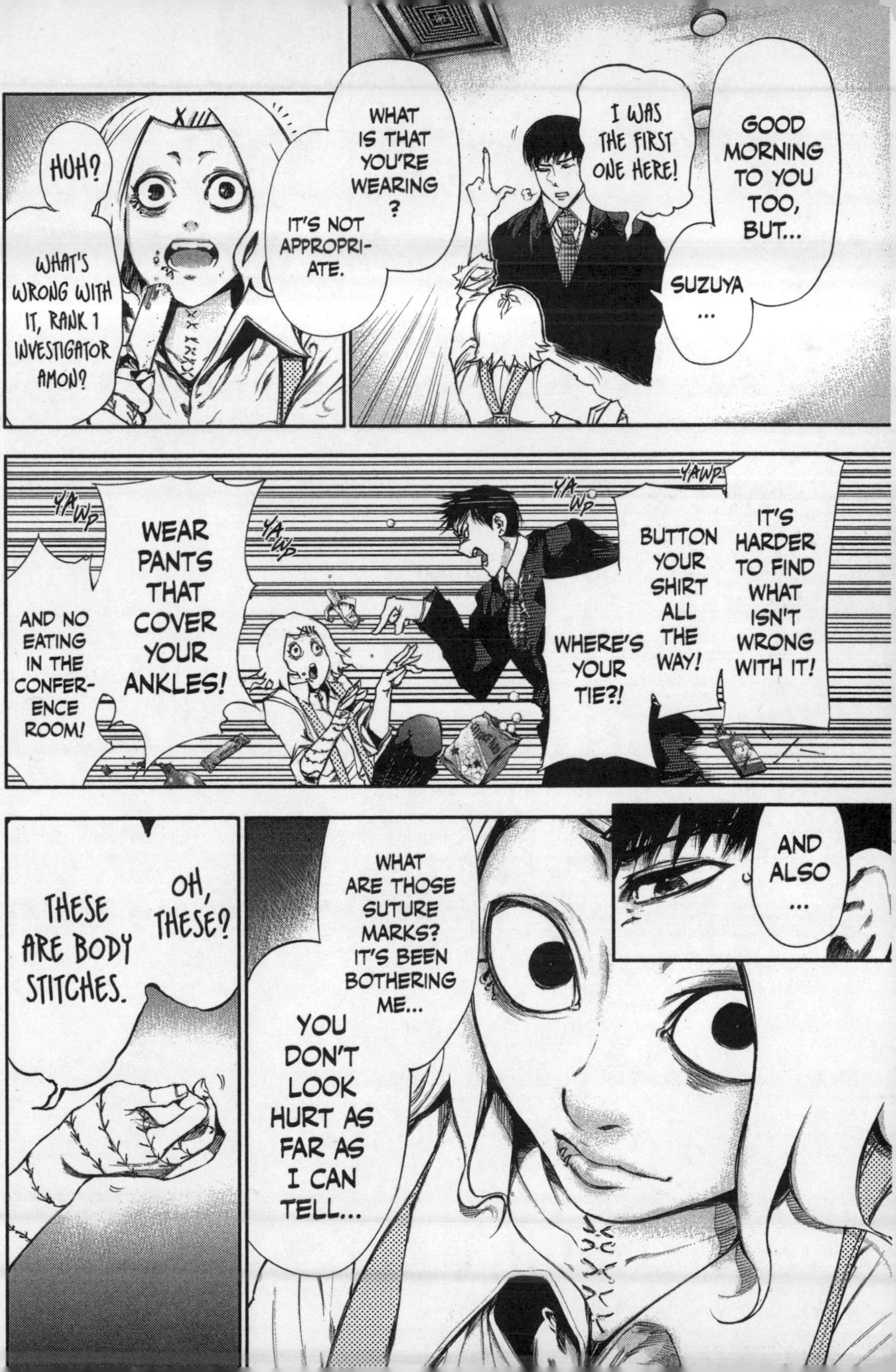
GOOD MORNING TO YOU TOO, BUT...
SUZUYA ...
I WAS THE FIRST ONE HERE!
WHAT IS THAT YOU'RE WEARING ?
IT'S NOT APPROPRI-ATE.
HUH?
WHAT'S WRONG WITH IT, RANK 1 INVESTIGATOR AMON?
YAWP
IT'S HARDER TO FIND WHAT ISN'T WRONG WITH IT!
YAWP
BUTTON YOUR SHIRT ALL THE WAY!
WHERE'S YOUR TIE?!
YAWP
WEAR PANTS THAT COVER YOUR ANKLES!
YAWP
AND NO EATING IN THE CONFER-ENCE ROOM!
AND ALSO ...
WHAT ARE THOSE SUTURE MARKS? IT'S BEEN BOTHERING ME...
YOU DON'T LOOK HURT AS FAR AS I CAN TELL...
OH, THESE?
THESE ARE BODY STITCHES.

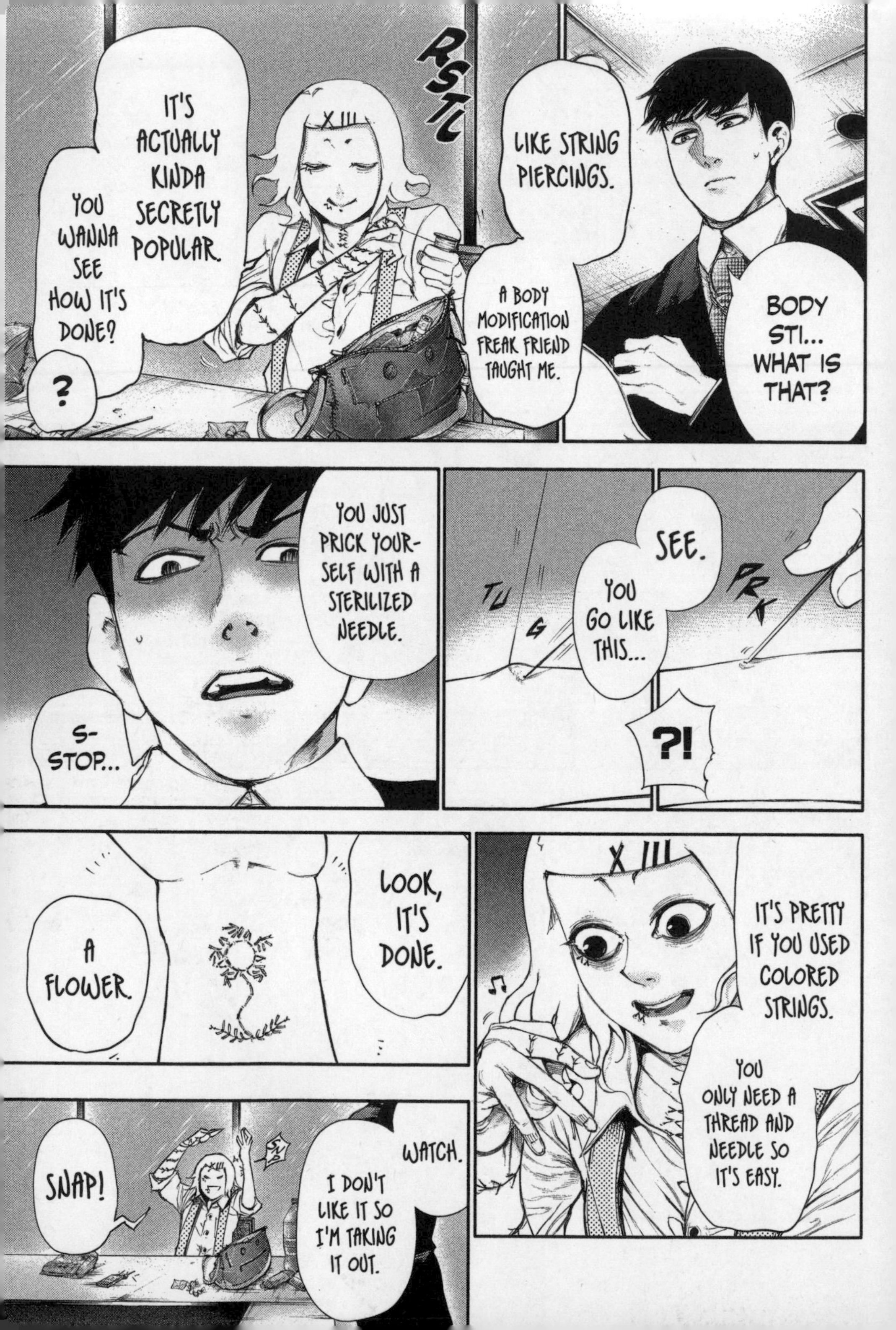
RSTL
LIKE STRING PIERCINGS.
BODY STI... WHAT IS THAT?
A BODY MODIFICATION FREAK FRIEND TAUGHT ME.
IT'S ACTUALLY KINDA SECRETLY POPULAR.
YOU WANNA SEE HOW IT'S DONE?
?
SEE.
YOU GO LIKE THIS...
PRK
?!
TUG
YOU JUST PRICK YOUR-SELF WITH A STERILIZED NEEDLE.
S-STOP...
IT'S PRETTY IF YOU USED COLORED STRINGS.
YOU ONLY NEED A THREAD AND NEEDLE SO IT'S EASY.
LOOK, IT'S DONE.
A FLOWER.
WATCH.
I DON'T LIKE IT SO I'M TAKING IT OUT.
SNAP!

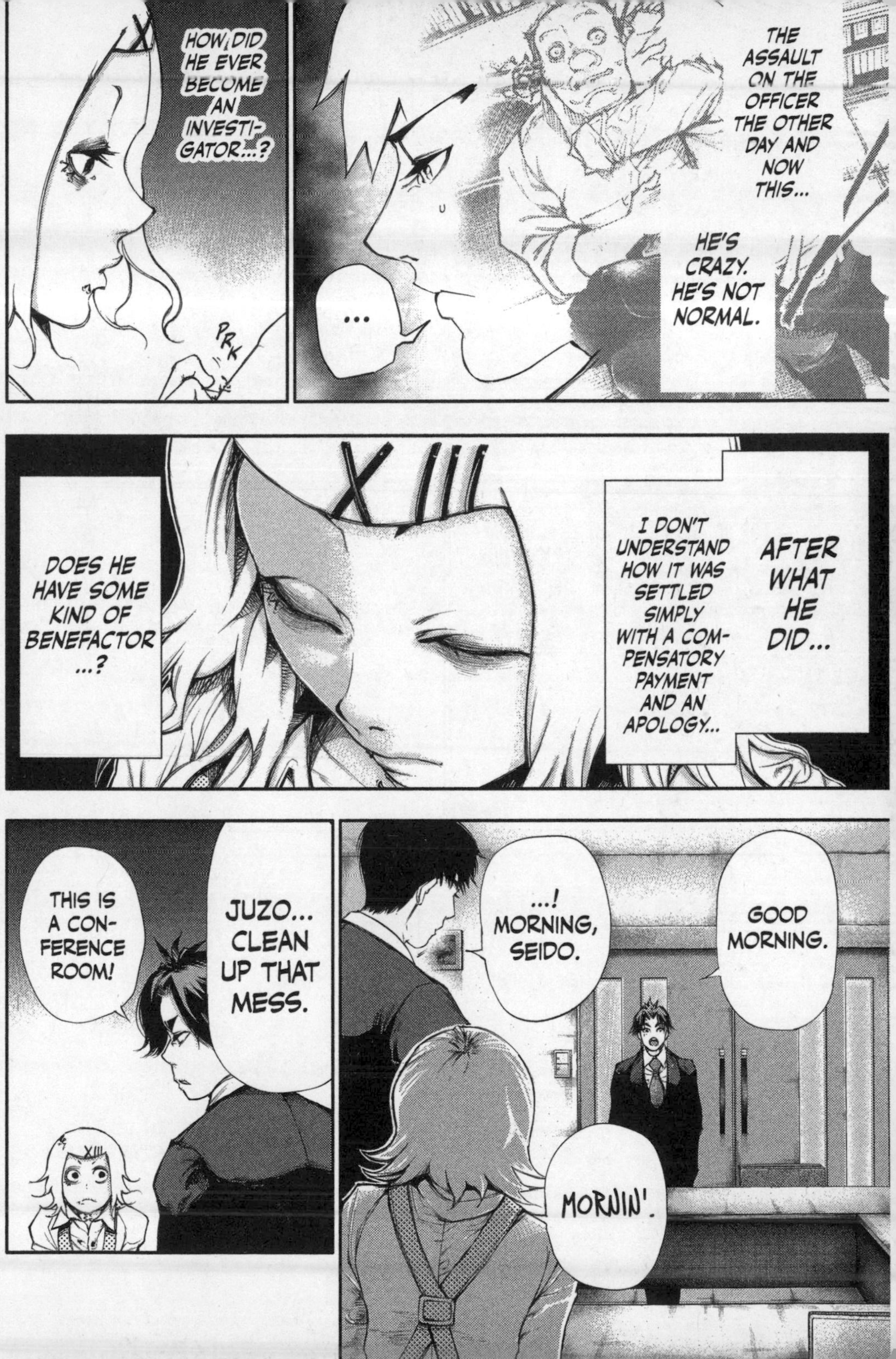
THE ASSAULT ON THE OFFICER THE OTHER DAY AND NOW THIS...
HE'S CRAZY. HE'S NOT NORMAL.
...
HOW DID HE EVER BECOME AN INVESTI-GATOR...?
PRK
AFTER WHAT HE DID...
I DON'T UNDERSTAND HOW IT WAS SETTLED SIMPLY WITH A COM-PENSATORY PAYMENT AND AN APOLOGY...
DOES HE HAVE SOME KIND OF BENEFACTOR ...?
GOOD MORNING.
...! MORNING, SEIDO.
MORNIN'.
JUZO... CLEAN UP THAT MESS.
THIS IS A CON-FERENCE ROOM!

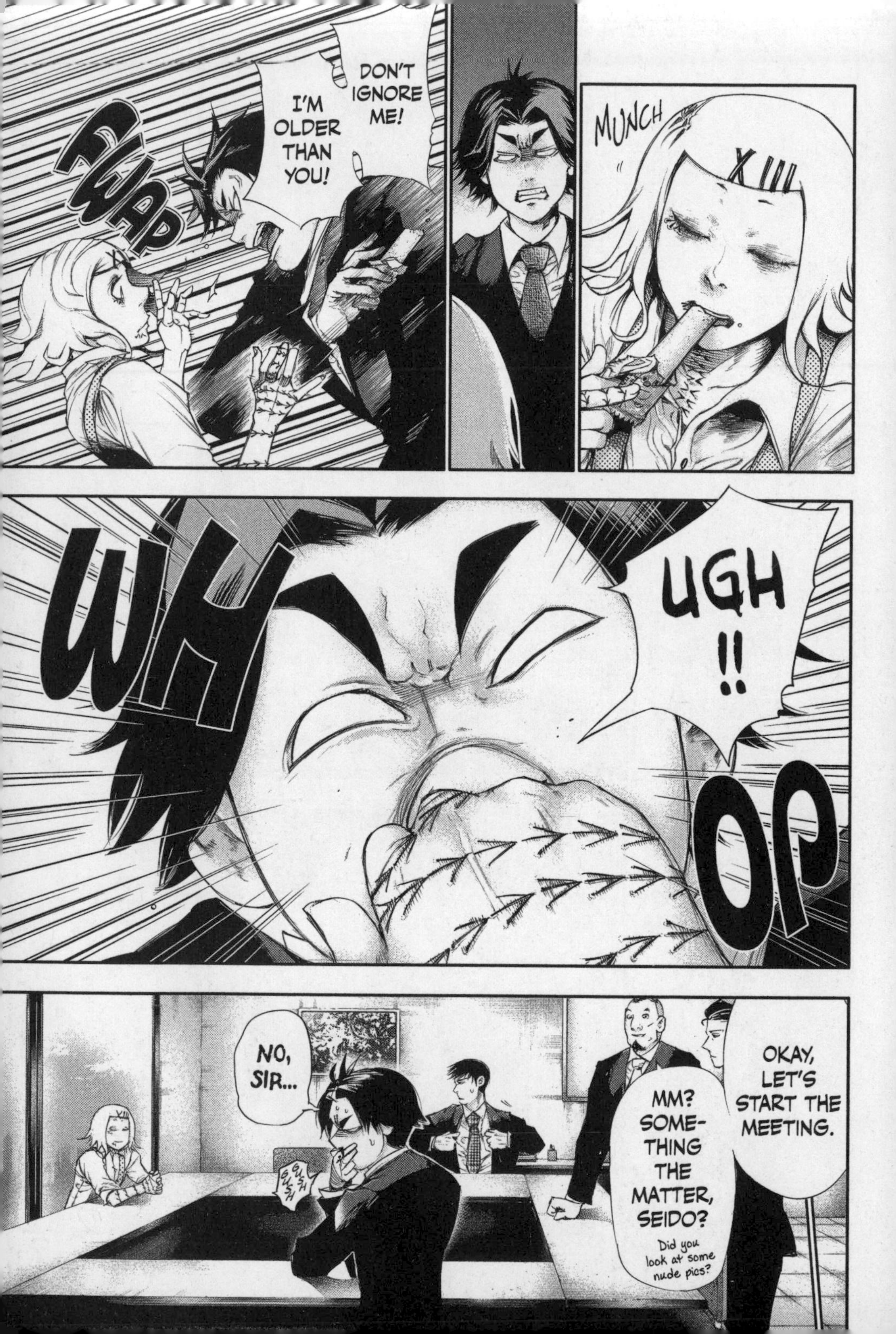
MUNCH
DON'T IGNORE ME!
I'M OLDER THAN YOU!
FWAP
UGH !!
WH
OP
OKAY, LET'S START THE MEETING.
MM? SOME-THING THE MATTER, SEIDO?
Did you look at some nude pics?
NO, SIR...

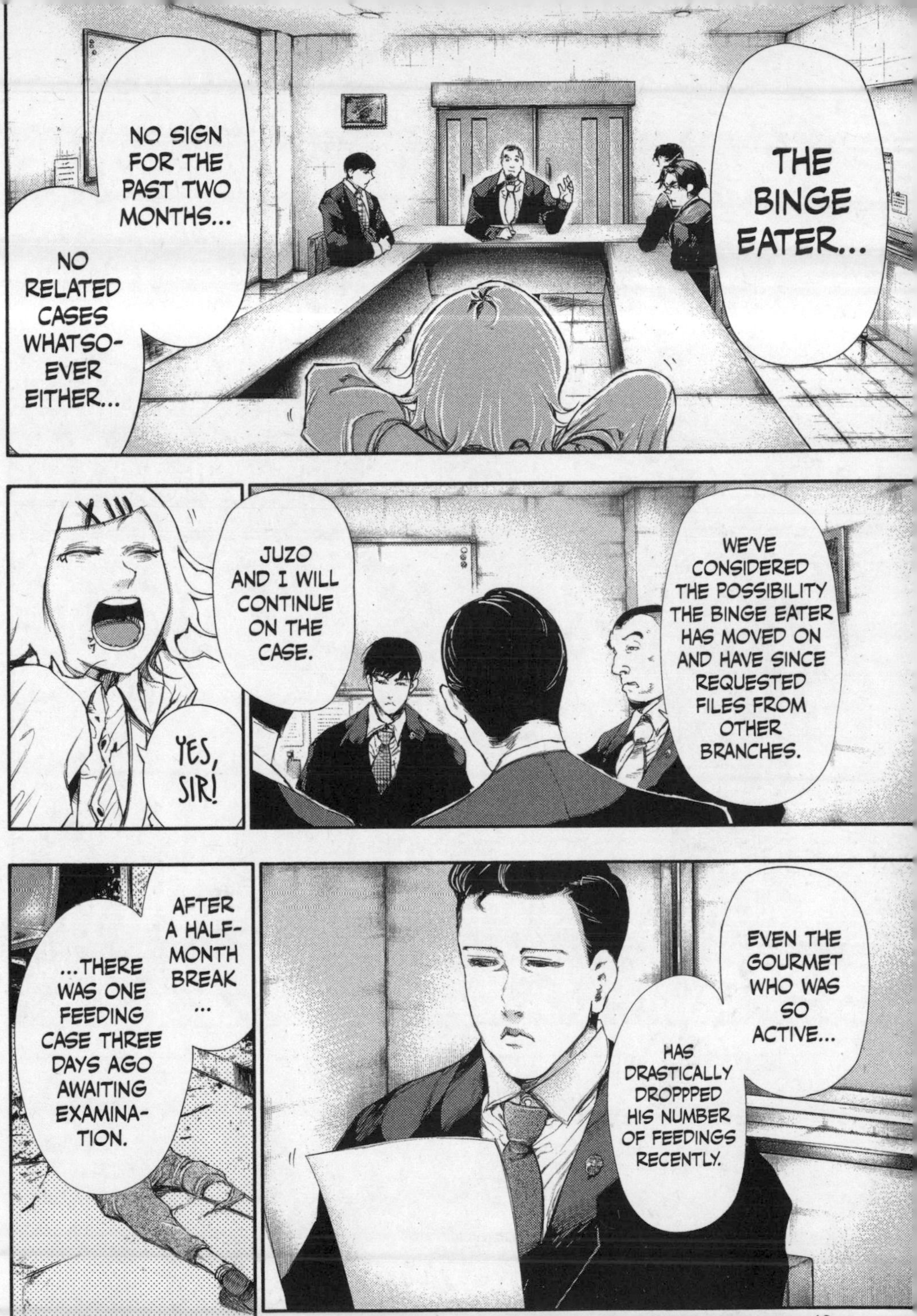
THE BINGE EATER...
NO SIGN FOR THE PAST TWO MONTHS...
NO RELATED CASES WHATSO-EVER EITHER...
WE'VE CONSIDERED THE POSSIBILITY THE BINGE EATER HAS MOVED ON AND HAVE SINCE REQUESTED FILES FROM OTHER BRANCHES.
JUZO AND I WILL CONTINUE ON THE CASE.
YES, SIR!
EVEN THE GOURMET WHO WAS SO ACTIVE...
HAS DRASTICALLY DROPPPED HIS NUMBER OF FEEDINGS RECENTLY.
AFTER A HALF-MONTH BREAK...
...THERE WAS ONE FEEDING CASE THREE DAYS AGO AWAITING EXAMINA-TION.

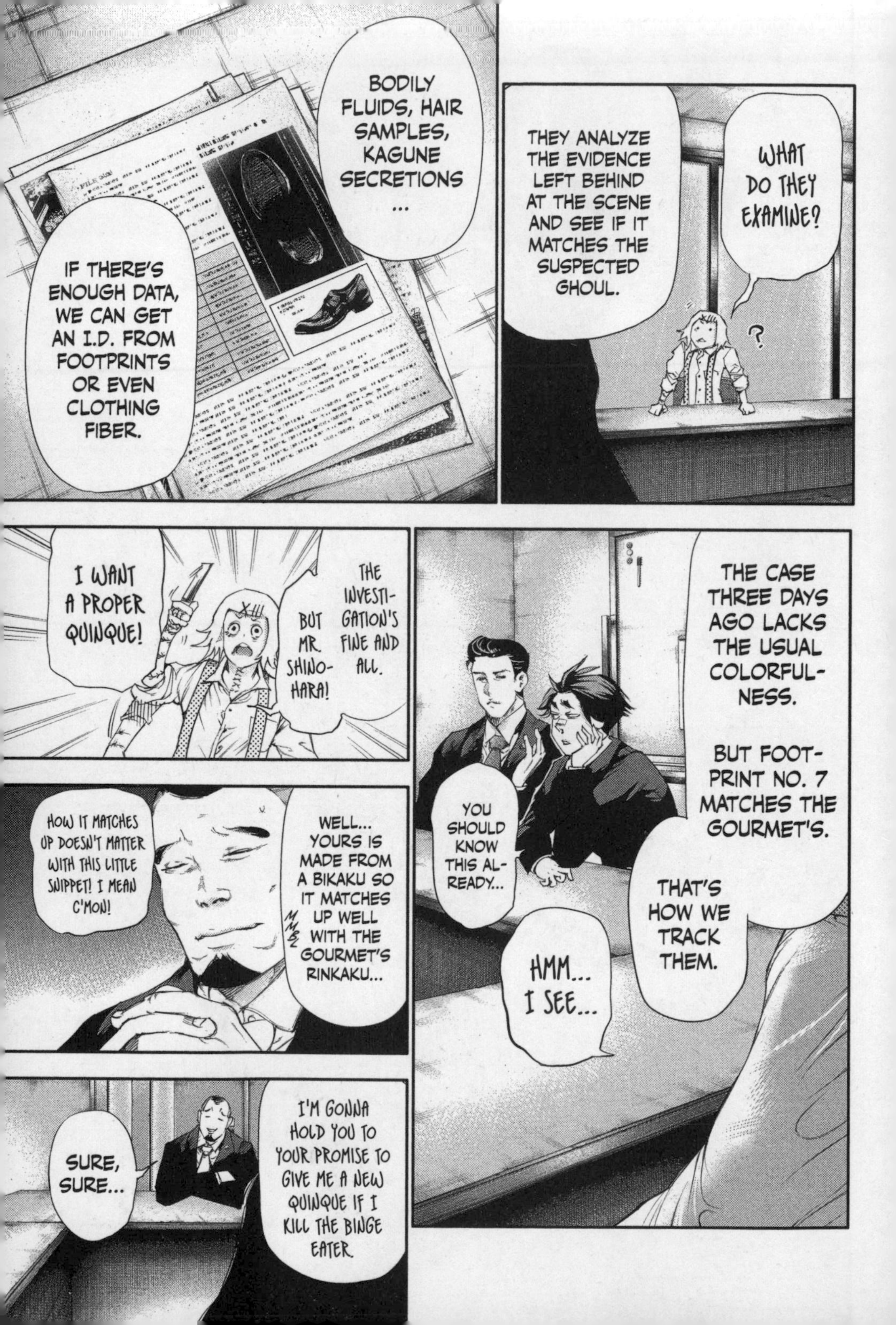
WHAT DO THEY EXAMINE?
THEY ANALYZE THE EVIDENCE LEFT BEHIND AT THE SCENE AND SEE IF IT MATCHES THE SUSPECTED GHOUL.
BODILY FLUIDS, HAIR SAMPLES, KAGUNE SECRETIONS ...
IF THERE'S ENOUGH DATA, WE CAN GET AN I.D. FROM FOOTPRINTS OR EVEN CLOTHING FIBER.
THE CASE THREE DAYS AGO LACKS THE USUAL COLORFULNESS.
BUT FOOTPRINT NO. 7 MATCHES THE GOURMET'S.
THAT'S HOW WE TRACK THEM.
YOU SHOULD KNOW THIS ALREADY...
HMM... I SEE...
THE INVESTIGATION'S FINE AND ALL.
BUT MR. SHINOHARA!
I WANT A PROPER QUINQUE!
WELL... YOURS IS MADE FROM A BIKAKU SO IT MATCHES UP WELL WITH THE GOURMET'S RINKAKU...
MMG
HOW IT MATCHES UP DOESN'T MATTER WITH THIS LITTLE SNIPPET! I MEAN C'MON!
I'M GONNA HOLD YOU TO YOUR PROMISE TO GIVE ME A NEW QUINQUE IF I KILL THE BINGE EATER.
SURE, SURE...

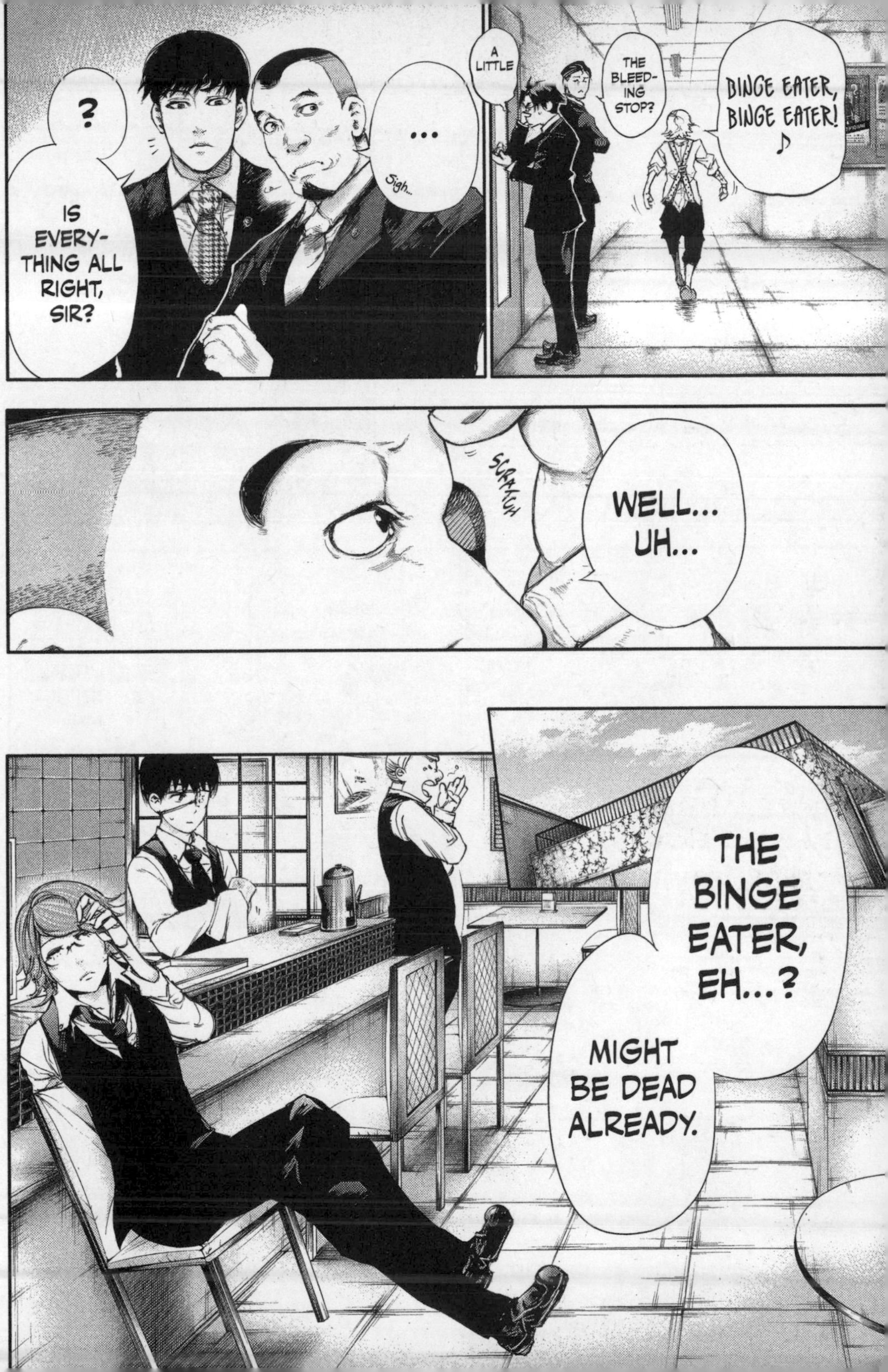
BINGE EATER, BINGE EATER! ♪
THE BLEED-ING STOP?
A LITTLE
...
Sigh...
?
IS EVERY-THING ALL RIGHT, SIR?
SCRATCH
WELL... UH...
THE BINGE EATER, EH...?
MIGHT BE DEAD ALREADY.

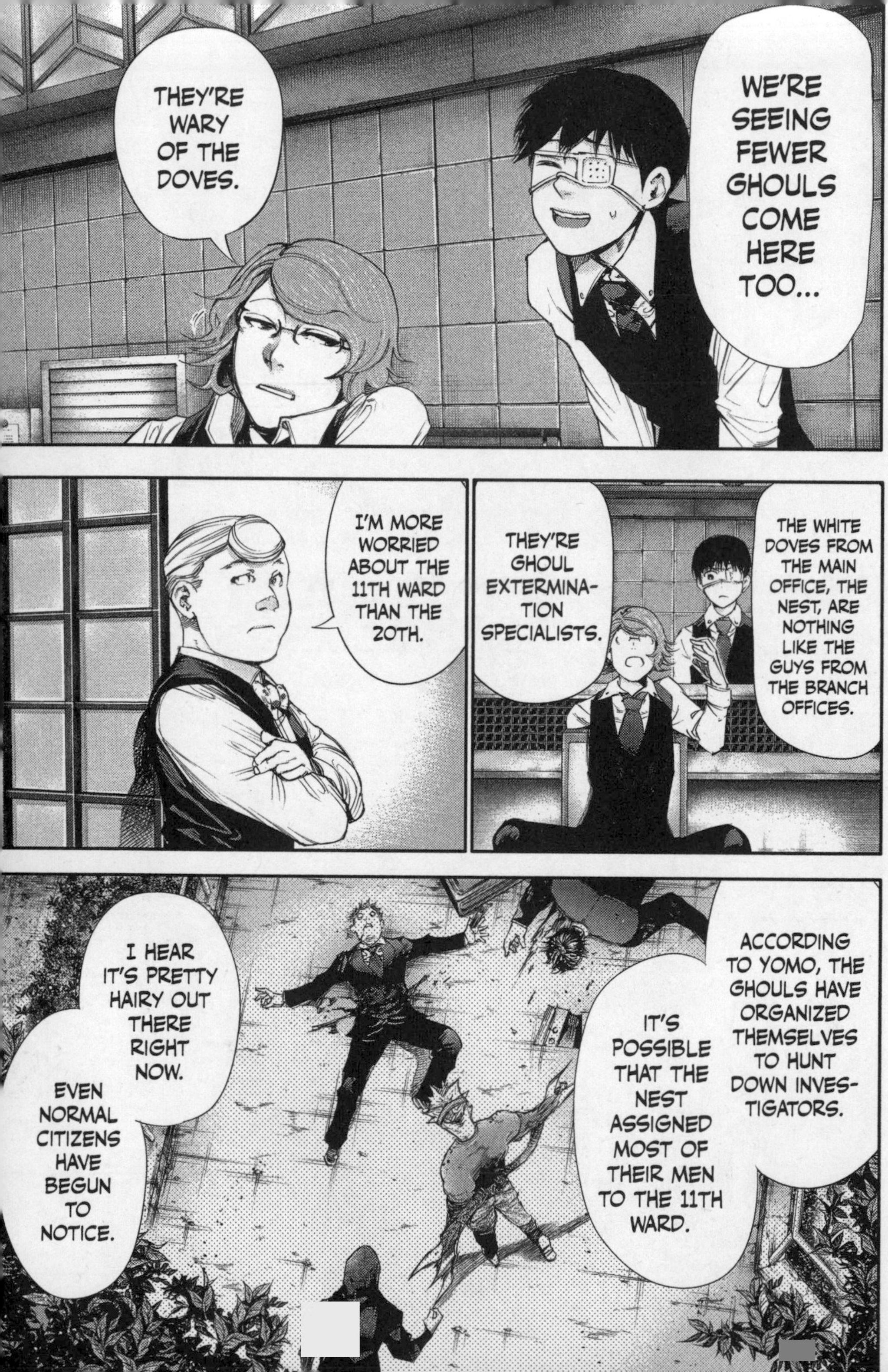
WE'RE SEEING FEWER GHOULS COME HERE TOO...
THEY'RE WARY OF THE DOVES.
THE WHITE DOVES FROM THE MAIN OFFICE, THE NEST, ARE NOTHING LIKE THE GUYS FROM THE BRANCH OFFICES.
THEY'RE GHOUL EXTERMINA-TION SPECIALISTS.
I'M MORE WORRIED ABOUT THE 11TH WARD THAN THE 20TH.
ACCORDING TO YOMO, THE GHOULS HAVE ORGANIZED THEMSELVES TO HUNT DOWN INVES-TIGATORS.
IT'S POSSIBLE THAT THE NEST ASSIGNED MOST OF THEIR MEN TO THE 11TH WARD.
I HEAR IT'S PRETTY HAIRY OUT THERE RIGHT NOW.
EVEN NORMAL CITIZENS HAVE BEGUN TO NOTICE.

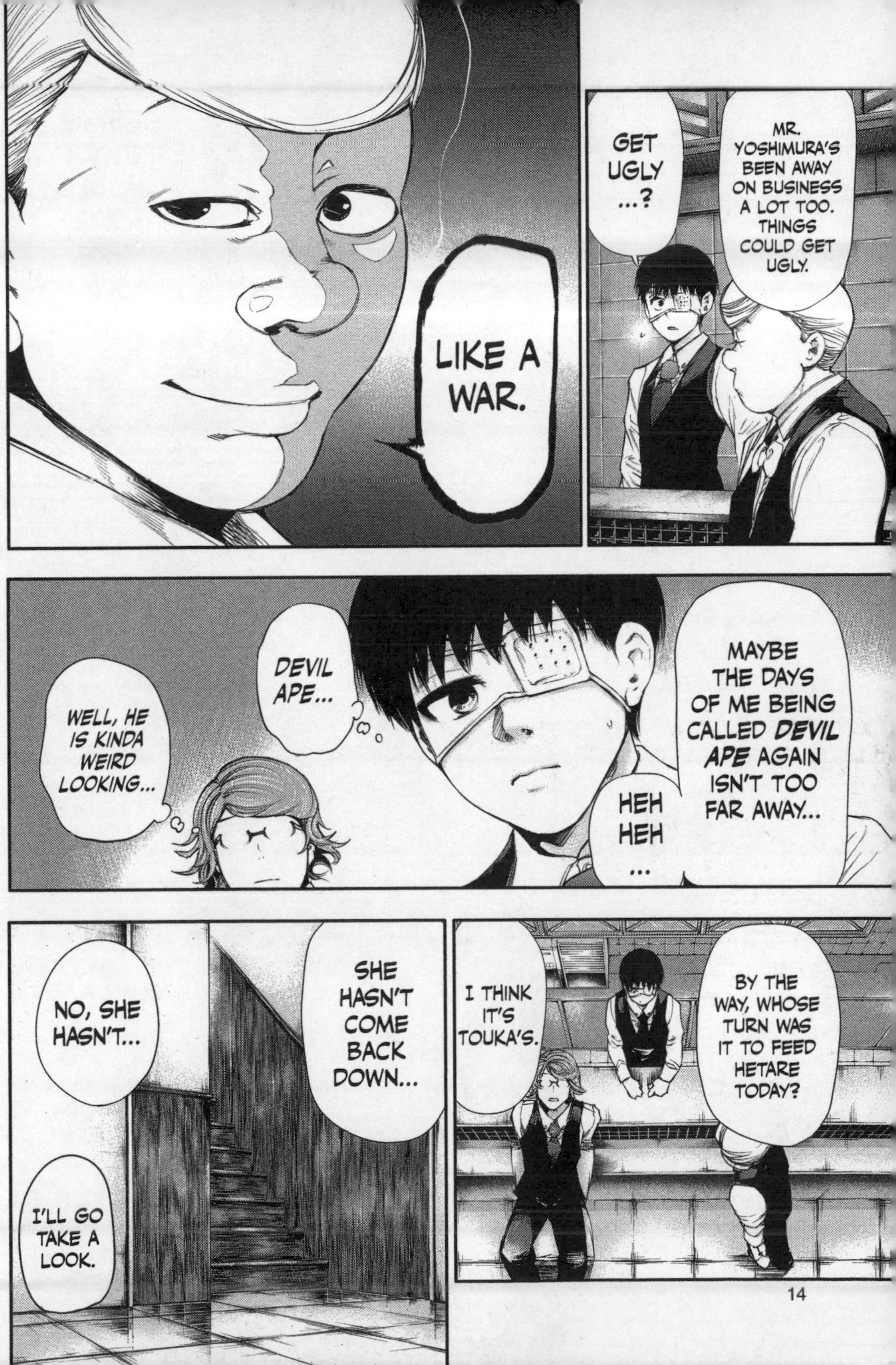
MR. YOSHIMURA'S BEEN AWAY ON BUSINESS A LOT TOO. THINGS COULD GET UGLY.
GET UGLY ...?
LIKE A WAR.
MAYBE THE DAYS OF ME BEING CALLED *DEVIL APE* AGAIN ISN'T TOO FAR AWAY...
HEH HEH ...
*DEVIL APE...*
*WELL, HE IS KINDA WEIRD LOOKING...*
BY THE WAY, WHOSE TURN WAS IT TO FEED HETARE TODAY?
I THINK IT'S TOUKA'S.
SHE HASN'T COME BACK DOWN...
NO, SHE HASN'T...
I'LL GO TAKE A LOOK.

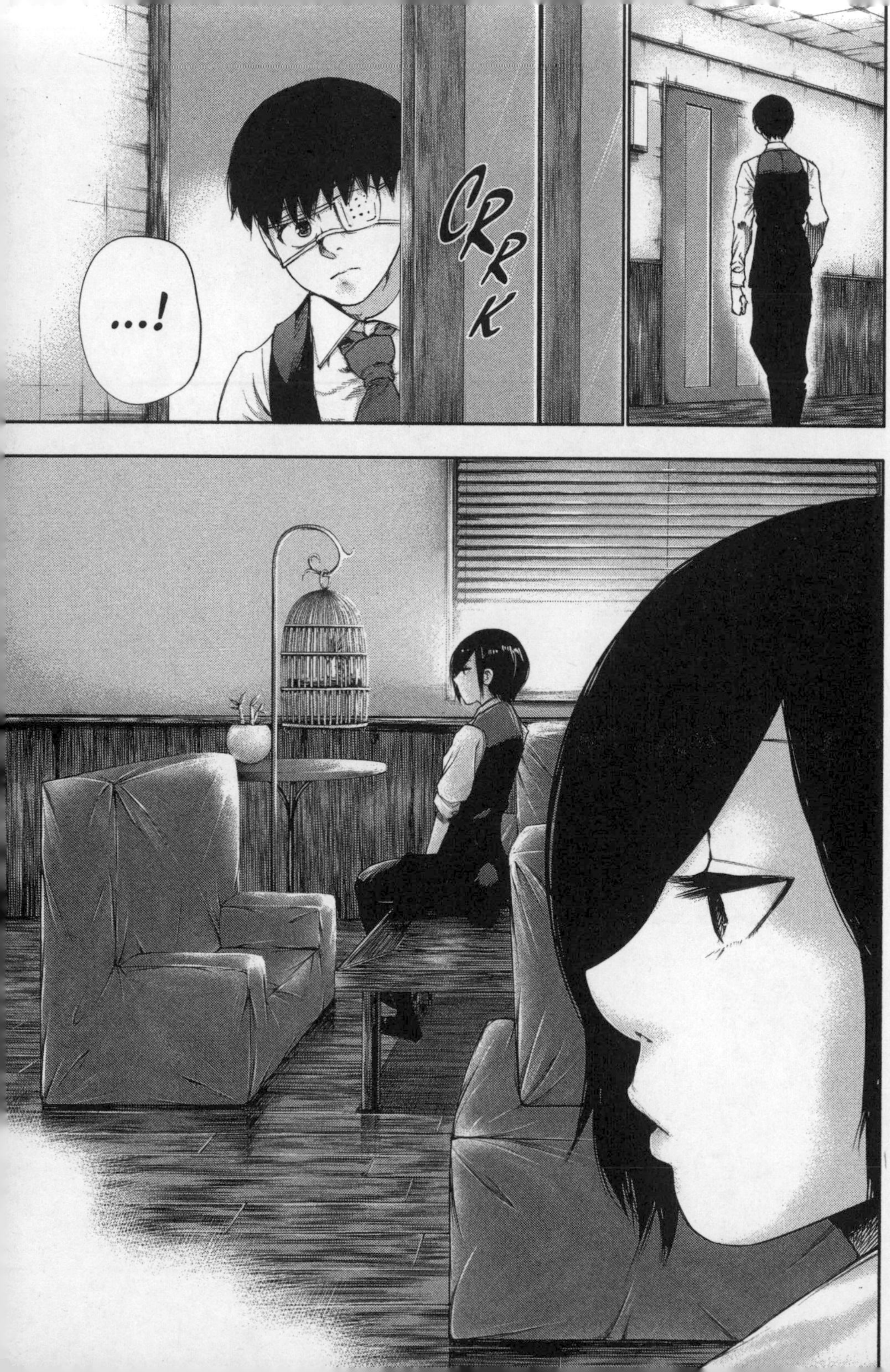
CRRKK
...!

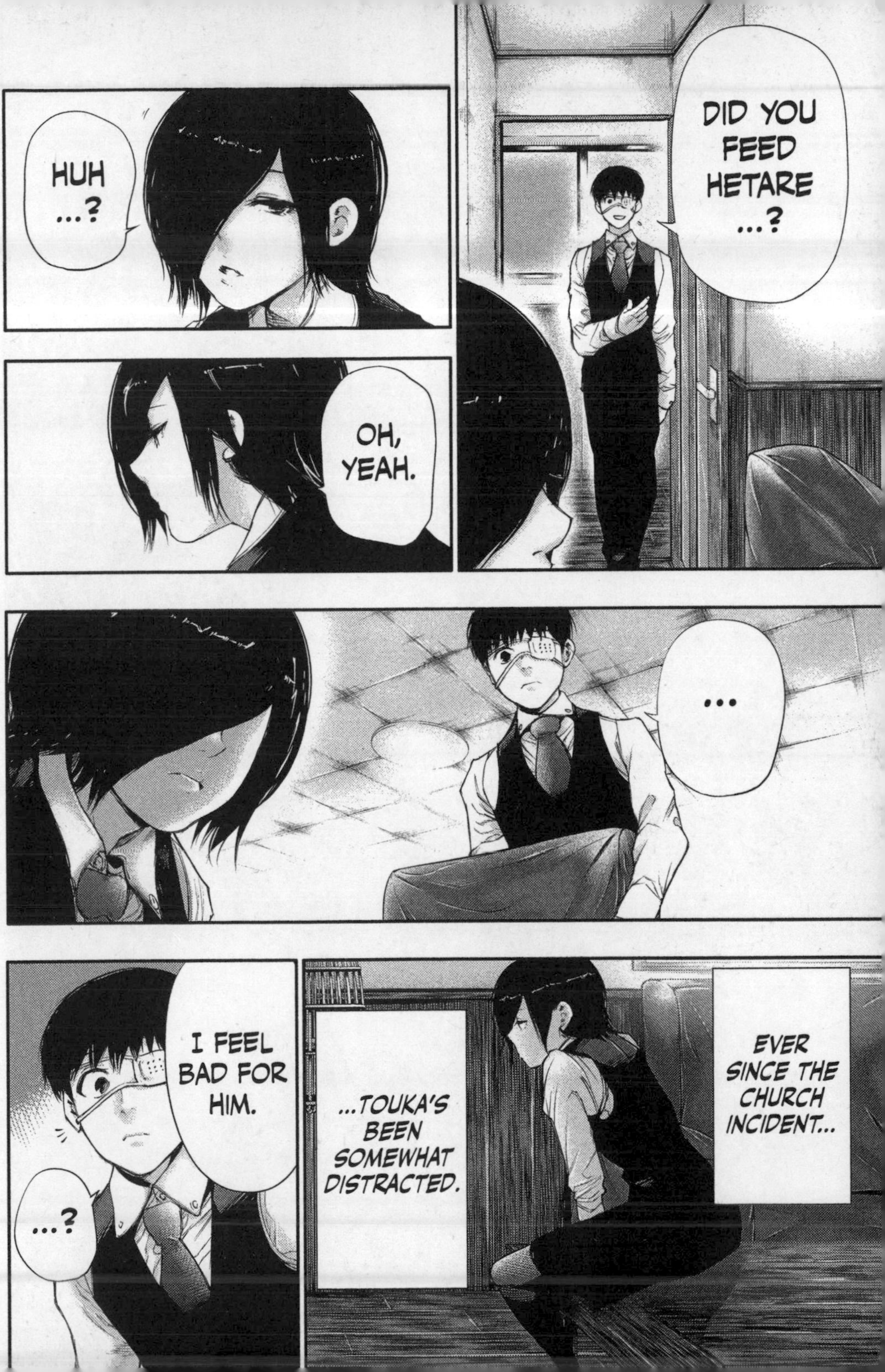
DID YOU FEED HETARE ...?
HUH ...?
OH, YEAH.
...
EVER SINCE THE CHURCH INCIDENT...
...TOUKA'S BEEN SOMEWHAT DISTRACTED.
I FEEL BAD FOR HIM.
...?

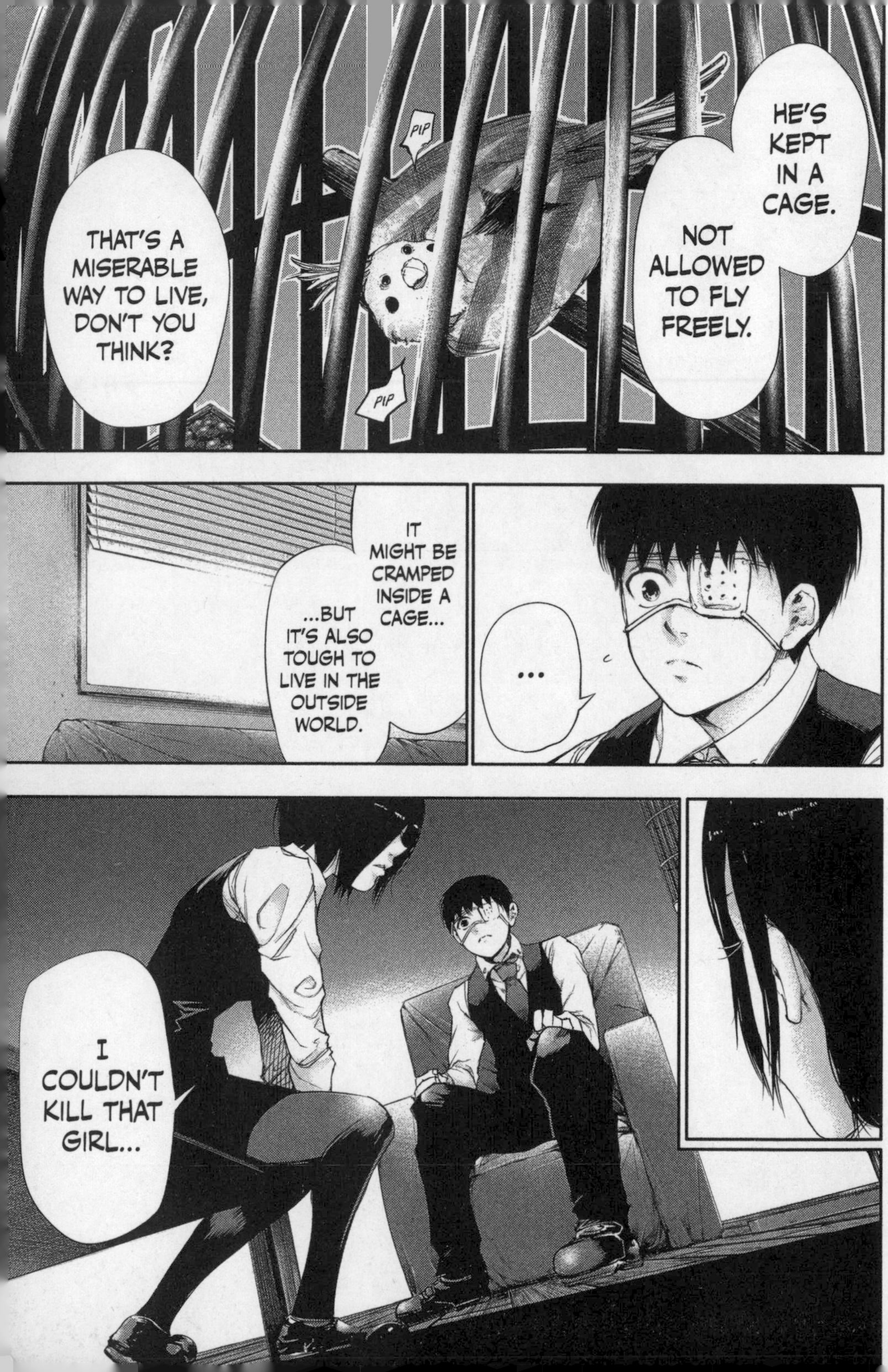
HE'S KEPT IN A CAGE.
NOT ALLOWED TO FLY FREELY.
PIP
THAT'S A MISERABLE WAY TO LIVE, DON'T YOU THINK?
PIP
...
IT MIGHT BE CRAMPED INSIDE A CAGE...
...BUT IT'S ALSO TOUGH TO LIVE IN THE OUTSIDE WORLD.
I COULDN'T KILL THAT GIRL...

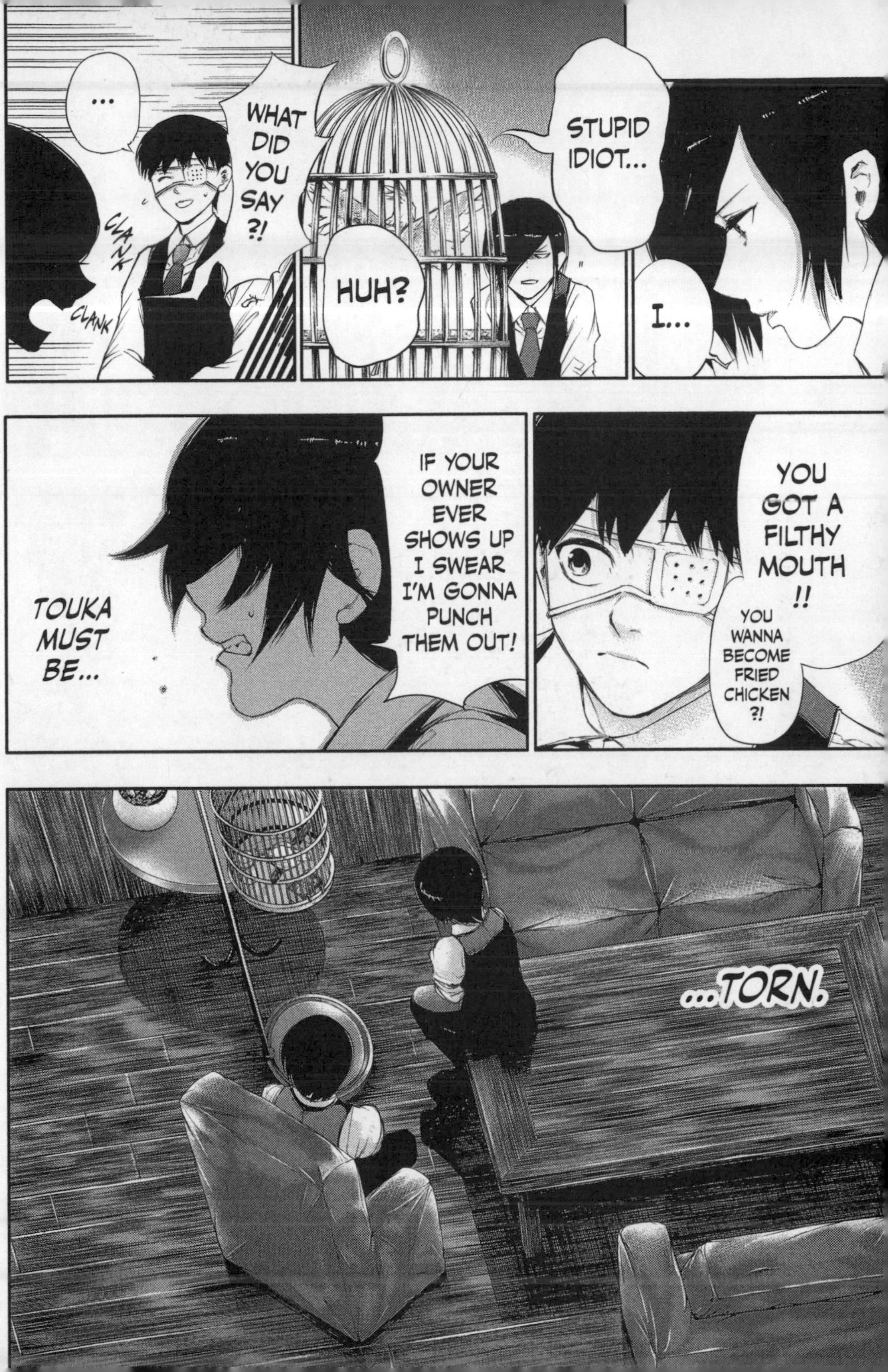
STUPID IDIOT...
I...
HUH?
WHAT DID YOU SAY?!
...
CLANK
CLANK
YOU GOT A FILTHY MOUTH!!
YOU WANNA BECOME FRIED CHICKEN?!
IF YOUR OWNER EVER SHOWS UP I SWEAR I'M GONNA PUNCH THEM OUT!
TOUKA MUST BE...
...TORN.

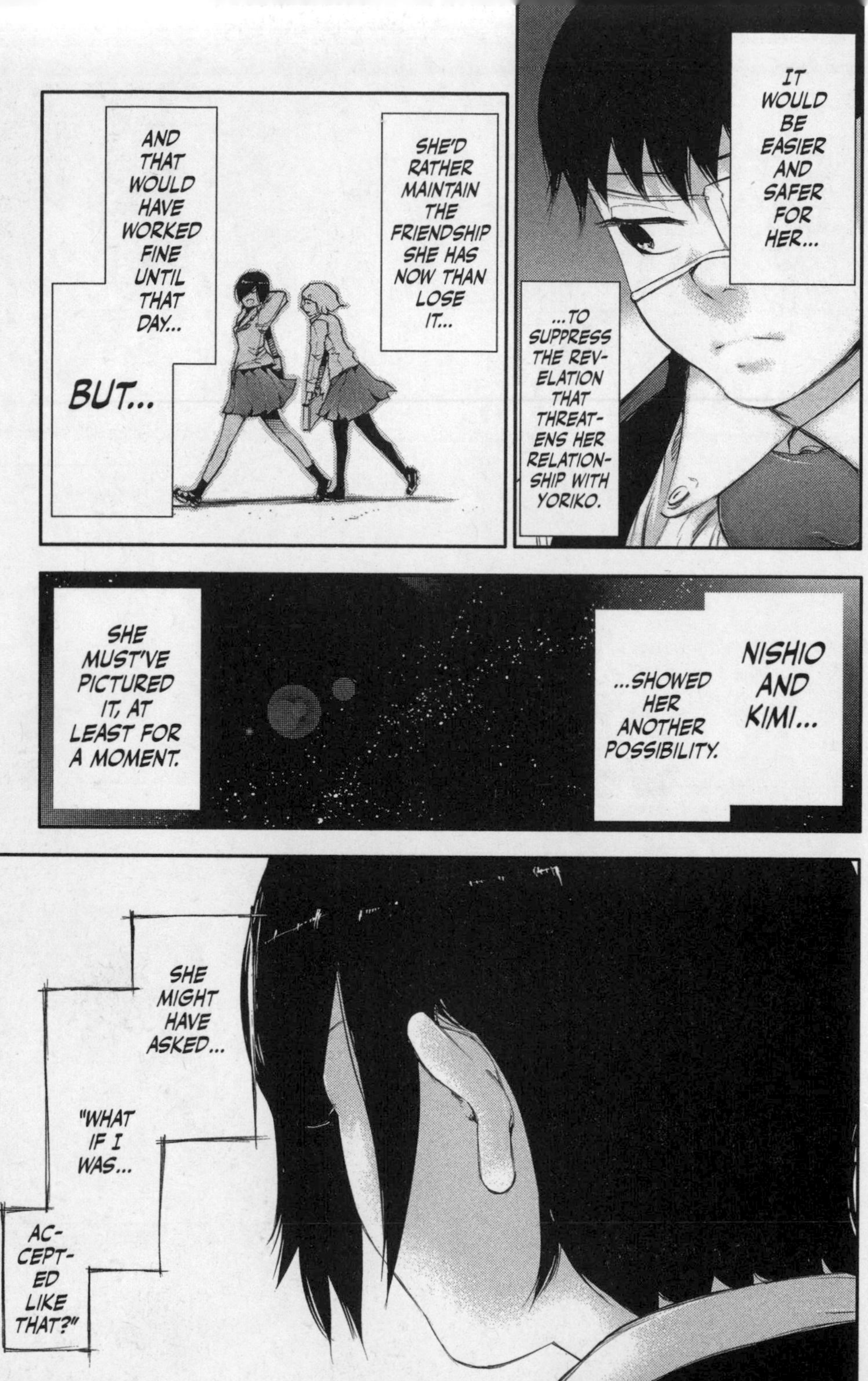
IT WOULD BE EASIER AND SAFER FOR HER...
...TO SUPPRESS THE REVELATION THAT THREATENS HER RELATIONSHIP WITH YORIKO.
SHE'D RATHER MAINTAIN THE FRIENDSHIP SHE HAS NOW THAN LOSE IT...
AND THAT WOULD HAVE WORKED FINE UNTIL THAT DAY...
BUT...
NISHIO AND KIMI...
...SHOWED HER ANOTHER POSSIBILITY.
SHE MUST'VE PICTURED IT, AT LEAST FOR A MOMENT.
SHE MIGHT HAVE ASKED...
"WHAT IF I WAS...
ACCEPTED LIKE THAT?"

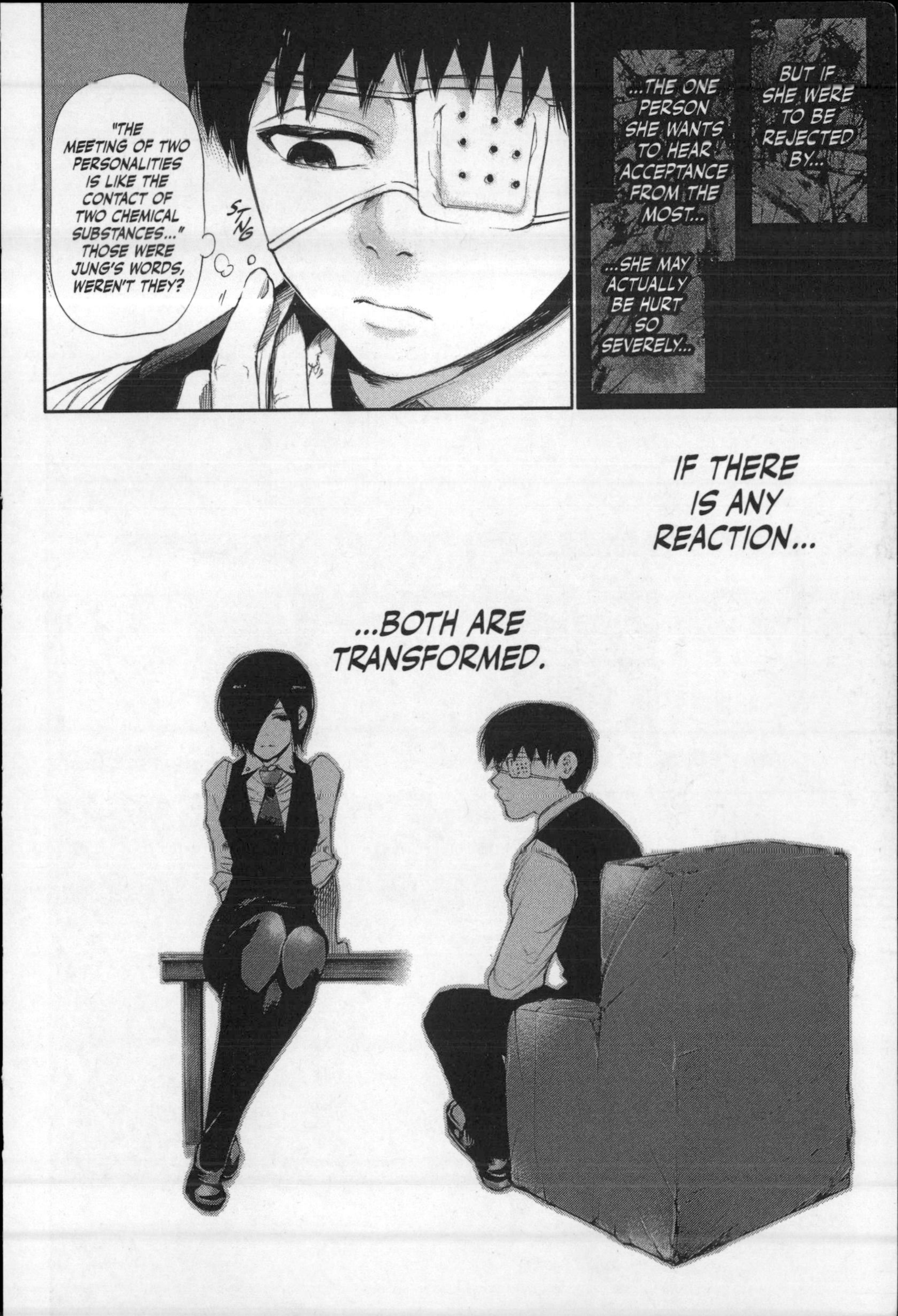
BUT IF SHE WERE TO BE REJECTED BY...
...THE ONE PERSON SHE WANTS TO HEAR ACCEPTANCE FROM THE MOST...
...SHE MAY ACTUALLY BE HURT SO SEVERELY...
"THE MEETING OF TWO PERSONALITIES IS LIKE THE CONTACT OF TWO CHEMICAL SUBSTANCES..." THOSE WERE JUNG'S WORDS, WEREN'T THEY?
STING
IF THERE IS ANY REACTION...
...BOTH ARE TRANSFORMED.

THE 20TH WARD... IT'S MY FIRST TIME HERE.

TIME SEEMS TO GO BY SLOWLY AT THIS PLACE.

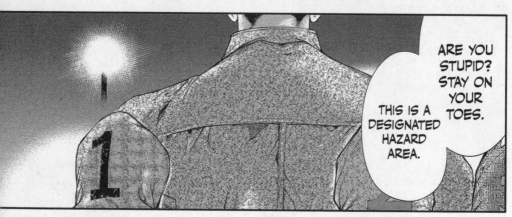

ARE YOU STUPID? STAY ON YOUR TOES.

THIS IS A DESIGNATED HAZARD AREA.

THERE SHOULD BE A NUMBER OF DOVES FROM THE NEST HERE TOO.

LET'S GET OUR BUSINESS DONE QUICKLY.

BEFORE THAT LITTLE BASTARD BOSSIN' ME AROUND GETS PISSED...

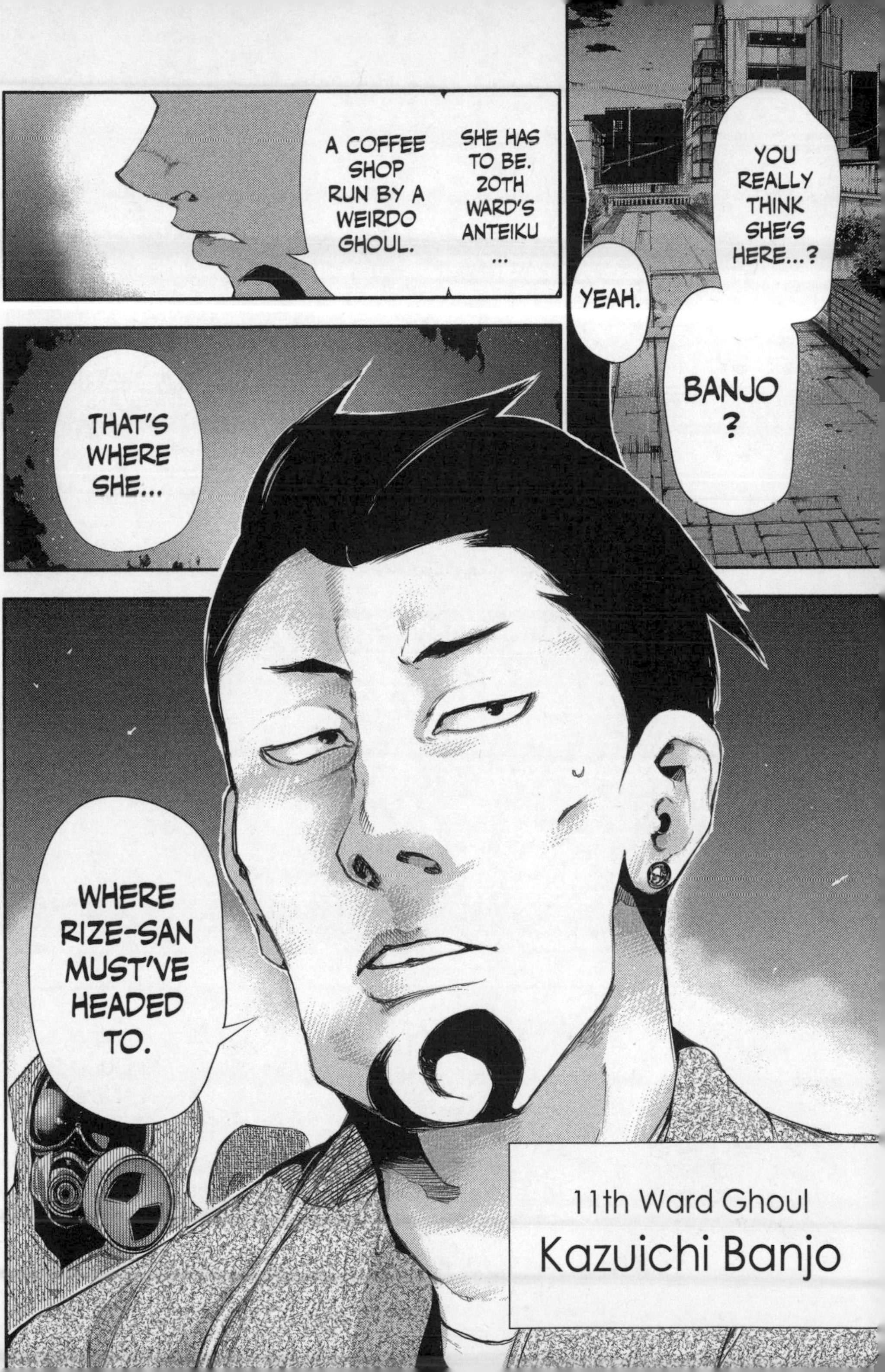
YOU REALLY THINK SHE'S HERE...?
YEAH.
BANJO?
SHE HAS TO BE. 20TH WARD'S ANTEIKU...
A COFFEE SHOP RUN BY A WEIRDO GHOUL.
THAT'S WHERE SHE...
WHERE RIZE-SAN MUST'VE HEADED TO.
11th Ward Ghoul
Kazuichi Banjo

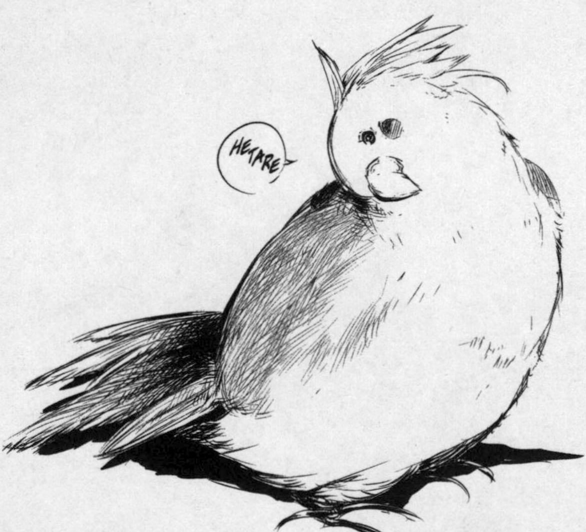
HETARE

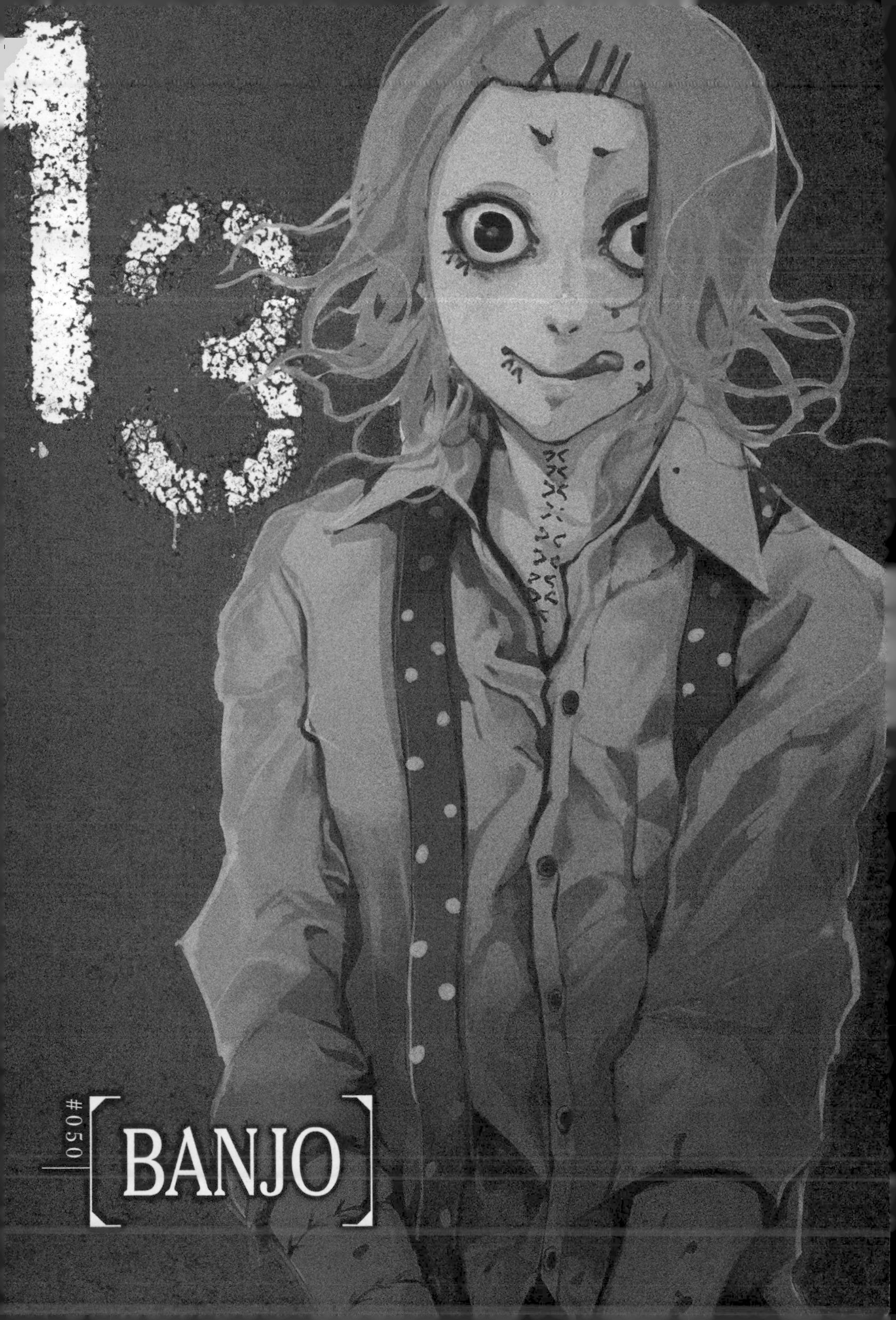
13
#050
BANJO

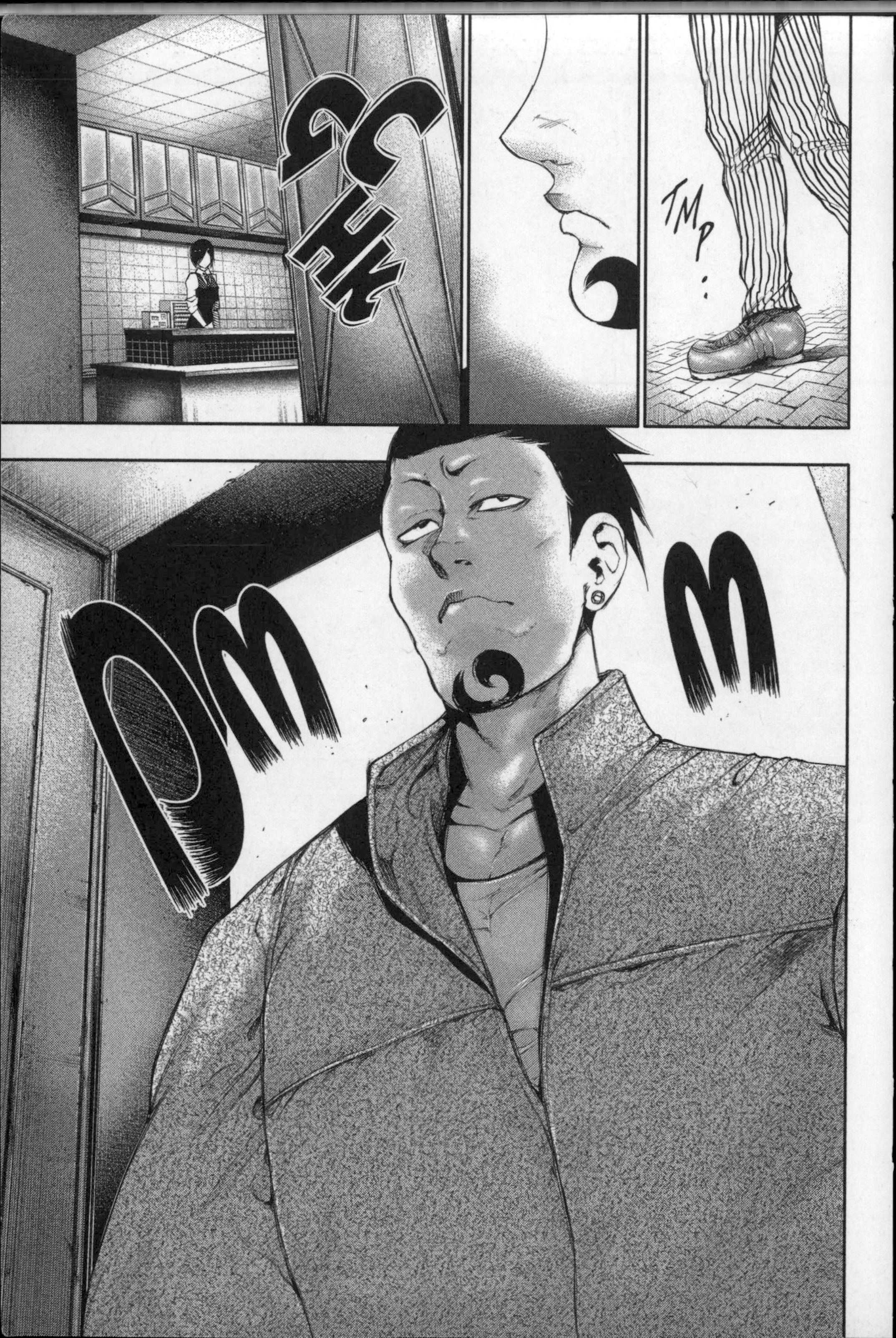
TMP
CHK
DMMM

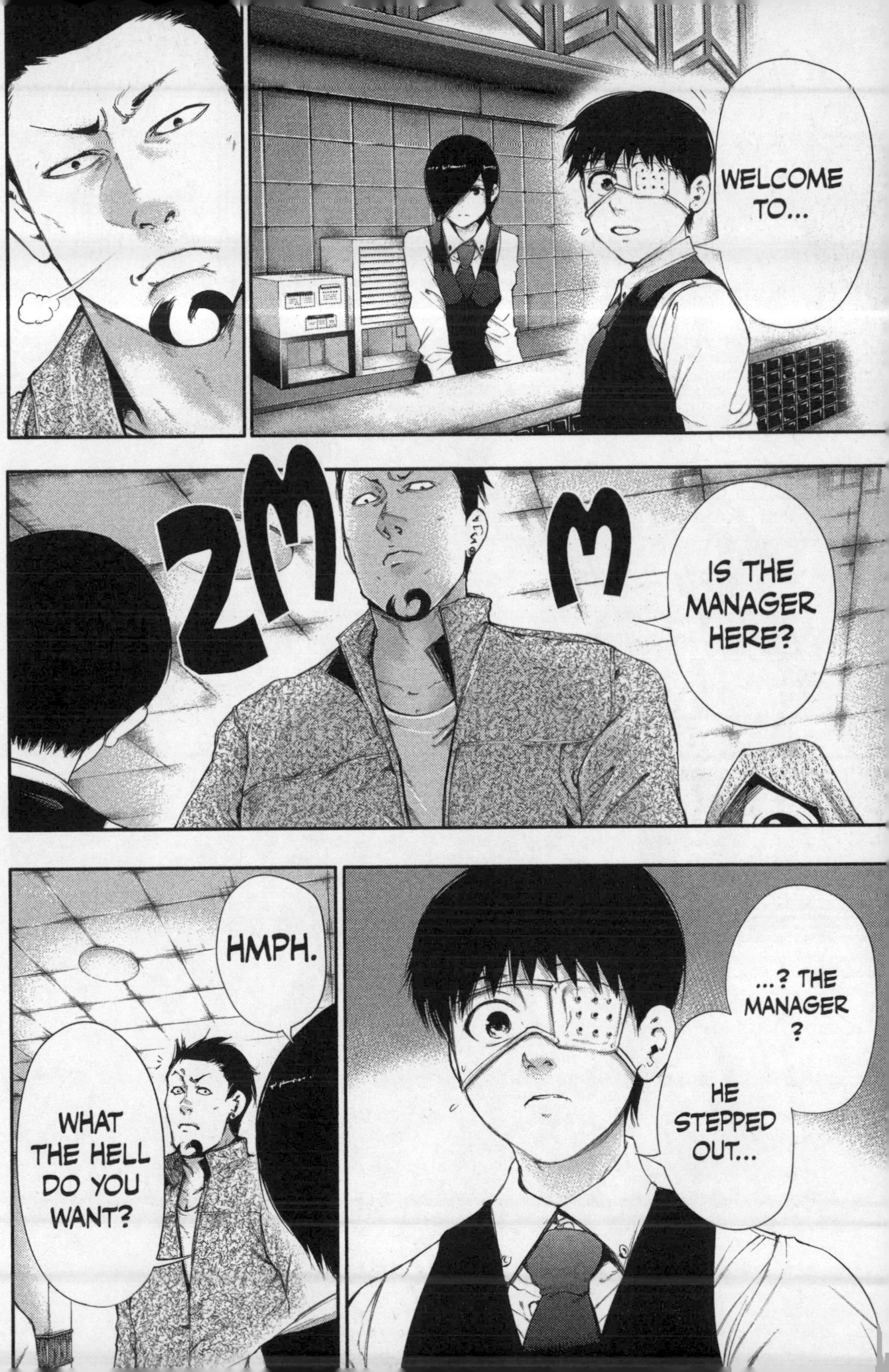
WELCOME TO...
ZMM
IS THE MANAGER HERE?
...? THE MANAGER ?
HE STEPPED OUT...
HMPH.
WHAT THE HELL DO YOU WANT?

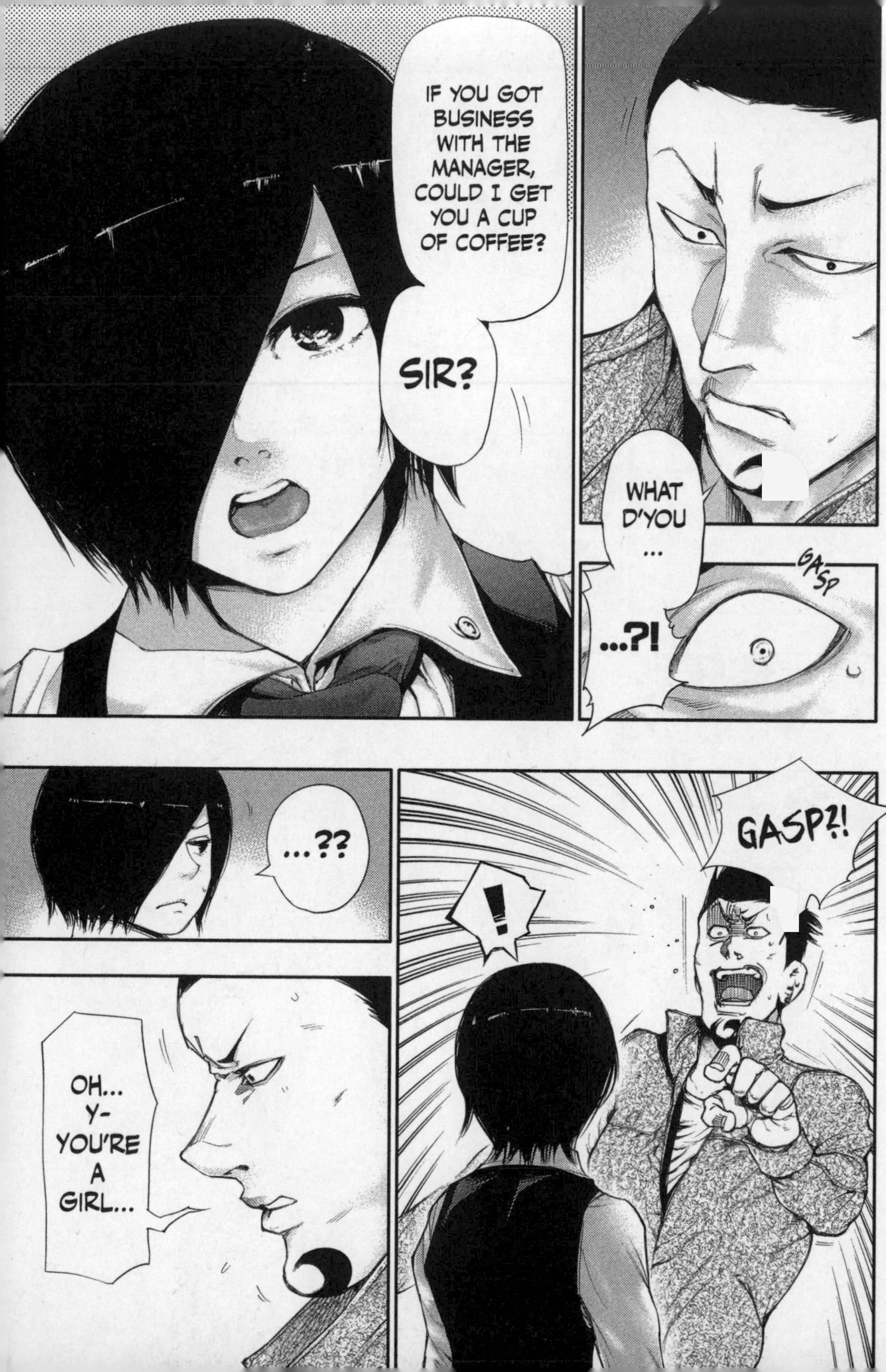
WHAT D'YOU ...
GASP
...?!
IF YOU GOT BUSINESS WITH THE MANAGER, COULD I GET YOU A CUP OF COFFEE?
SIR?
GASP?!
!
...??
OH... Y- YOU'RE A GIRL...

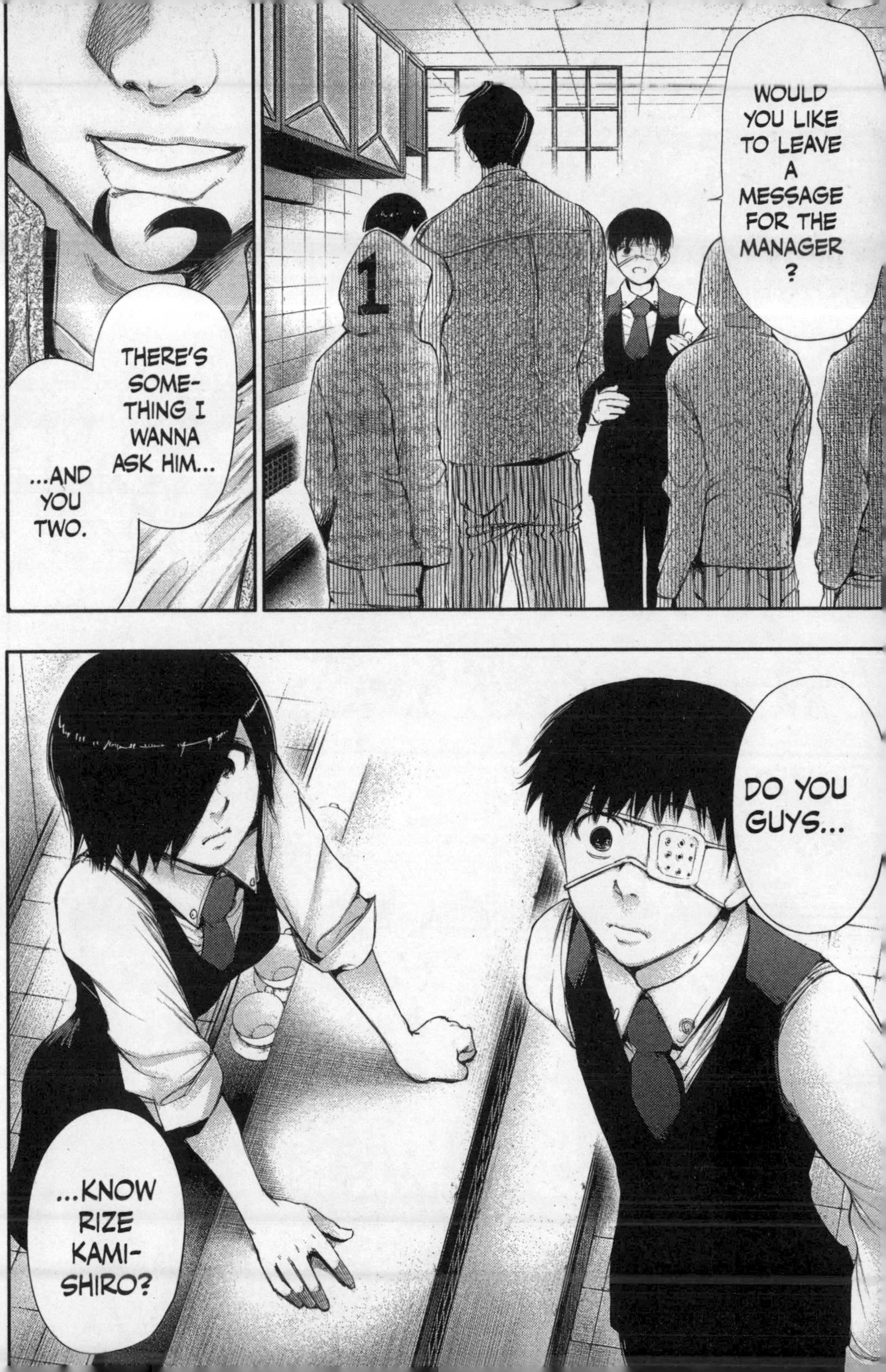
WOULD YOU LIKE TO LEAVE A MESSAGE FOR THE MANAGER?
THERE'S SOMETHING I WANNA ASK HIM...
...AND YOU TWO.
DO YOU GUYS...
...KNOW RIZE KAMISHIRO?

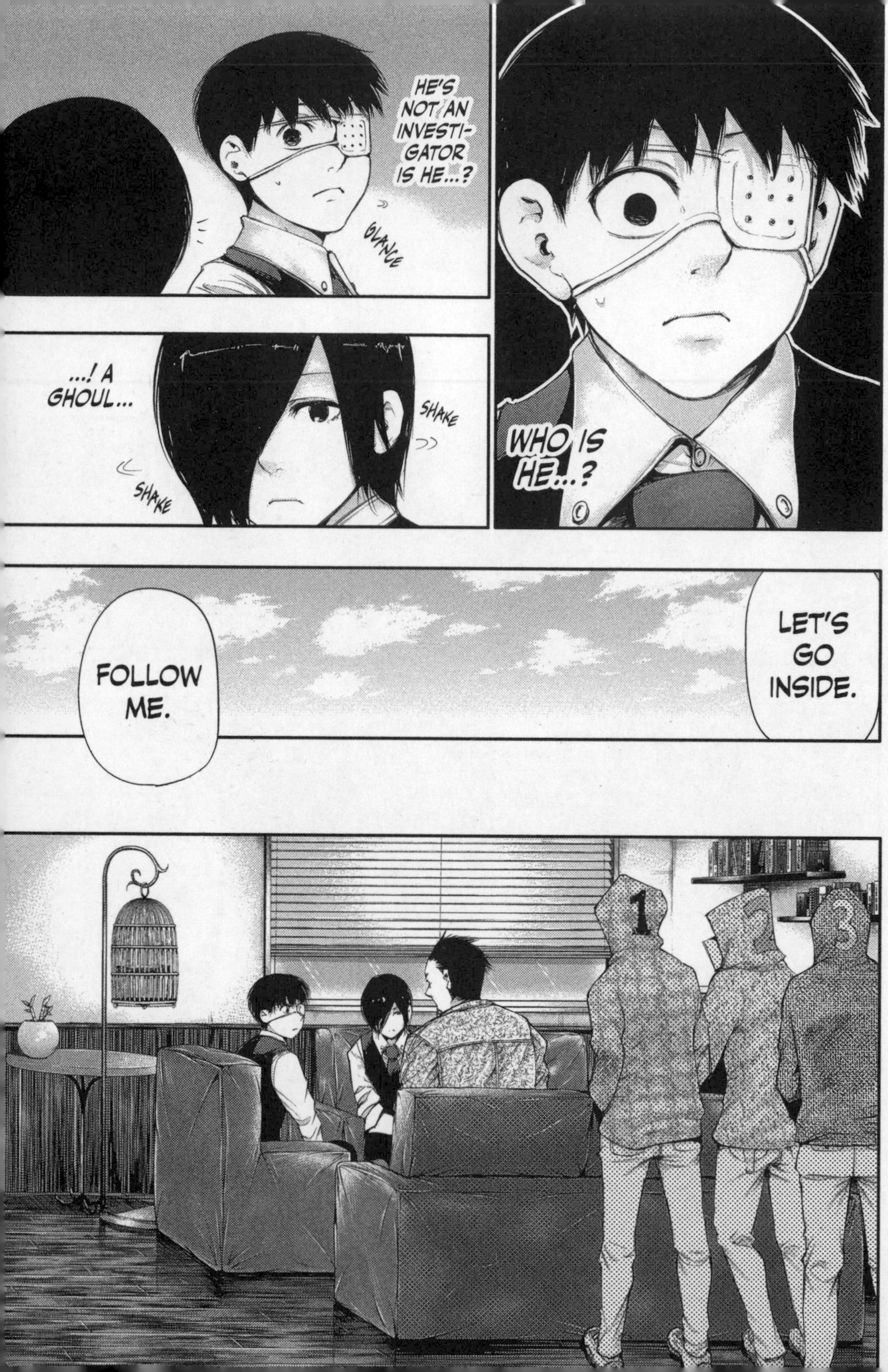
WHO IS HE...?
HE'S NOT AN INVESTIGATOR IS HE...?
GLANCE
...! A GHOUL...
SHAKE
SHAKE
LET'S GO INSIDE.
FOLLOW ME.

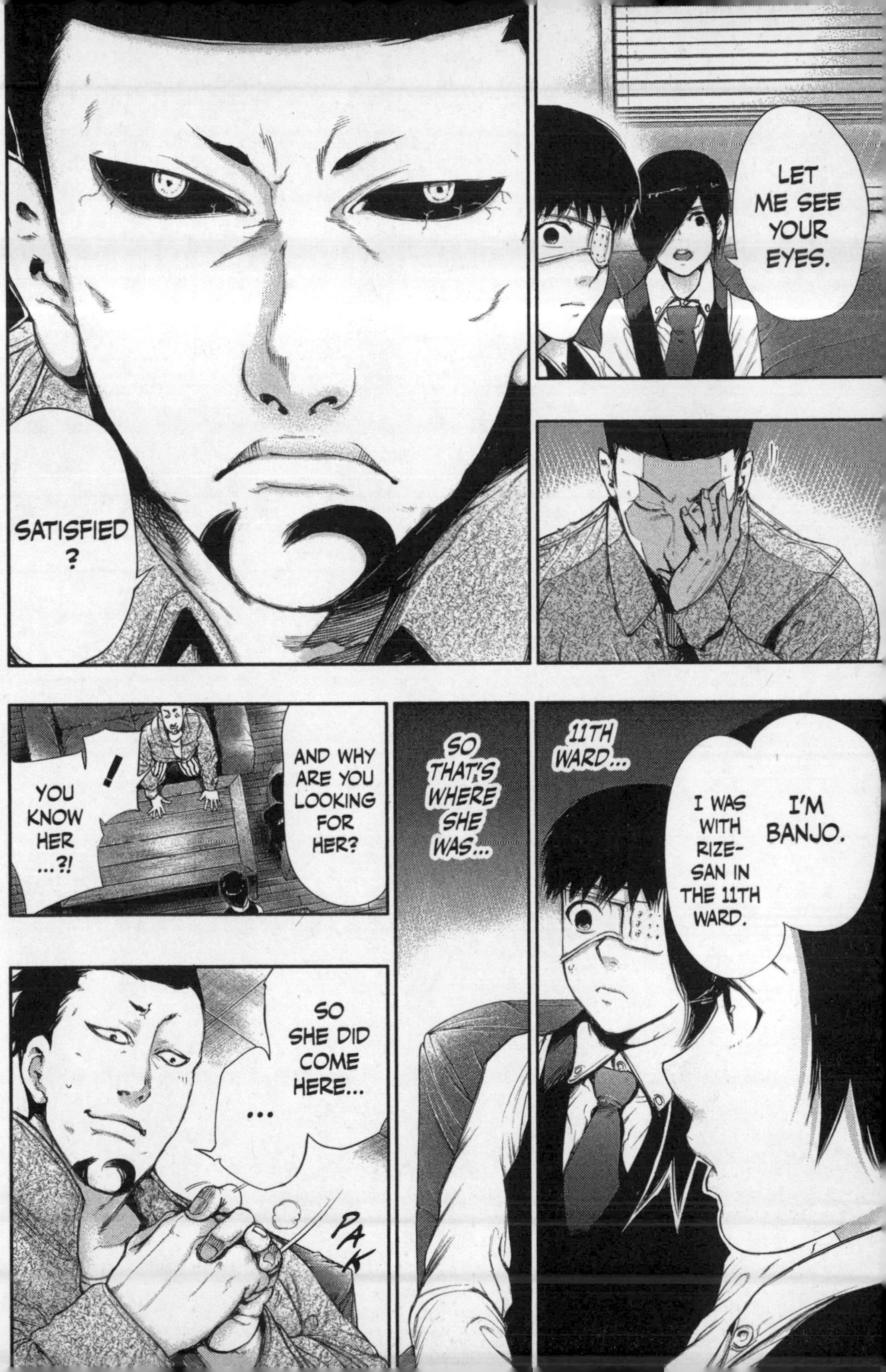
LET ME SEE YOUR EYES.
SATISFIED ?
I'M BANJO.
I WAS WITH RIZE-SAN IN THE 11TH WARD.
11TH WARD...
SO THAT'S WHERE SHE WAS...
AND WHY ARE YOU LOOKING FOR HER?
YOU KNOW HER ...?!
SO SHE DID COME HERE...
...
PAK

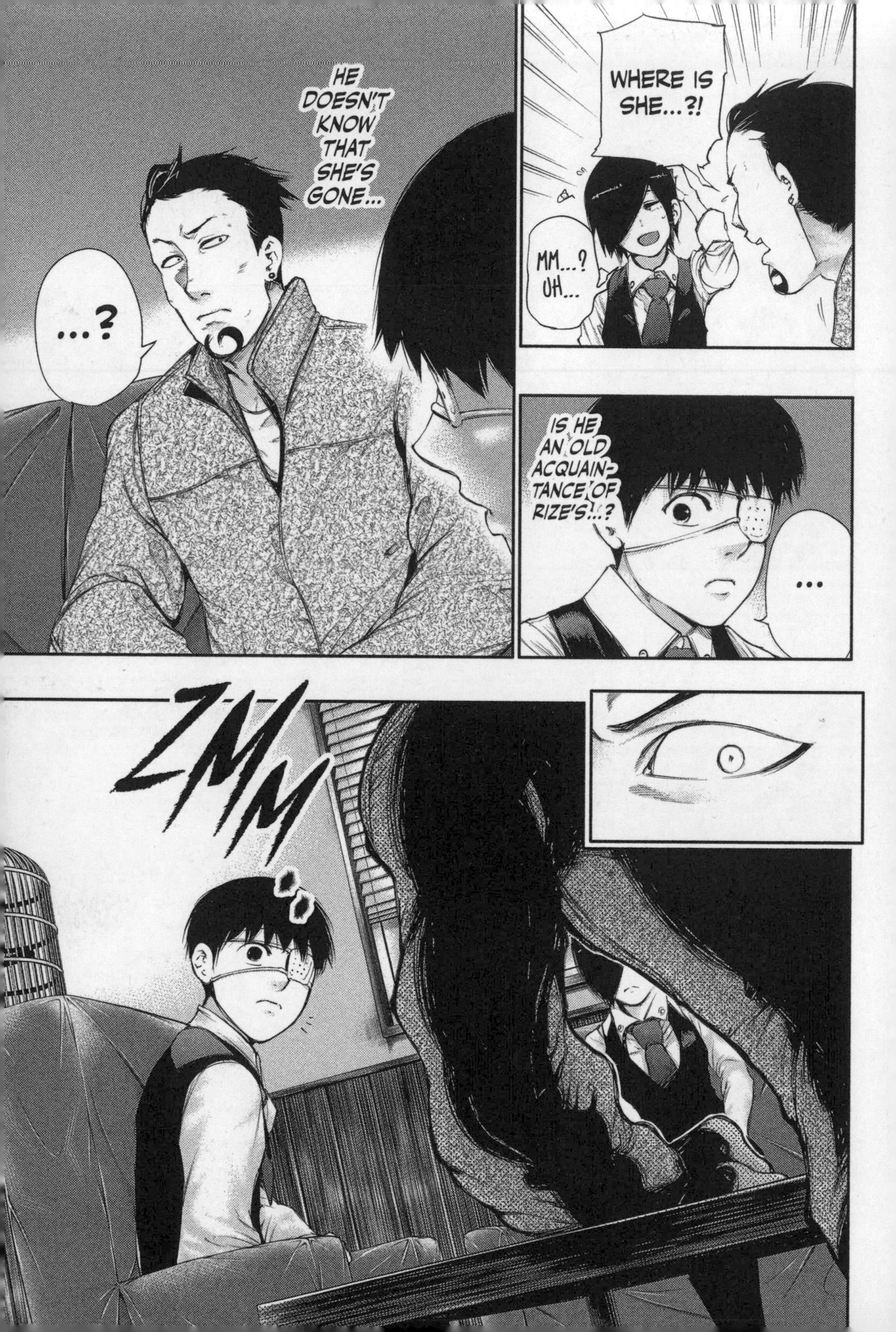
WHERE IS SHE...?!
MM...? UH...
IS HE AN OLD ACQUAINTANCE OF RIZE'S...?
...
HE DOESN'T KNOW THAT SHE'S GONE...
...?
ZMM

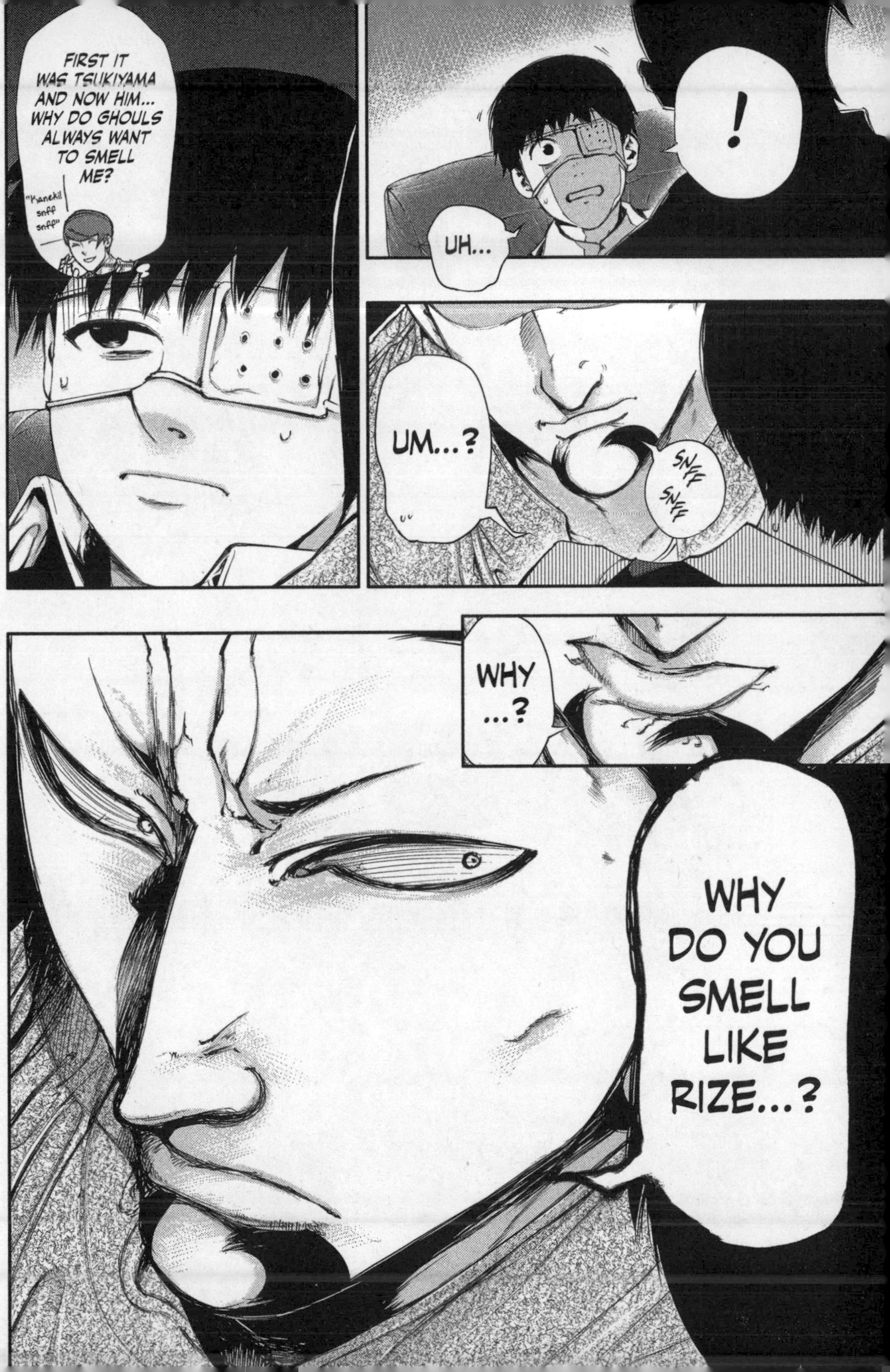
!
UH...
UM...?
SNFF SNFF
FIRST IT WAS TSUKIYAMA AND NOW HIM... WHY DO GHOULS ALWAYS WANT TO SMELL ME?
"Kaneki! snff snff"
WHY ...?
WHY DO YOU SMELL LIKE RIZE...?

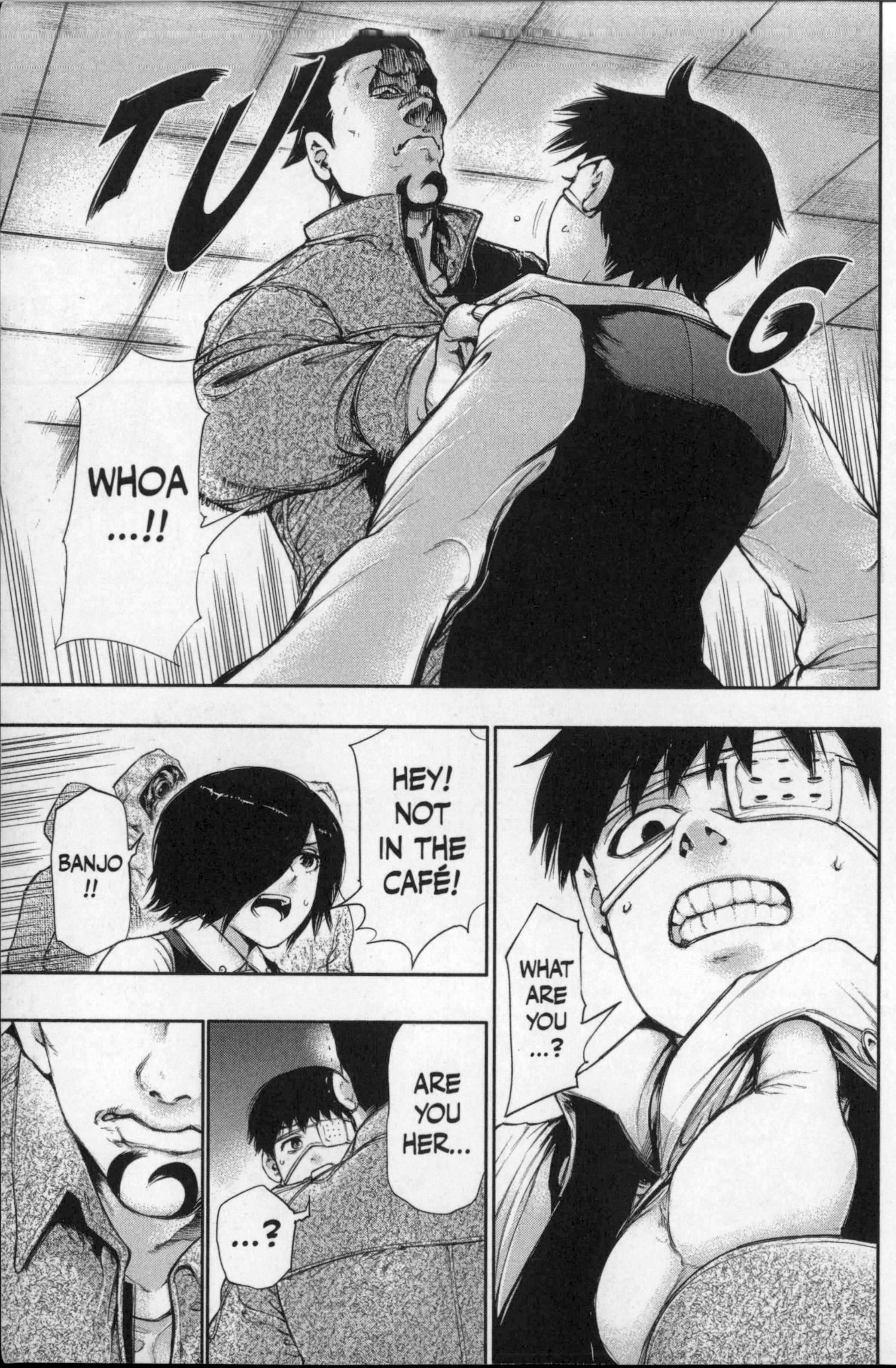
TUG
WHOA ...!!
WHAT ARE YOU ...?
HEY! NOT IN THE CAFÉ!
BANJO !!
ARE YOU HER...
...?

ARE YOU RIZE-SAN'S BOY-FRIEND?!

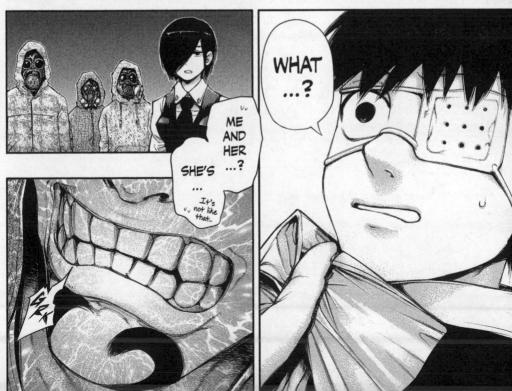

WHAT ...?

ME AND HER ...?

SHE'S ...

It's not like that...

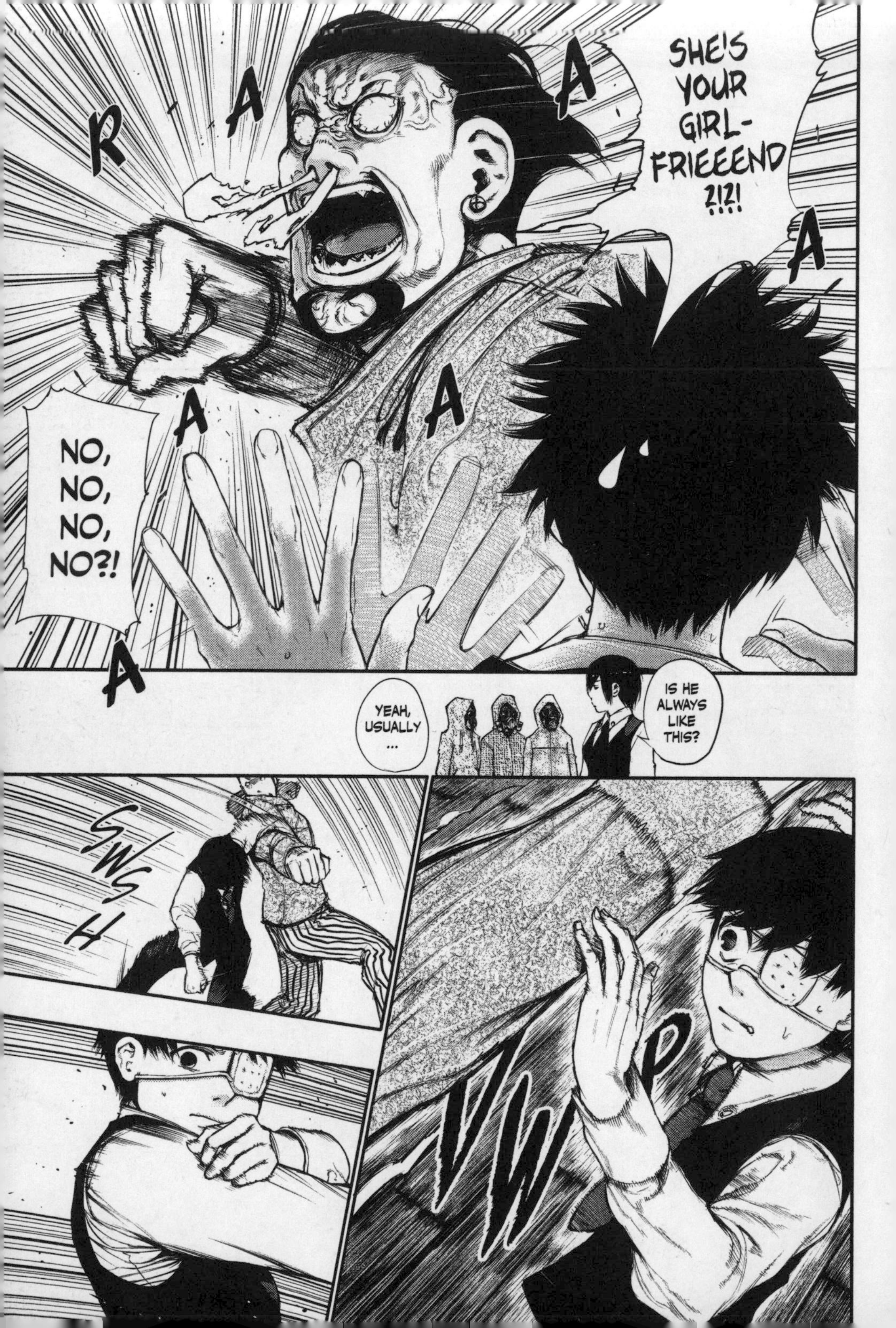
SHE'S YOUR GIRL-FRIEEEND ?!?!
RAAAAAA
NO, NO, NO, NO?!
IS HE ALWAYS LIKE THIS?
YEAH, USUALLY ...
VWP
SWSH

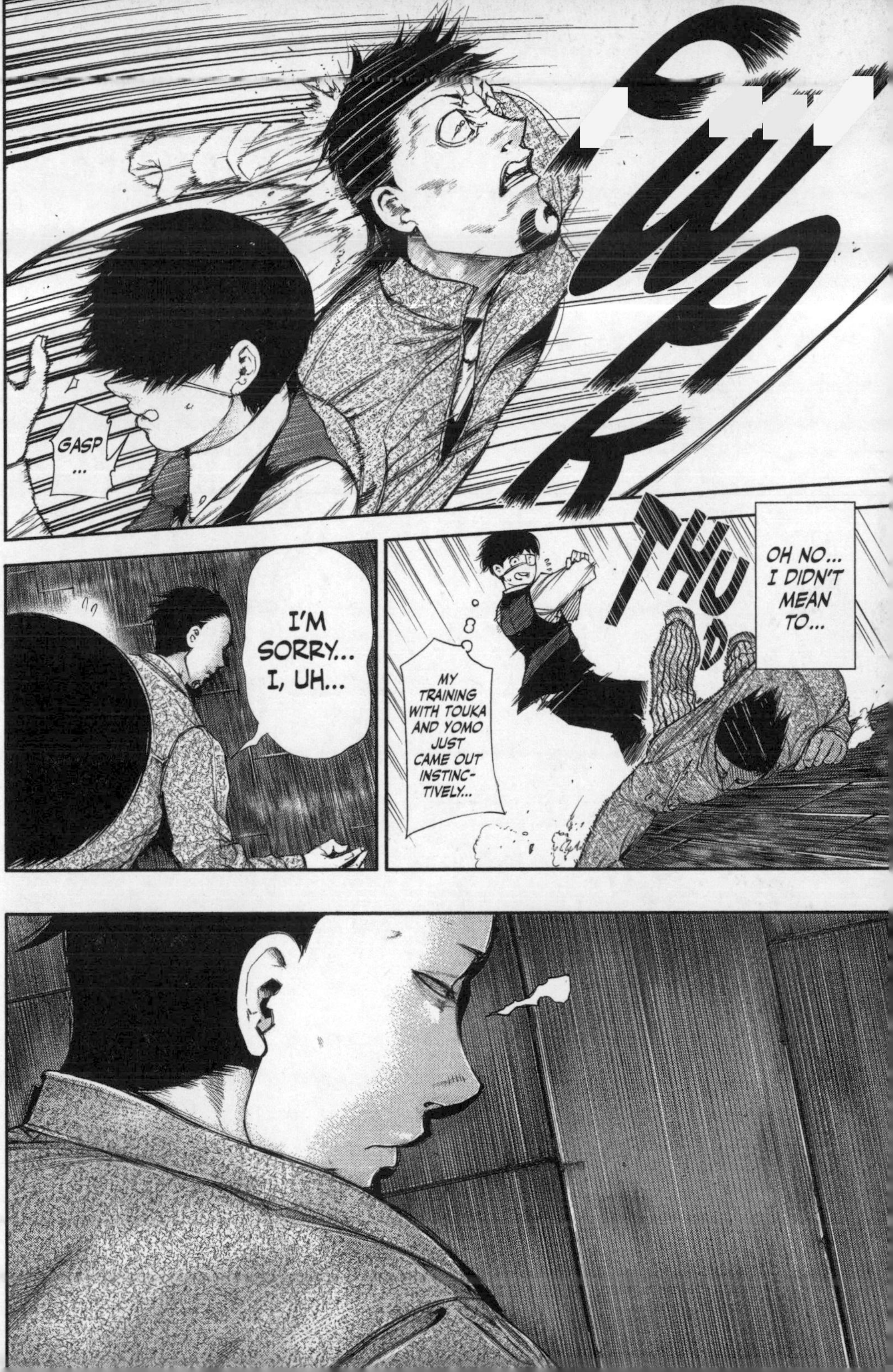
GASP...
OH NO... I DIDN'T MEAN TO...
THUD
MY TRAINING WITH TOUKA AND YOMO JUST CAME OUT INSTINCTIVELY...
I'M SORRY... I, UH...

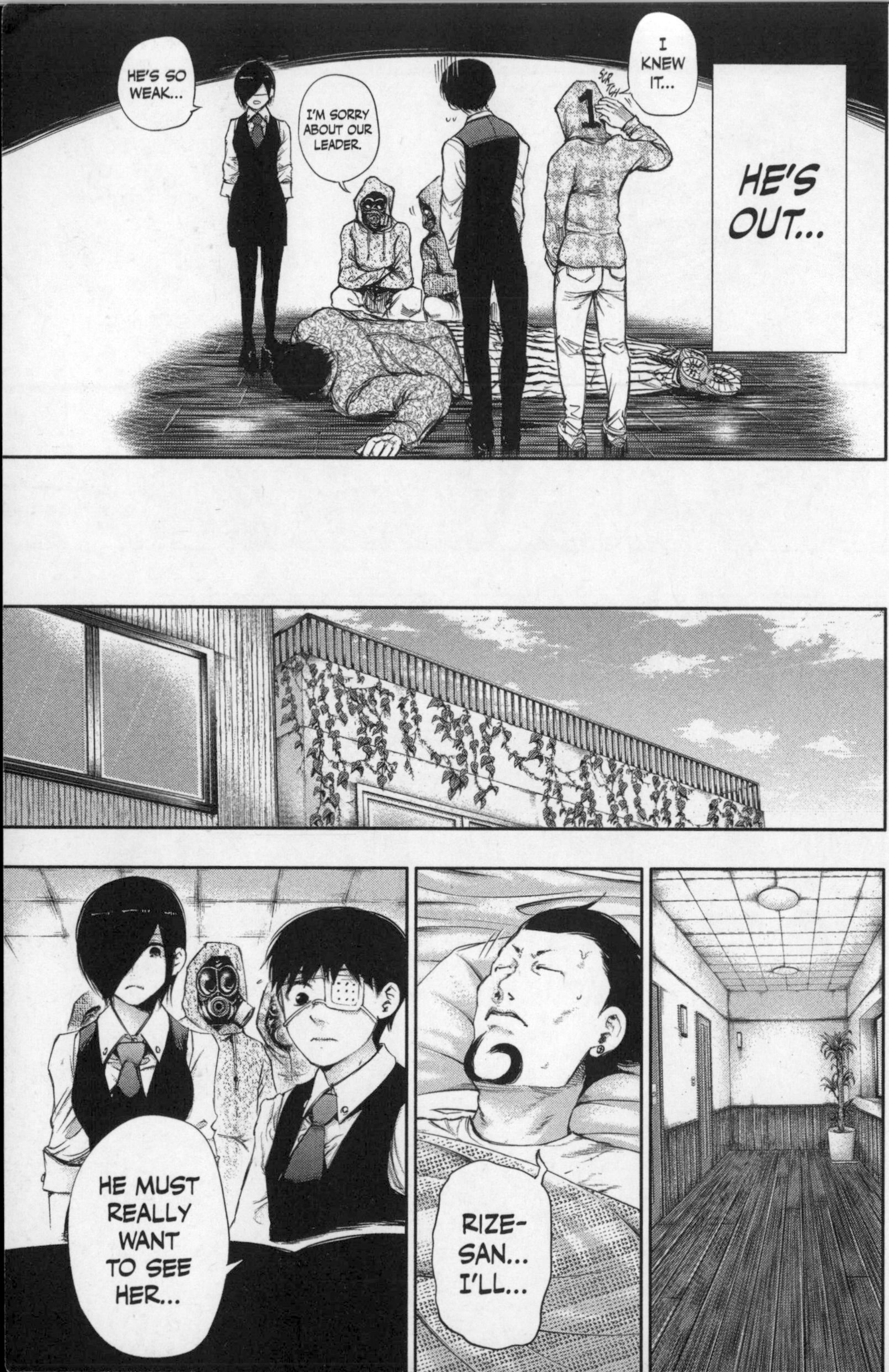
HE'S OUT...
I KNEW IT...
I'M SORRY ABOUT OUR LEADER.
HE'S SO WEAK...
RIZE-SAN... I'LL...
HE MUST REALLY WANT TO SEE HER...

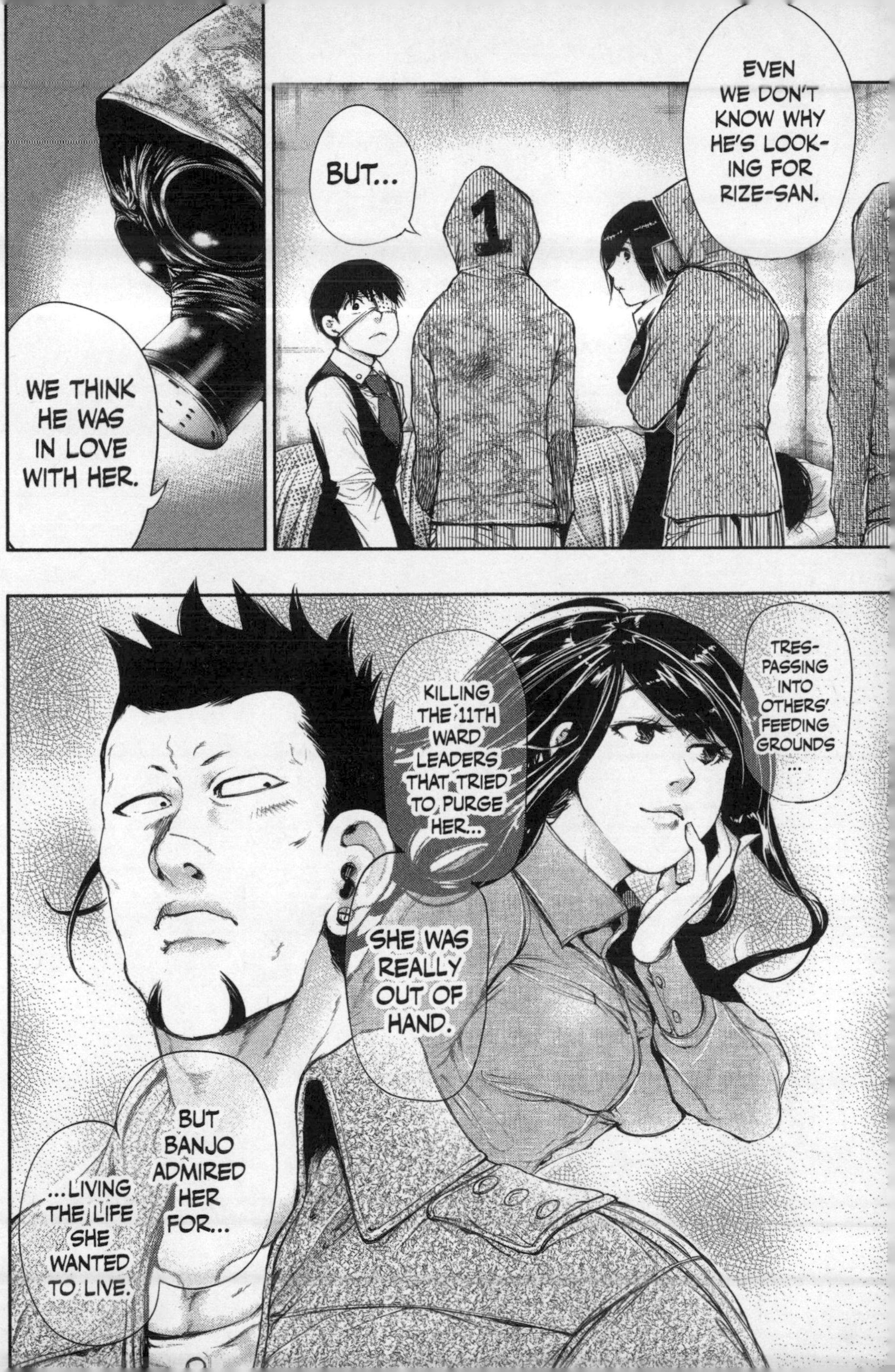
EVEN WE DON'T KNOW WHY HE'S LOOKING FOR RIZE-SAN.
BUT...
WE THINK HE WAS IN LOVE WITH HER.
TRES-PASSING INTO OTHERS' FEEDING GROUNDS...
KILLING THE 11TH WARD LEADERS THAT TRIED TO PURGE HER...
SHE WAS REALLY OUT OF HAND.
BUT BANJO ADMIRED HER FOR...
...LIVING THE LIFE SHE WANTED TO LIVE.

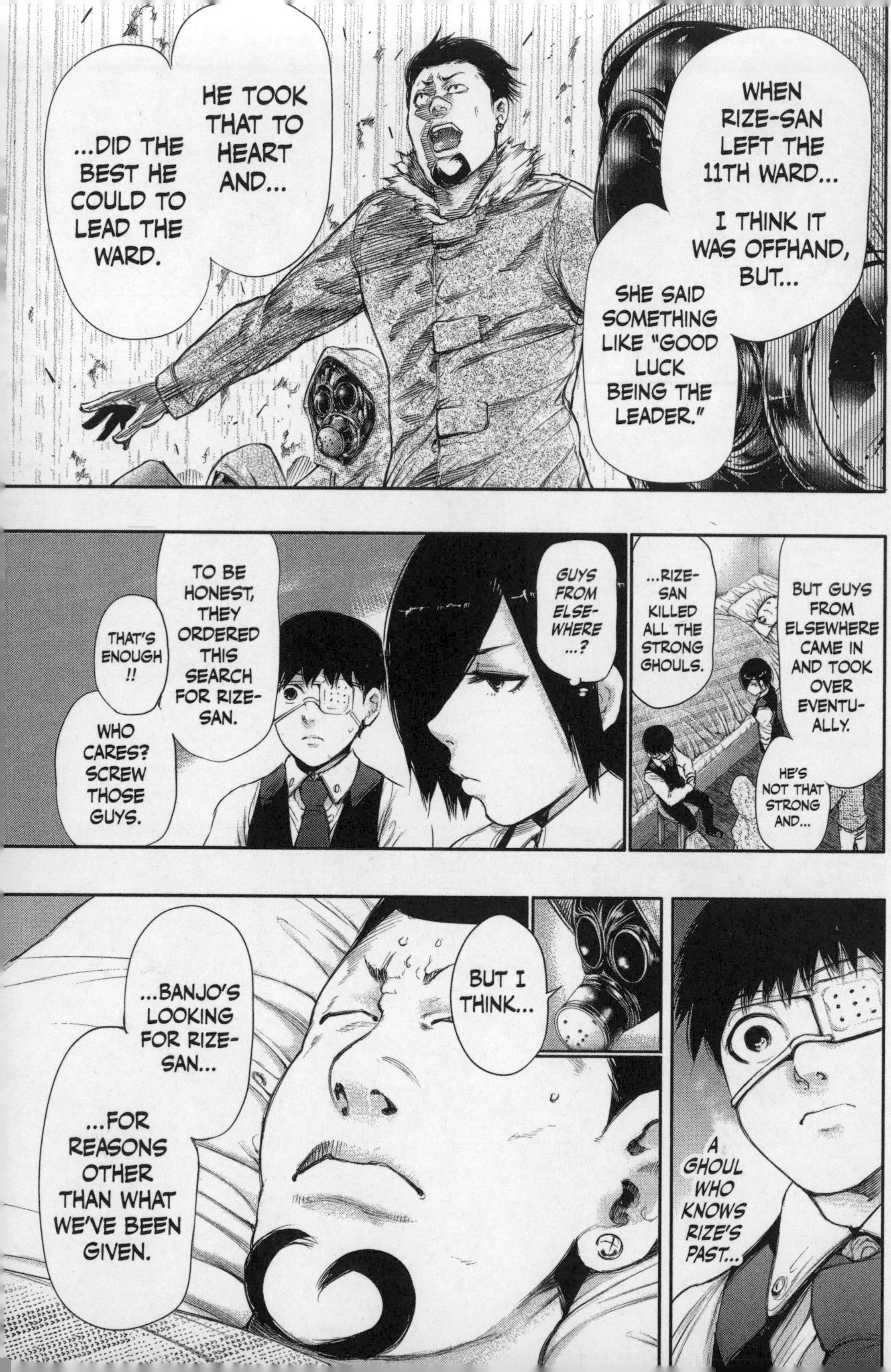
WHEN RIZE-SAN LEFT THE 11TH WARD...
I THINK IT WAS OFFHAND, BUT...
SHE SAID SOMETHING LIKE "GOOD LUCK BEING THE LEADER."
HE TOOK THAT TO HEART AND...
...DID THE BEST HE COULD TO LEAD THE WARD.
...RIZE-SAN KILLED ALL THE STRONG GHOULS.
BUT GUYS FROM ELSEWHERE CAME IN AND TOOK OVER EVENTUALLY.
HE'S NOT THAT STRONG AND...
GUYS FROM ELSEWHERE ...?
TO BE HONEST, THEY ORDERED THIS SEARCH FOR RIZE-SAN.
THAT'S ENOUGH !!
WHO CARES? SCREW THOSE GUYS.
A GHOUL WHO KNOWS RIZE'S PAST...
BUT I THINK...
...BANJO'S LOOKING FOR RIZE-SAN...
...FOR REASONS OTHER THAN WHAT WE'VE BEEN GIVEN.

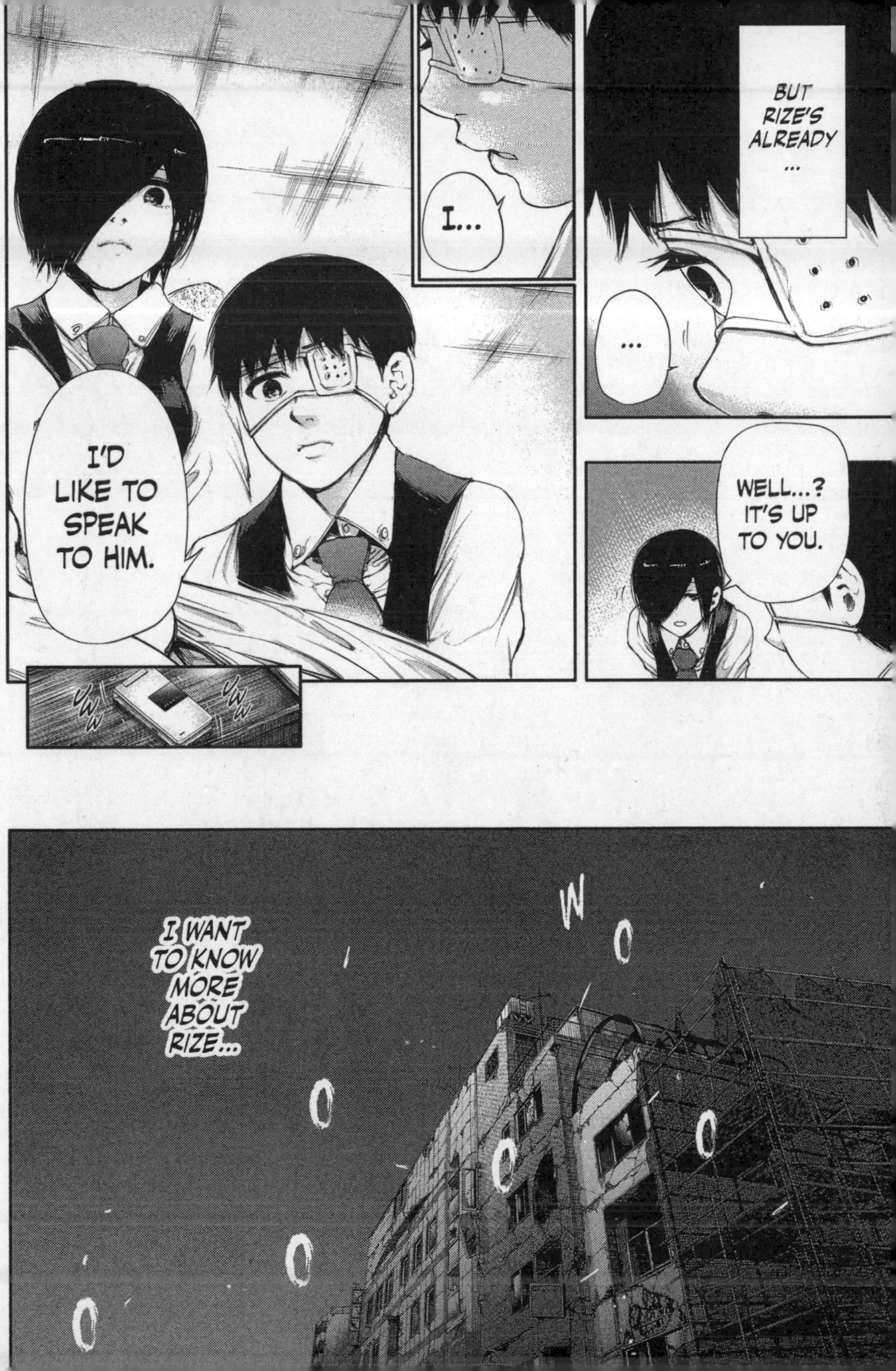
BUT RIZE'S ALREADY ...
...
I...
WELL...? IT'S UP TO YOU.
I'D LIKE TO SPEAK TO HIM.
VWW
VWW
I WANT TO KNOW MORE ABOUT RIZE...
WOOOOOO

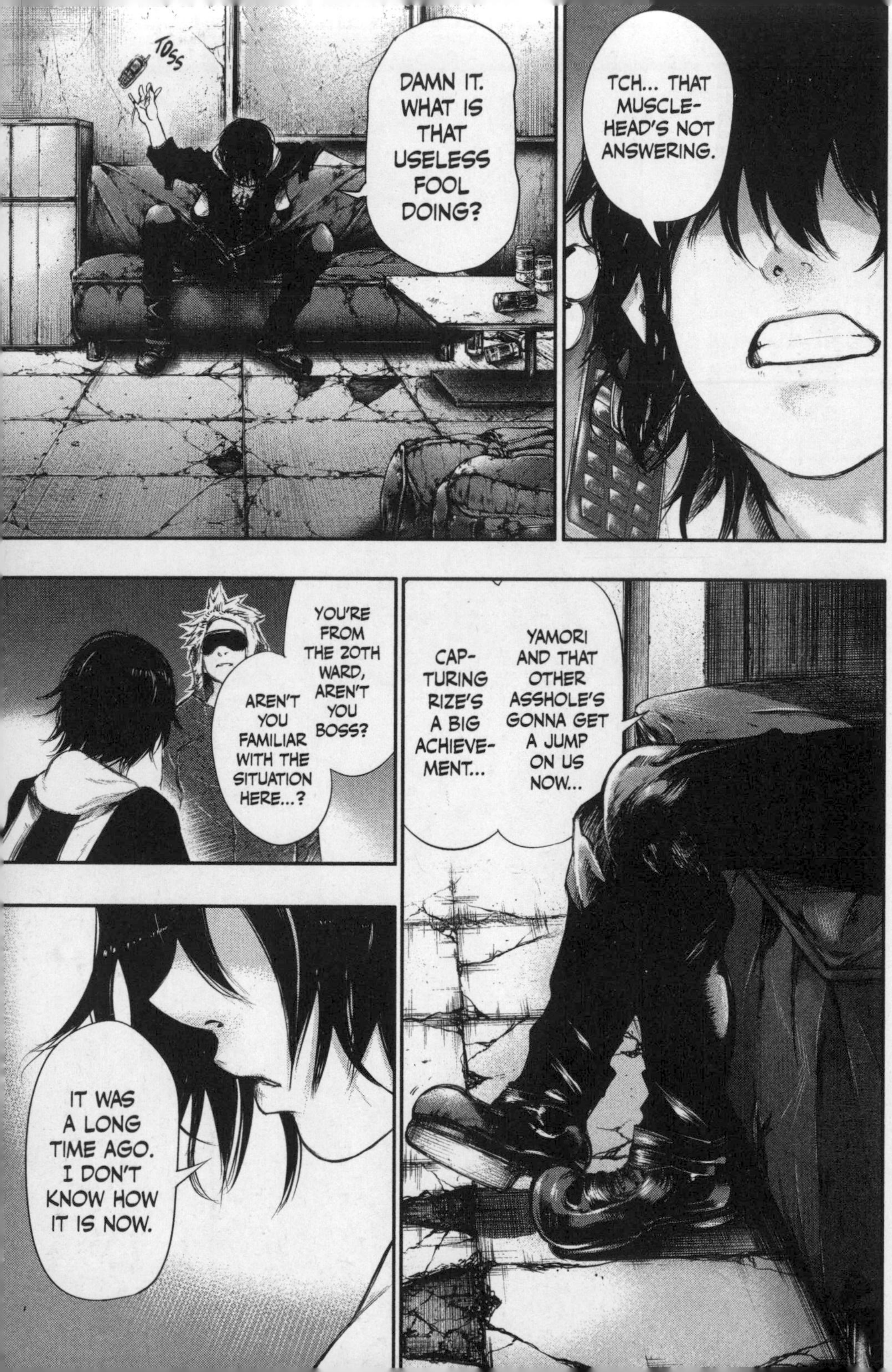
TCH... THAT MUSCLE-HEAD'S NOT ANSWERING.
TOSS
DAMN IT. WHAT IS THAT USELESS FOOL DOING?
YAMORI AND THAT OTHER ASSHOLE'S GONNA GET A JUMP ON US NOW...
CAP-TURING RIZE'S A BIG ACHIEVE-MENT...
YOU'RE FROM THE 20TH WARD, AREN'T YOU BOSS?
AREN'T YOU FAMILIAR WITH THE SITUATION HERE...?
IT WAS A LONG TIME AGO. I DON'T KNOW HOW IT IS NOW.

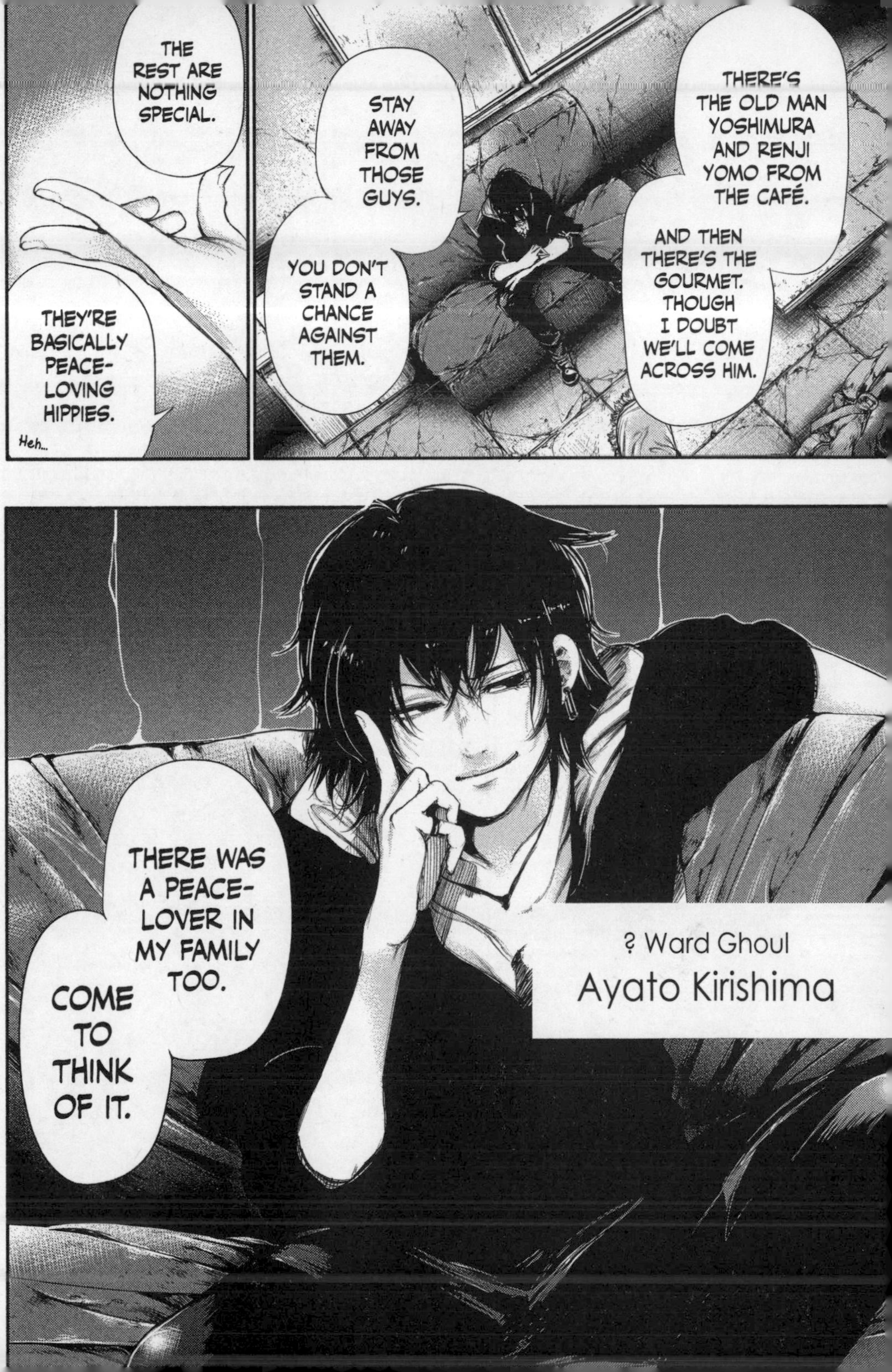
THERE'S THE OLD MAN YOSHIMURA AND RENJI YOMO FROM THE CAFÉ.
AND THEN THERE'S THE GOURMET. THOUGH I DOUBT WE'LL COME ACROSS HIM.
STAY AWAY FROM THOSE GUYS.
YOU DON'T STAND A CHANCE AGAINST THEM.
THE REST ARE NOTHING SPECIAL.
THEY'RE BASICALLY PEACE-LOVING HIPPIES.
Heh...
? Ward Ghoul
Ayato Kirishima
THERE WAS A PEACE-LOVER IN MY FAMILY TOO.
COME TO THINK OF IT.

東京喰種
トーキョーグール
Tokyo
Ghoul

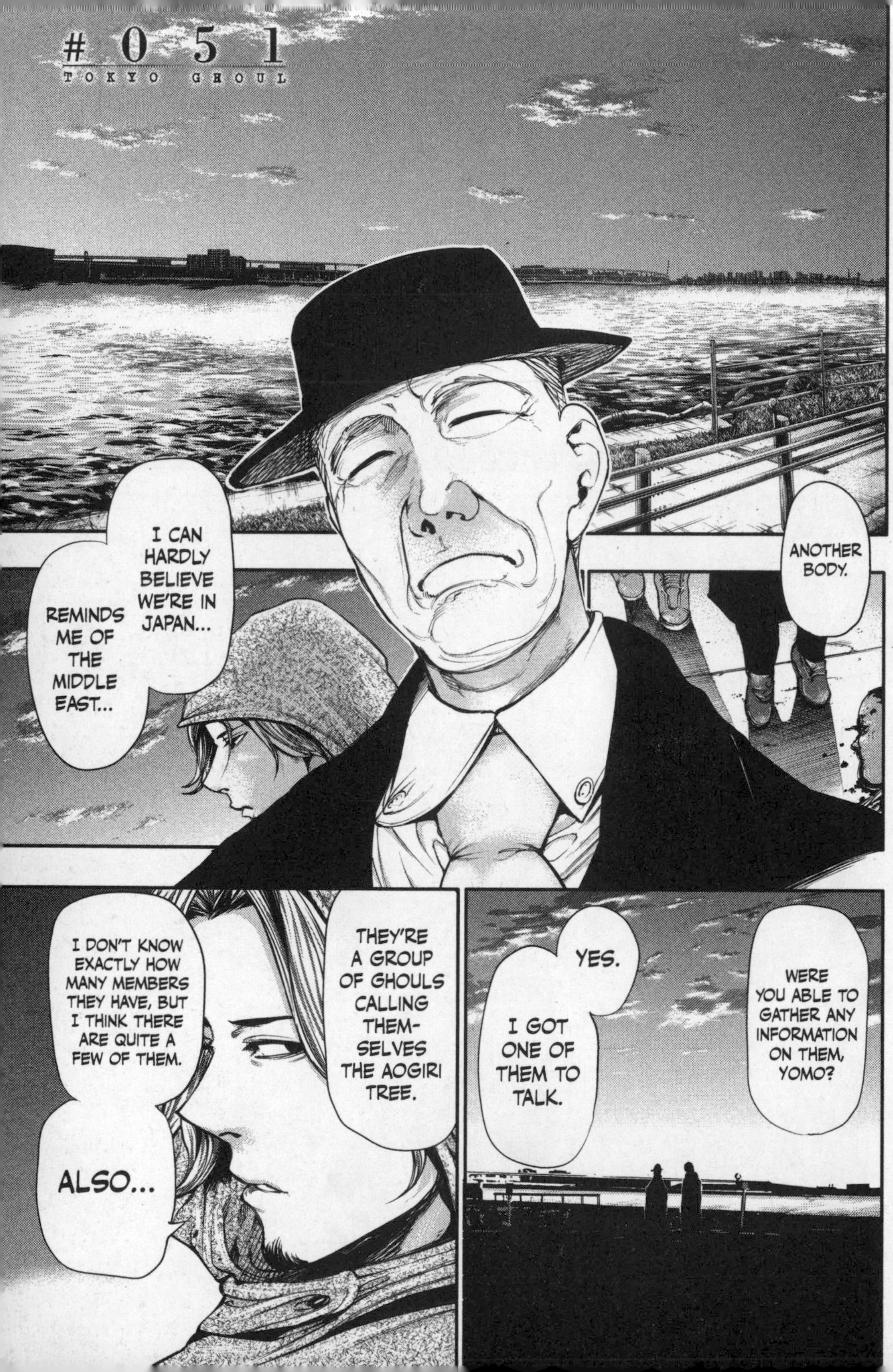
#051
TOKYO GHOUL
ANOTHER BODY.
I CAN HARDLY BELIEVE WE'RE IN JAPAN...
REMINDS ME OF THE MIDDLE EAST...
WERE YOU ABLE TO GATHER ANY INFORMATION ON THEM, YOMO?
YES.
I GOT ONE OF THEM TO TALK.
THEY'RE A GROUP OF GHOULS CALLING THEM-SELVES THE AOGIRI TREE.
I DON'T KNOW EXACTLY HOW MANY MEMBERS THEY HAVE, BUT I THINK THERE ARE QUITE A FEW OF THEM.
ALSO...

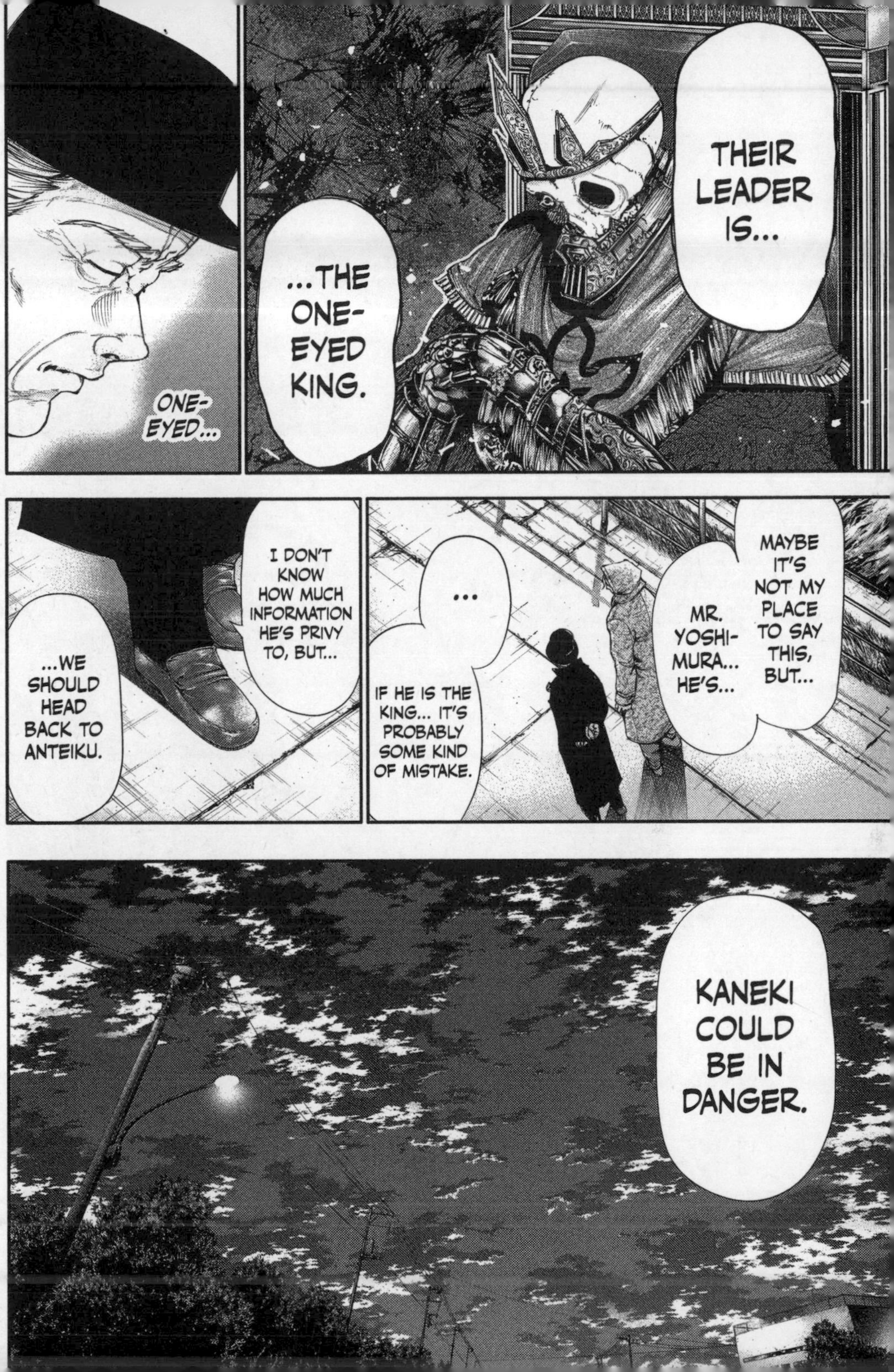
THEIR LEADER IS...
...THE ONE-EYED KING.
ONE-EYED...
MAYBE IT'S NOT MY PLACE TO SAY THIS, BUT...
MR. YOSHIMURA... HE'S...
...
IF HE IS THE KING... IT'S PROBABLY SOME KIND OF MISTAKE.
I DON'T KNOW HOW MUCH INFORMATION HE'S PRIVY TO, BUT...
...WE SHOULD HEAD BACK TO ANTEIKU.
KANEKI COULD BE IN DANGER.

# #051 [EDICT]

TOKYO GHOUL

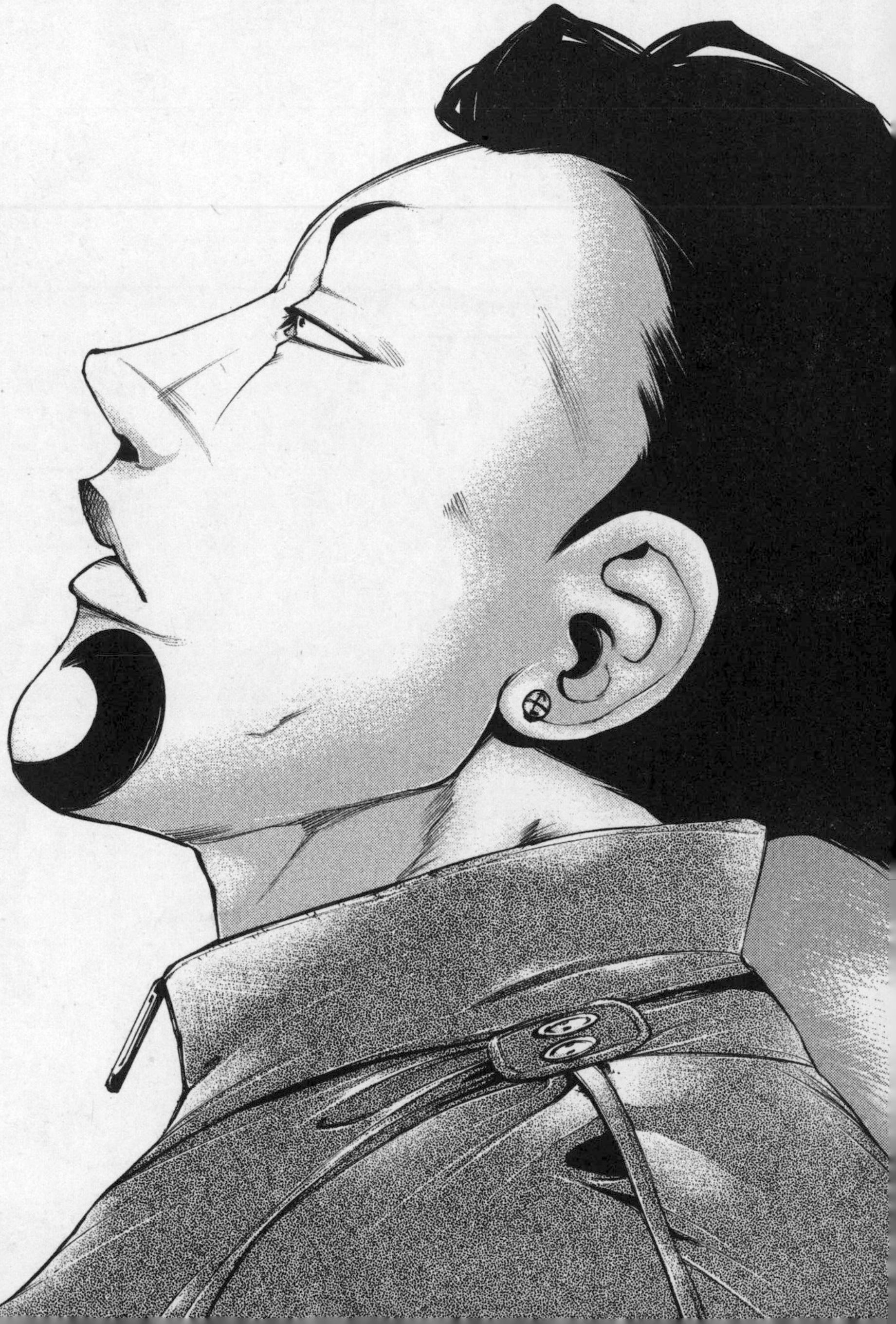

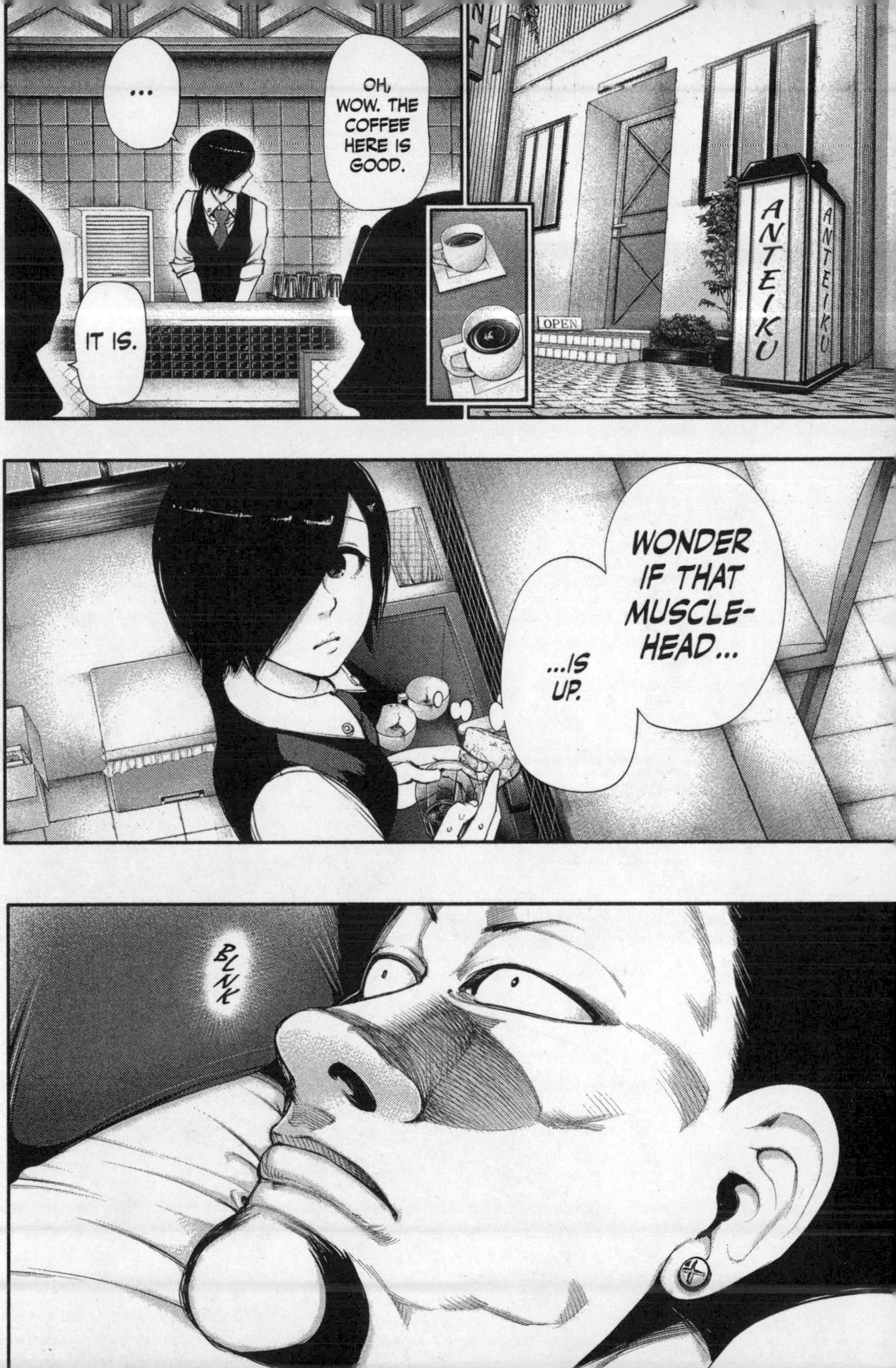
ANTEIKU
ANTEIKU
OPEN
OH, WOW. THE COFFEE HERE IS GOOD.
...
IT IS.
WONDER IF THAT MUSCLE-HEAD...
...IS UP.
BLNK

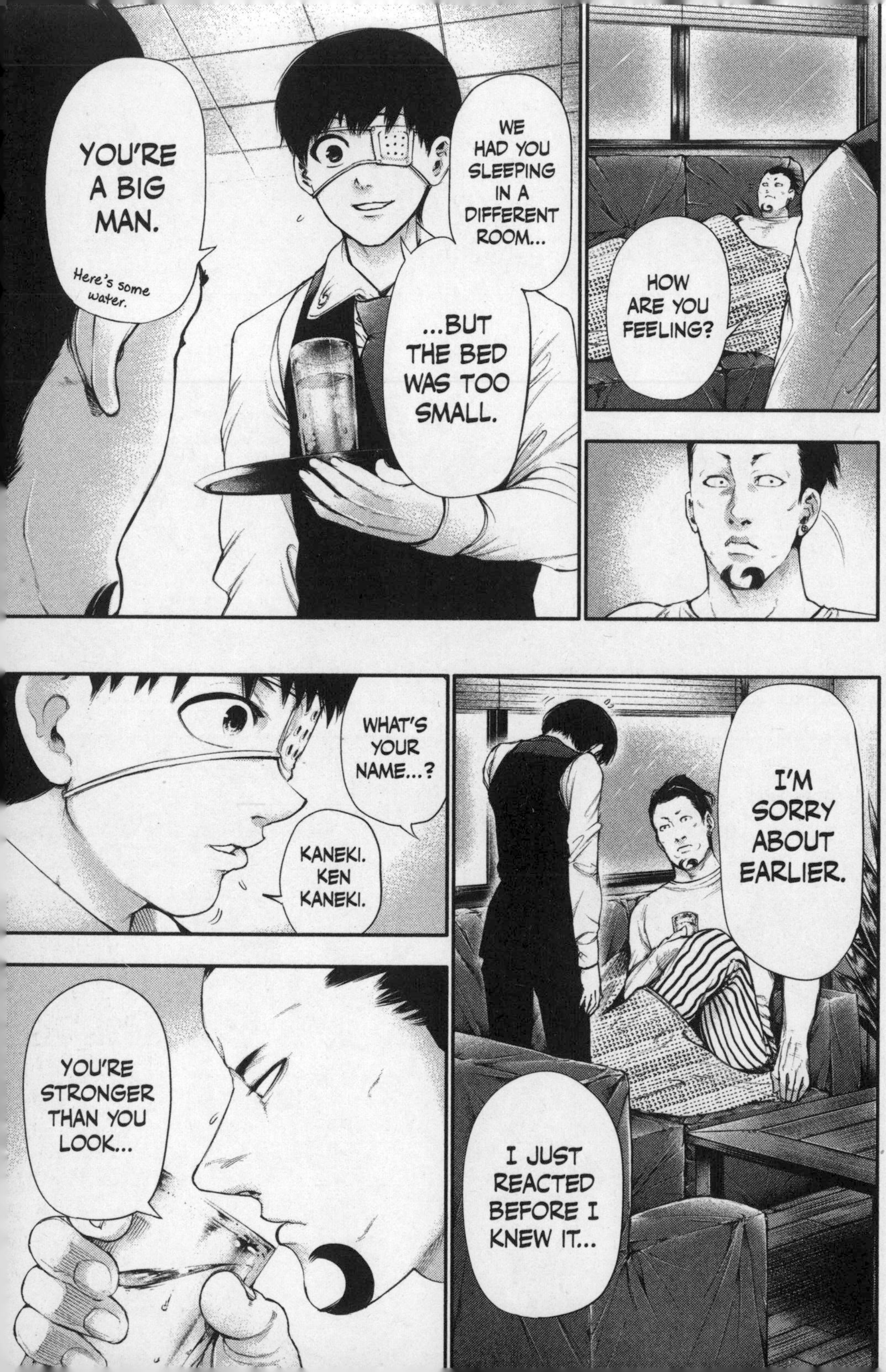
HOW ARE YOU FEELING?
WE HAD YOU SLEEPING IN A DIFFERENT ROOM...
...BUT THE BED WAS TOO SMALL.
YOU'RE A BIG MAN.
Here's some water.
I'M SORRY ABOUT EARLIER.
I JUST REACTED BEFORE I KNEW IT...
WHAT'S YOUR NAME...?
KANEKI. KEN KANEKI.
YOU'RE STRONGER THAN YOU LOOK...

WE WERE BASICALLY CASUAL ACQUAINTANCES...

...

OH...

MAYBE THAT'S WHY SHE CHOSE YOU...

I DIDN'T HAVE THAT KIND OF RELATIONSHIP WITH RIZE...

UM, BANJO...

I'M NOT...

P-PLEASE! THERE'S NO NEED TO...

I'M SORRY! I REALLY AM!

NO! THIS IS THE LEAST I CAN DO!

I'M SORRY!!

COME TO THINK OF IT, YOUR SCENT'S A BIT DIFFERENT THAN HERS...

I'M SORRY I LOST IT...

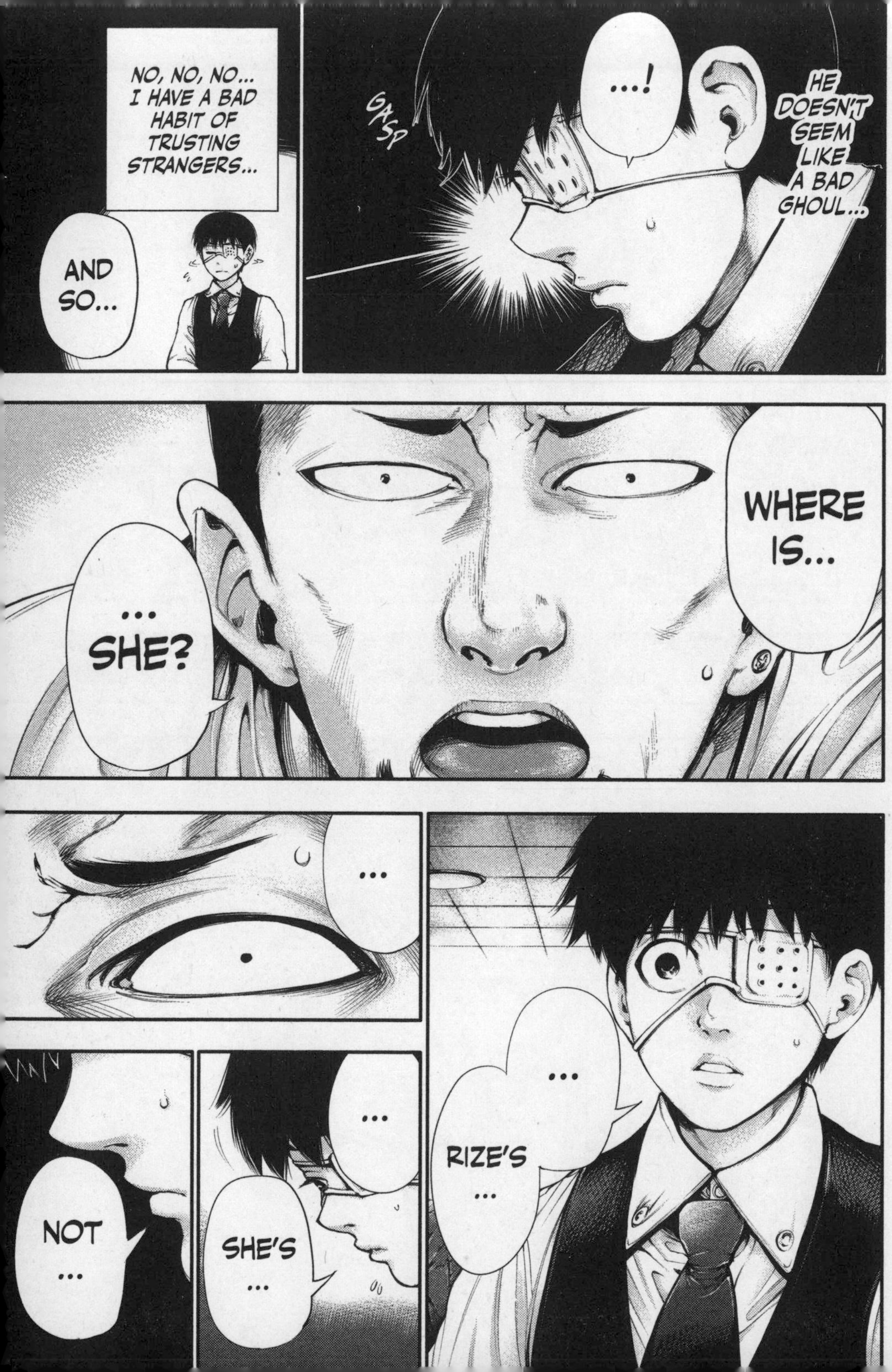
...!
GASP
HE DOESN'T SEEM LIKE A BAD GHOUL...
NO, NO, NO... I HAVE A BAD HABIT OF TRUSTING STRANGERS...
AND SO...
WHERE IS...
... SHE?
...
RIZE'S ...
...
...
SHE'S ...
NOT ...

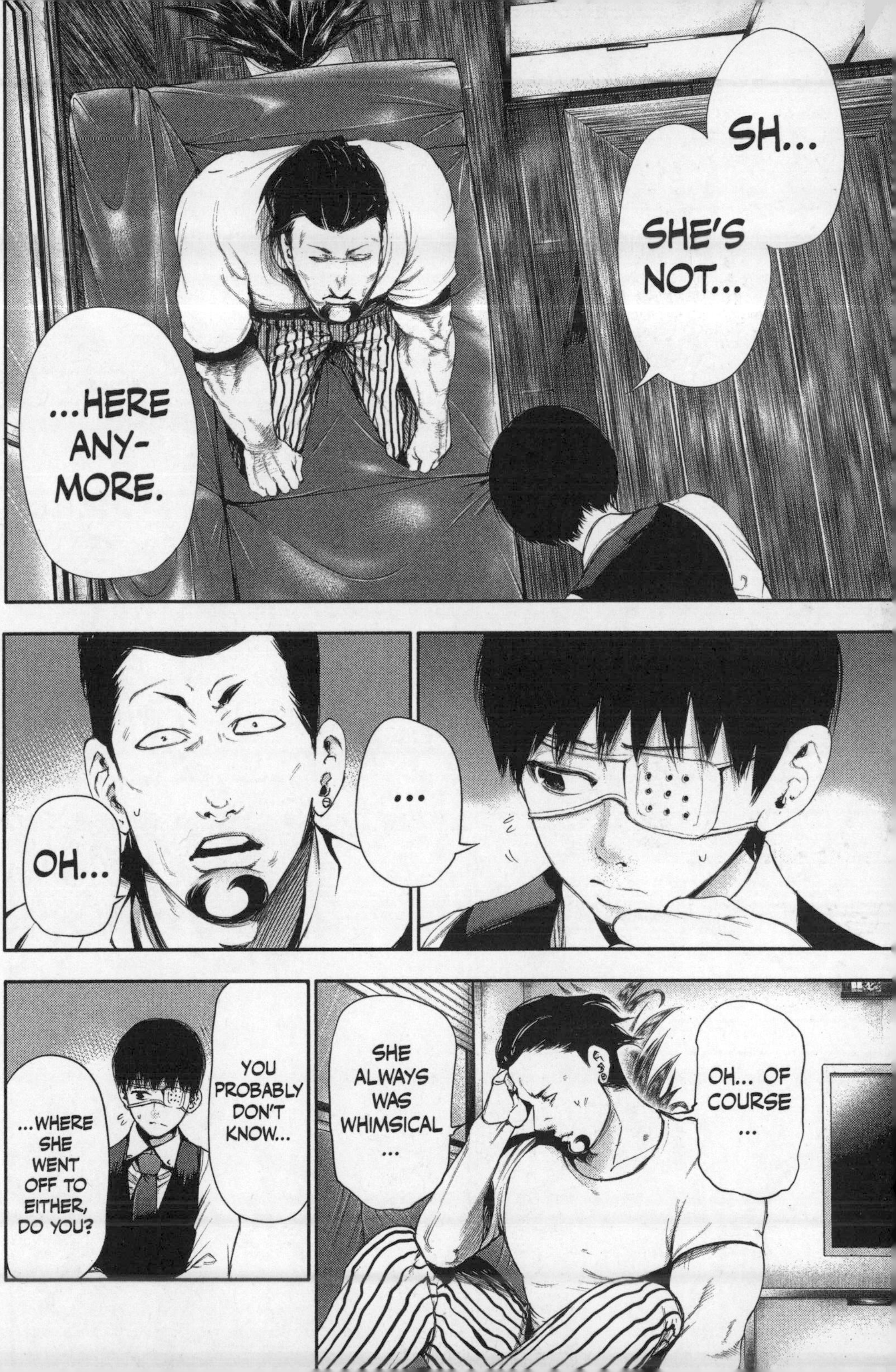
SH...
SHE'S NOT...
...HERE ANYMORE.
...
OH...
OH... OF COURSE ...
SHE ALWAYS WAS WHIMSICAL ...
YOU PROBABLY DON'T KNOW...
...WHERE SHE WENT OFF TO EITHER, DO YOU?

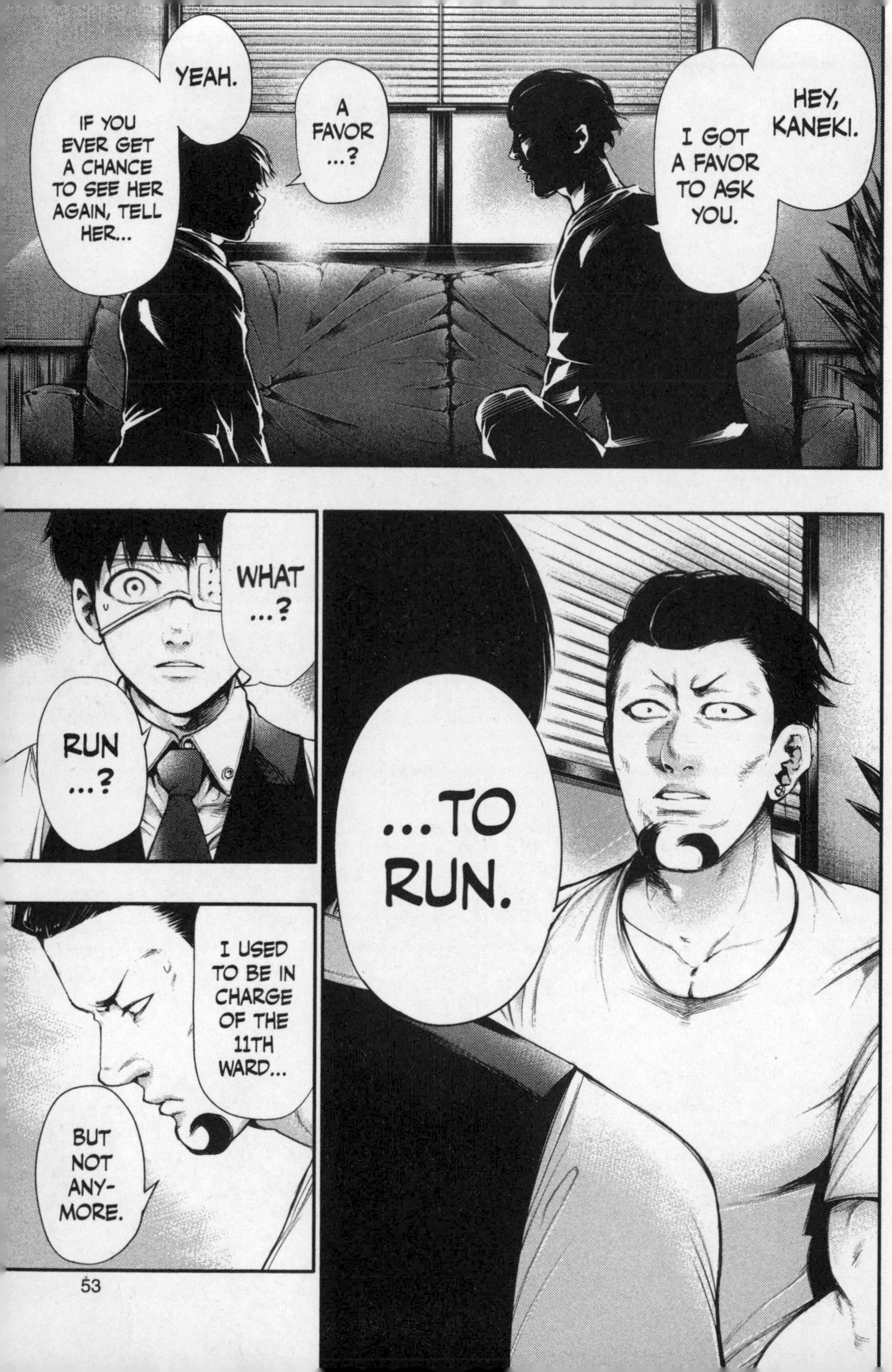
HEY, KANEKI.
I GOT A FAVOR TO ASK YOU.
A FAVOR ...?
YEAH.
IF YOU EVER GET A CHANCE TO SEE HER AGAIN, TELL HER...
...TO RUN.
WHAT ...?
RUN ...?
I USED TO BE IN CHARGE OF THE 11TH WARD...
BUT NOT ANYMORE.

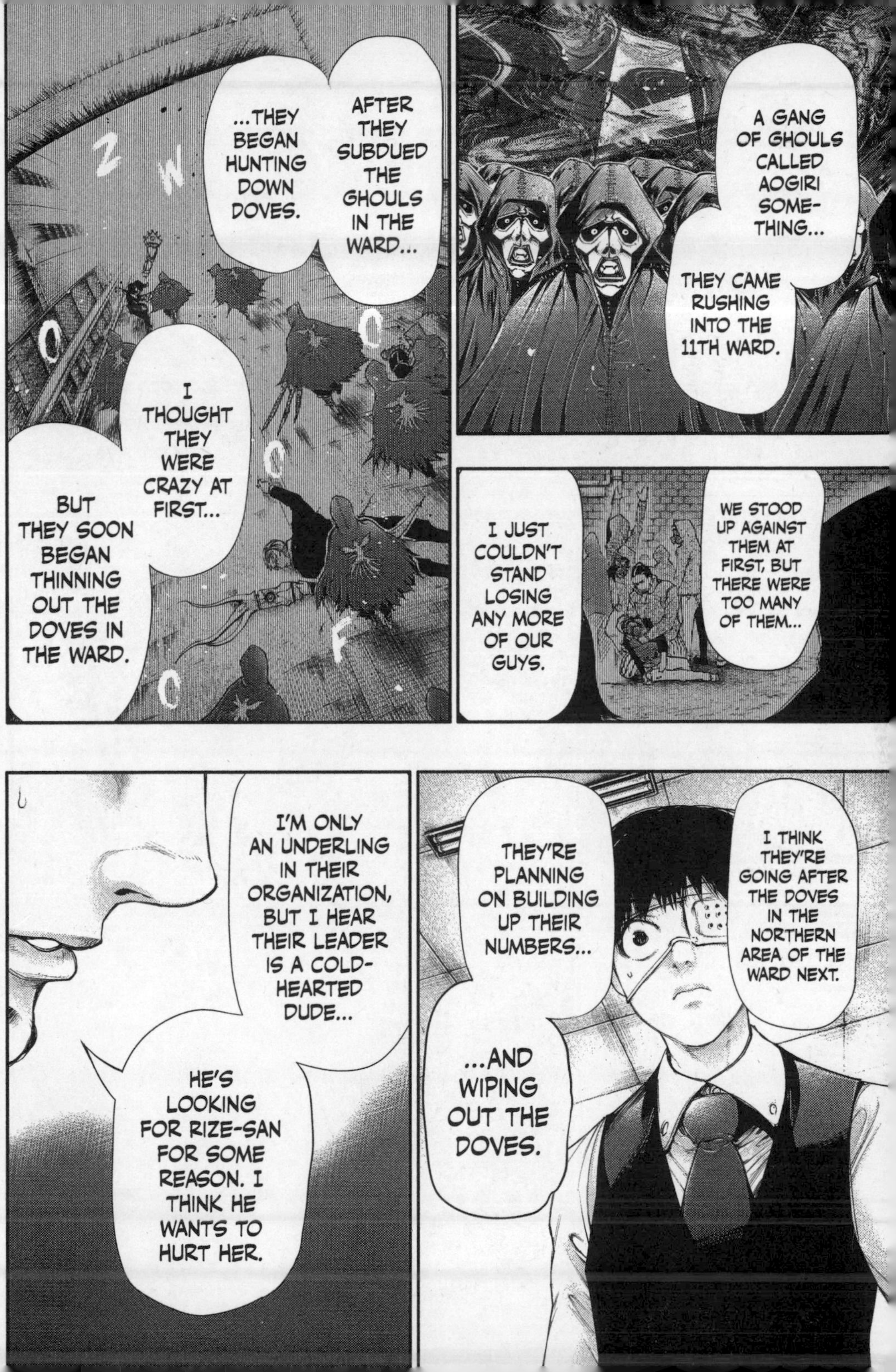
A GANG OF GHOULS CALLED AOGIRI SOME-THING...
THEY CAME RUSHING INTO THE 11TH WARD.
WE STOOD UP AGAINST THEM AT FIRST, BUT THERE WERE TOO MANY OF THEM...
I JUST COULDN'T STAND LOSING ANY MORE OF OUR GUYS.
AFTER THEY SUBDUED THE GHOULS IN THE WARD...
...THEY BEGAN HUNTING DOWN DOVES.
I THOUGHT THEY WERE CRAZY AT FIRST...
BUT THEY SOON BEGAN THINNING OUT THE DOVES IN THE WARD.
I THINK THEY'RE GOING AFTER THE DOVES IN THE NORTHERN AREA OF THE WARD NEXT.
THEY'RE PLANNING ON BUILDING UP THEIR NUMBERS...
...AND WIPING OUT THE DOVES.
I'M ONLY AN UNDERLING IN THEIR ORGANIZATION, BUT I HEAR THEIR LEADER IS A COLD-HEARTED DUDE...
HE'S LOOKING FOR RIZE-SAN FOR SOME REASON. I THINK HE WANTS TO HURT HER.

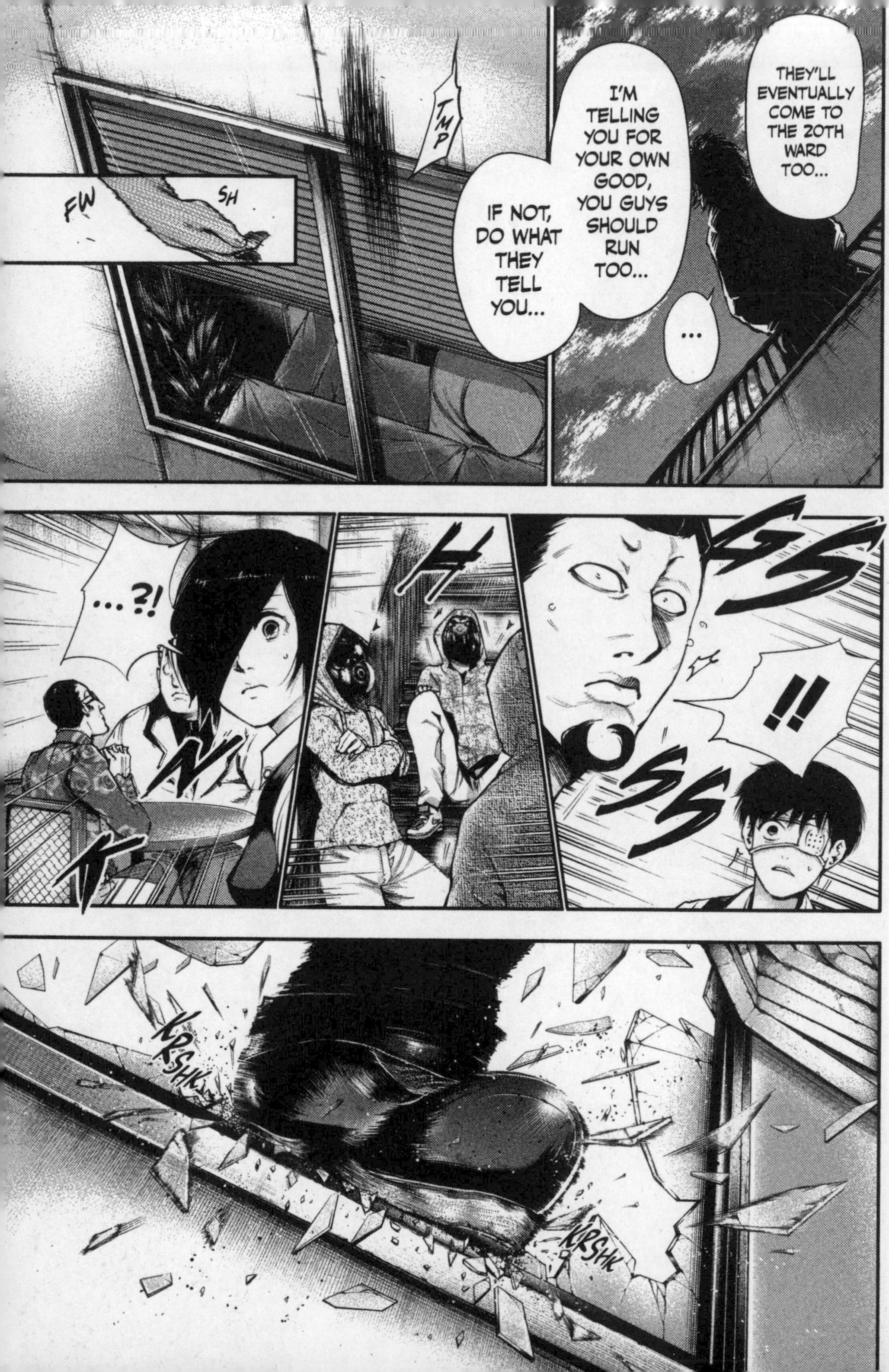
THEY'LL EVENTUALLY COME TO THE 20TH WARD TOO...
I'M TELLING YOU FOR YOUR OWN GOOD, YOU GUYS SHOULD RUN TOO...
IF NOT, DO WHAT THEY TELL YOU...
...
TMP
FWSH
GS
!!
SS
H
...?!
WK
KRSHK
KRSHK

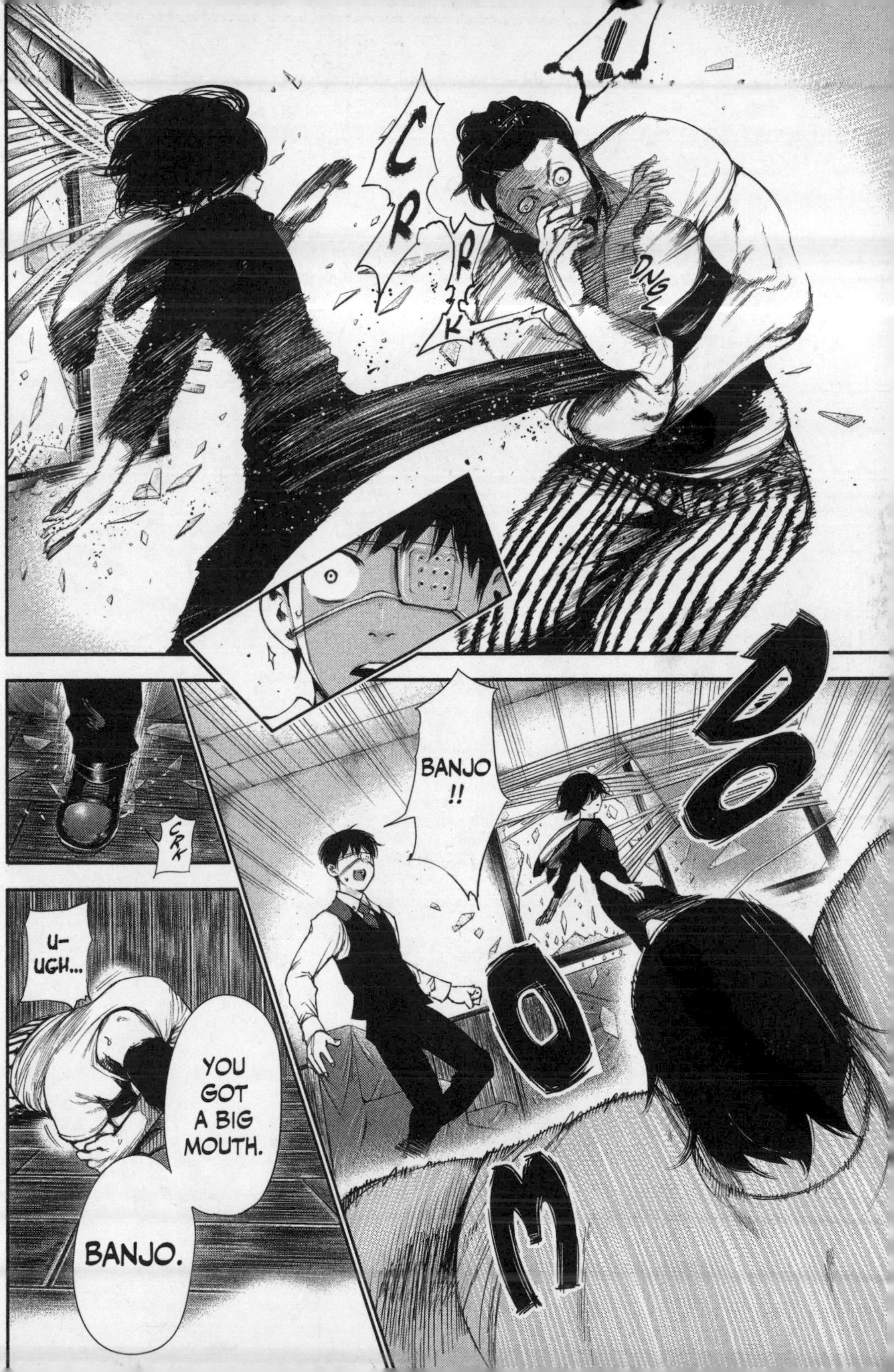
!
CRRRK
DNGL
BANJO !!
DOOM
CRK
U-UGH...
YOU GOT A BIG MOUTH.
BANJO.

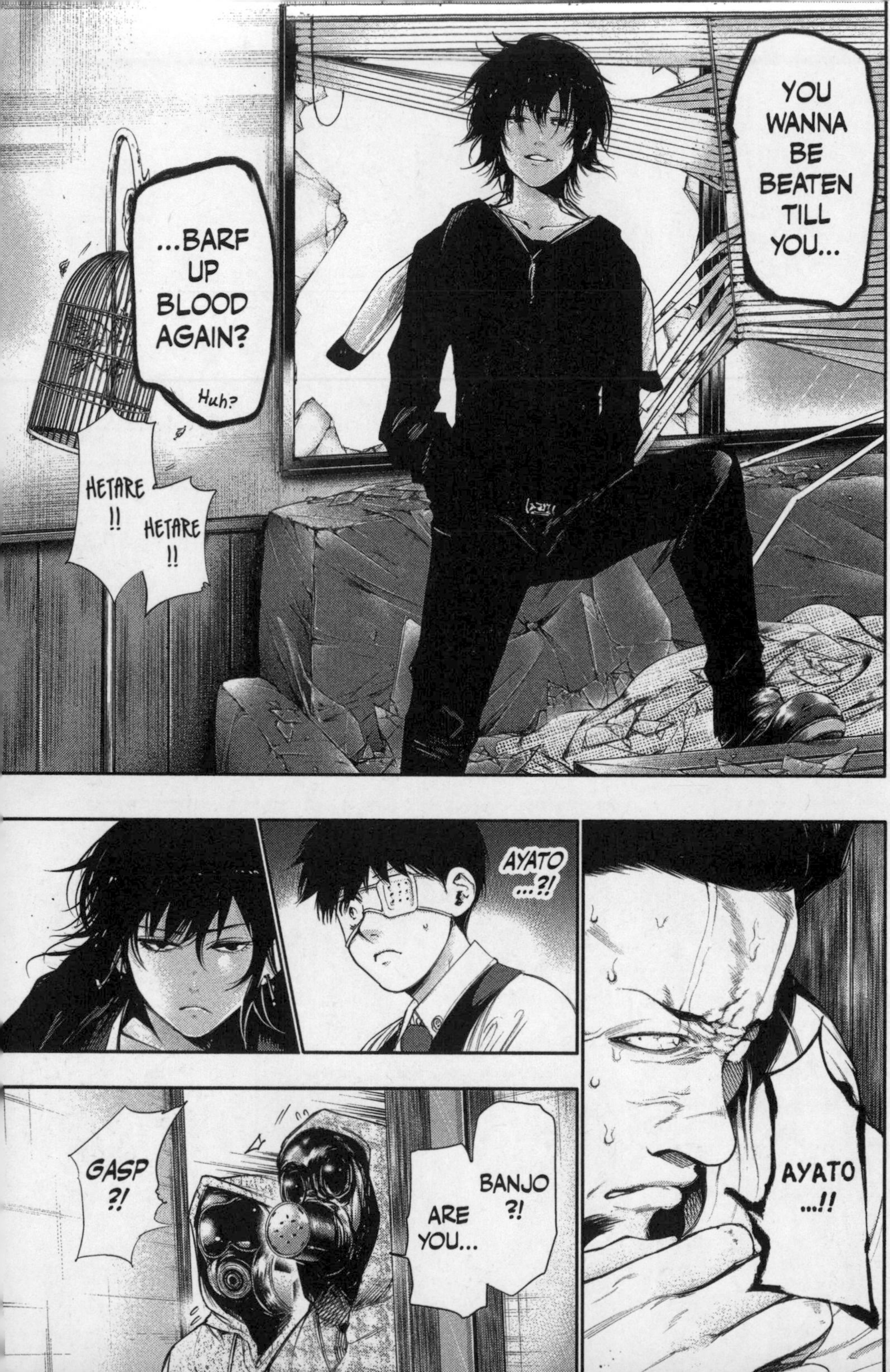
YOU WANNA BE BEATEN TILL YOU...
...BARF UP BLOOD AGAIN?
Huh?
HETARE !!
HETARE !!
AYATO ...!!
AYATO ...?!
BANJO ?!
ARE YOU...
GASP ?!

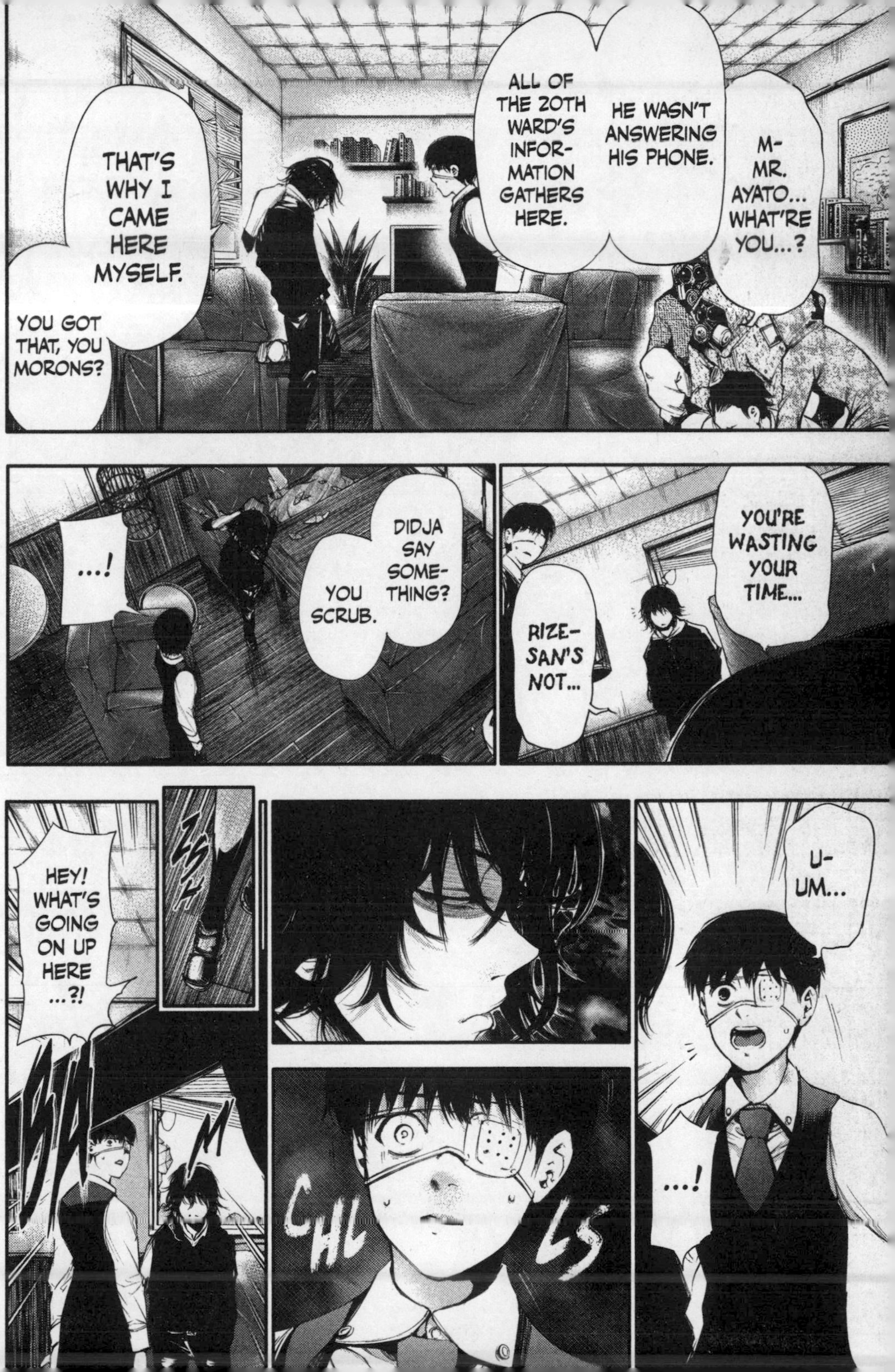
M-MR. AYATO... WHAT'RE YOU...?
HE WASN'T ANSWERING HIS PHONE.
ALL OF THE 20TH WARD'S INFORMATION GATHERS HERE.
THAT'S WHY I CAME HERE MYSELF.
YOU GOT THAT, YOU MORONS?
YOU'RE WASTING YOUR TIME...
RIZE-SAN'S NOT...
DIDJA SAY SOMETHING?
YOU SCRUB.
...!
U-UM...
...!
HEY! WHAT'S GOING ON UP HERE ...?!

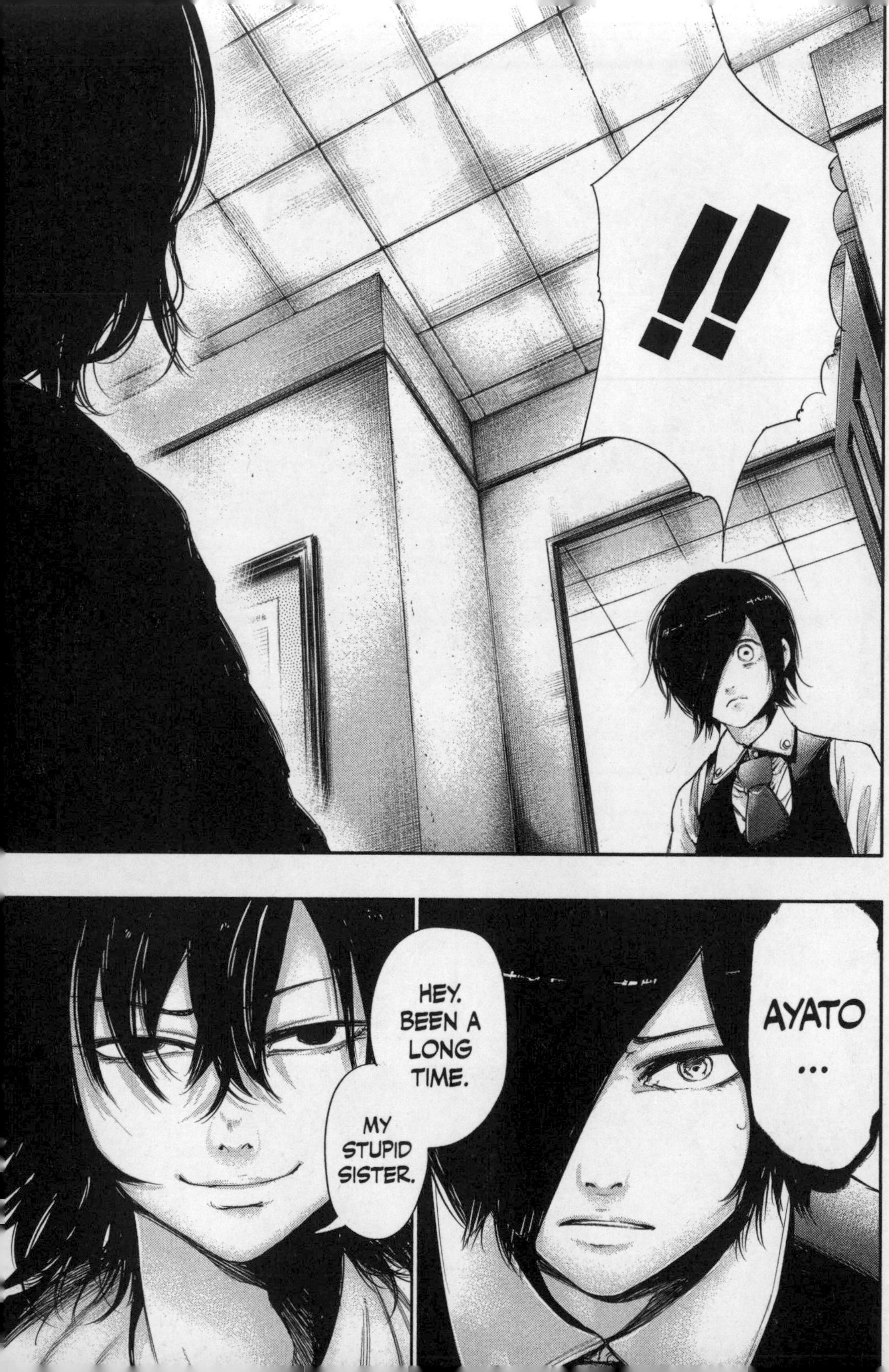
!!
AYATO ...
HEY. BEEN A LONG TIME.
MY STUPID SISTER.

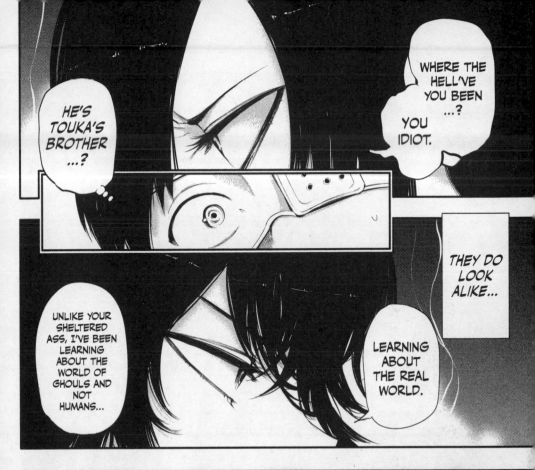

WHERE THE HELL'VE YOU BEEN ...? YOU IDIOT.

HE'S TOUKA'S BROTHER ...?

THEY DO LOOK ALIKE...

UNLIKE YOUR SHELTERED ASS, I'VE BEEN LEARNING ABOUT THE WORLD OF GHOULS AND NOT HUMANS...

LEARNING ABOUT THE REAL WORLD.

OH MY...

?!

YOU LITTLE PUNK...

YOU'RE THE PUNK. OPEN YOUR EYES TO REALITY.

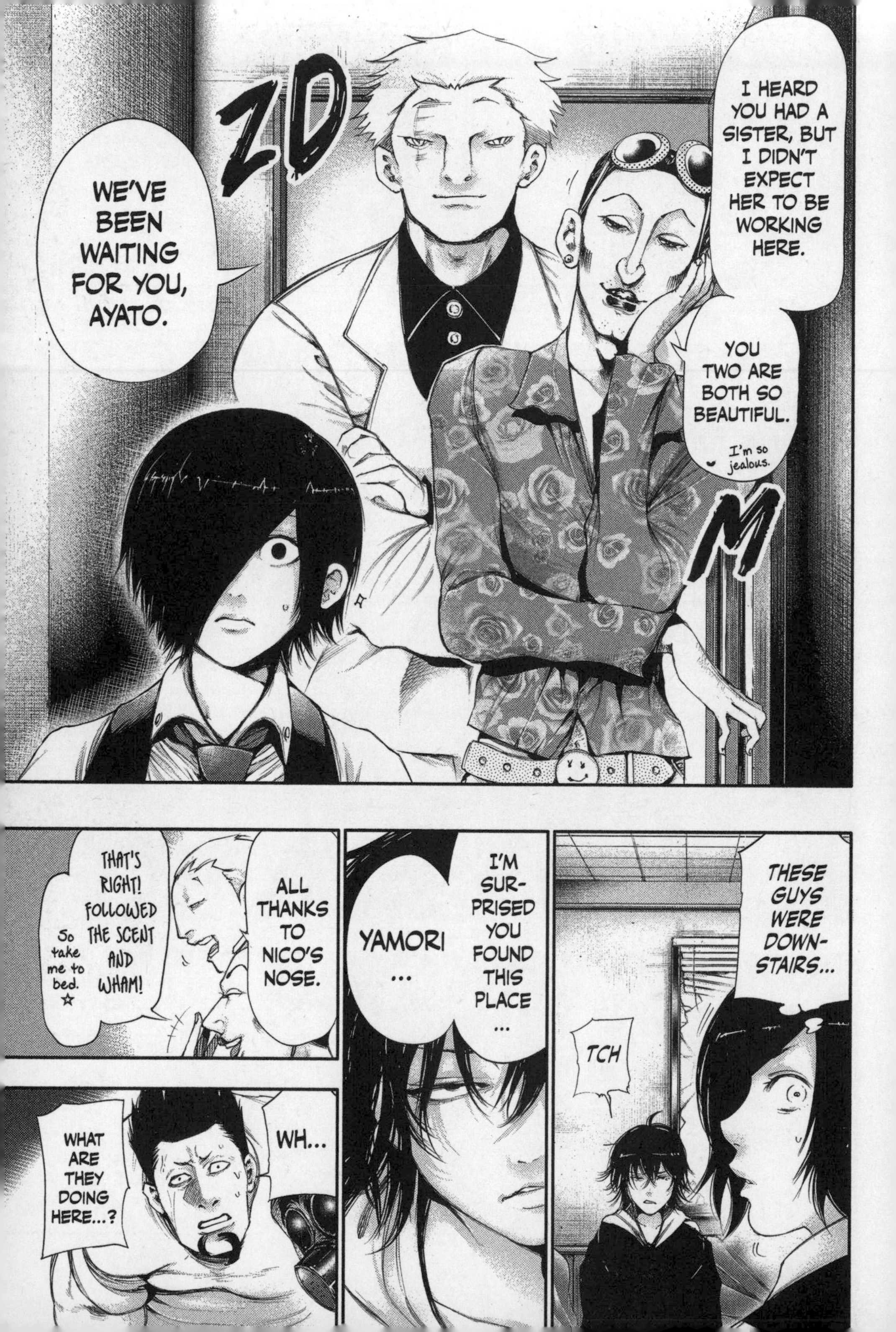
I HEARD YOU HAD A SISTER, BUT I DIDN'T EXPECT HER TO BE WORKING HERE.
YOU TWO ARE BOTH SO BEAUTIFUL.
I'm so jealous.
M
ZD
WE'VE BEEN WAITING FOR YOU, AYATO.
THESE GUYS WERE DOWN-STAIRS...
TCH
I'M SUR-PRISED YOU FOUND THIS PLACE ...
YAMORI ...
ALL THANKS TO NICO'S NOSE.
THAT'S RIGHT! FOLLOWED THE SCENT AND WHAM!
So take me to bed. ☆
WH...
WHAT ARE THEY DOING HERE...?

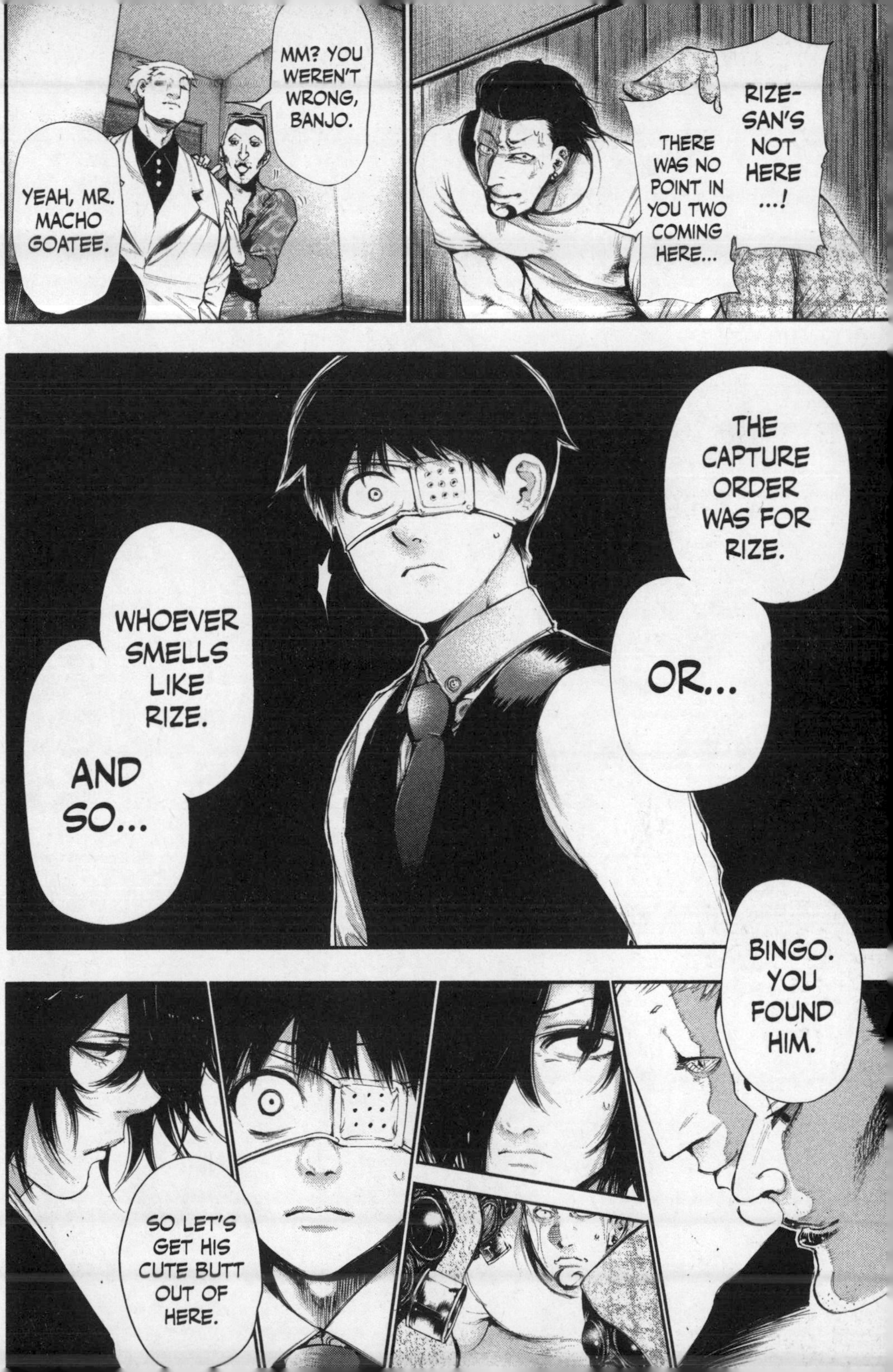
RIZE-SAN'S NOT HERE ...!
THERE WAS NO POINT IN YOU TWO COMING HERE...
MM? YOU WEREN'T WRONG, BANJO.
YEAH, MR. MACHO GOATEE.
THE CAPTURE ORDER WAS FOR RIZE.
OR...
WHOEVER SMELLS LIKE RIZE.
AND SO...
BINGO. YOU FOUND HIM.
SO LET'S GET HIS CUTE BUTT OUT OF HERE.

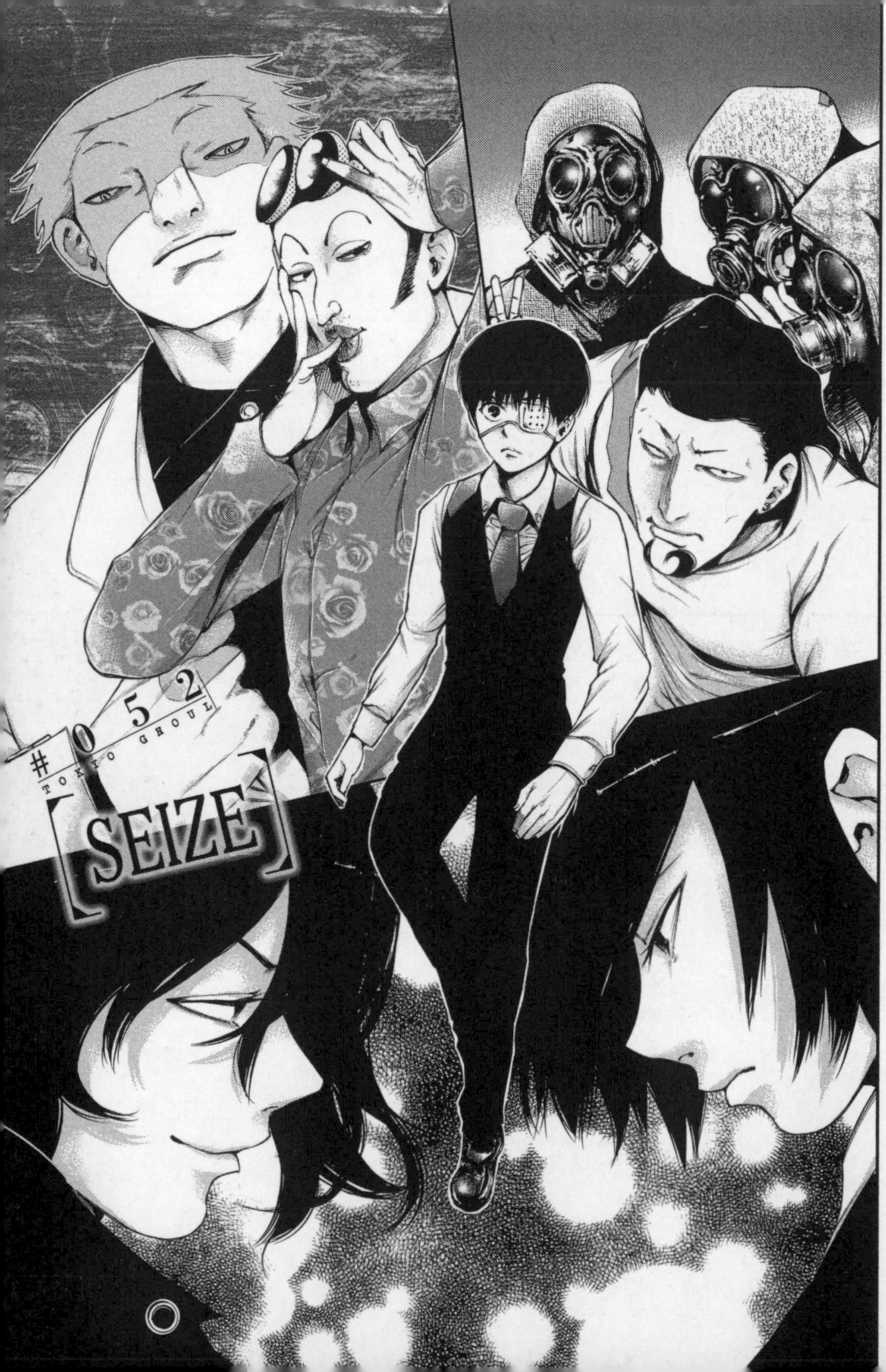

#052
TOKYO GHOUL
SEIZE

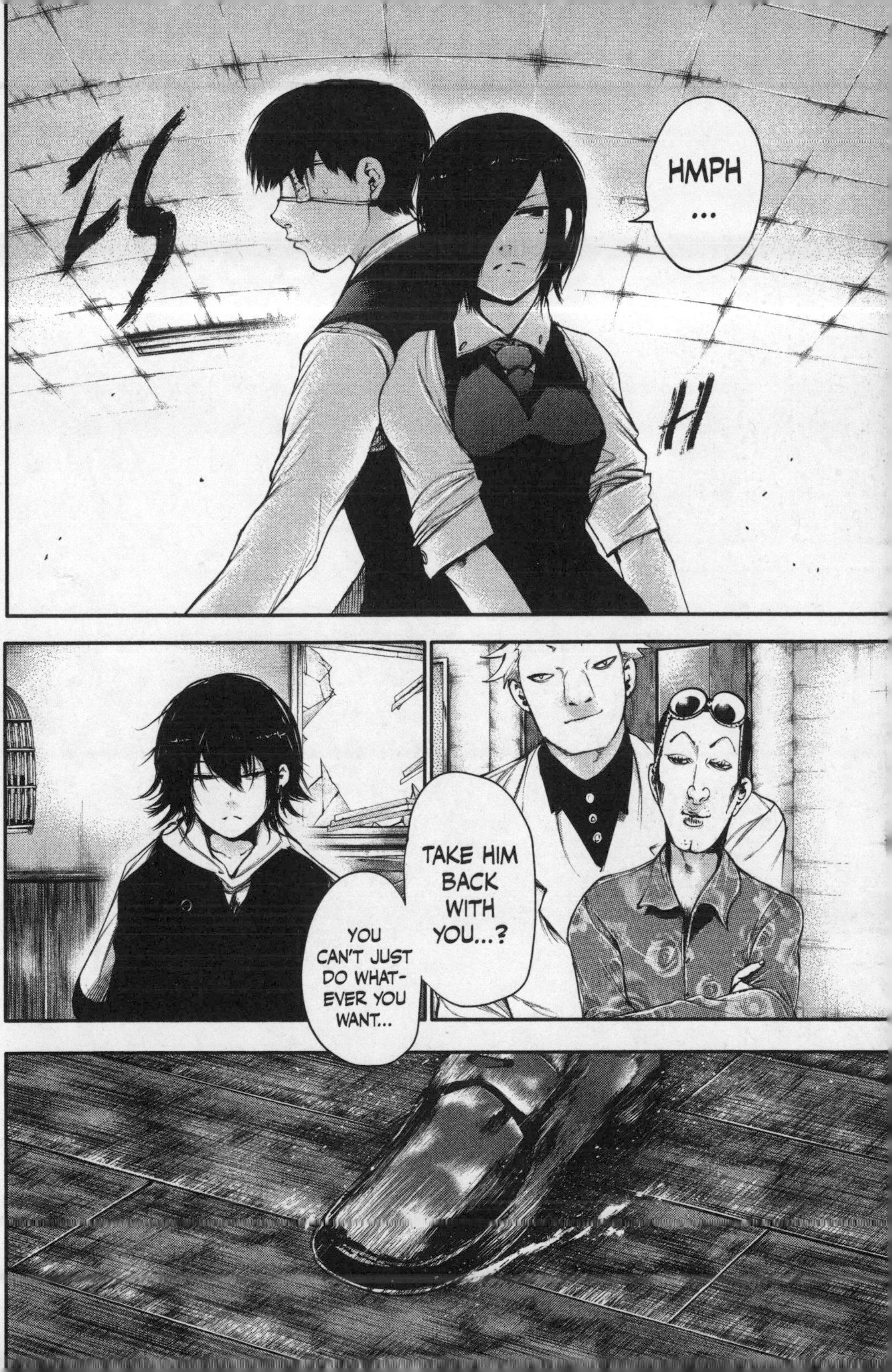
HMPH ...
TAKE HIM BACK WITH YOU...?
YOU CAN'T JUST DO WHAT-EVER YOU WANT...

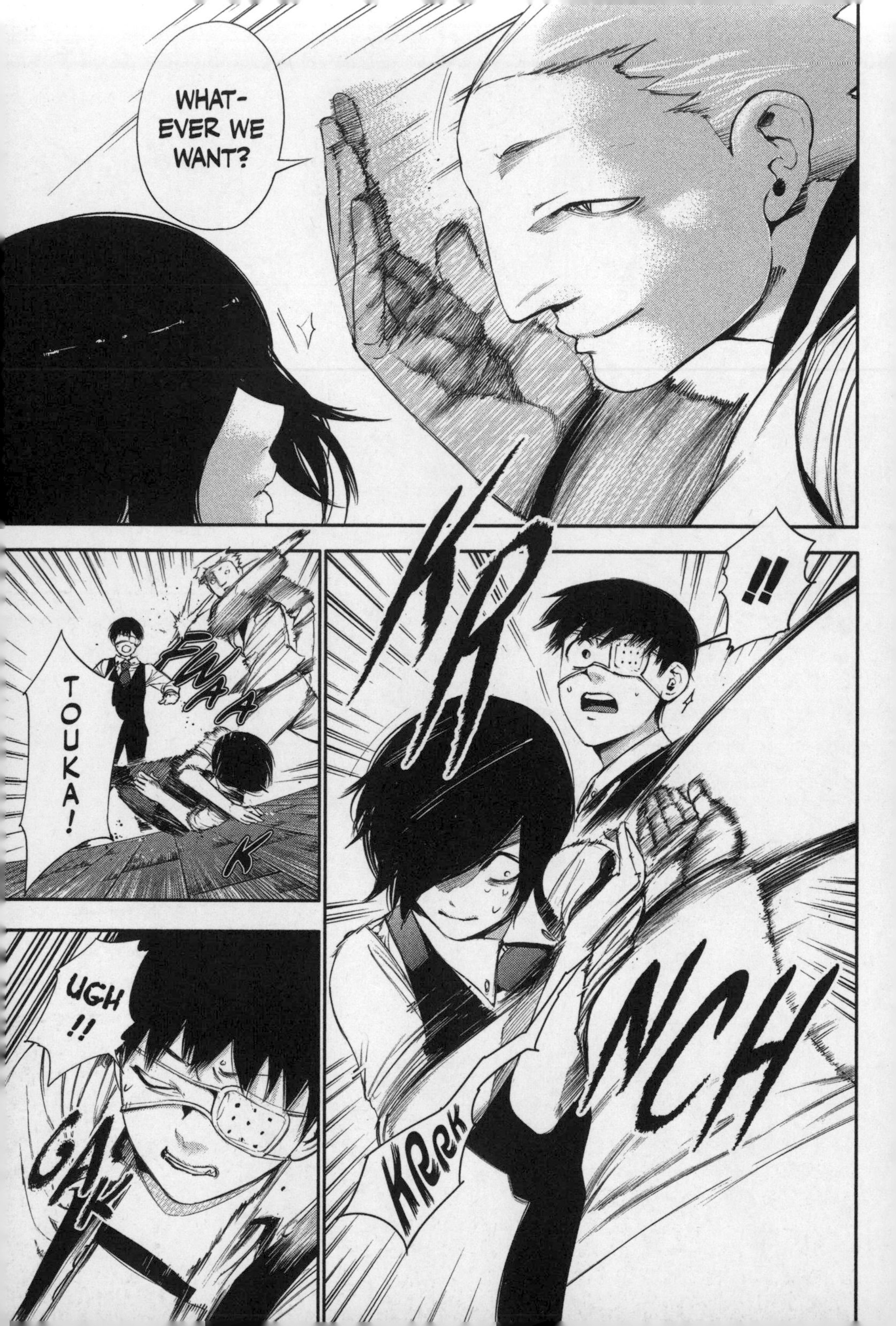
WHAT-EVER WE WANT?
KR
!!
NCH
KRRK
TOUKA!
FWAA
K
UGH !!
GAK

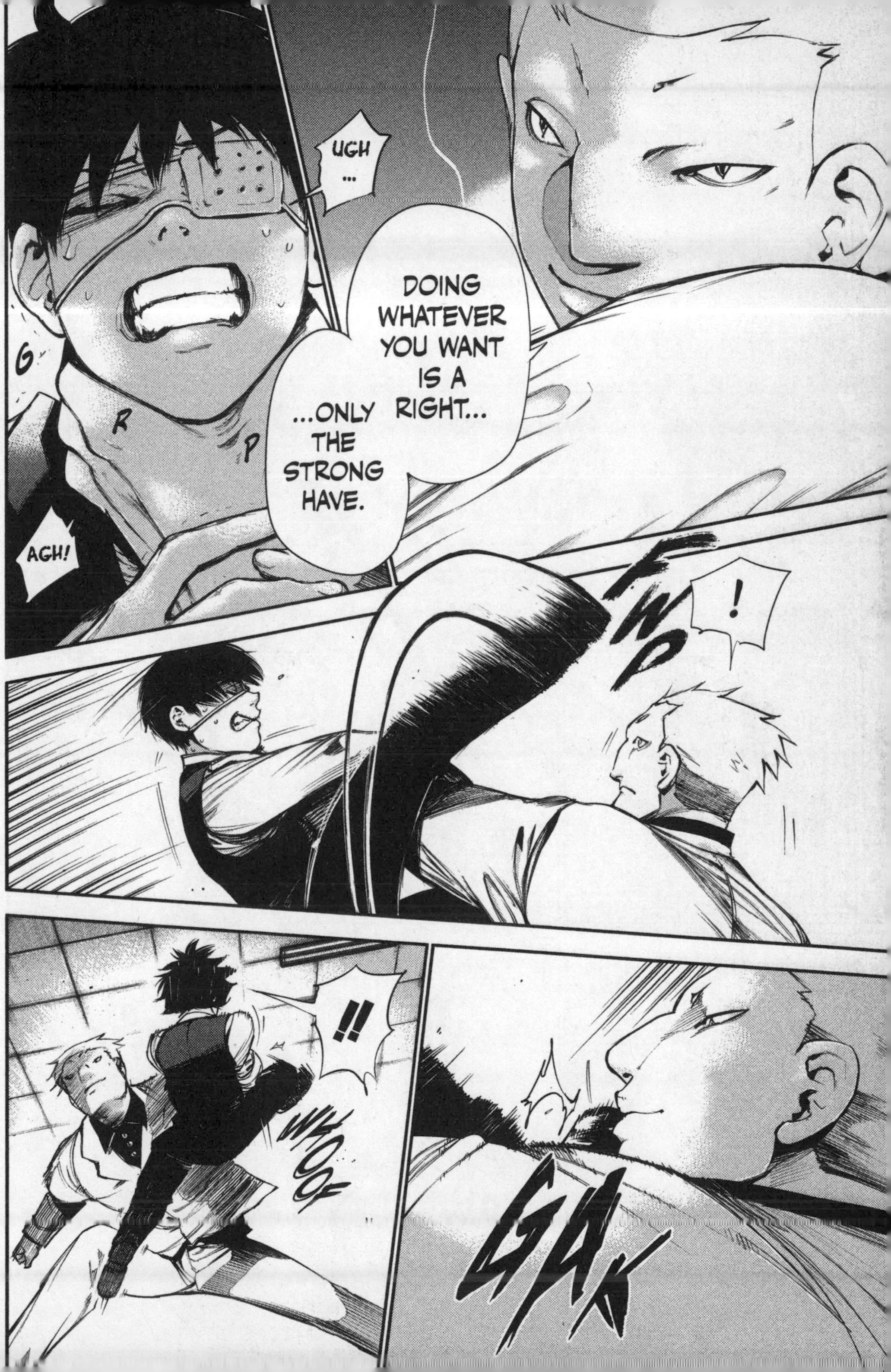
UGH ...
DOING WHATEVER YOU WANT IS A RIGHT...
...ONLY THE STRONG HAVE.
GRP
AGH!
FWP
!
GAK
!!
WHOOF

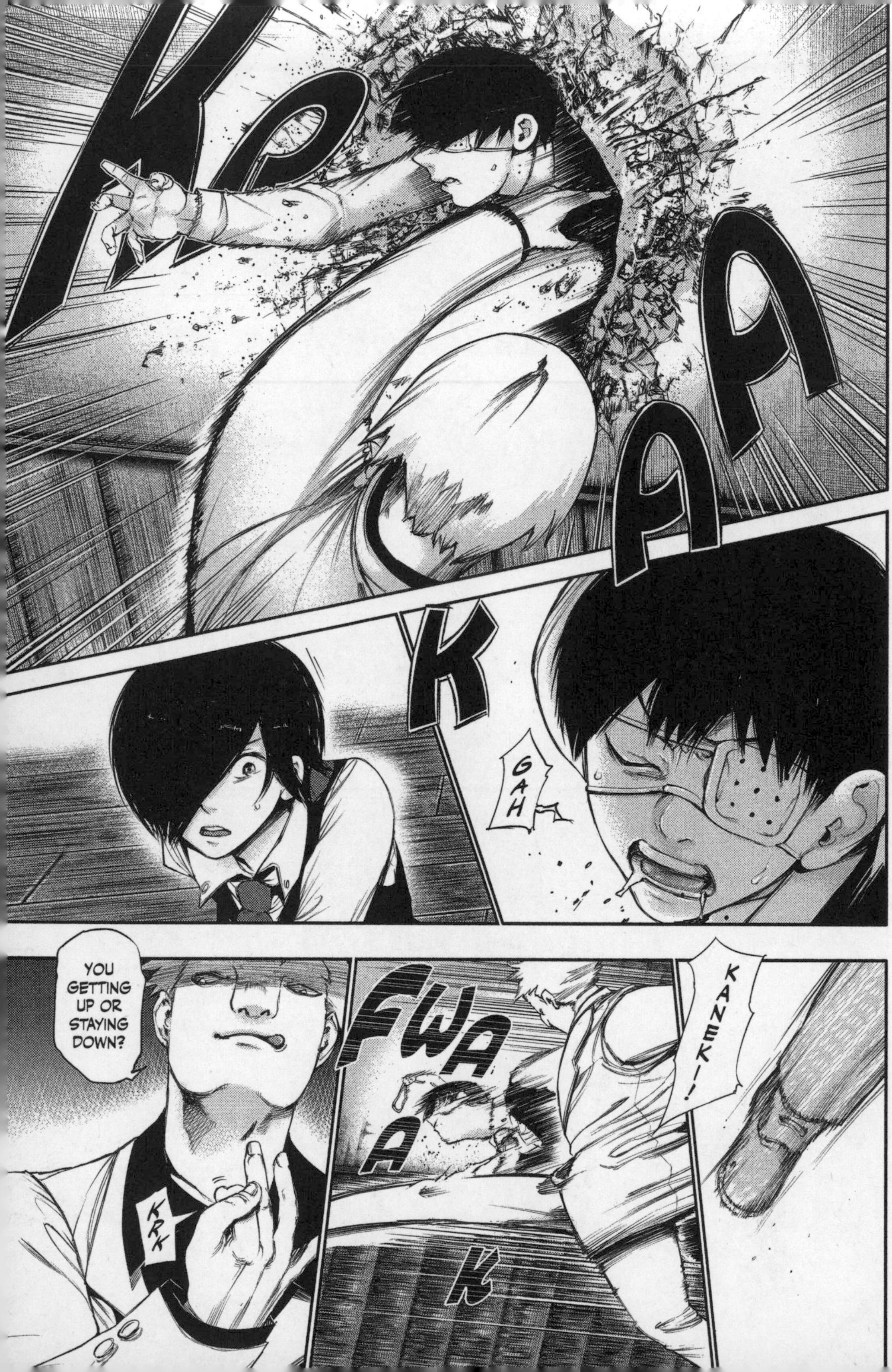
GAH
KANEKI!
FWA
A
K
YOU GETTING UP OR STAYING DOWN?
KRK

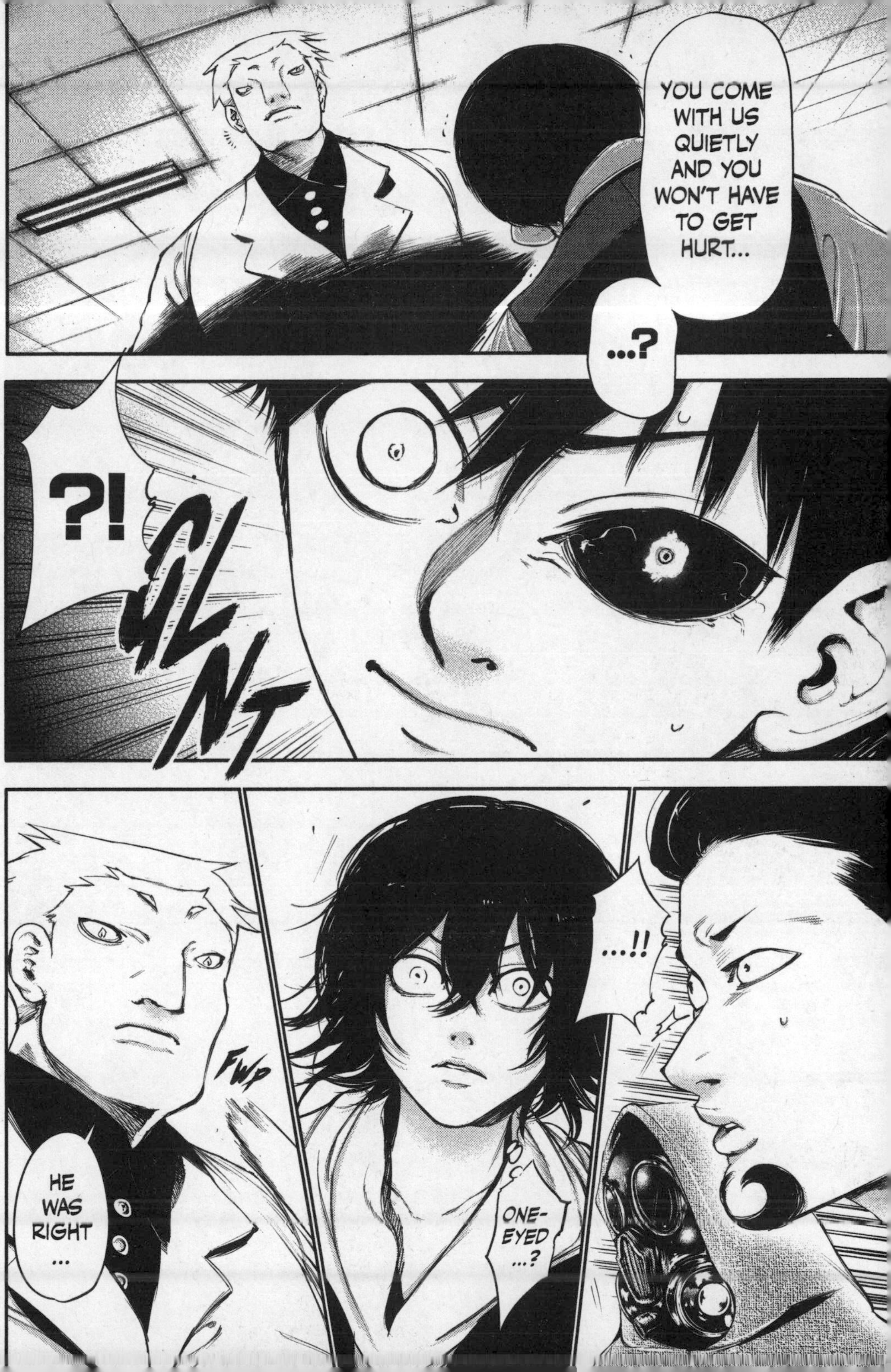
YOU COME WITH US QUIETLY AND YOU WON'T HAVE TO GET HURT...
...?
?!
GLINT
...!!
ONE-EYED ...?
FWP
HE WAS RIGHT ...

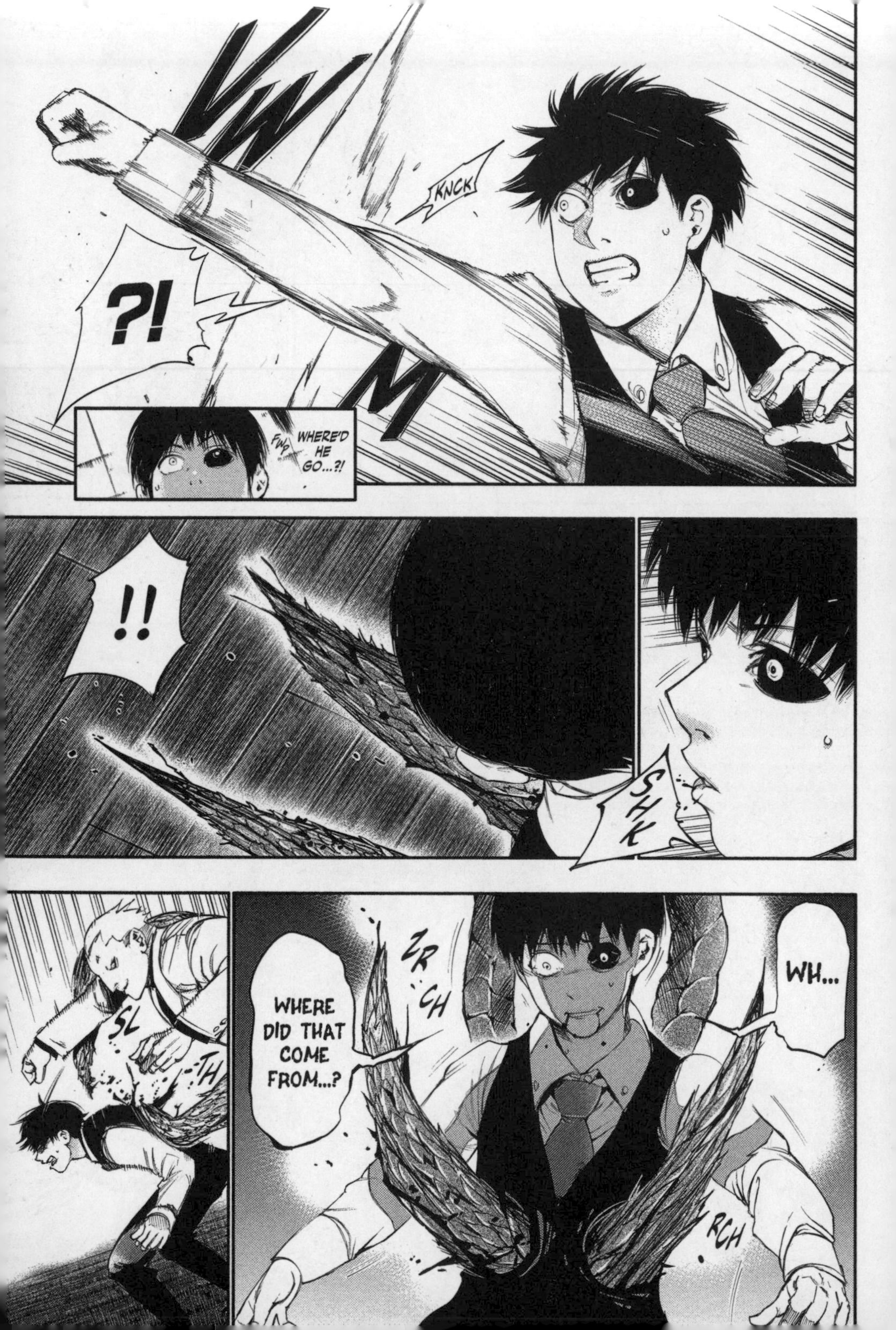
VWM
KNCK
?!
FWP
WHERE'D HE GO...?!
SHK
!!
WH...
ZRCH
WHERE DID THAT COME FROM...?
RCH
SL-TH

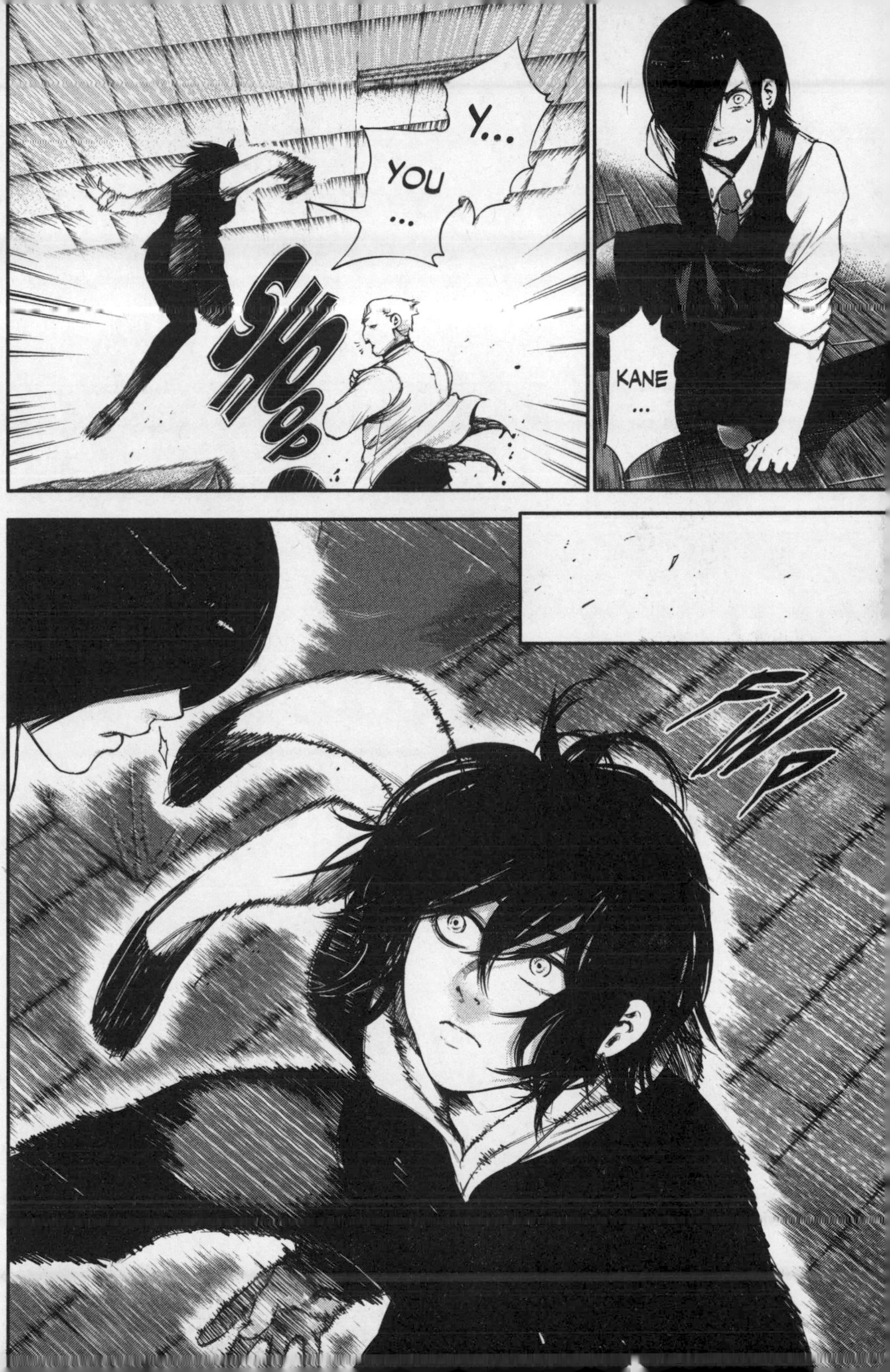
KANE ...
Y... YOU ...
SHOOP

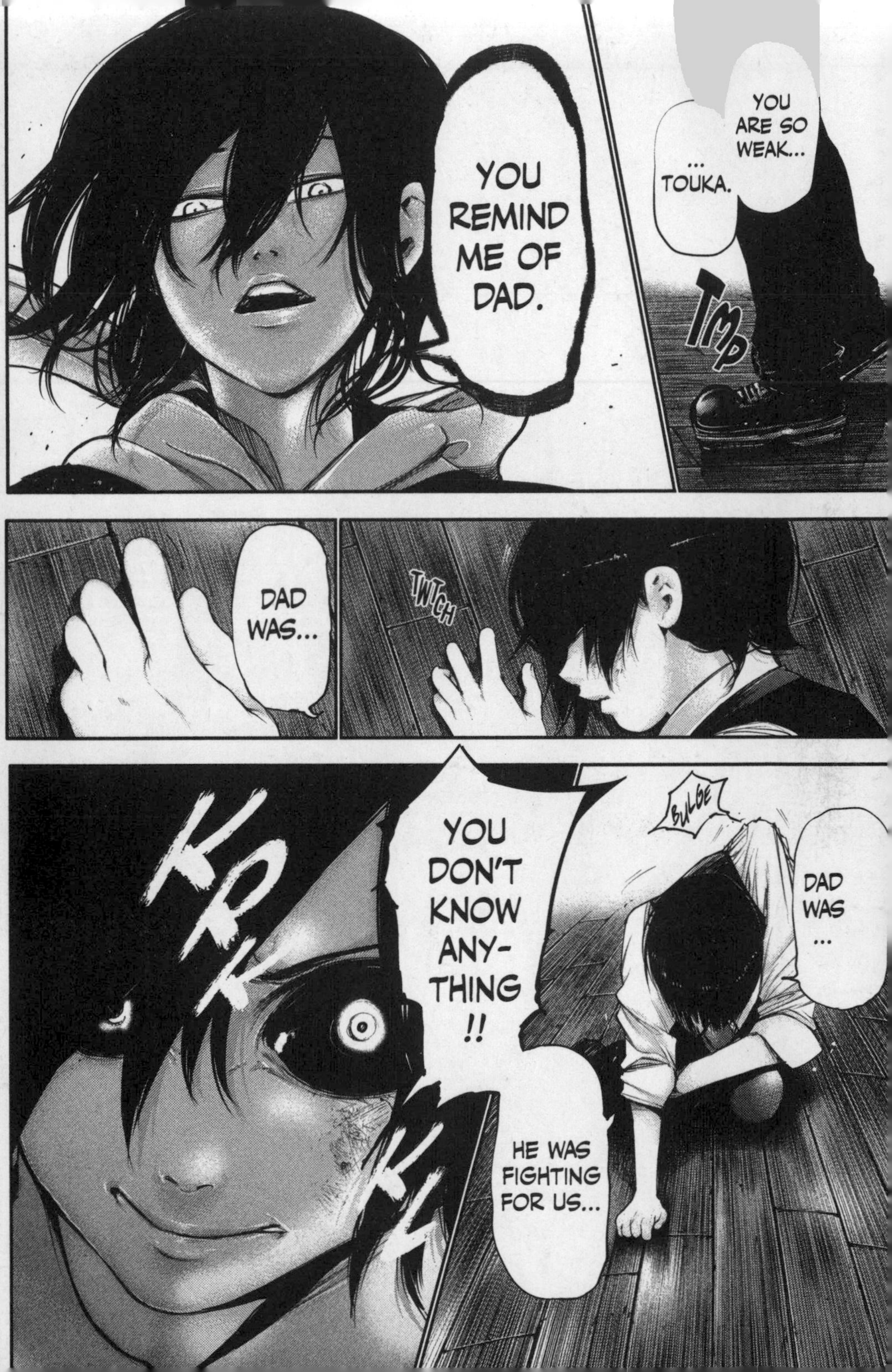
YOU ARE SO WEAK...
...TOUKA.
TMP
YOU REMIND ME OF DAD.
TWITCH
DAD WAS...
BULGE
DAD WAS ...
YOU DON'T KNOW ANY-THING!!
KRK
HE WAS FIGHTING FOR US...

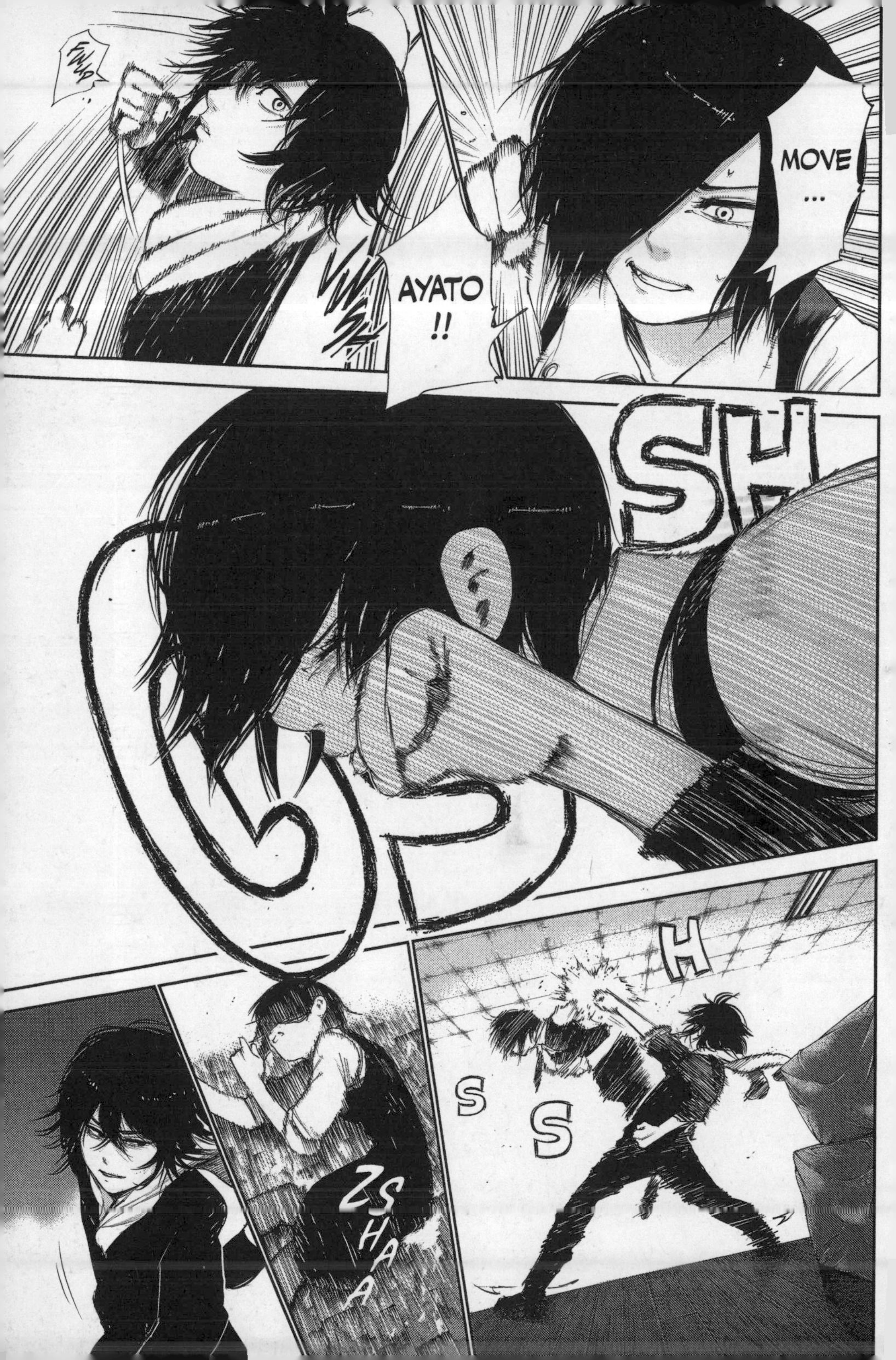
MOVE
...
AYATO
!!
VWSH
SH
H
S
S
ZSHAA

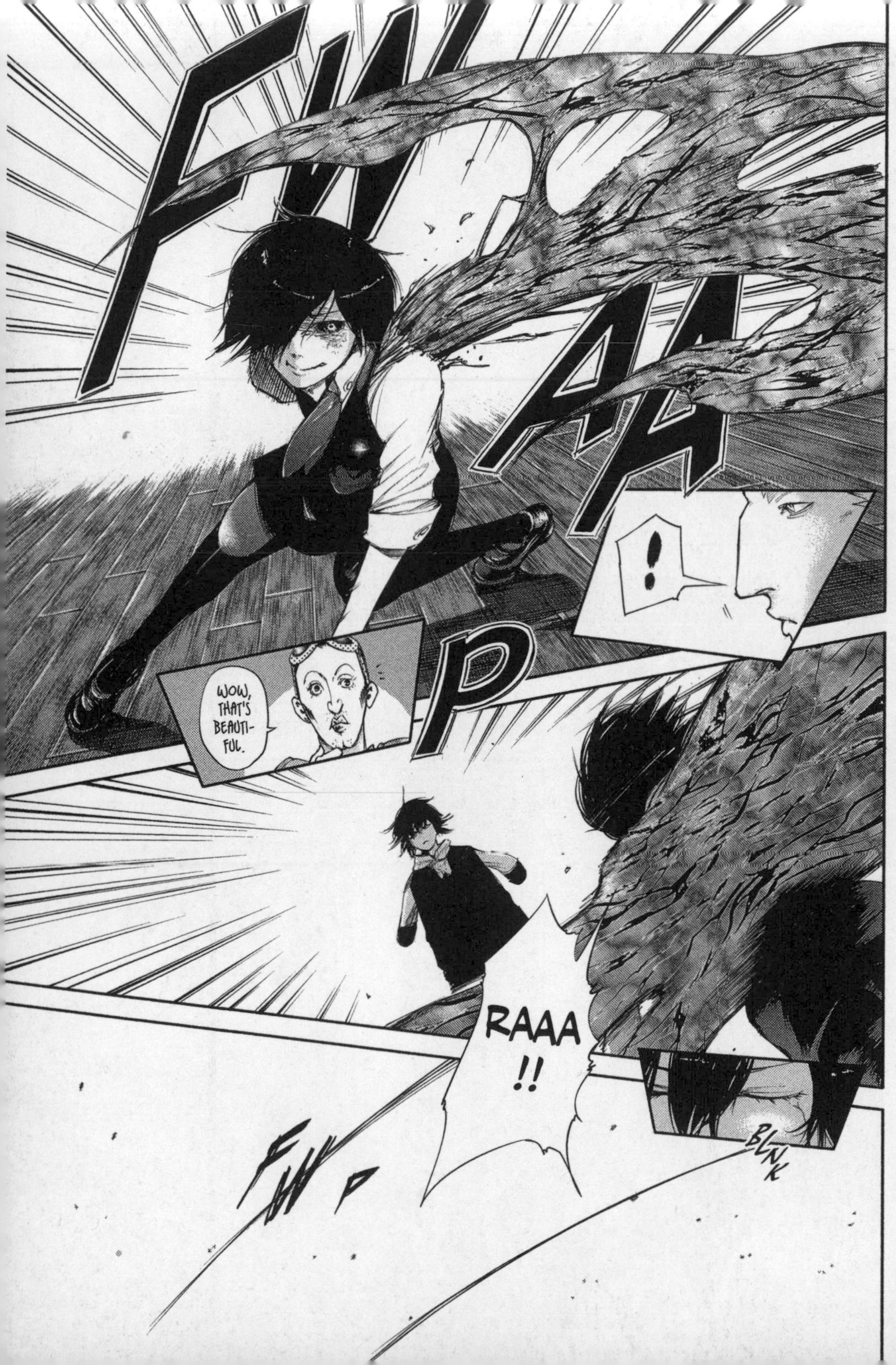
FWAAP
!
WOW, THAT'S BEAUTIFUL.
RAAA!!
BLNK
FWP

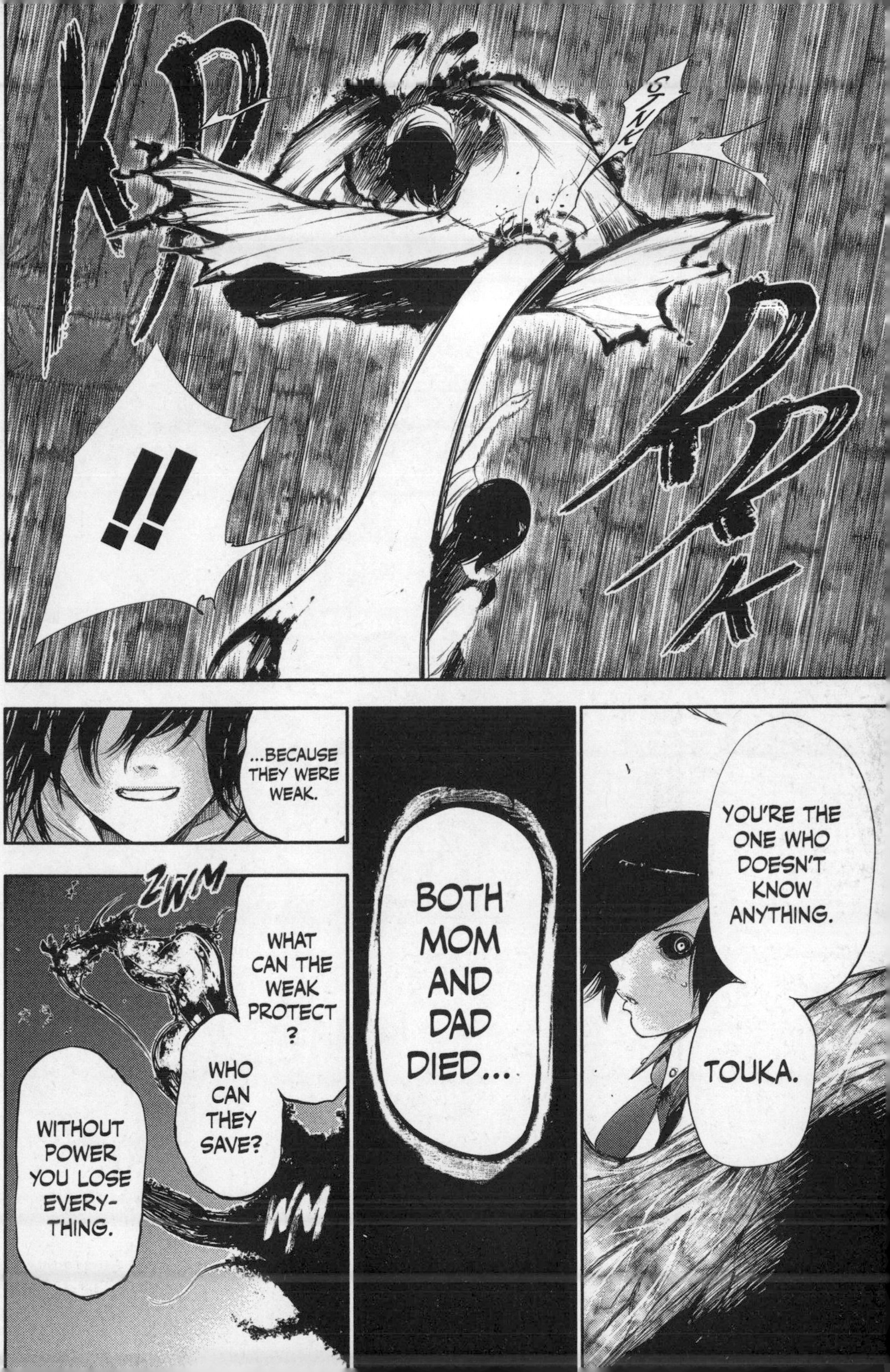
!!
YOU'RE THE ONE WHO DOESN'T KNOW ANYTHING.
TOUKA.
BOTH MOM AND DAD DIED...
...BECAUSE THEY WERE WEAK.
ZWM
WHAT CAN THE WEAK PROTECT?
WHO CAN THEY SAVE?
WITHOUT POWER YOU LOSE EVERY-THING.
WM

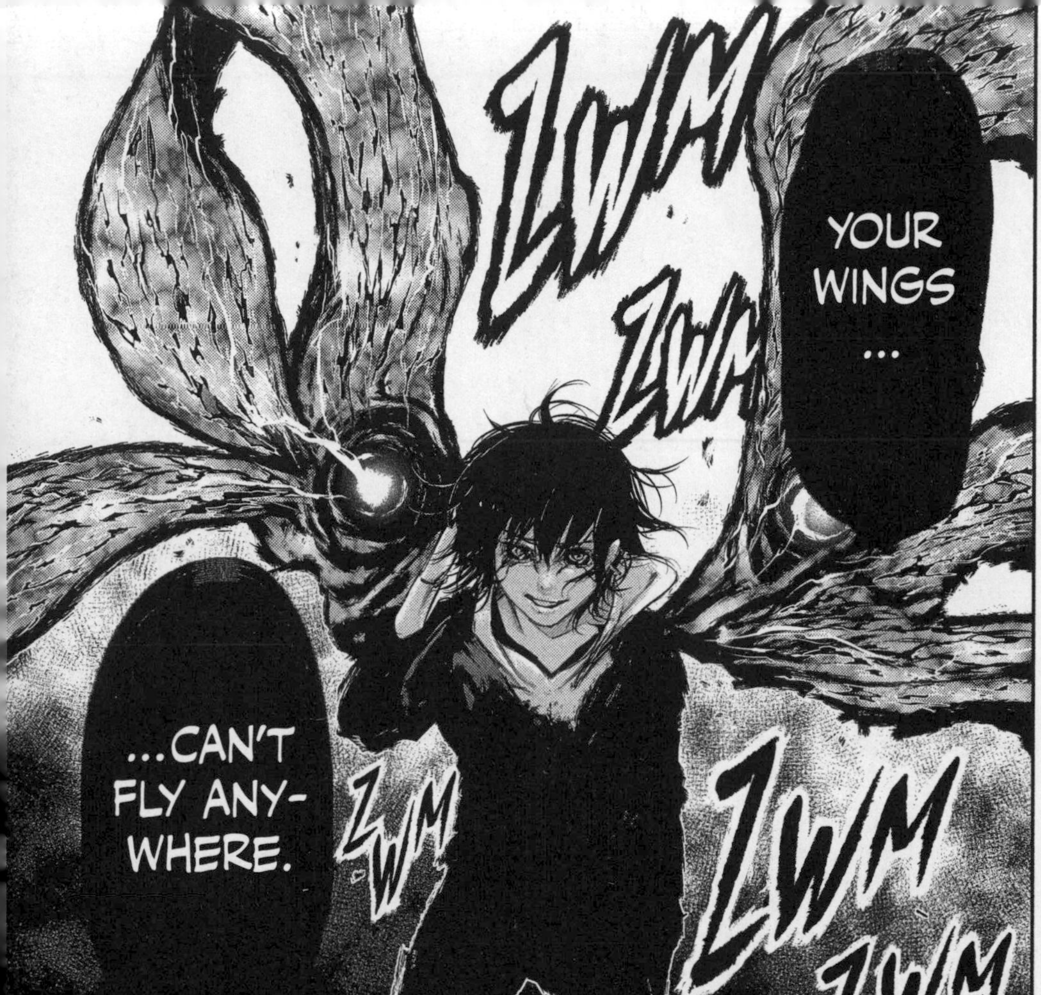
ZWM
ZWM
YOUR WINGS ...
...CAN'T FLY ANY-WHERE.
ZWM
ZWM
ZWM

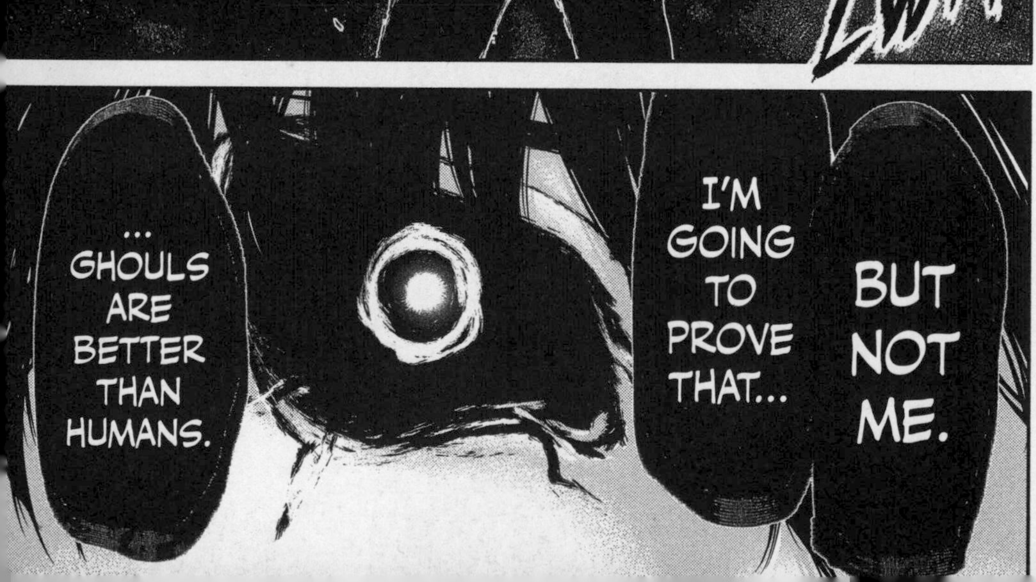
BUT NOT ME.
I'M GOING TO PROVE THAT...
... GHOULS ARE BETTER THAN HUMANS.

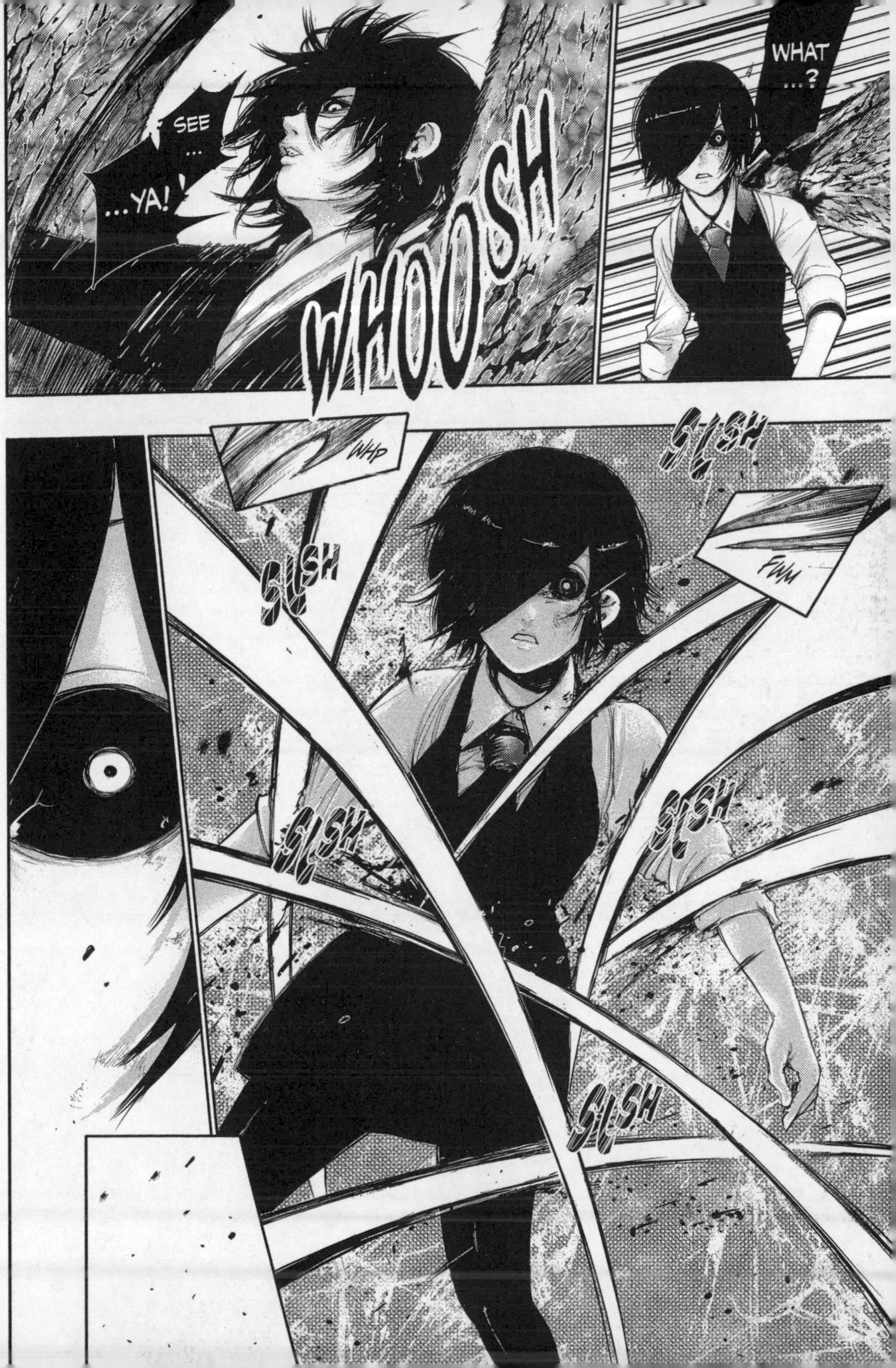
WHAT ...?
SEE ...
...YA!
WHOOSH
SLISH
WHP
FWM
SLISH
SLISH
SLISH
SLISH

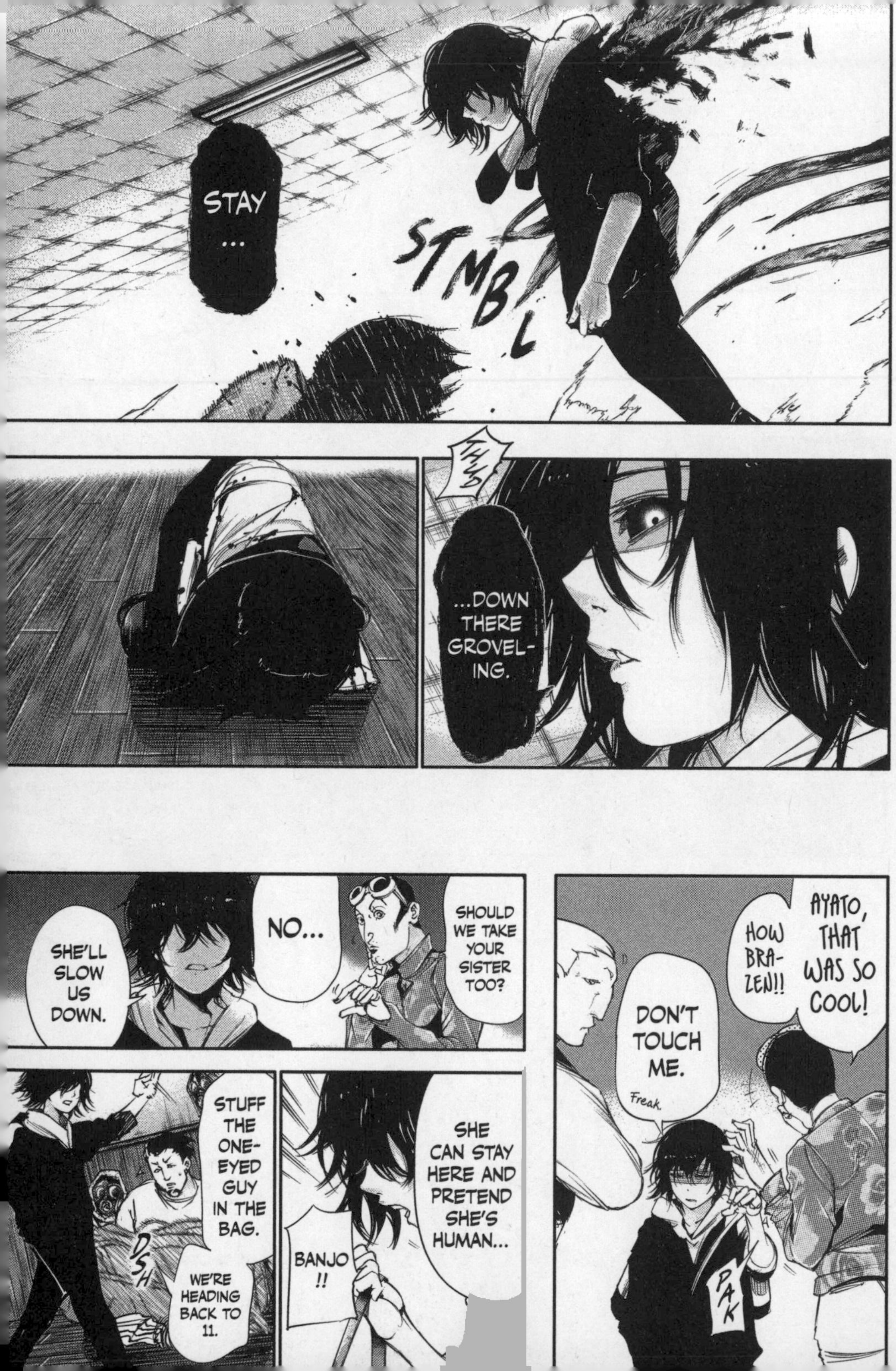
STAY ...
STMBL
THUD
...DOWN THERE GROVEL-ING.
AYATO, THAT WAS SO COOL!
HOW BRA-ZEN!!
DON'T TOUCH ME.
Freak.
PAK
SHOULD WE TAKE YOUR SISTER TOO?
NO...
SHE'LL SLOW US DOWN.
SHE CAN STAY HERE AND PRETEND SHE'S HUMAN...
BANJO !!
STUFF THE ONE-EYED GUY IN THE BAG.
WE'RE HEADING BACK TO 11.
DSH

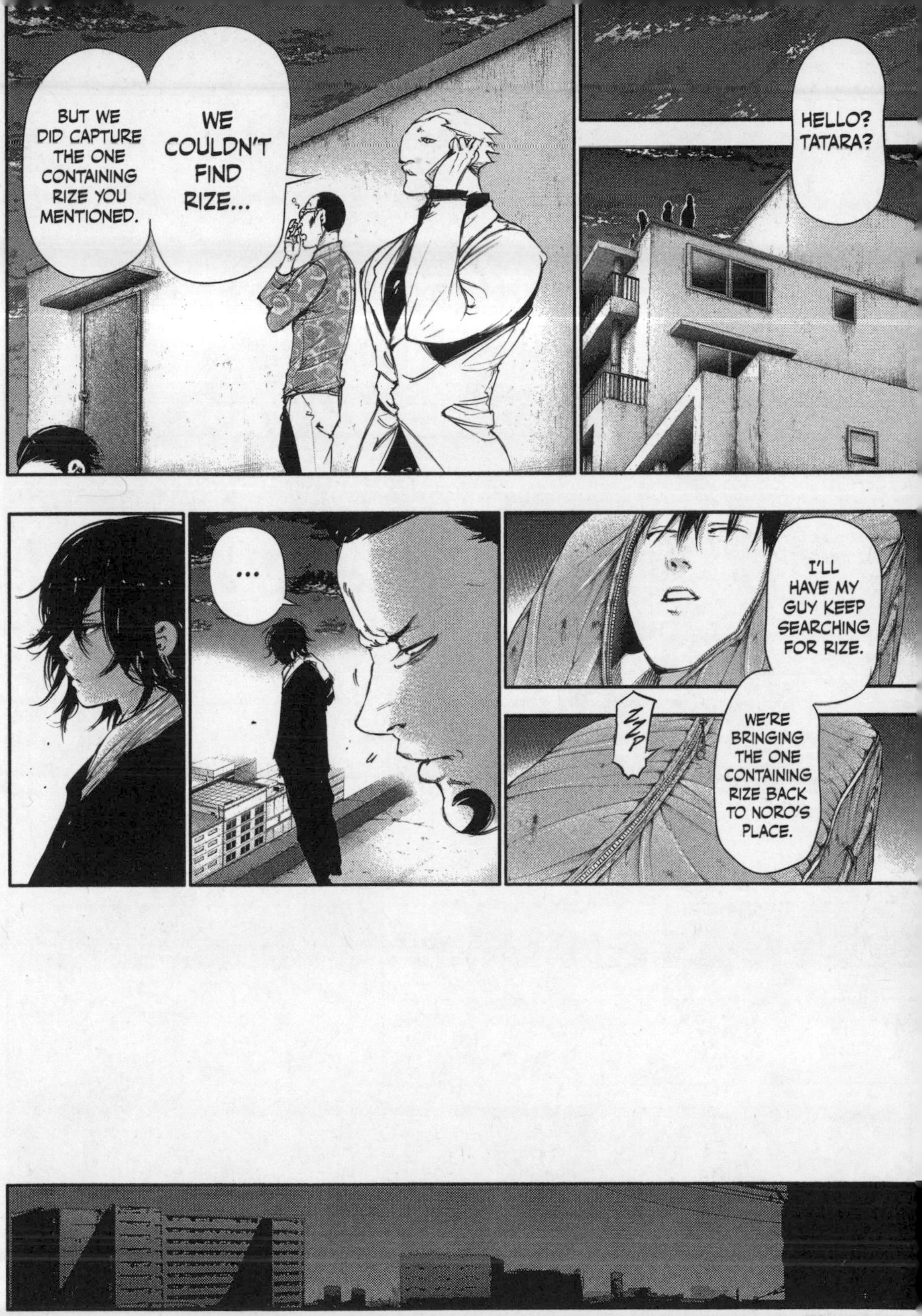
HELLO? TATARA?
WE COULDN'T FIND RIZE...
BUT WE DID CAPTURE THE ONE CONTAINING RIZE YOU MENTIONED.
I'LL HAVE MY GUY KEEP SEARCHING FOR RIZE.
WE'RE BRINGING THE ONE CONTAINING RIZE BACK TO NORO'S PLACE.
...

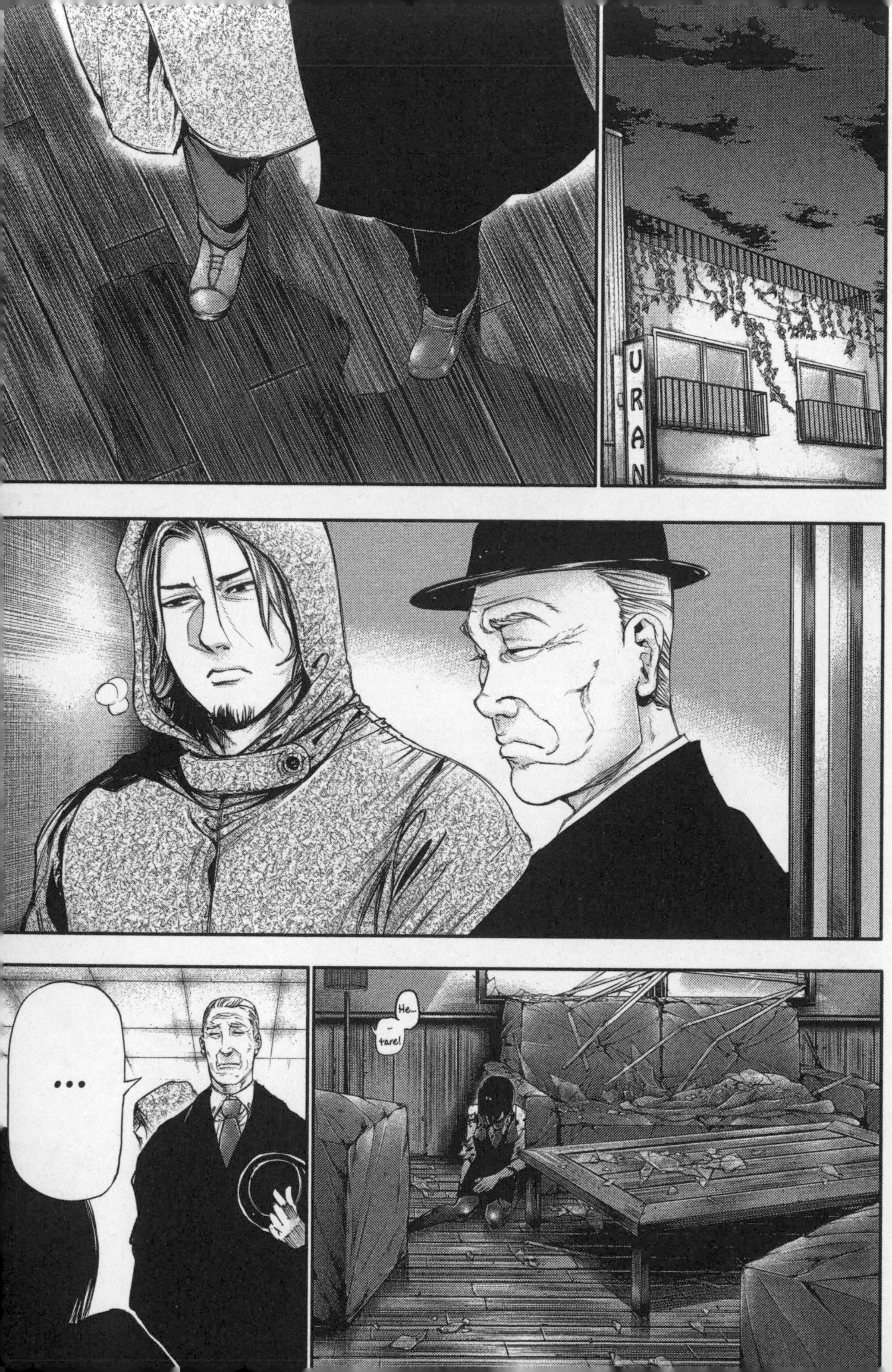
URAN
He...
...tare!
...

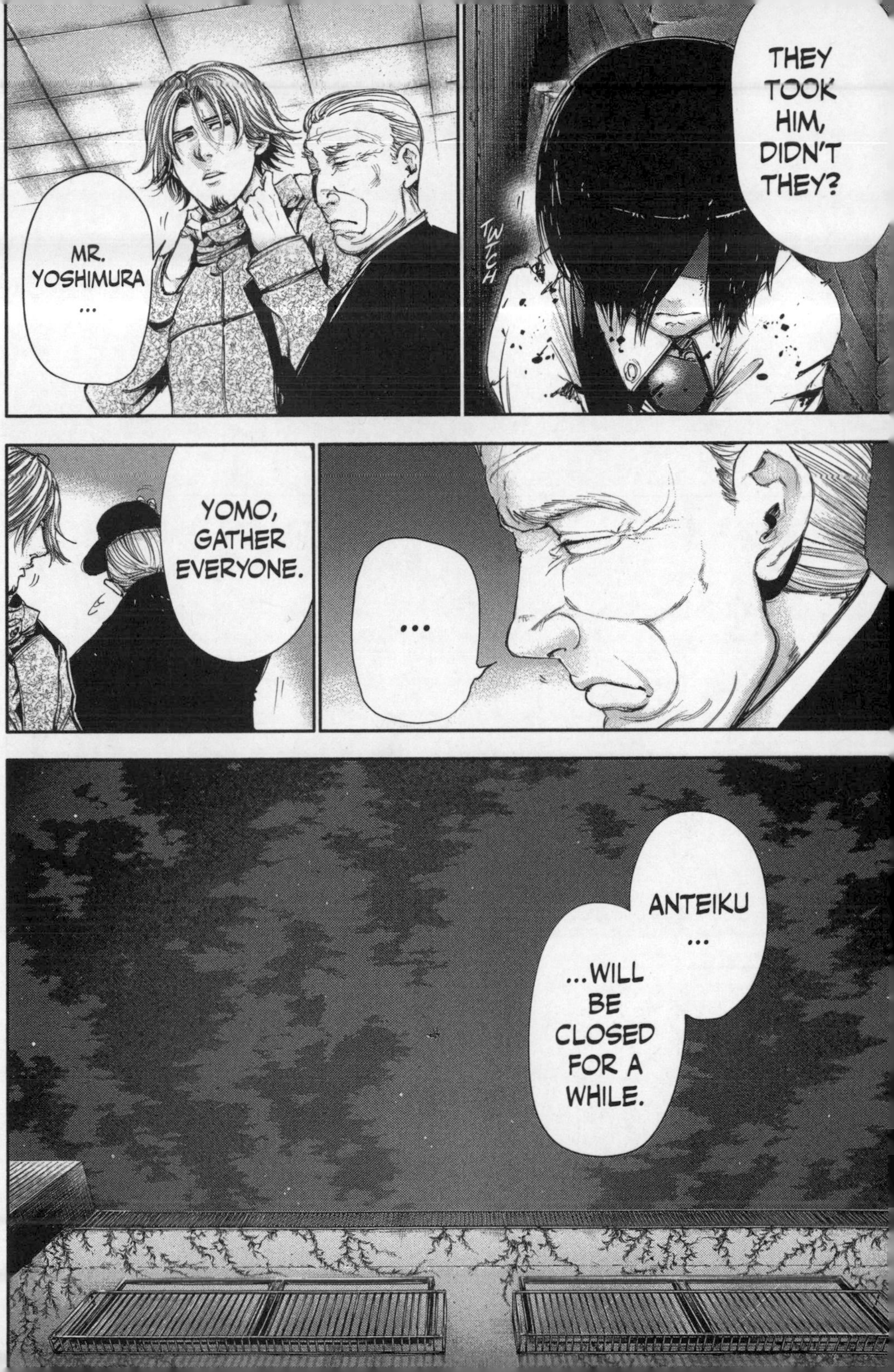
THEY TOOK HIM, DIDN'T THEY?
TWITCH
MR. YOSHIMURA ...
...
YOMO, GATHER EVERYONE.
ANTEIKU ...
...WILL BE CLOSED FOR A WHILE.

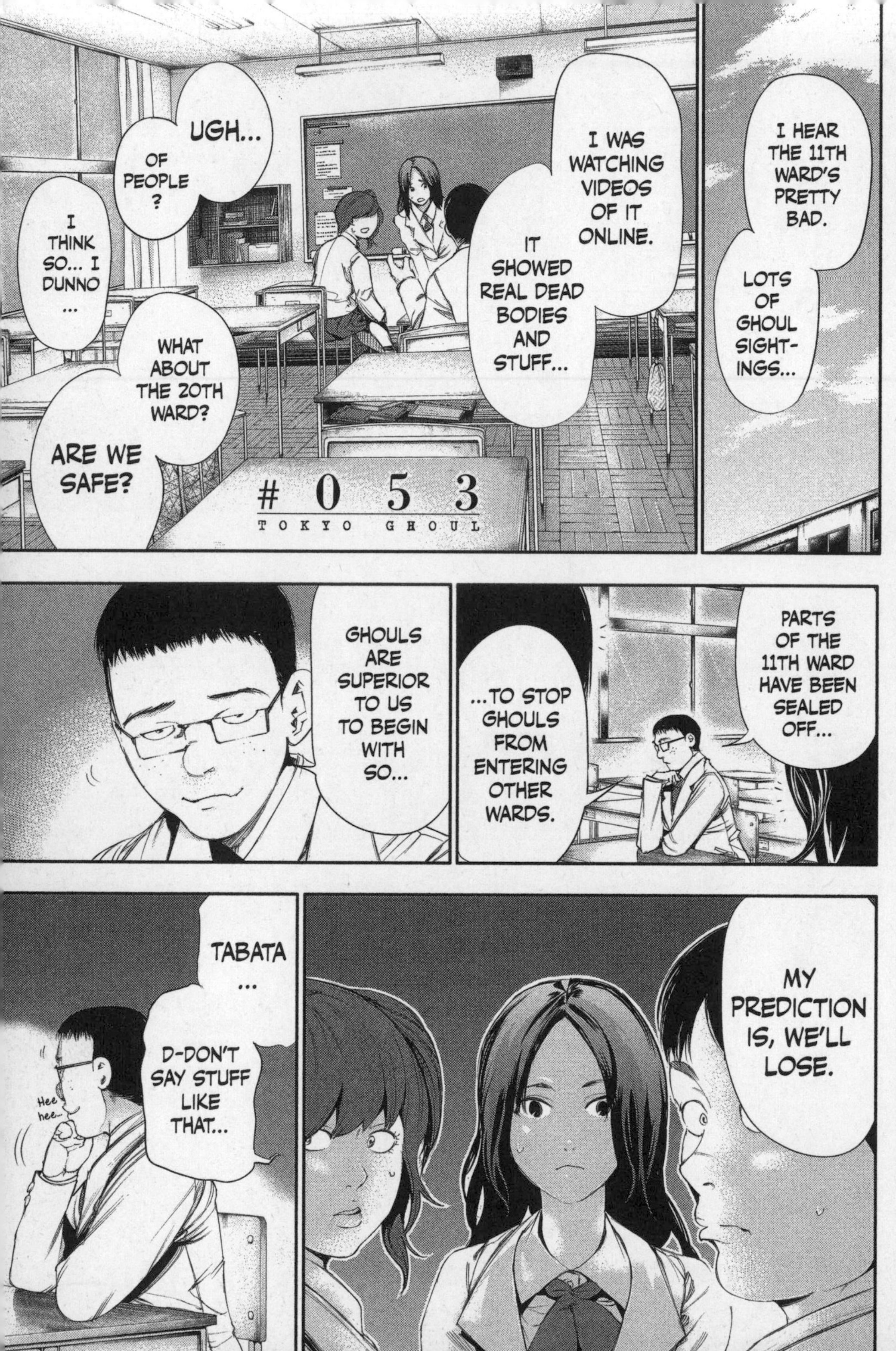
I HEAR THE 11TH WARD'S PRETTY BAD.
LOTS OF GHOUL SIGHTINGS...
I WAS WATCHING VIDEOS OF IT ONLINE.
IT SHOWED REAL DEAD BODIES AND STUFF...
UGH...
OF PEOPLE?
I THINK SO... I DUNNO...
WHAT ABOUT THE 20TH WARD?
ARE WE SAFE?
#053
TOKYO GHOUL
PARTS OF THE 11TH WARD HAVE BEEN SEALED OFF...
...TO STOP GHOULS FROM ENTERING OTHER WARDS.
GHOULS ARE SUPERIOR TO US TO BEGIN WITH SO...
MY PREDICTION IS, WE'LL LOSE.
TABATA...
D-DON'T SAY STUFF LIKE THAT...
Hee hee...

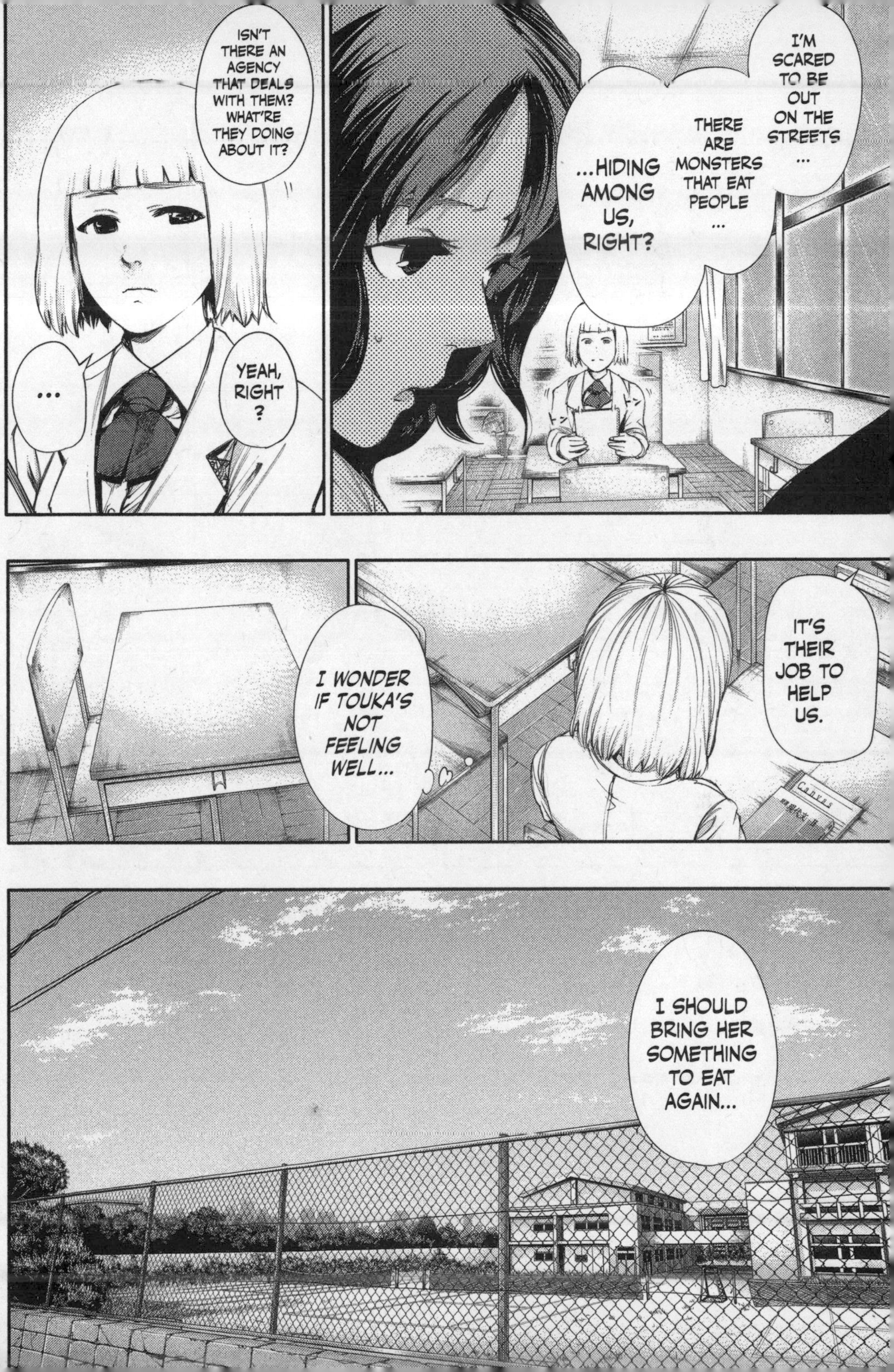
I'M SCARED TO BE OUT ON THE STREETS...
THERE ARE MONSTERS THAT EAT PEOPLE...
...HIDING AMONG US, RIGHT?
ISN'T THERE AN AGENCY THAT DEALS WITH THEM? WHAT'RE THEY DOING ABOUT IT?
YEAH, RIGHT?
...
IT'S THEIR JOB TO HELP US.
Canvas
I WONDER IF TOUKA'S NOT FEELING WELL...
I SHOULD BRING HER SOMETHING TO EAT AGAIN...

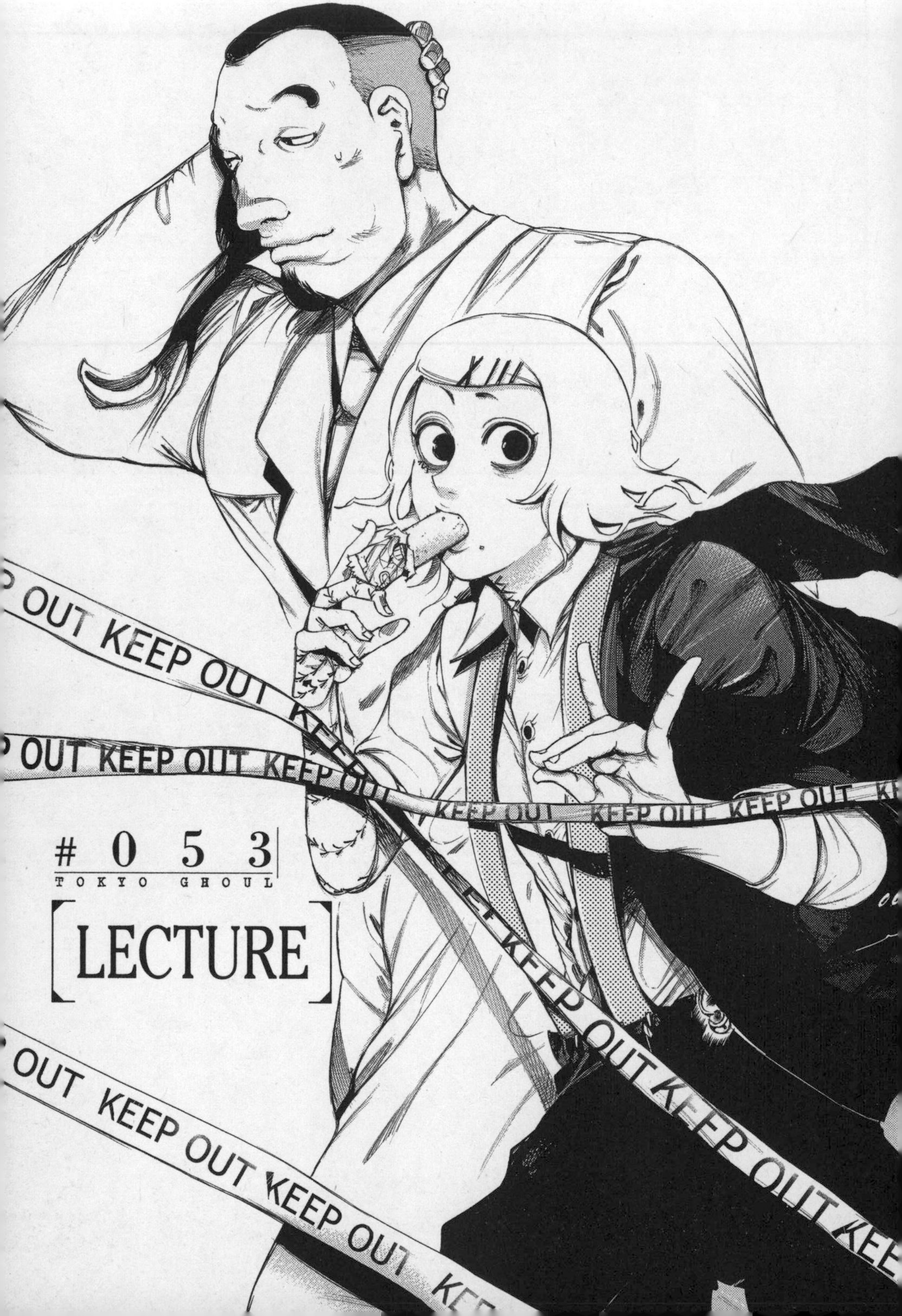
#053
TOKYO GHOUL
LECTURE

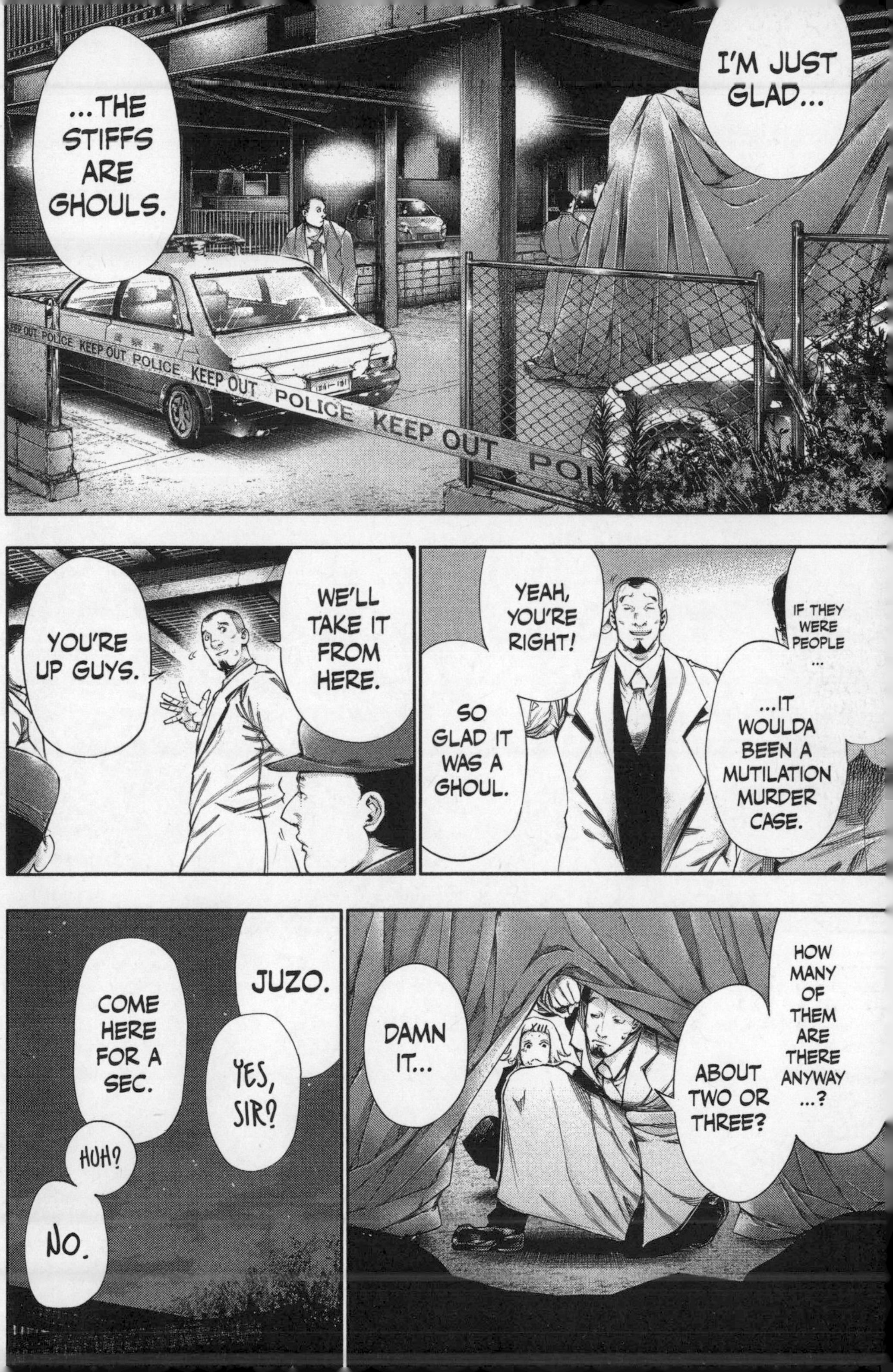
I'M JUST GLAD...
...THE STIFFS ARE GHOULS.
KEEP OUT POLICE KEEP OUT POLICE KEEP OUT POLICE KEEP OUT
IF THEY WERE PEOPLE ...
...IT WOULDA BEEN A MUTILATION MURDER CASE.
YEAH, YOU'RE RIGHT!
SO GLAD IT WAS A GHOUL.
WE'LL TAKE IT FROM HERE.
YOU'RE UP GUYS.
HOW MANY OF THEM ARE THERE ANYWAY ...?
ABOUT TWO OR THREE?
DAMN IT...
JUZO.
COME HERE FOR A SEC.
YES, SIR?
HUH?
NO.

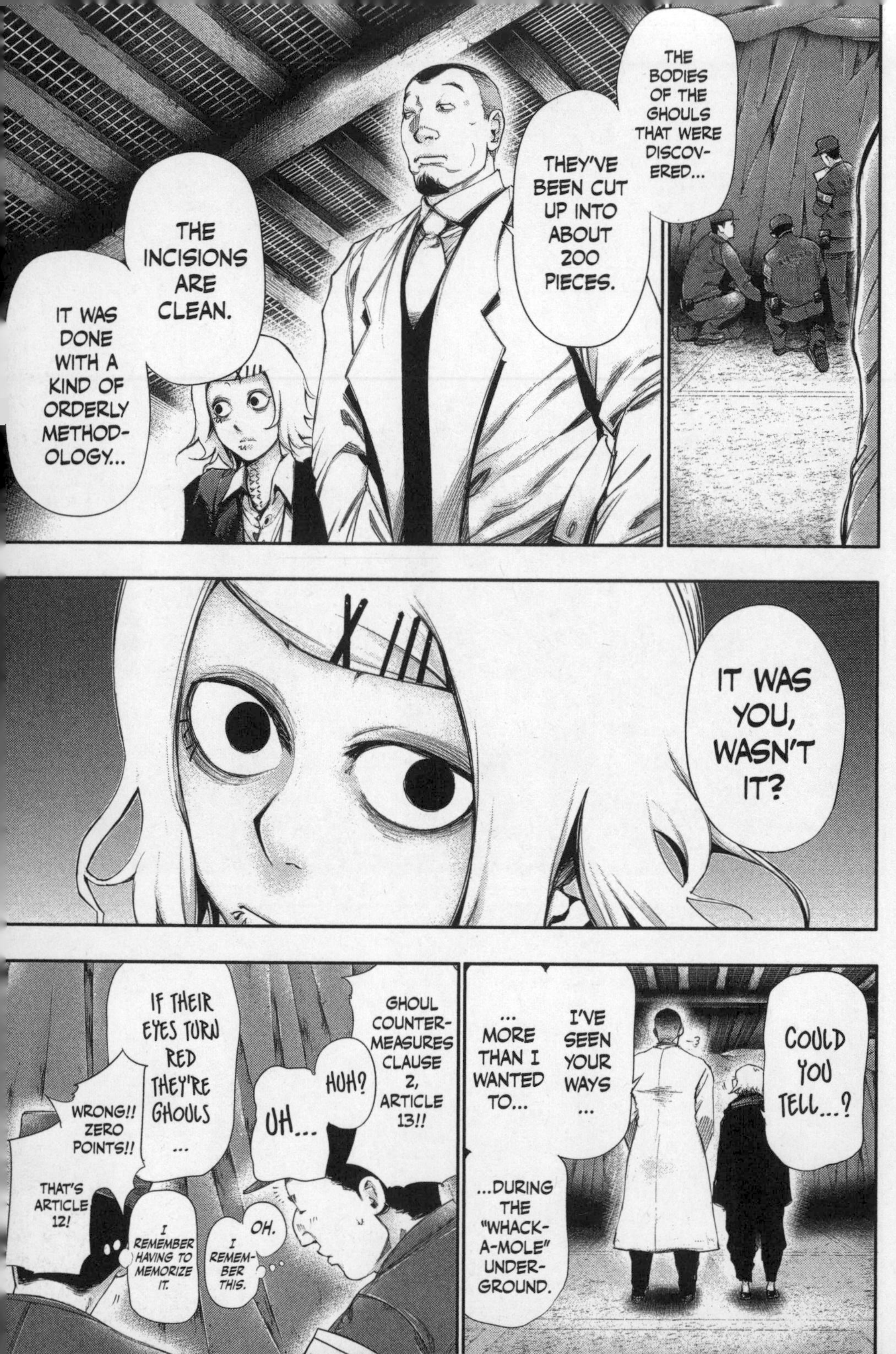
THE BODIES OF THE GHOULS THAT WERE DISCOVERED...
THEY'VE BEEN CUT UP INTO ABOUT 200 PIECES.
THE INCISIONS ARE CLEAN.
IT WAS DONE WITH A KIND OF ORDERLY METHODOLOGY...
IT WAS YOU, WASN'T IT?
COULD YOU TELL...?
I'VE SEEN YOUR WAYS...
...MORE THAN I WANTED TO...
...DURING THE "WHACK-A-MOLE" UNDERGROUND.
GHOUL COUNTERMEASURES CLAUSE 2, ARTICLE 13!!
HUH?
UH...
IF THEIR EYES TURN RED THEY'RE GHOULS...
WRONG!! ZERO POINTS!!
THAT'S ARTICLE 12!
OH.
I REMEMBER THIS.
I REMEMBER HAVING TO MEMORIZE IT.

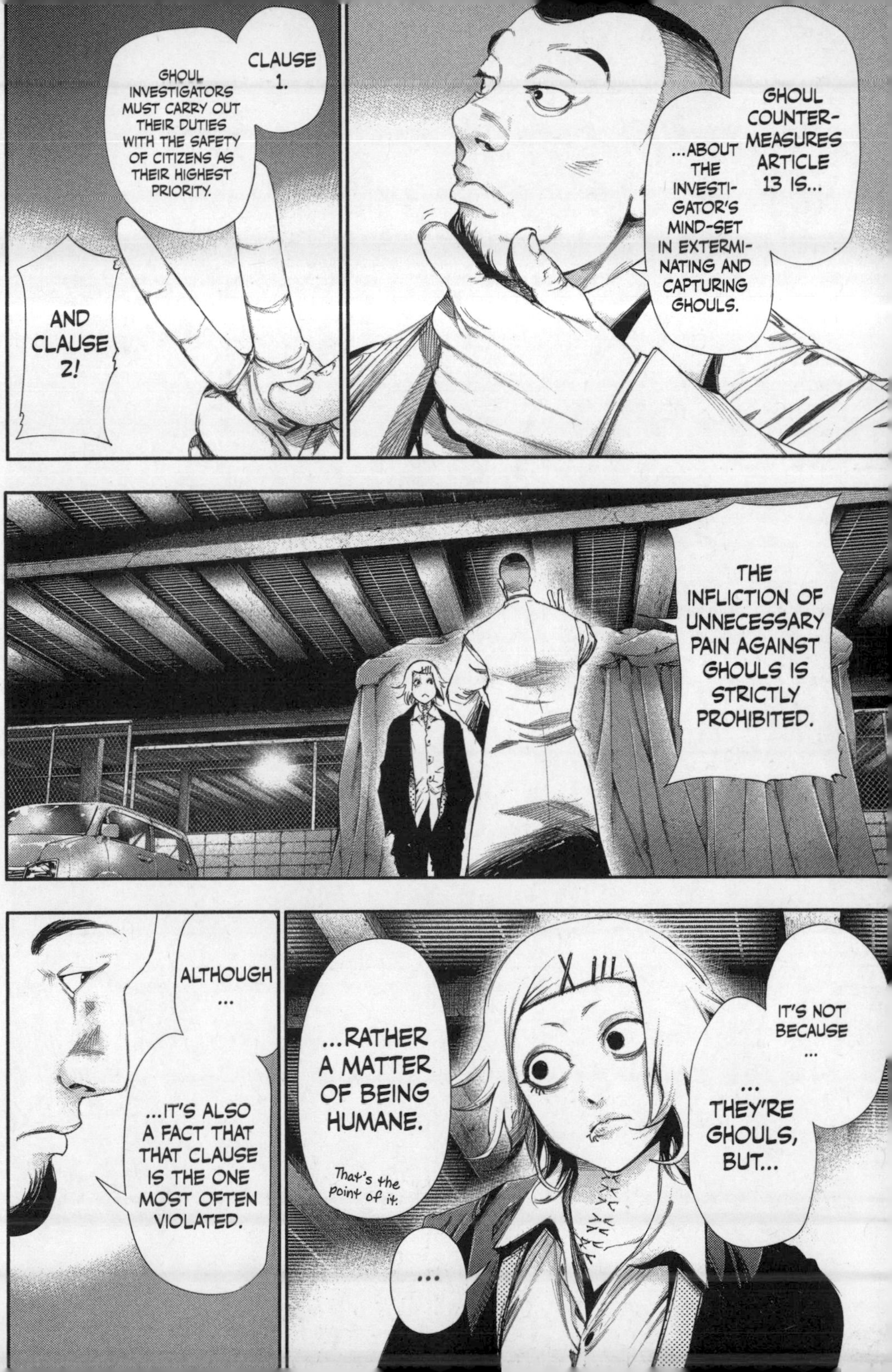
GHOUL COUNTER-MEASURES ARTICLE 13 IS...
...ABOUT THE INVESTIGATOR'S MIND-SET IN EXTERMINATING AND CAPTURING GHOULS.
CLAUSE 1.
GHOUL INVESTIGATORS MUST CARRY OUT THEIR DUTIES WITH THE SAFETY OF CITIZENS AS THEIR HIGHEST PRIORITY.
AND CLAUSE 2!
THE INFLICTION OF UNNECESSARY PAIN AGAINST GHOULS IS STRICTLY PROHIBITED.
IT'S NOT BECAUSE ...
... THEY'RE GHOULS, BUT...
...RATHER A MATTER OF BEING HUMANE.
That's the point of it.
...
ALTHOUGH ...
...IT'S ALSO A FACT THAT THAT CLAUSE IS THE ONE MOST OFTEN VIOLATED.

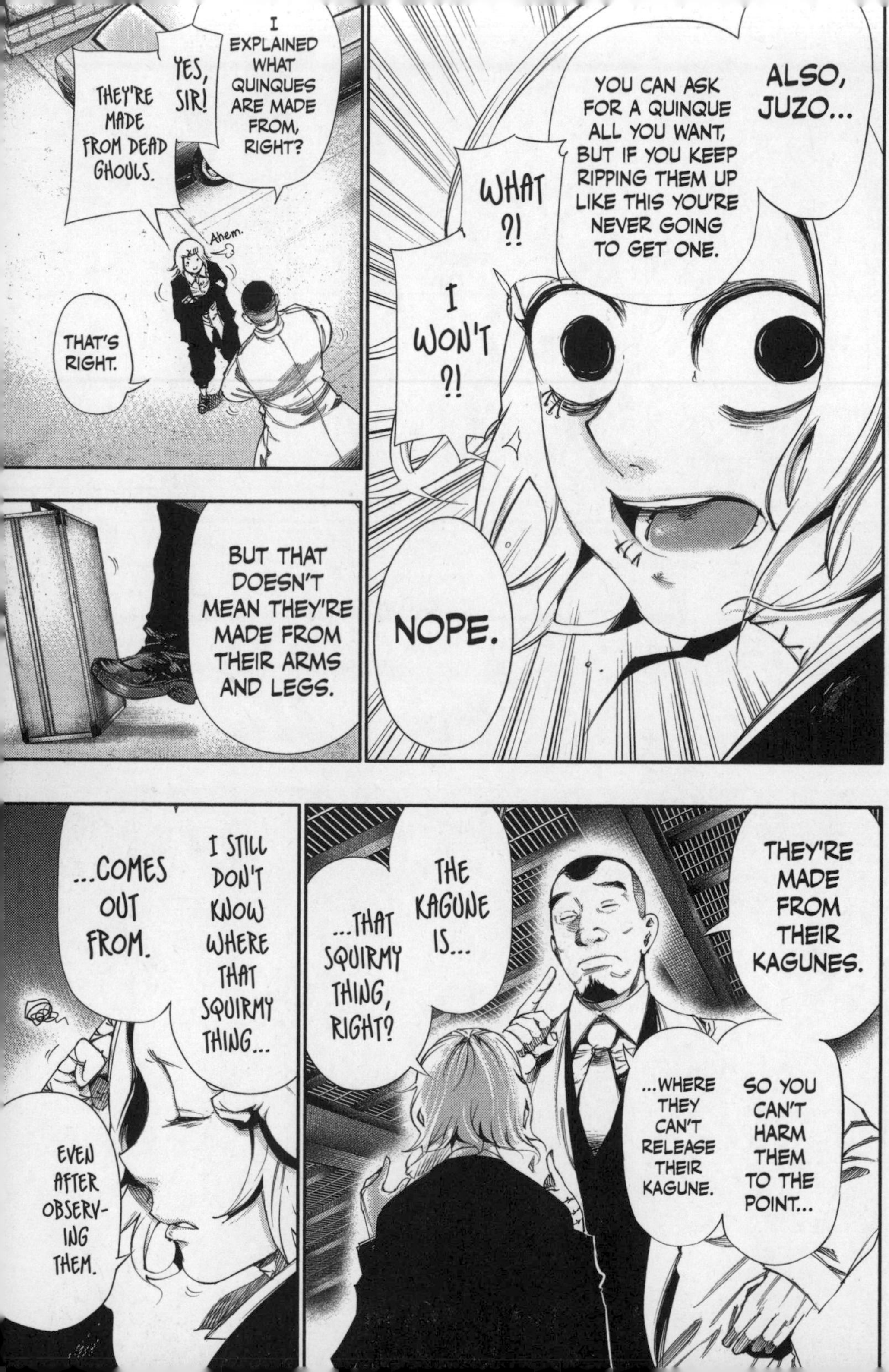
ALSO, JUZO...
YOU CAN ASK FOR A QUINQUE ALL YOU WANT, BUT IF YOU KEEP RIPPING THEM UP LIKE THIS YOU'RE NEVER GOING TO GET ONE.
WHAT ?!
I WON'T ?!
NOPE.
I EXPLAINED WHAT QUINQUES ARE MADE FROM, RIGHT?
YES, SIR!
THEY'RE MADE FROM DEAD GHOULS.
Ahem.
THAT'S RIGHT.
BUT THAT DOESN'T MEAN THEY'RE MADE FROM THEIR ARMS AND LEGS.
THEY'RE MADE FROM THEIR KAGUNES.
SO YOU CAN'T HARM THEM TO THE POINT...
...WHERE THEY CAN'T RELEASE THEIR KAGUNE.
THE KAGUNE IS...
...THAT SQUIRMY THING, RIGHT?
I STILL DON'T KNOW WHERE THAT SQUIRMY THING...
...COMES OUT FROM.
EVEN AFTER OBSERV-ING THEM.

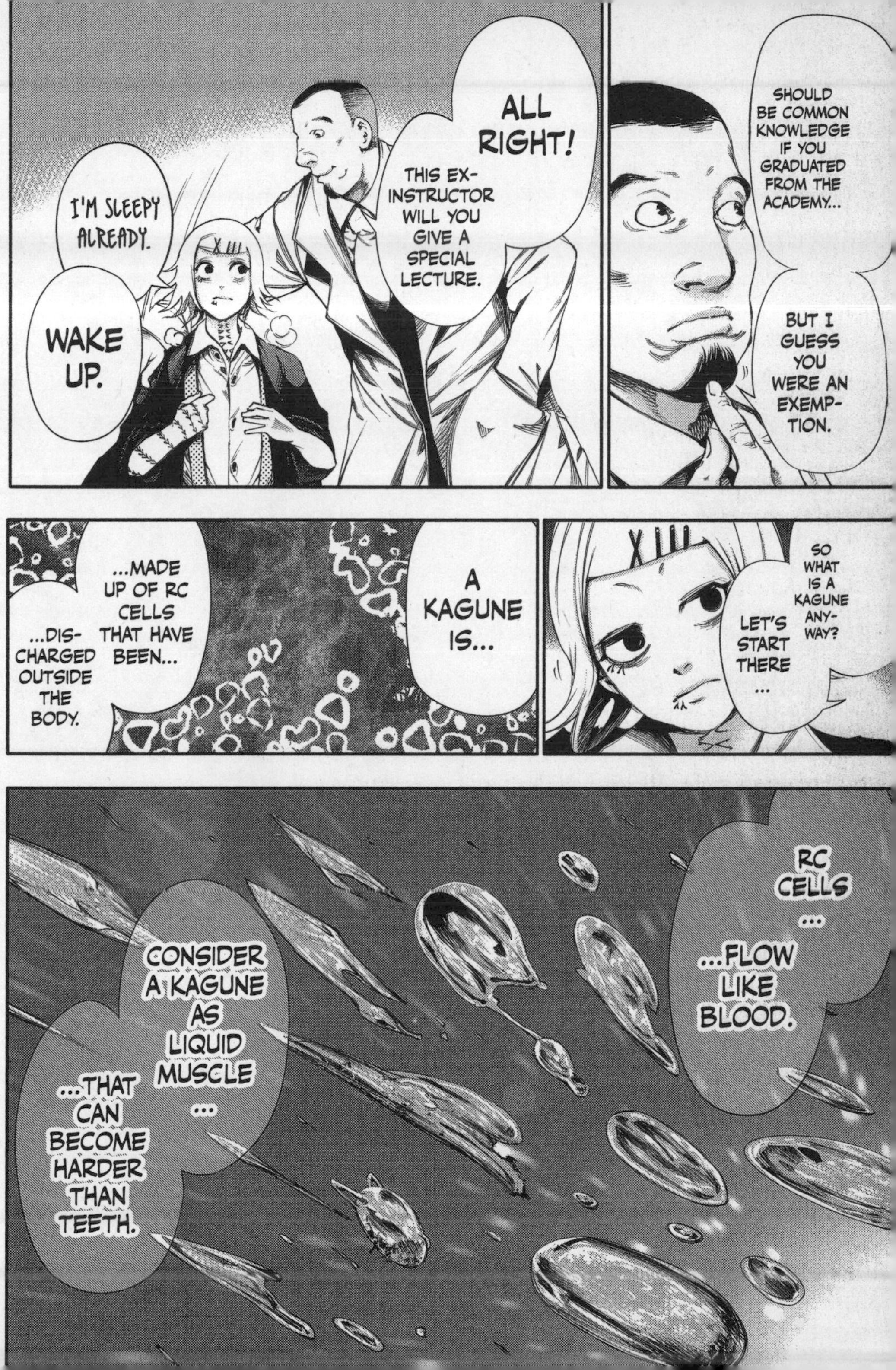
SHOULD BE COMMON KNOWLEDGE IF YOU GRADUATED FROM THE ACADEMY...
BUT I GUESS YOU WERE AN EXEMPTION.
ALL RIGHT!
THIS EX-INSTRUCTOR WILL YOU GIVE A SPECIAL LECTURE.
I'M SLEEPY ALREADY.
WAKE UP.
SO WHAT IS A KAGUNE ANYWAY?
LET'S START THERE...
A KAGUNE IS...
...MADE UP OF RC CELLS THAT HAVE BEEN...
...DIS-CHARGED OUTSIDE THE BODY.
RC CELLS...
...FLOW LIKE BLOOD.
CONSIDER A KAGUNE AS LIQUID MUSCLE...
...THAT CAN BECOME HARDER THAN TEETH.

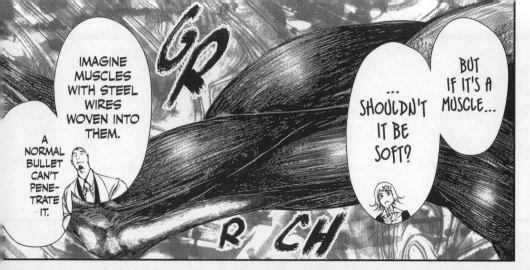

BUT IF IT'S A MUSCLE...
...SHOULDN'T IT BE SOFT?
GR
IMAGINE MUSCLES WITH STEEL WIRES WOVEN INTO THEM.
A NORMAL BULLET CAN'T PENE-TRATE IT.
R CH
GHOULS ACCUMU-LATE RC CELLS IN THEIR BLOOD ...
...BY CONSUMING HUMANS.
Rc
AND THE ACCUMU-LATED RC CELLS...
...ARE SENT TO A SAC KNOWN AS THE KAKUHO ...
...AND STORED THERE.
Rc
Kakuho
RC CELLS THAT ARE STORED IN THE KAKUHO...
Kakuho
Rc
...EITHER CON-SCIOUSLY ...
...OR FROM MENTAL AGITATION ...
...BREAK THROUGH THE SKIN AND ARE DIS-CHARGED.

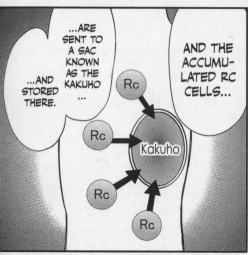

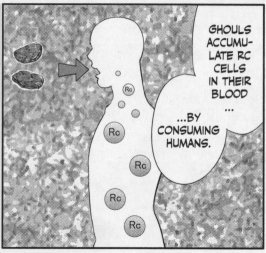

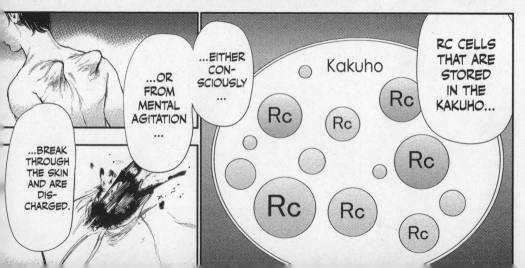

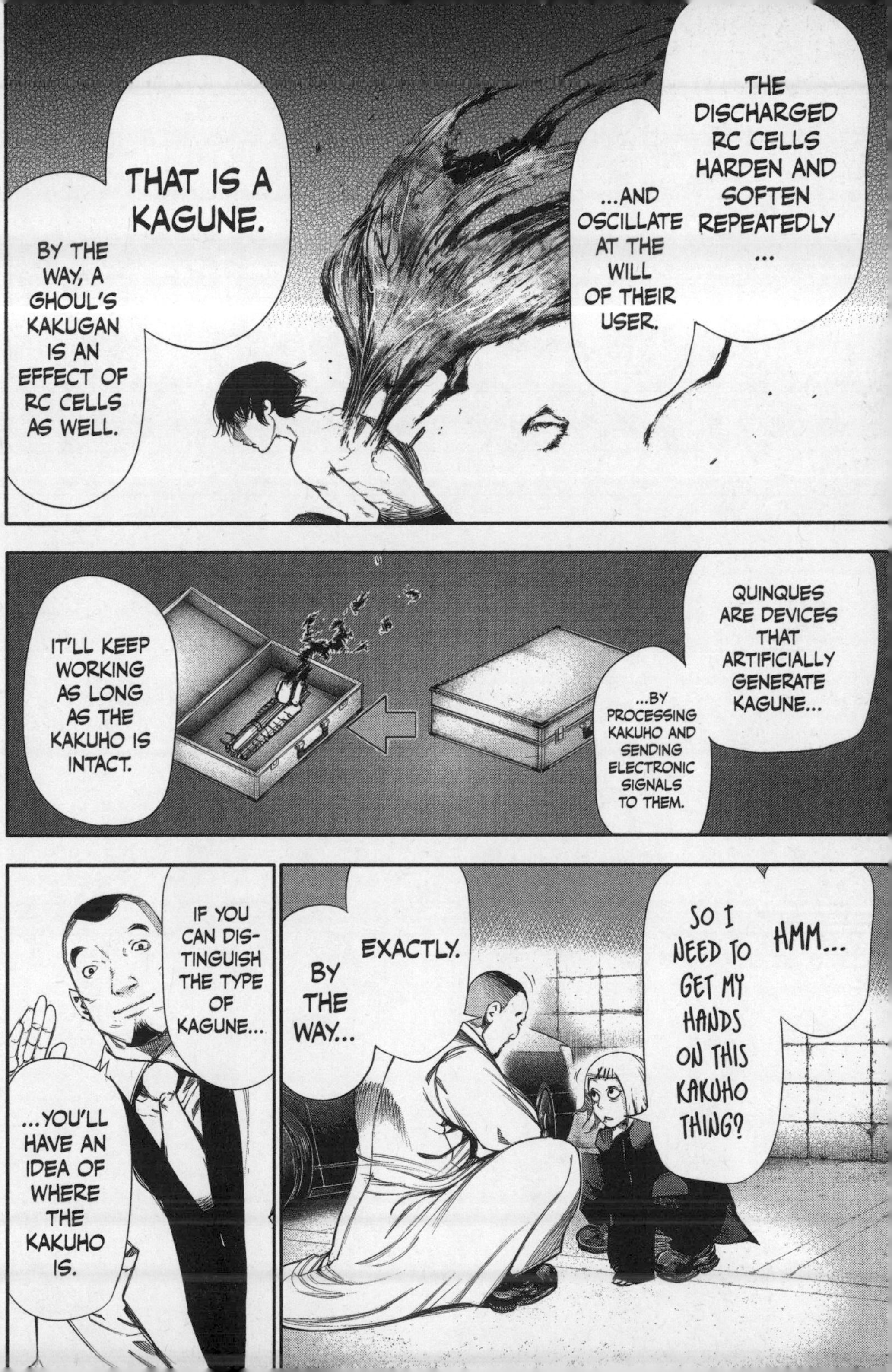
THE DISCHARGED RC CELLS HARDEN AND SOFTEN REPEATEDLY...
...AND OSCILLATE AT THE WILL OF THEIR USER.
THAT IS A KAGUNE.
BY THE WAY, A GHOUL'S KAKUGAN IS AN EFFECT OF RC CELLS AS WELL.
QUINQUES ARE DEVICES THAT ARTIFICIALLY GENERATE KAGUNE...
...BY PROCESSING KAKUHO AND SENDING ELECTRONIC SIGNALS TO THEM.
IT'LL KEEP WORKING AS LONG AS THE KAKUHO IS INTACT.
HMM...
SO I NEED TO GET MY HANDS ON THIS KAKUHO THING?
EXACTLY.
BY THE WAY...
IF YOU CAN DIS-TINGUISH THE TYPE OF KAGUNE...
...YOU'LL HAVE AN IDEA OF WHERE THE KAKUHO IS.

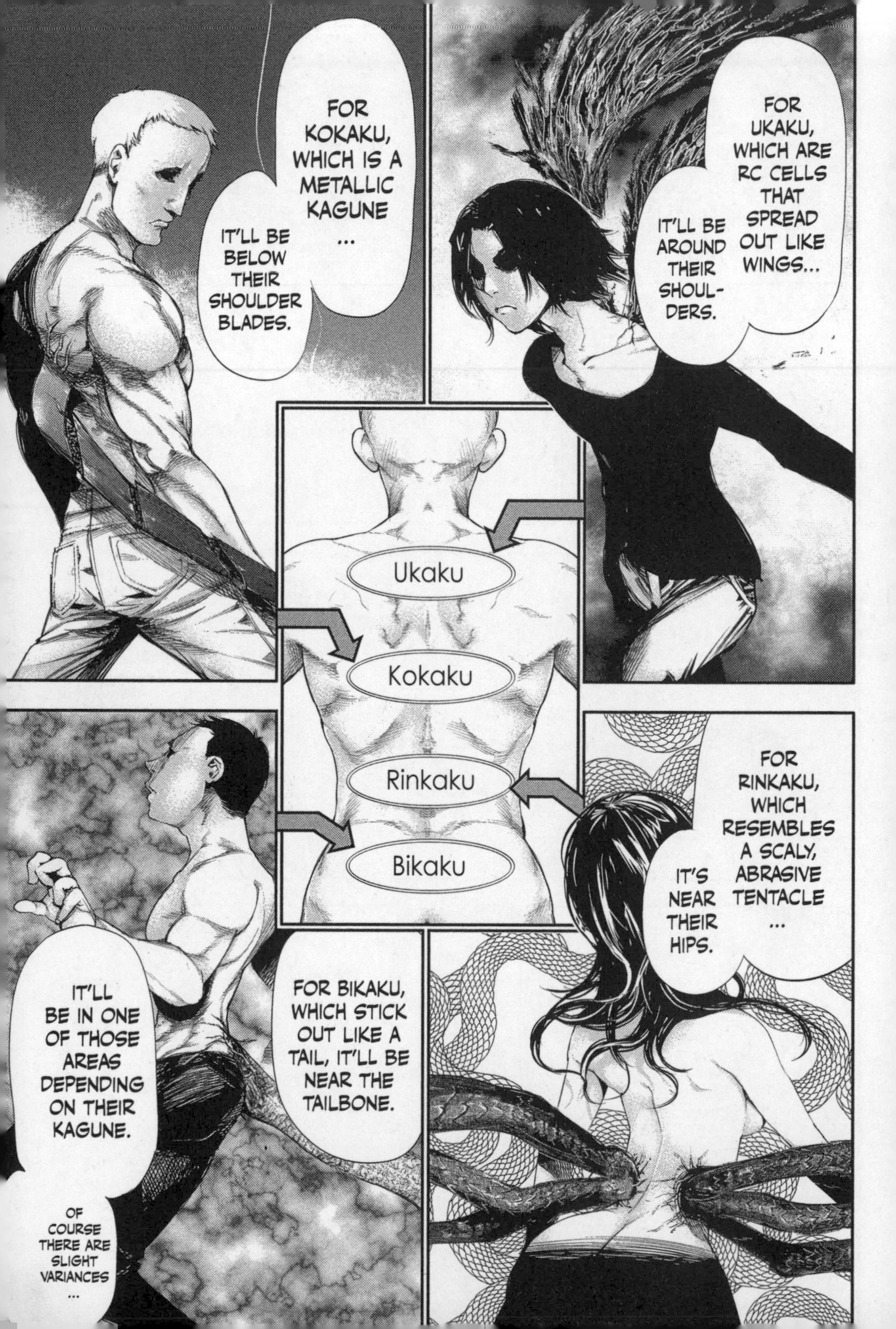
FOR UKAKU, WHICH ARE RC CELLS THAT SPREAD OUT LIKE WINGS...
IT'LL BE AROUND THEIR SHOUL-DERS.
FOR KOKAKU, WHICH IS A METALLIC KAGUNE...
IT'LL BE BELOW THEIR SHOULDER BLADES.
Ukaku
Kokaku
Rinkaku
Bikaku
FOR RINKAKU, WHICH RESEMBLES A SCALY, ABRASIVE TENTACLE...
IT'S NEAR THEIR HIPS.
FOR BIKAKU, WHICH STICK OUT LIKE A TAIL, IT'LL BE NEAR THE TAILBONE.
IT'LL BE IN ONE OF THOSE AREAS DEPENDING ON THEIR KAGUNE.
OF COURSE THERE ARE SLIGHT VARIANCES...

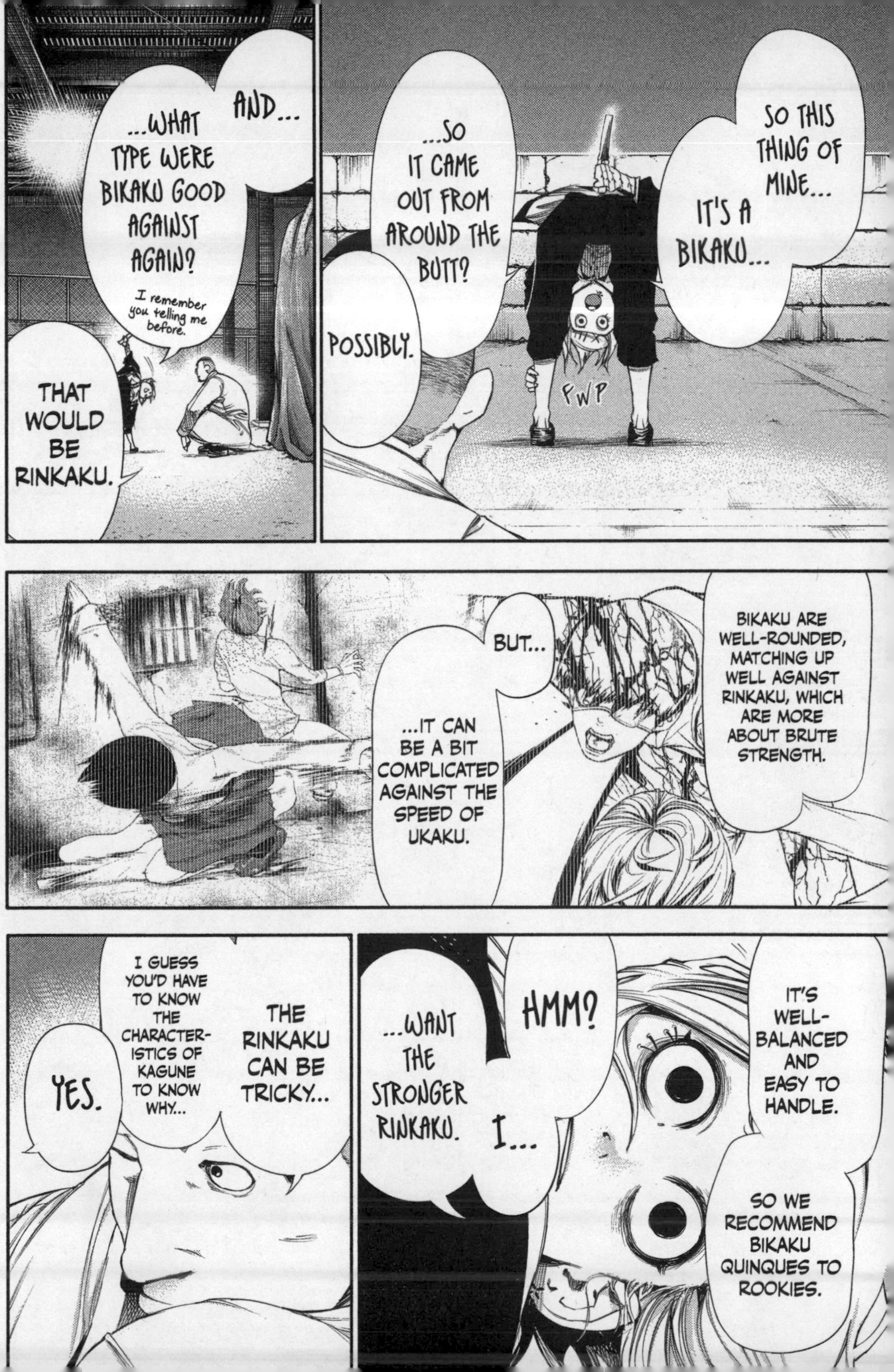
SO THIS THING OF MINE...
IT'S A BIKAKU...
...SO IT CAME OUT FROM AROUND THE BUTT?
POSSIBLY.
FWP
AND...
...WHAT TYPE WERE BIKAKU GOOD AGAINST AGAIN?
I remember you telling me before.
THAT WOULD BE RINKAKU.
BIKAKU ARE WELL-ROUNDED, MATCHING UP WELL AGAINST RINKAKU, WHICH ARE MORE ABOUT BRUTE STRENGTH.
BUT...
...IT CAN BE A BIT COMPLICATED AGAINST THE SPEED OF UKAKU.
IT'S WELL-BALANCED AND EASY TO HANDLE.
SO WE RECOMMEND BIKAKU QUINQUES TO ROOKIES.
HMM?
I...
...WANT THE STRONGER RINKAKU.
THE RINKAKU CAN BE TRICKY...
I GUESS YOU'D HAVE TO KNOW THE CHARACTER-ISTICS OF KAGUNE TO KNOW WHY...
YES.

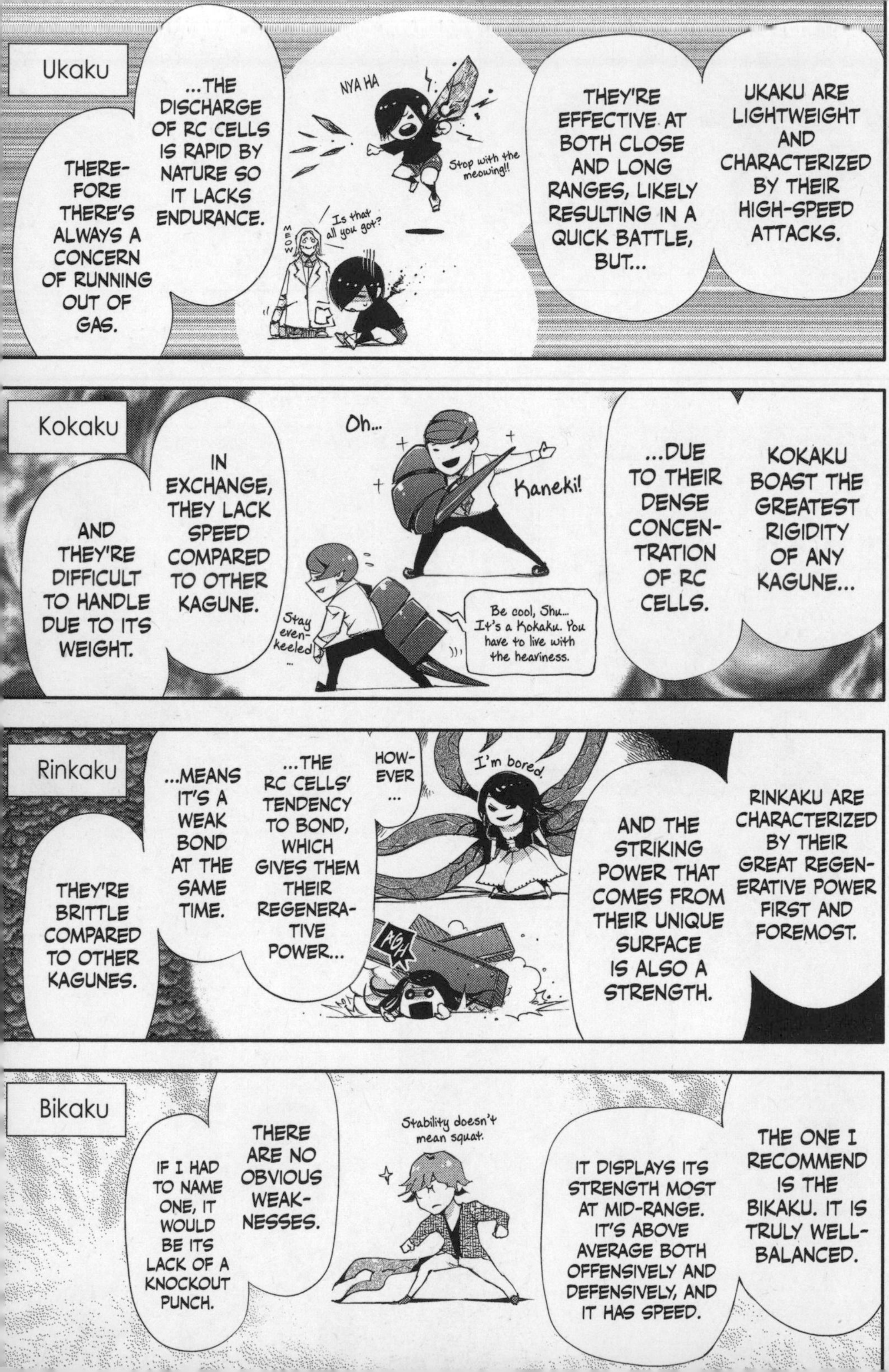
Ukaku
UKAKU ARE LIGHTWEIGHT AND CHARACTERIZED BY THEIR HIGH-SPEED ATTACKS.
THEY'RE EFFECTIVE AT BOTH CLOSE AND LONG RANGES, LIKELY RESULTING IN A QUICK BATTLE, BUT...
NYA HA
Stop with the meowing!!
Is that all you got?
MEOW
...THE DISCHARGE OF RC CELLS IS RAPID BY NATURE SO IT LACKS ENDURANCE.
THERE-FORE THERE'S ALWAYS A CONCERN OF RUNNING OUT OF GAS.
Kokaku
KOKAKU BOAST THE GREATEST RIGIDITY OF ANY KAGUNE...
...DUE TO THEIR DENSE CONCEN-TRATION OF RC CELLS.
Oh...
Kaneki!
Be cool, Shu... It's a Kokaku. You have to live with the heaviness.
Stay even-keeled...
IN EXCHANGE, THEY LACK SPEED COMPARED TO OTHER KAGUNE.
AND THEY'RE DIFFICULT TO HANDLE DUE TO ITS WEIGHT.
Rinkaku
RINKAKU ARE CHARACTERIZED BY THEIR GREAT REGEN-ERATIVE POWER FIRST AND FOREMOST.
AND THE STRIKING POWER THAT COMES FROM THEIR UNIQUE SURFACE IS ALSO A STRENGTH.
I'm bored.
HOW-EVER...
...THE RC CELLS' TENDENCY TO BOND, WHICH GIVES THEM THEIR REGENERA-TIVE POWER...
AGH
...MEANS IT'S A WEAK BOND AT THE SAME TIME.
THEY'RE BRITTLE COMPARED TO OTHER KAGUNES.
Bikaku
THE ONE I RECOMMEND IS THE BIKAKU. IT IS TRULY WELL-BALANCED.
IT DISPLAYS ITS STRENGTH MOST AT MID-RANGE. IT'S ABOVE AVERAGE BOTH OFFENSIVELY AND DEFENSIVELY, AND IT HAS SPEED.
Stability doesn't mean squat.
THERE ARE NO OBVIOUS WEAK-NESSES.
IF I HAD TO NAME ONE, IT WOULD BE ITS LACK OF A KNOCKOUT PUNCH.

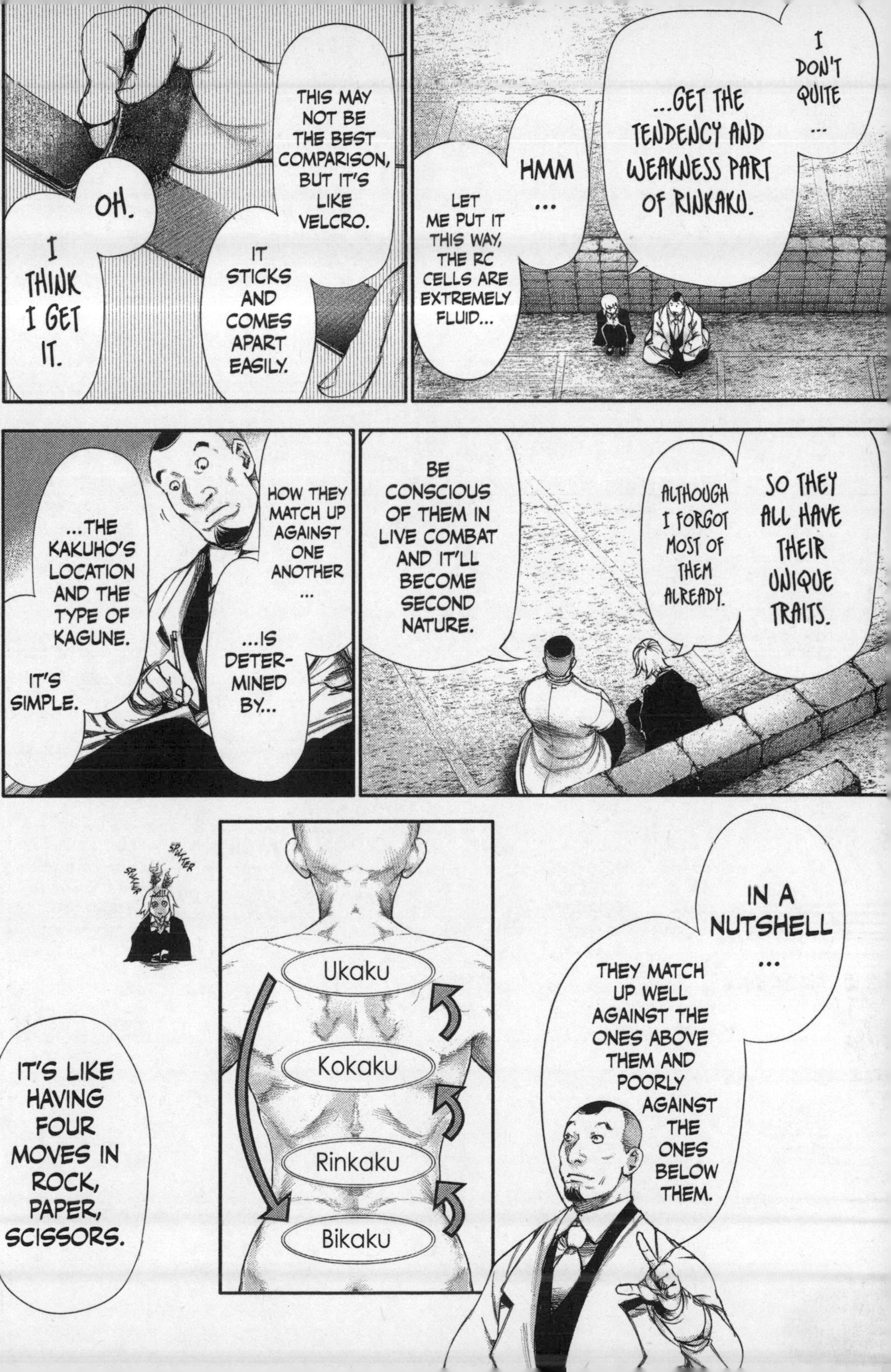
I DON'T QUITE ...
...GET THE TENDENCY AND WEAKNESS PART OF RINKAKU.
HMM ...
LET ME PUT IT THIS WAY, THE RC CELLS ARE EXTREMELY FLUID...
THIS MAY NOT BE THE BEST COMPARISON, BUT IT'S LIKE VELCRO.
IT STICKS AND COMES APART EASILY.
OH.
I THINK I GET IT.
SO THEY ALL HAVE THEIR UNIQUE TRAITS.
ALTHOUGH I FORGOT MOST OF THEM ALREADY.
BE CONSCIOUS OF THEM IN LIVE COMBAT AND IT'LL BECOME SECOND NATURE.
HOW THEY MATCH UP AGAINST ONE ANOTHER ...
...IS DETERMINED BY...
...THE KAKUHO'S LOCATION AND THE TYPE OF KAGUNE.
IT'S SIMPLE.
IN A NUTSHELL ...
THEY MATCH UP WELL AGAINST THE ONES ABOVE THEM AND POORLY AGAINST THE ONES BELOW THEM.
Ukaku
Kokaku
Rinkaku
Bikaku
IT'S LIKE HAVING FOUR MOVES IN ROCK, PAPER, SCISSORS.

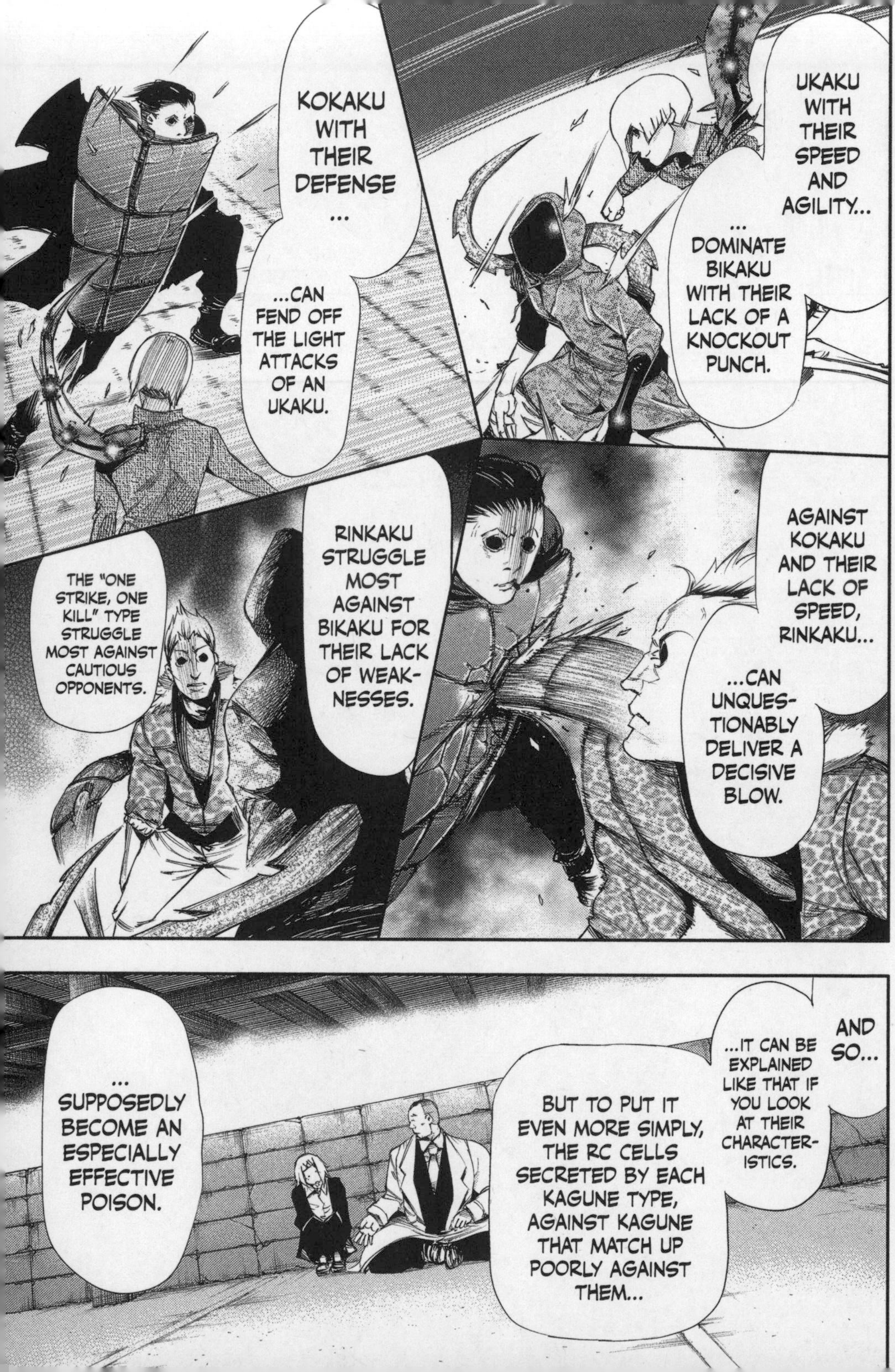
UKAKU WITH THEIR SPEED AND AGILITY...
...DOMINATE BIKAKU WITH THEIR LACK OF A KNOCKOUT PUNCH.
KOKAKU WITH THEIR DEFENSE...
...CAN FEND OFF THE LIGHT ATTACKS OF AN UKAKU.
AGAINST KOKAKU AND THEIR LACK OF SPEED, RINKAKU...
...CAN UNQUESTIONABLY DELIVER A DECISIVE BLOW.
RINKAKU STRUGGLE MOST AGAINST BIKAKU FOR THEIR LACK OF WEAKNESSES.
THE "ONE STRIKE, ONE KILL" TYPE STRUGGLE MOST AGAINST CAUTIOUS OPPONENTS.
AND SO...
...IT CAN BE EXPLAINED LIKE THAT IF YOU LOOK AT THEIR CHARACTERISTICS.
BUT TO PUT IT EVEN MORE SIMPLY, THE RC CELLS SECRETED BY EACH KAGUNE TYPE, AGAINST KAGUNE THAT MATCH UP POORLY AGAINST THEM...
...SUPPOSEDLY BECOME AN ESPECIALLY EFFECTIVE POISON.

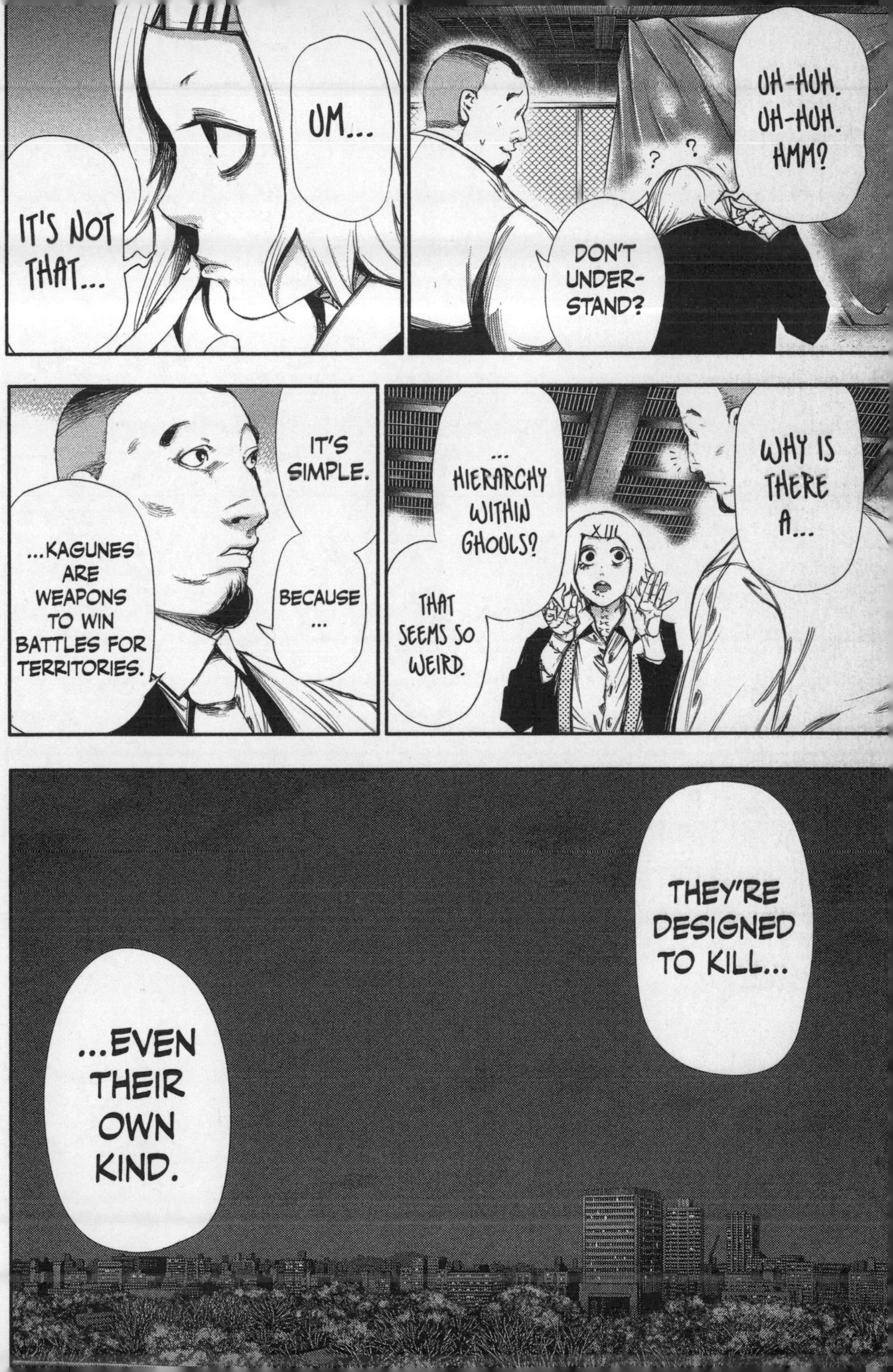
UH-HUH. UH-HUH. HMM?
DON'T UNDER-STAND?
UM...
IT'S NOT THAT...
WHY IS THERE A...
...HIERARCHY WITHIN GHOULS?
THAT SEEMS SO WEIRD.
IT'S SIMPLE.
BECAUSE...
...KAGUNES ARE WEAPONS TO WIN BATTLES FOR TERRITORIES.
THEY'RE DESIGNED TO KILL...
...EVEN THEIR OWN KIND.

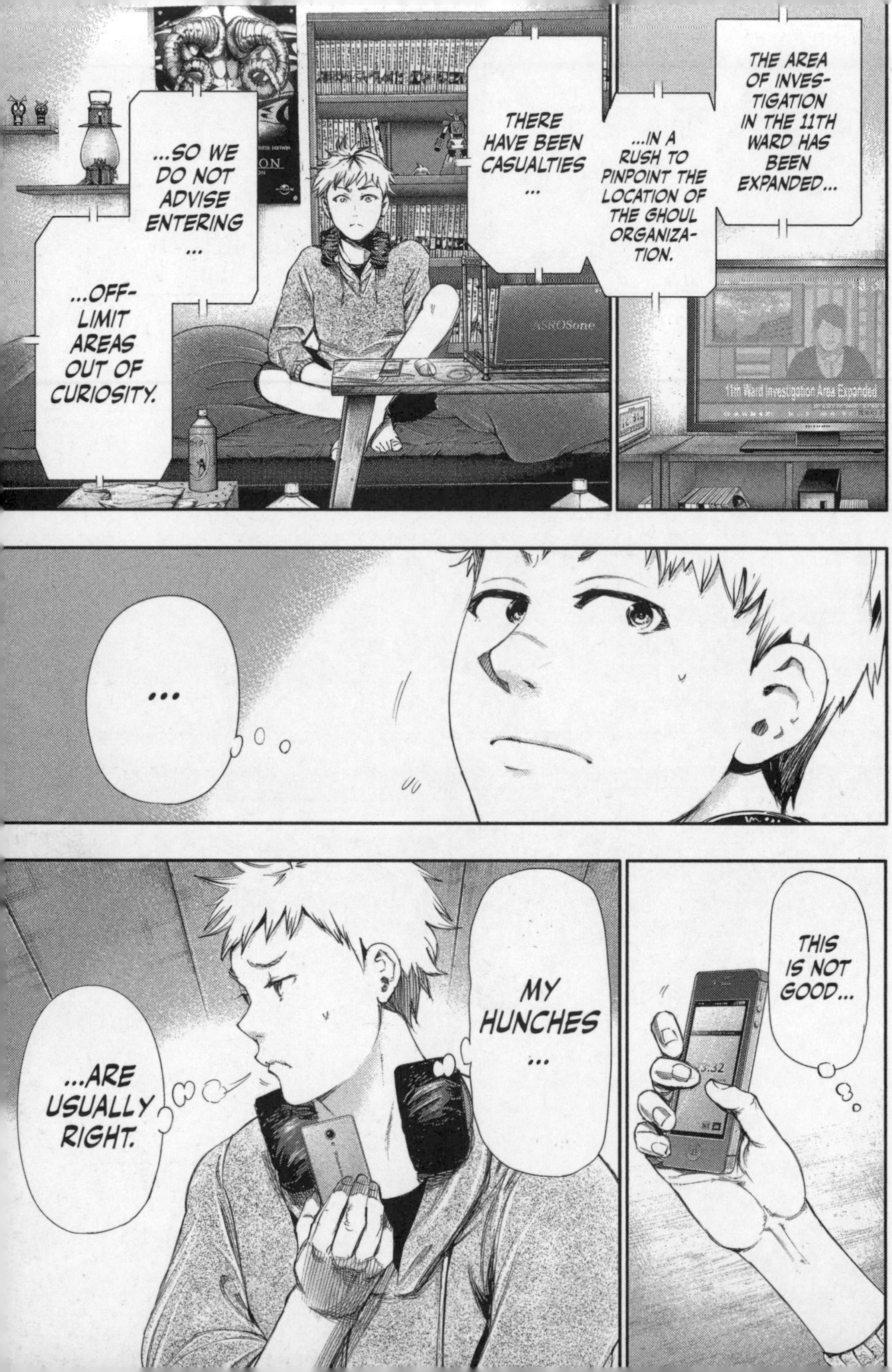
THE AREA OF INVESTIGATION IN THE 11TH WARD HAS BEEN EXPANDED...
...IN A RUSH TO PINPOINT THE LOCATION OF THE GHOUL ORGANIZATION.
11th Ward Investigation Area Expanded
THERE HAVE BEEN CASUALTIES...
...SO WE DO NOT ADVISE ENTERING...
...OFF-LIMIT AREAS OUT OF CURIOSITY.
...
THIS IS NOT GOOD...
MY HUNCHES...
...ARE USUALLY RIGHT.

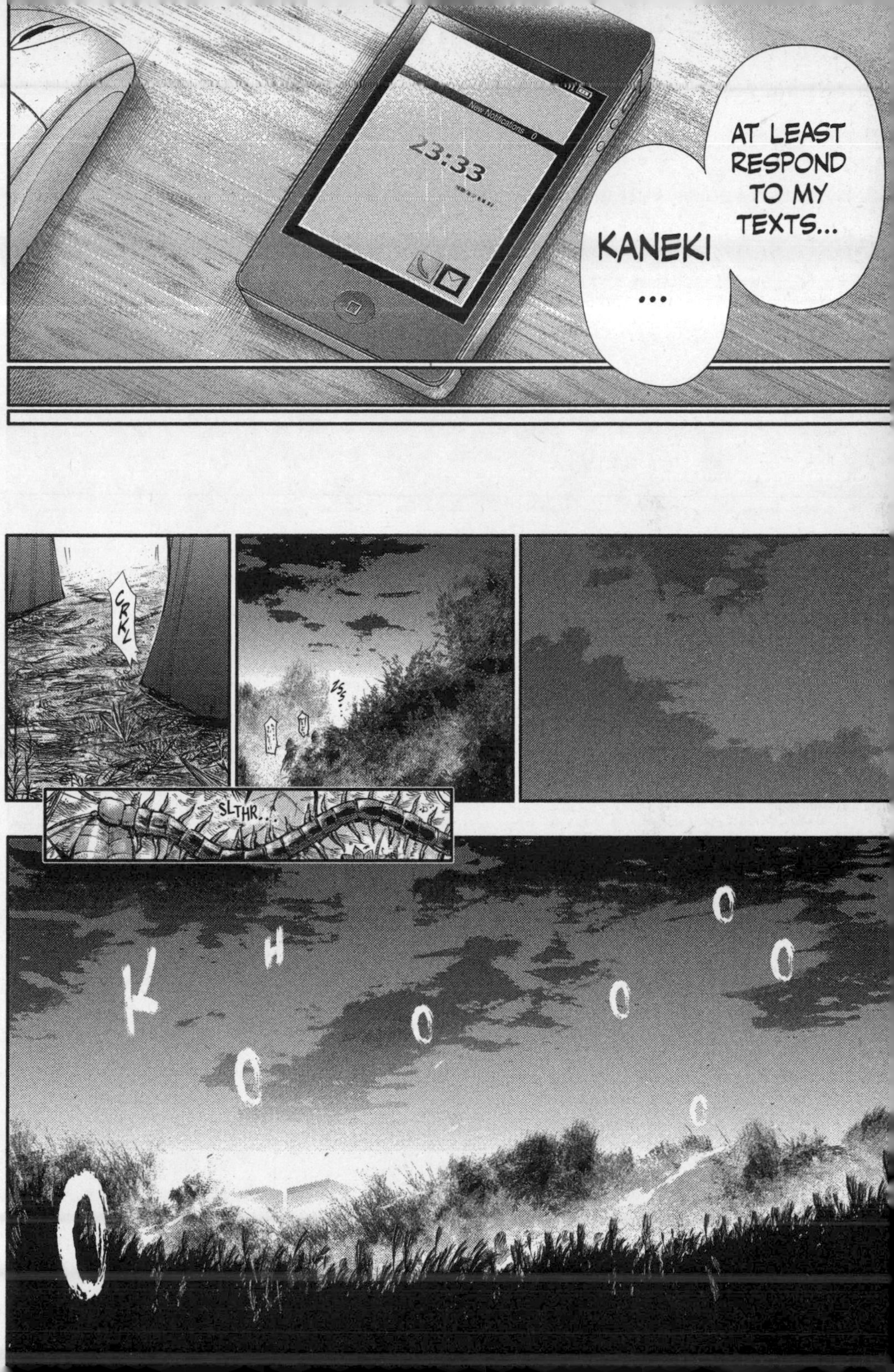
AT LEAST RESPOND TO MY TEXTS...
KANEKI ...
New Notifications 0
23:33
ZSS...
CRKL
SLTHR...
KHOOOOOOO

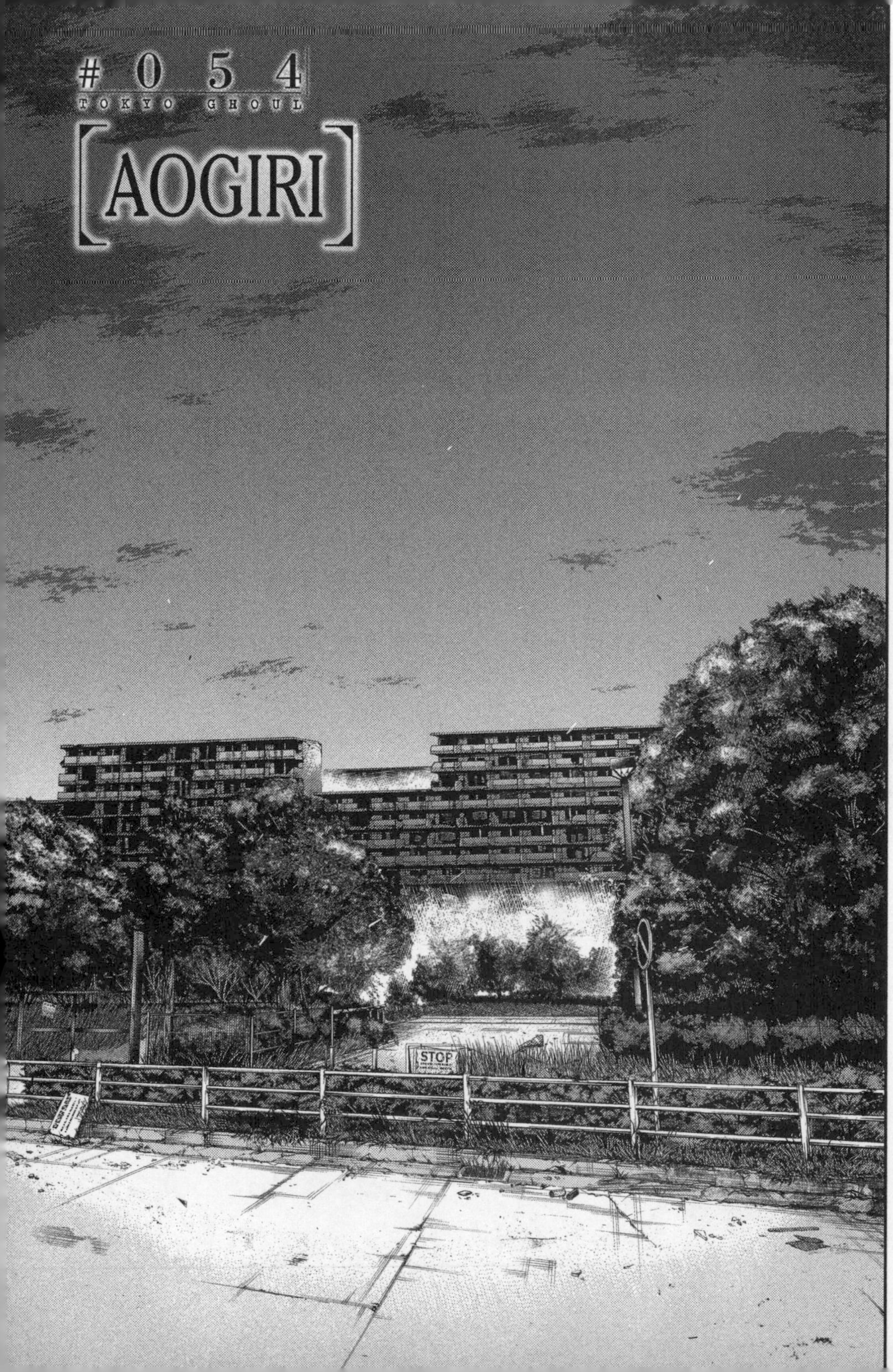
#054
TOKYO GHOUL
[AOGIRI]
STOP

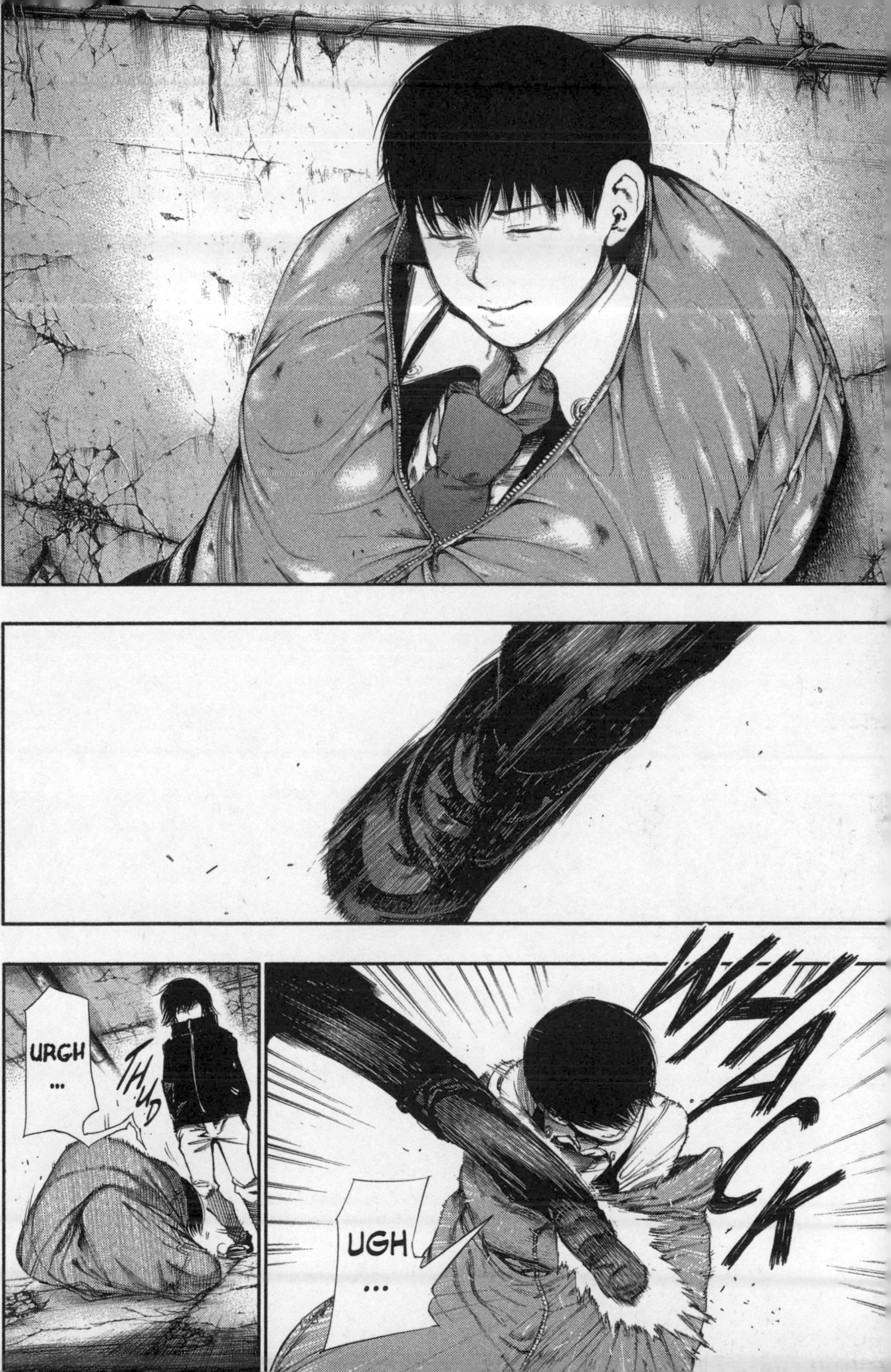
WHACK
UGH ...
URGH ...
THUD

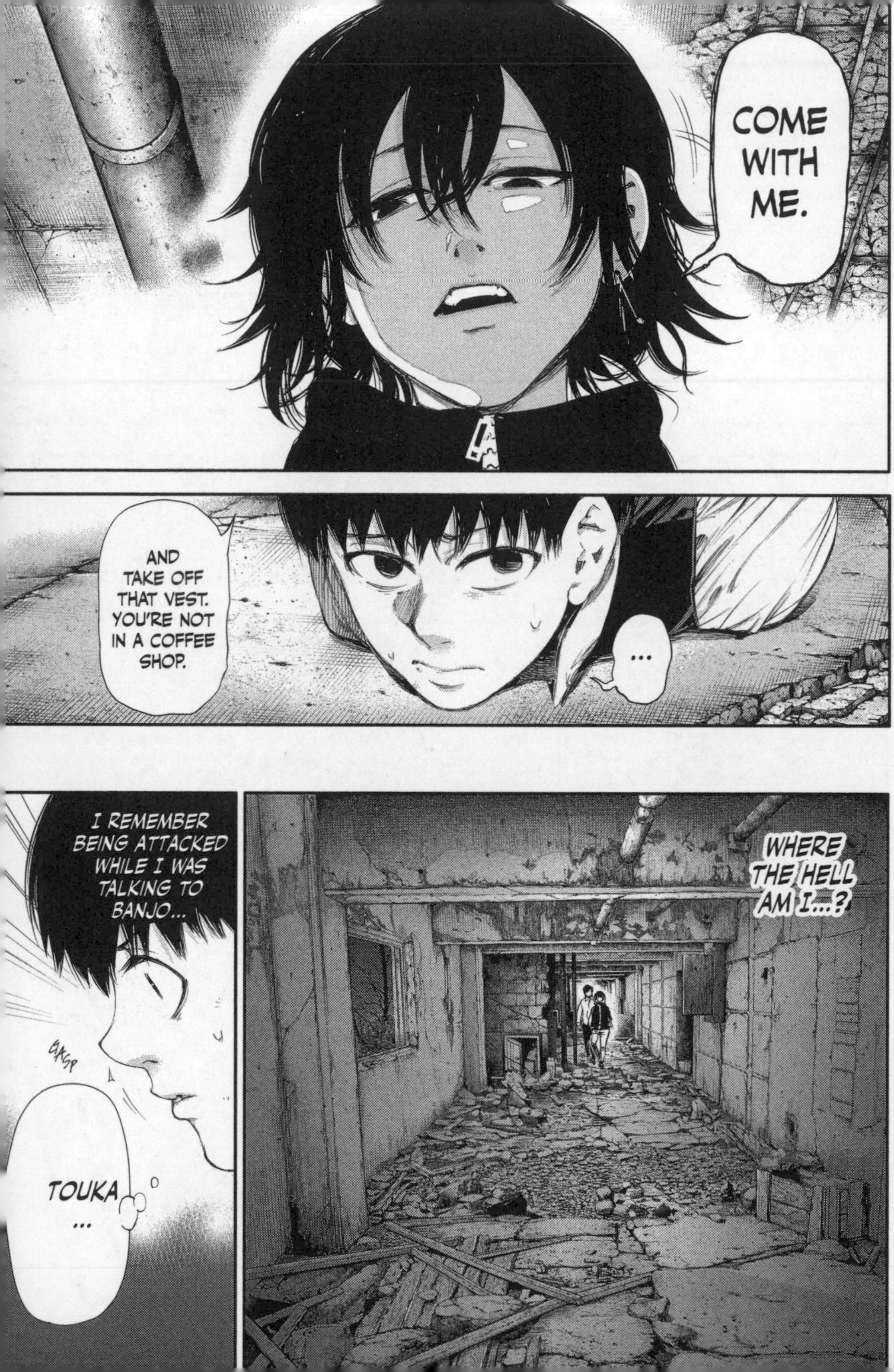
COME WITH ME.
AND TAKE OFF THAT VEST. YOU'RE NOT IN A COFFEE SHOP.
...
WHERE THE HELL AM I...?
I REMEMBER BEING ATTACKED WHILE I WAS TALKING TO BANJO...
GASP
TOUKA ...

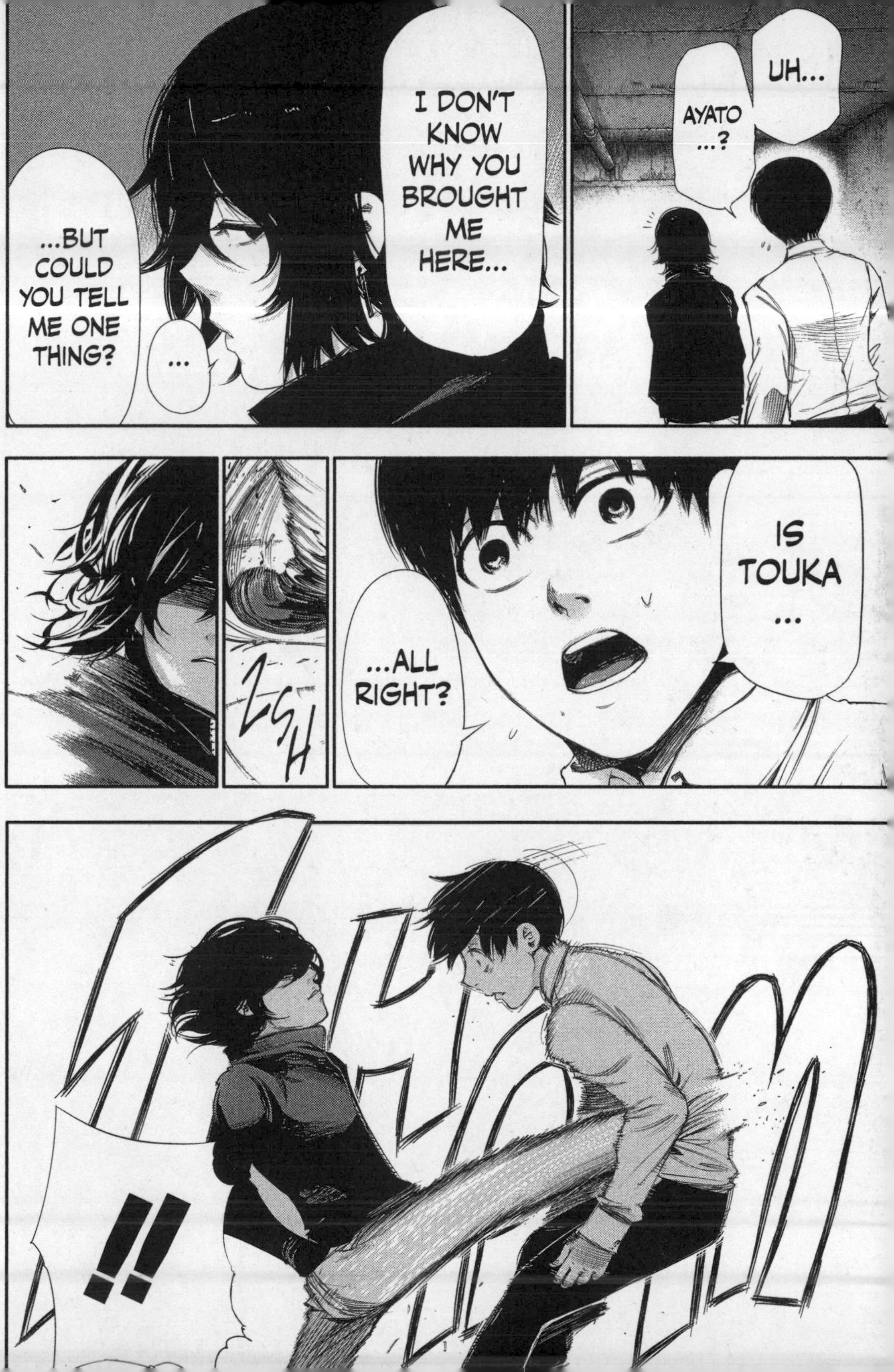
UH...
AYATO ...?
I DON'T KNOW WHY YOU BROUGHT ME HERE...
...BUT COULD YOU TELL ME ONE THING?
...
IS TOUKA ...
...ALL RIGHT?
ZSH
!!

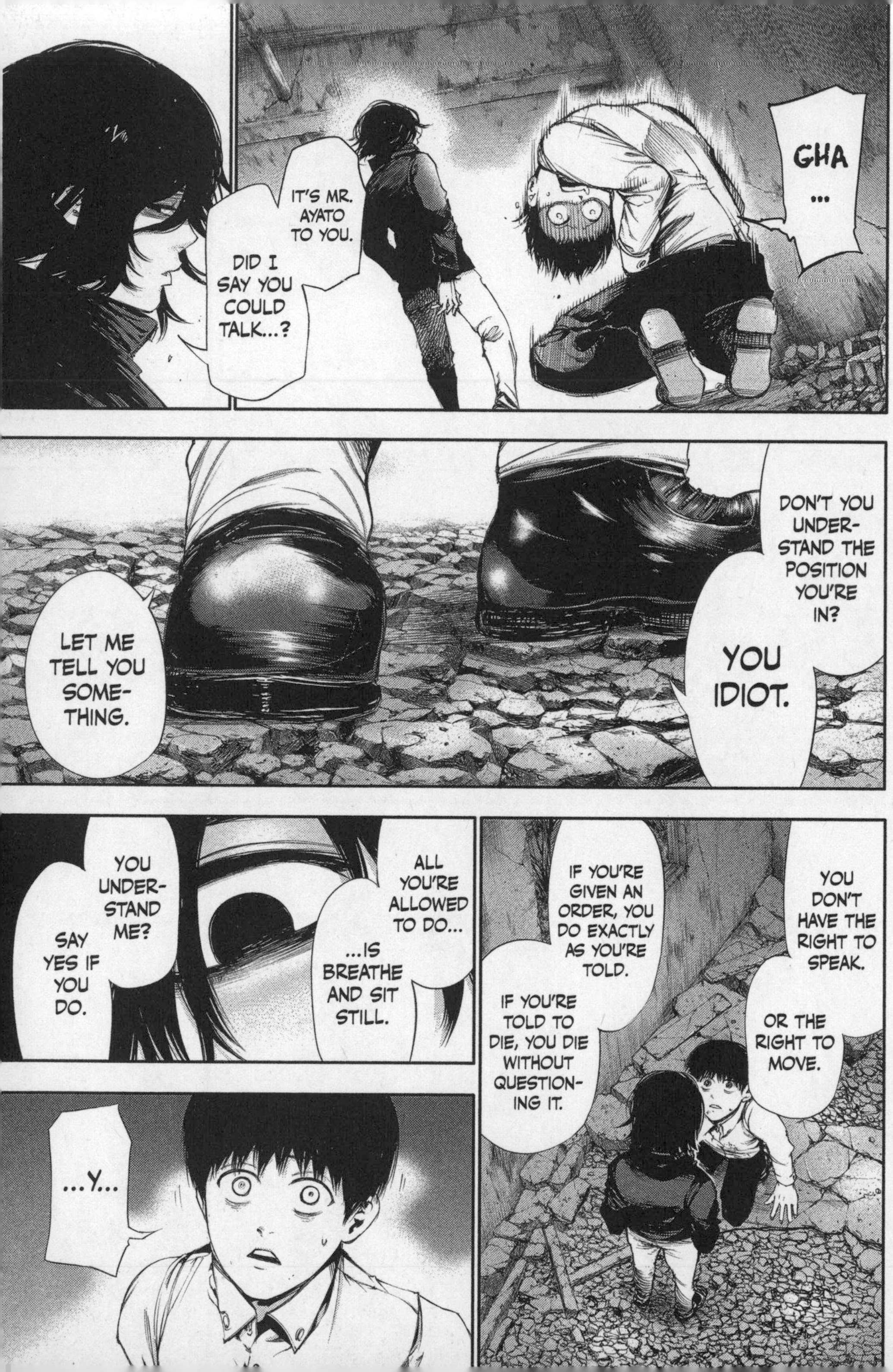
GHA ...
IT'S MR. AYATO TO YOU.
DID I SAY YOU COULD TALK...?
DON'T YOU UNDER-STAND THE POSITION YOU'RE IN?
YOU IDIOT.
LET ME TELL YOU SOME-THING.
YOU DON'T HAVE THE RIGHT TO SPEAK.
OR THE RIGHT TO MOVE.
IF YOU'RE GIVEN AN ORDER, YOU DO EXACTLY AS YOU'RE TOLD.
IF YOU'RE TOLD TO DIE, YOU DIE WITHOUT QUESTION-ING IT.
ALL YOU'RE ALLOWED TO DO...
...IS BREATHE AND SIT STILL.
YOU UNDER-STAND ME?
SAY YES IF YOU DO.
...Y...

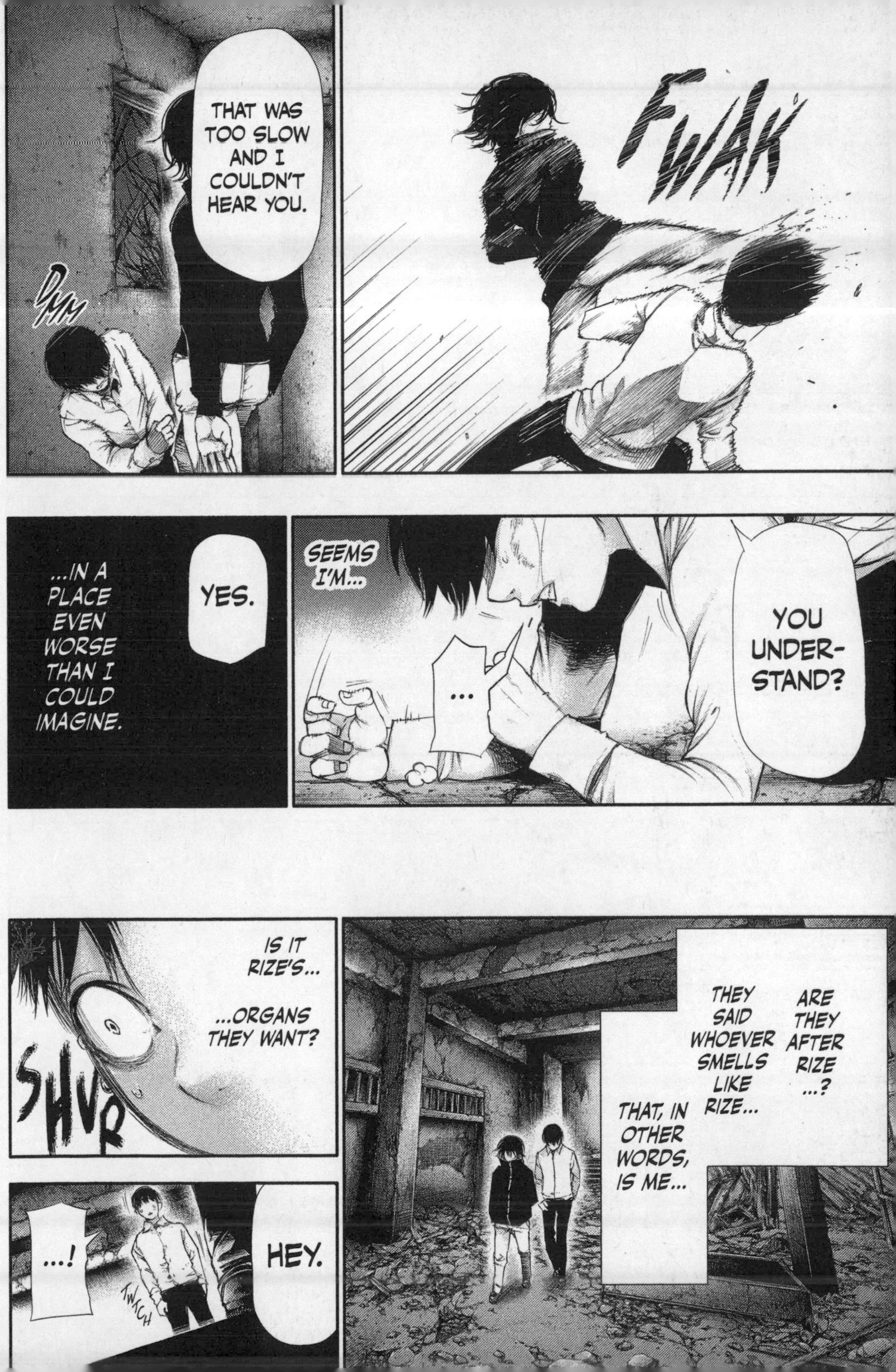
FWAK
THAT WAS TOO SLOW AND I COULDN'T HEAR YOU.
DMM
YOU UNDER-STAND?
SEEMS I'M...
...
YES.
...IN A PLACE EVEN WORSE THAN I COULD IMAGINE.
ARE THEY AFTER RIZE ...?
THEY SAID WHOEVER SMELLS LIKE RIZE...
THAT, IN OTHER WORDS, IS ME...
IS IT RIZE'S...
...ORGANS THEY WANT?
SHVR
HEY.
...!
TWACH

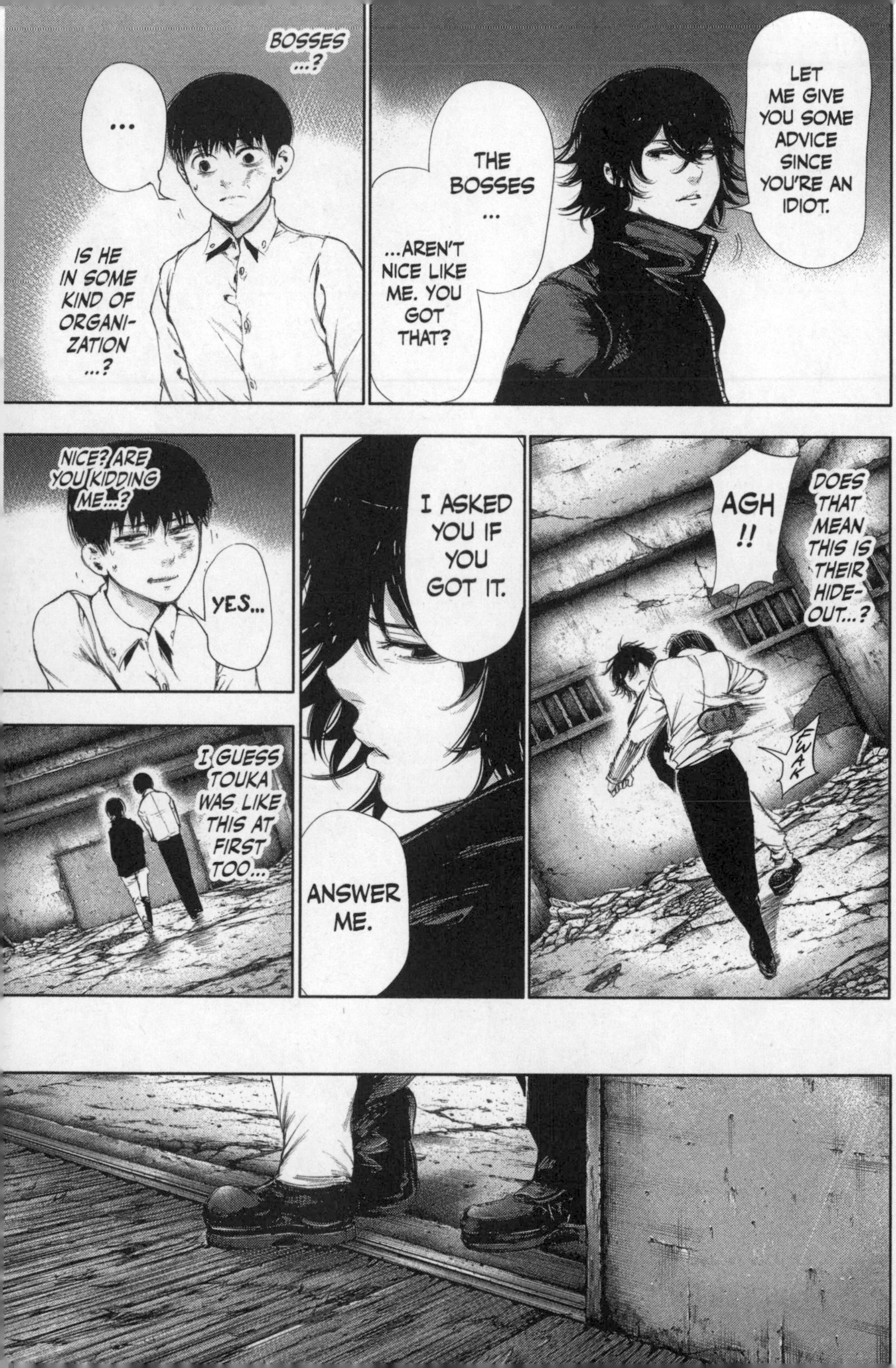
LET ME GIVE YOU SOME ADVICE SINCE YOU'RE AN IDIOT.
THE BOSSES...
...AREN'T NICE LIKE ME. YOU GOT THAT?
BOSSES...?
...
IS HE IN SOME KIND OF ORGANIZATION...?
AGH!!
DOES THAT MEAN THIS IS THEIR HIDE-OUT...?
FWAK
I ASKED YOU IF YOU GOT IT.
ANSWER ME.
NICE? ARE YOU KIDDING ME...?
YES...
I GUESS TOUKA WAS LIKE THIS AT FIRST TOO...

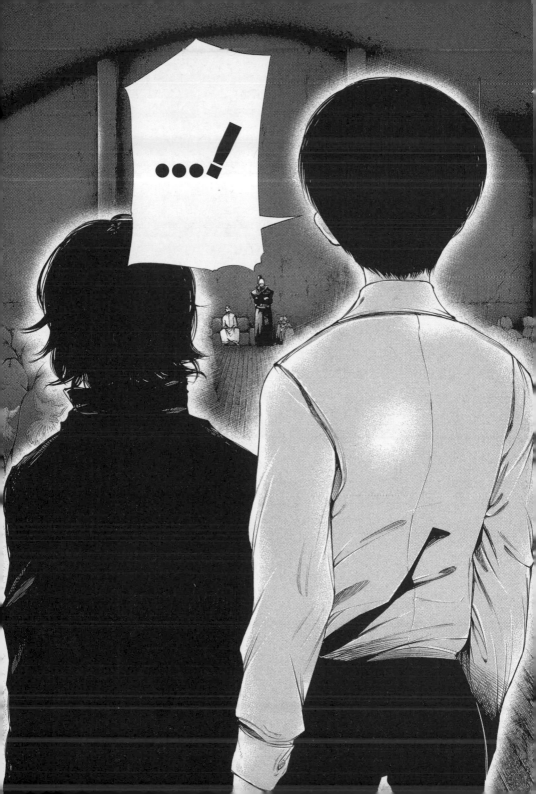

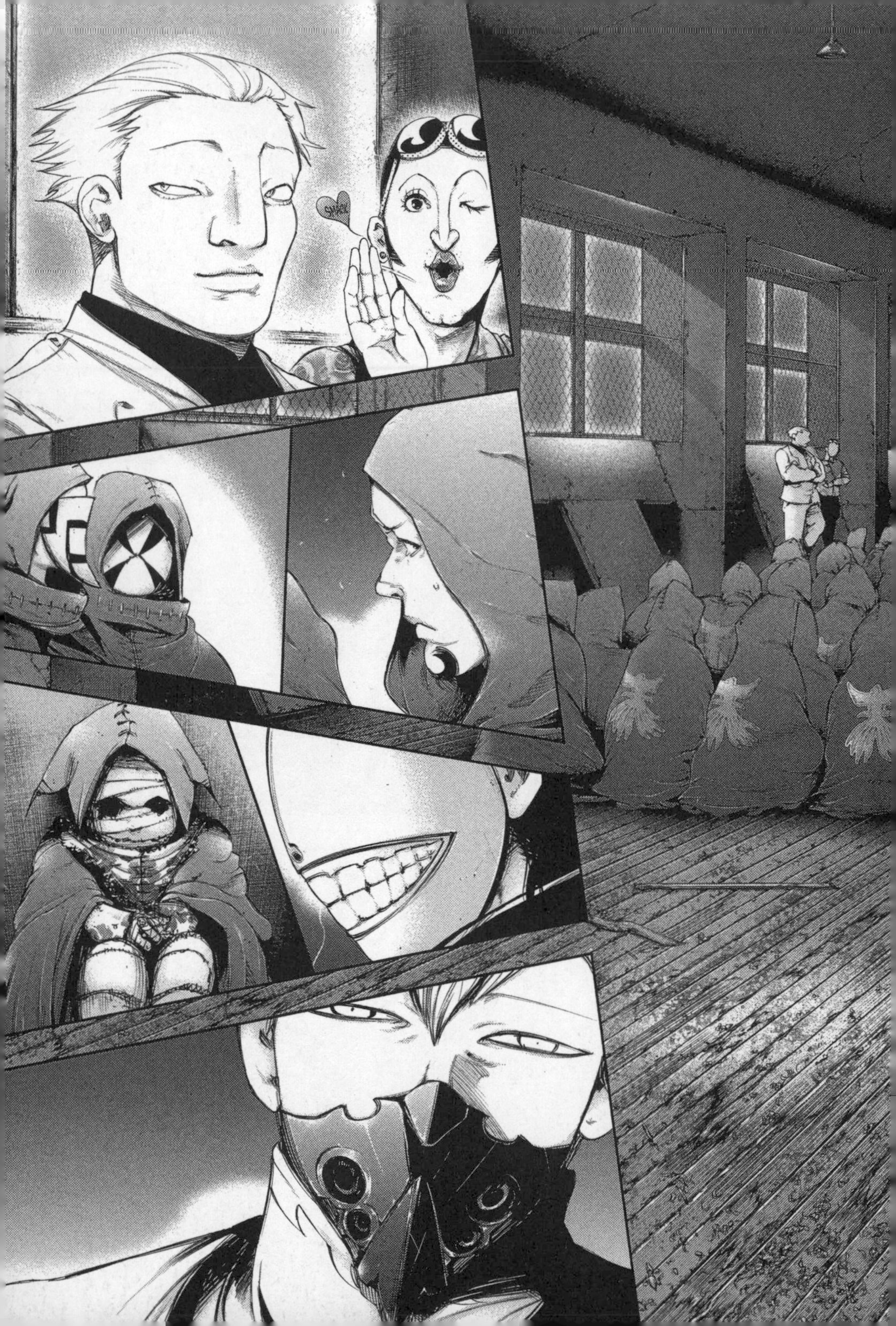
SMACK

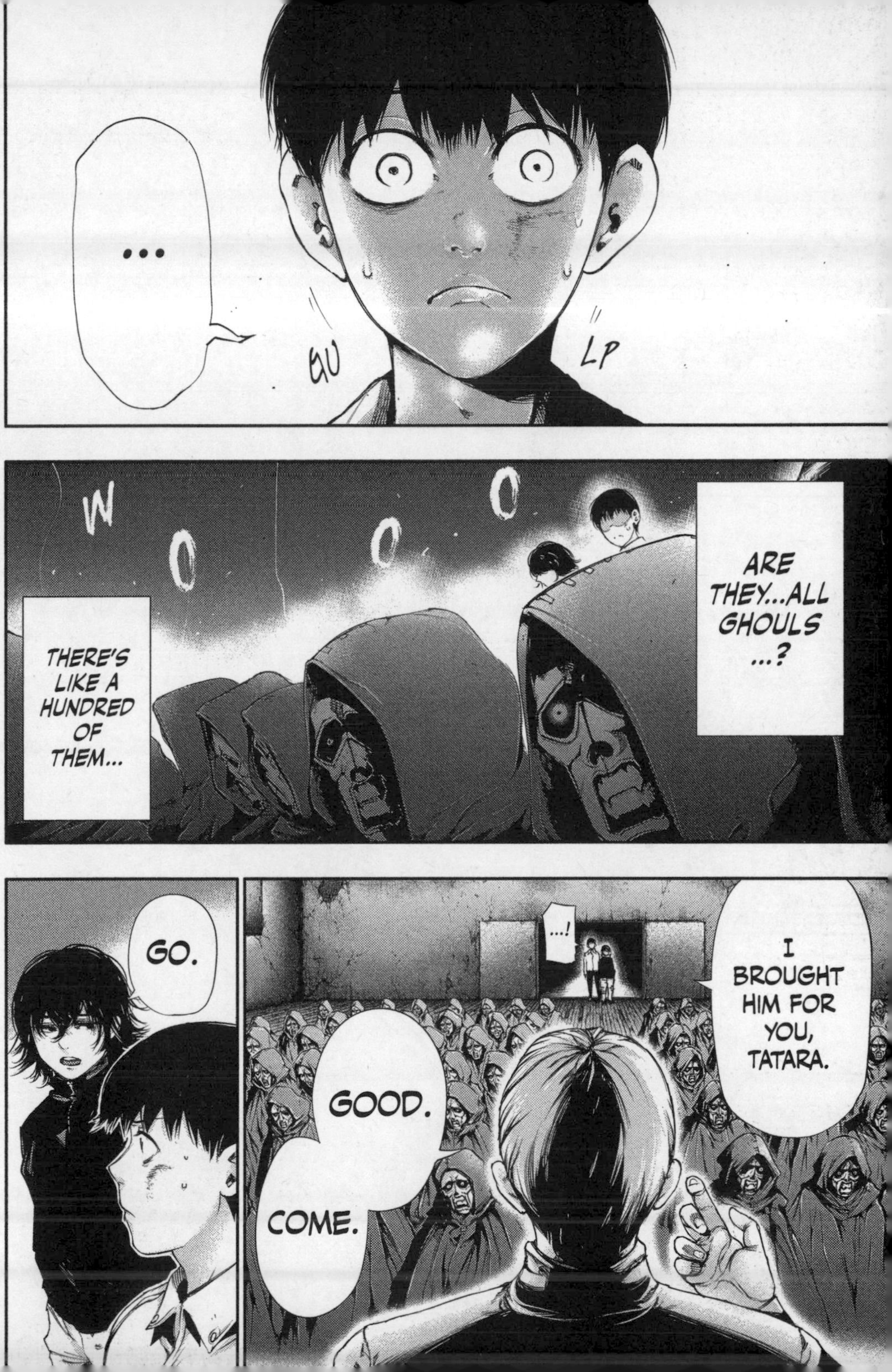
...
GU
LP
ARE THEY...ALL GHOULS ...?
WOOO
THERE'S LIKE A HUNDRED OF THEM...
I BROUGHT HIM FOR YOU, TATARA.
...!
GOOD.
COME.
GO.

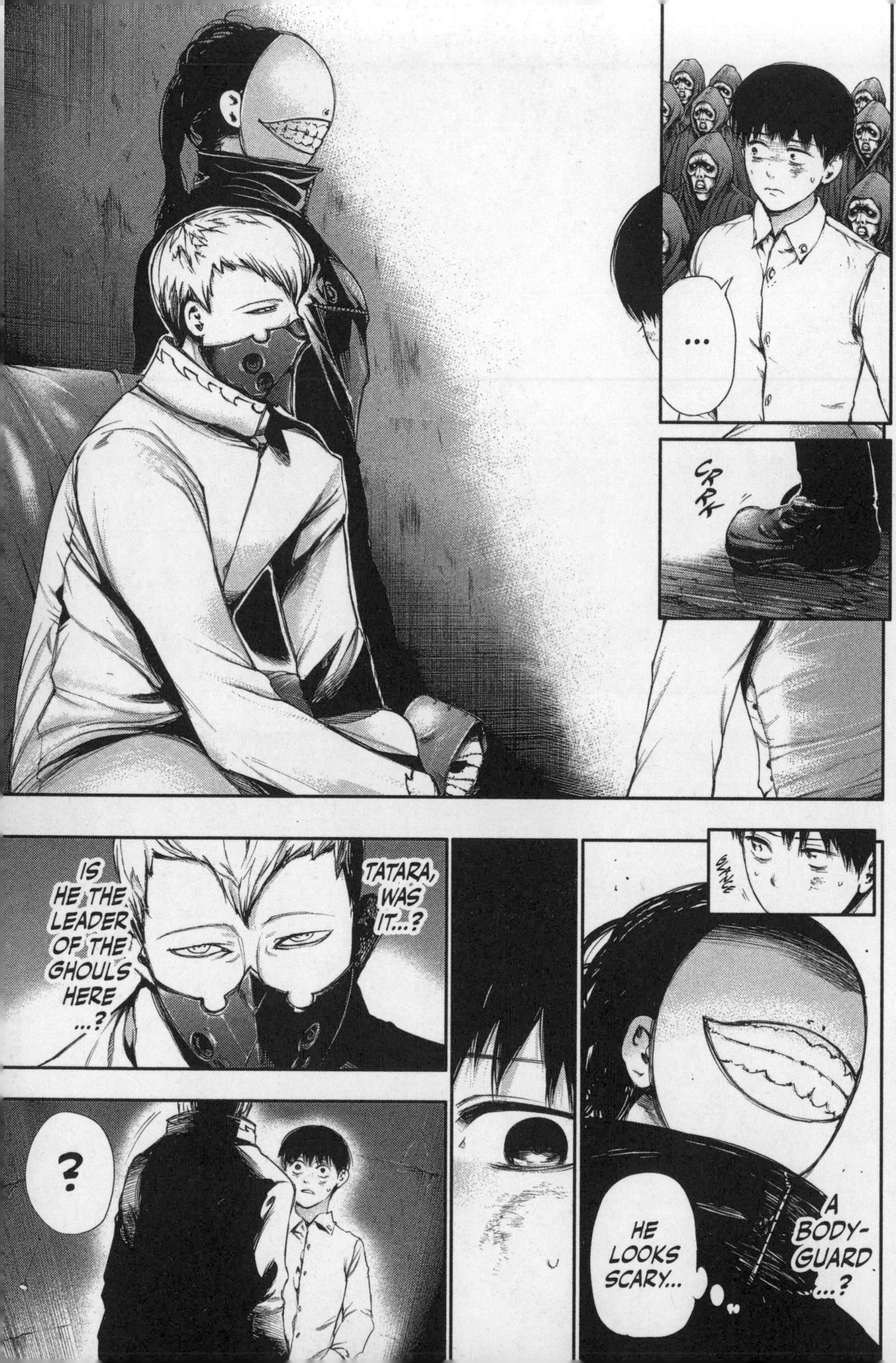
...
CRRK
A BODY-GUARD ...?
HE LOOKS SCARY...
TATARA, WAS IT...?
IS HE THE LEADER OF THE GHOULS HERE ...?
?

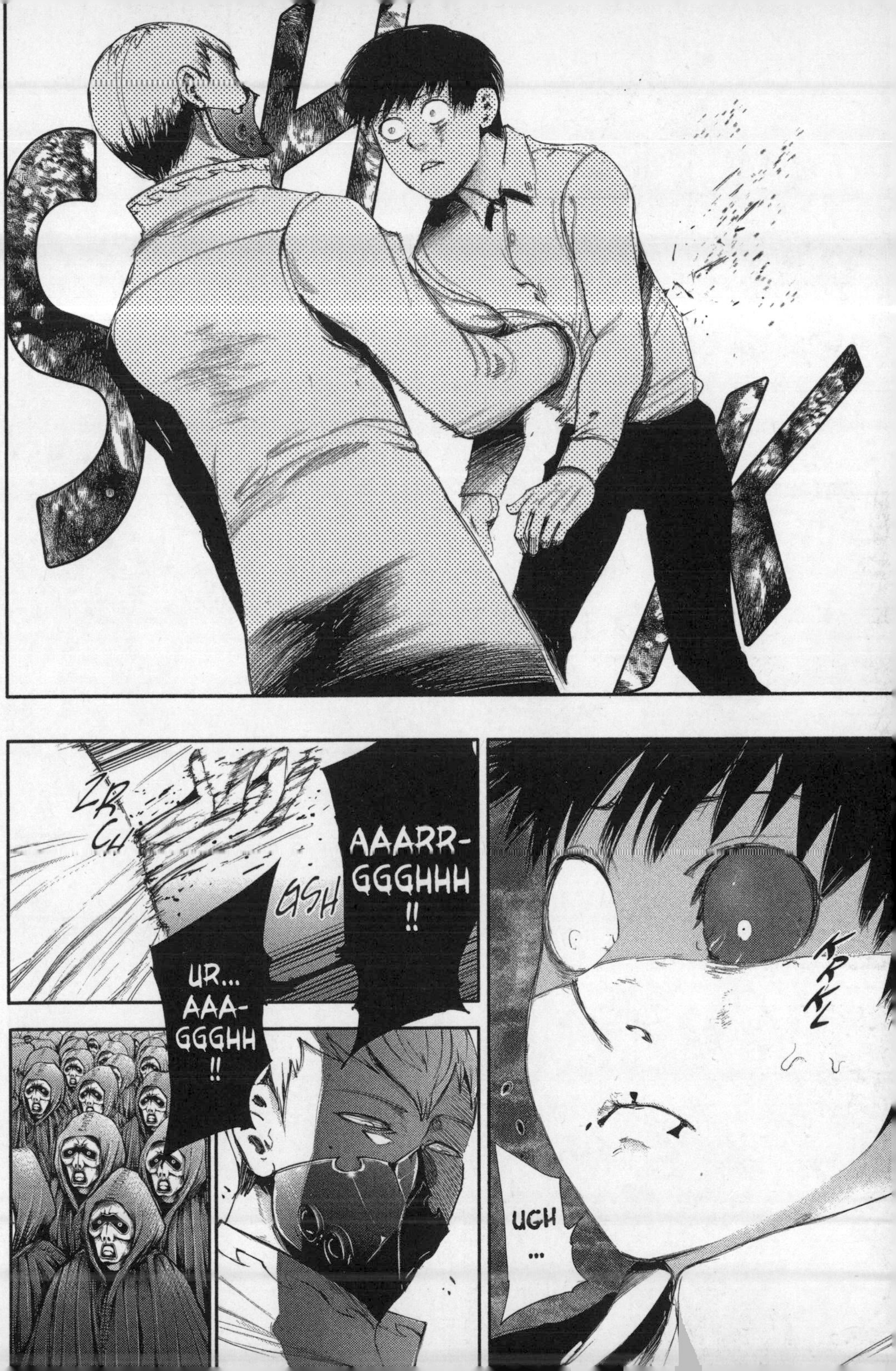
KRKL
UGH
...
AAARR-
GGGHHH
!!
ZRCH
GSH
UR...
AAA-
GGGHH
!!

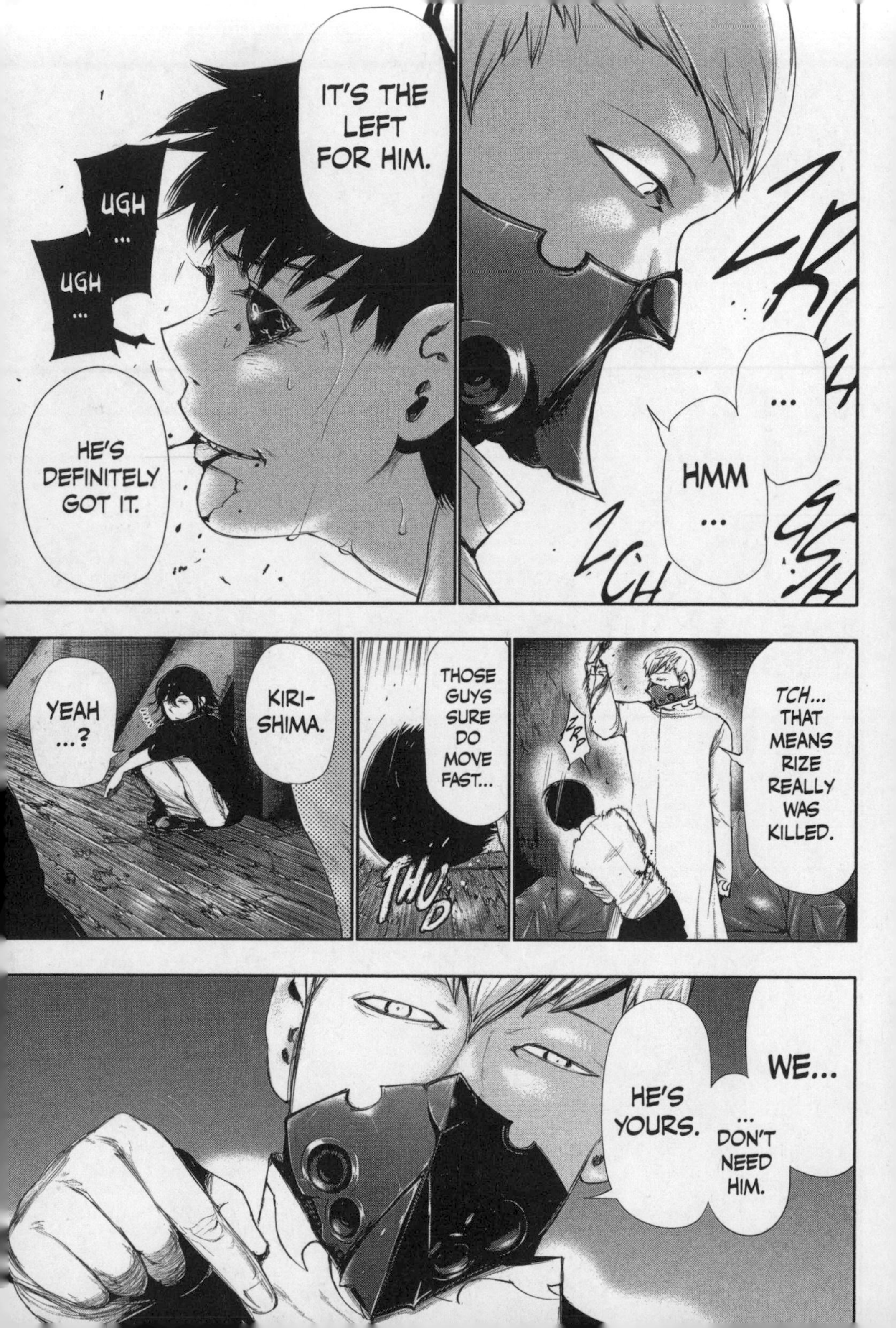
... HMM ...
IT'S THE LEFT FOR HIM.
UGH ... UGH ...
HE'S DEFINITELY GOT IT.
TCH... THAT MEANS RIZE REALLY WAS KILLED.
THOSE GUYS SURE DO MOVE FAST...
THUD
KIRI-SHIMA.
YEAH ...?
WE... ... DON'T NEED HIM.
HE'S YOURS.

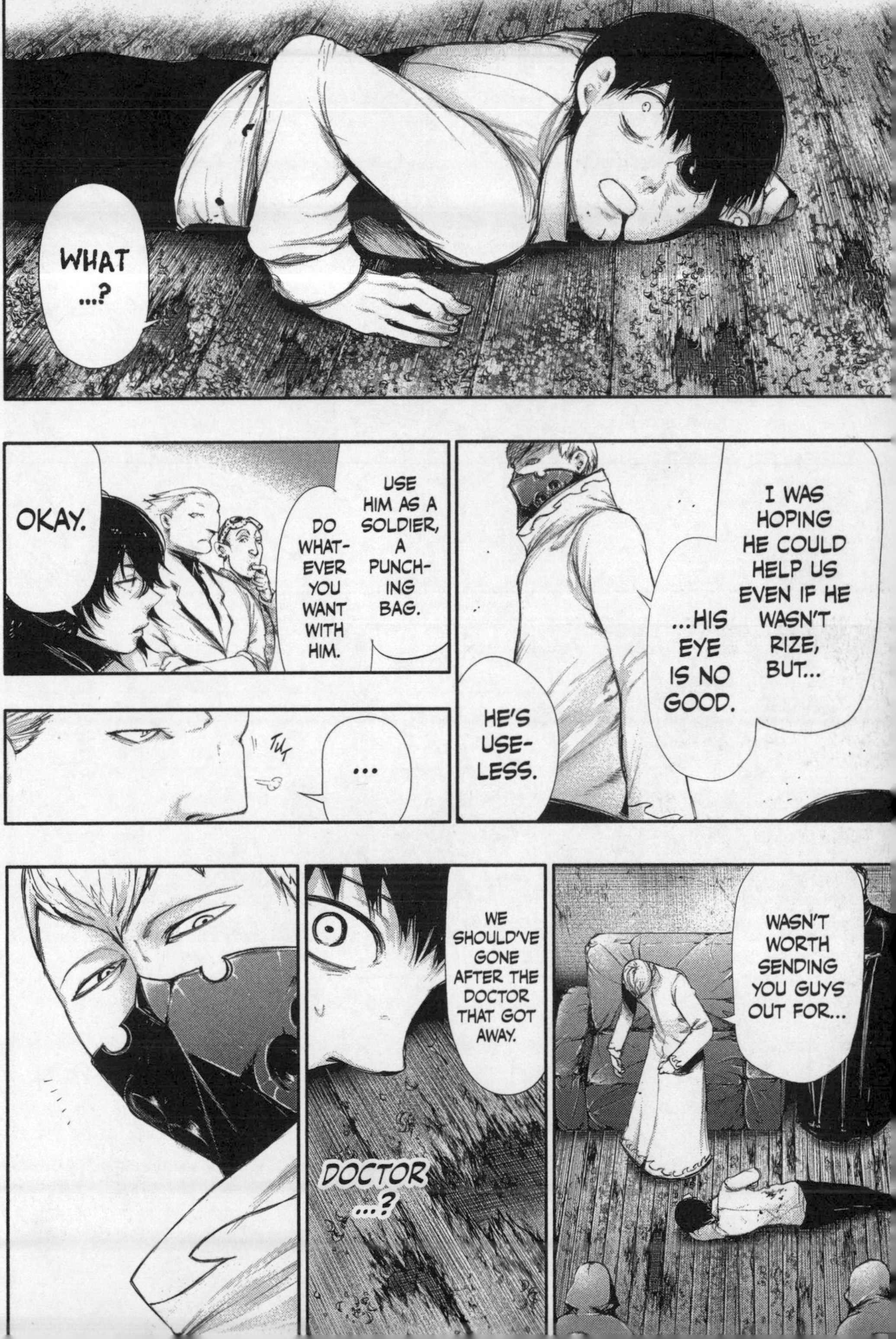
WHAT ...?
I WAS HOPING HE COULD HELP US EVEN IF HE WASN'T RIZE, BUT...
...HIS EYE IS NO GOOD.
HE'S USE-LESS.
USE HIM AS A SOLDIER, A PUNCH-ING BAG.
DO WHAT-EVER YOU WANT WITH HIM.
OKAY.
...
WASN'T WORTH SENDING YOU GUYS OUT FOR...
WE SHOULD'VE GONE AFTER THE DOCTOR THAT GOT AWAY.
DOCTOR ...?

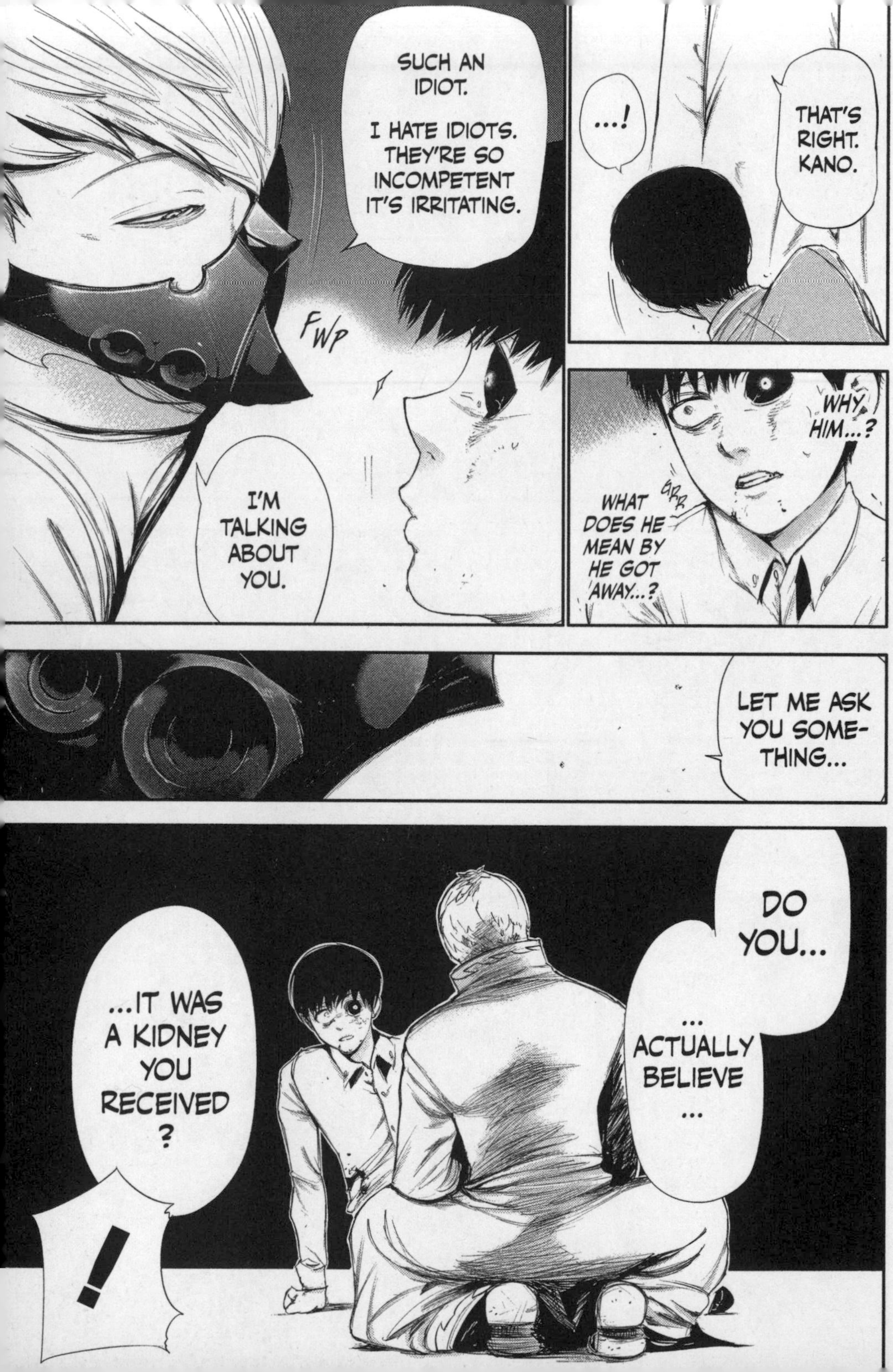
THAT'S RIGHT. KANO.
...!
WHY HIM...?
WHAT DOES HE MEAN BY HE GOT AWAY...?
SUCH AN IDIOT.
I HATE IDIOTS. THEY'RE SO INCOMPETENT IT'S IRRITATING.
FWP
I'M TALKING ABOUT YOU.
LET ME ASK YOU SOMETHING...
DO YOU...
... ACTUALLY BELIEVE ...
...IT WAS A KIDNEY YOU RECEIVED ?
!

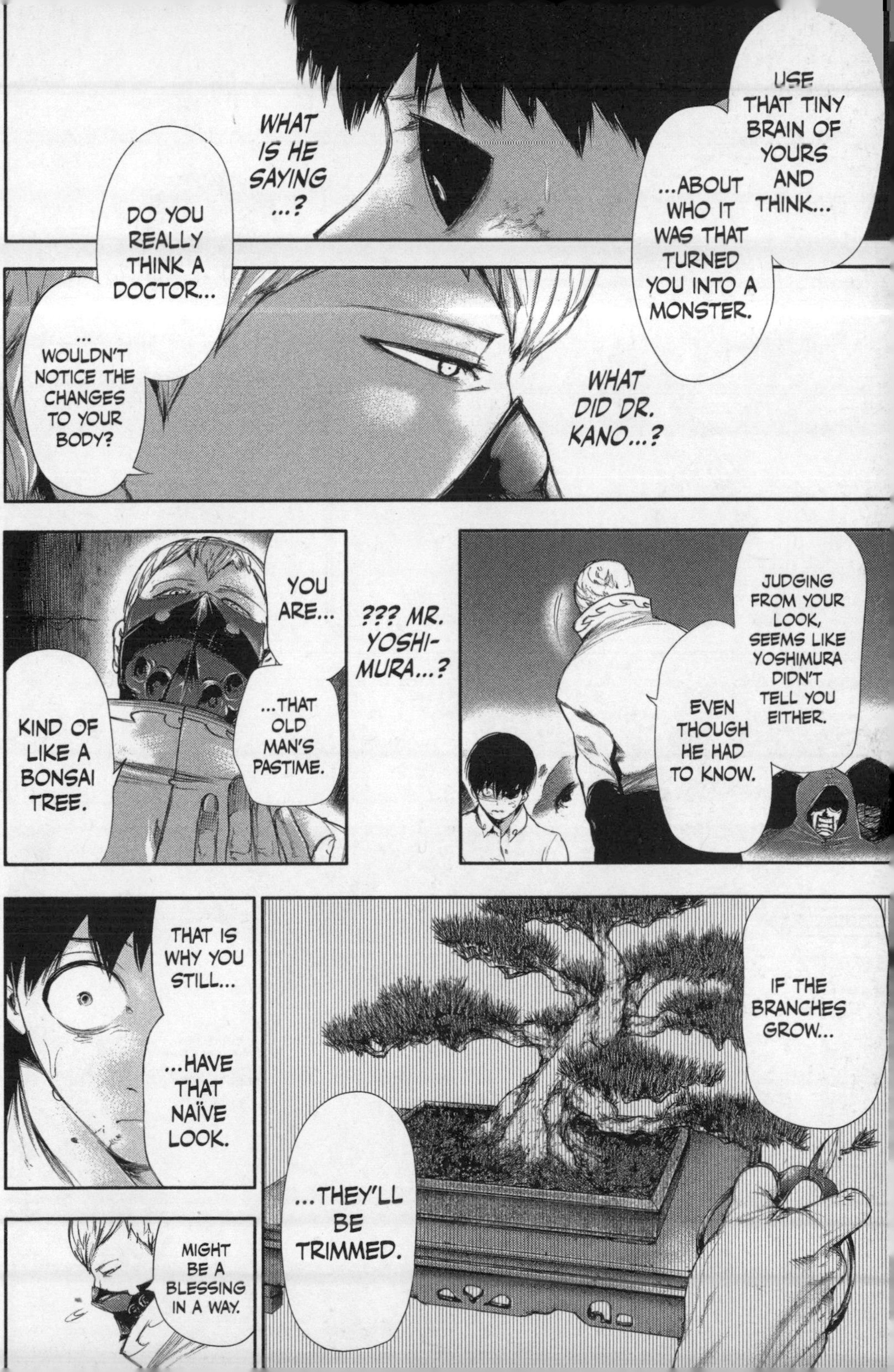
USE THAT TINY BRAIN OF YOURS AND THINK...
...ABOUT WHO IT WAS THAT TURNED YOU INTO A MONSTER.
WHAT IS HE SAYING...?
WHAT DID DR. KANO...?
DO YOU REALLY THINK A DOCTOR...
...WOULDN'T NOTICE THE CHANGES TO YOUR BODY?
JUDGING FROM YOUR LOOK, SEEMS LIKE YOSHIMURA DIDN'T TELL YOU EITHER.
EVEN THOUGH HE HAD TO KNOW.
??? MR. YOSHI-MURA...?
YOU ARE...
...THAT OLD MAN'S PASTIME.
KIND OF LIKE A BONSAI TREE.
IF THE BRANCHES GROW...
...THEY'LL BE TRIMMED.
THAT IS WHY YOU STILL...
...HAVE THAT NAÏVE LOOK.
MIGHT BE A BLESSING IN A WAY.

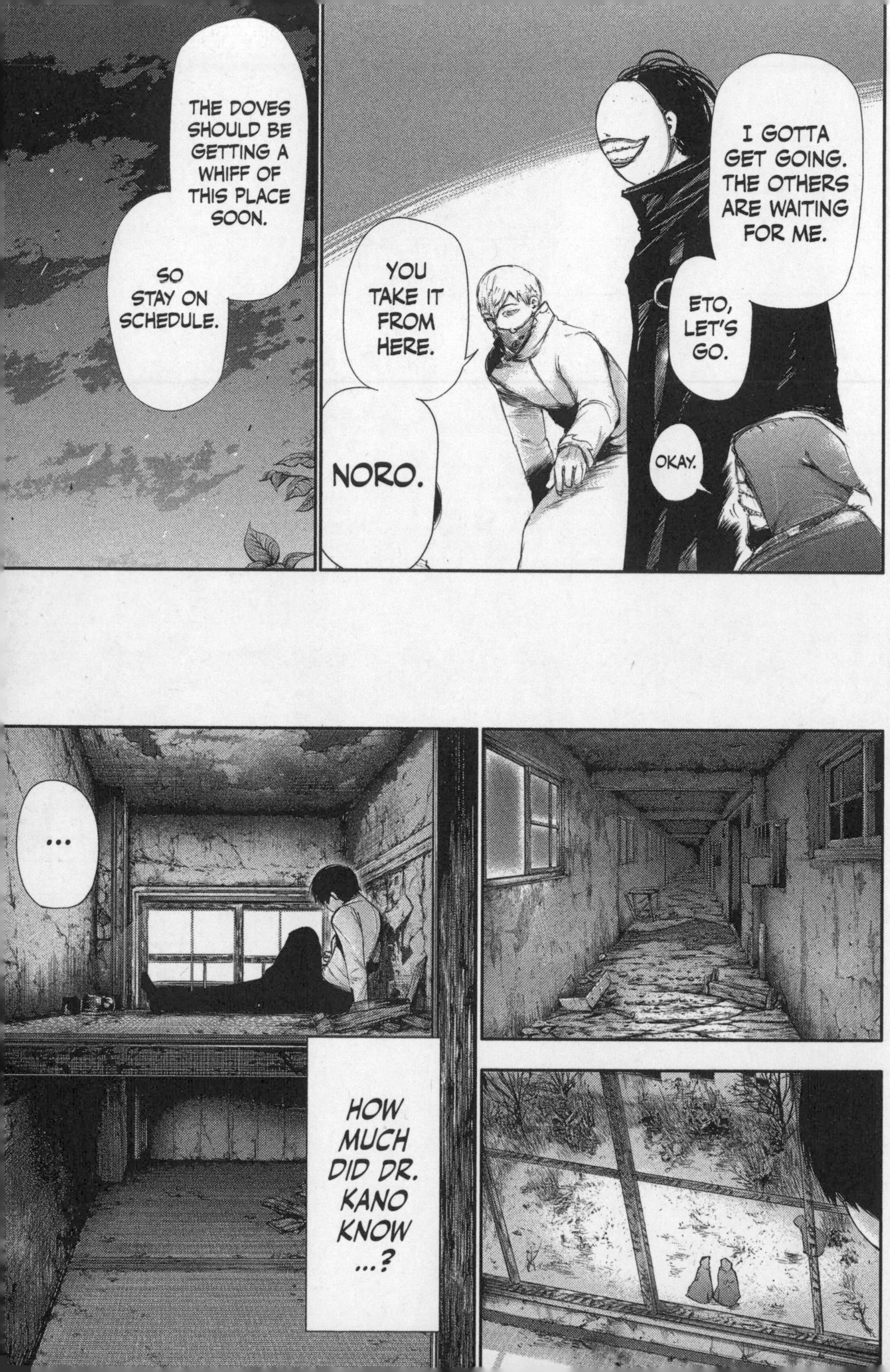
I GOTTA GET GOING. THE OTHERS ARE WAITING FOR ME.
ETO, LET'S GO.
OKAY.
YOU TAKE IT FROM HERE.
NORO.
THE DOVES SHOULD BE GETTING A WHIFF OF THIS PLACE SOON.
SO STAY ON SCHEDULE.
...
HOW MUCH DID DR. KANO KNOW ...?

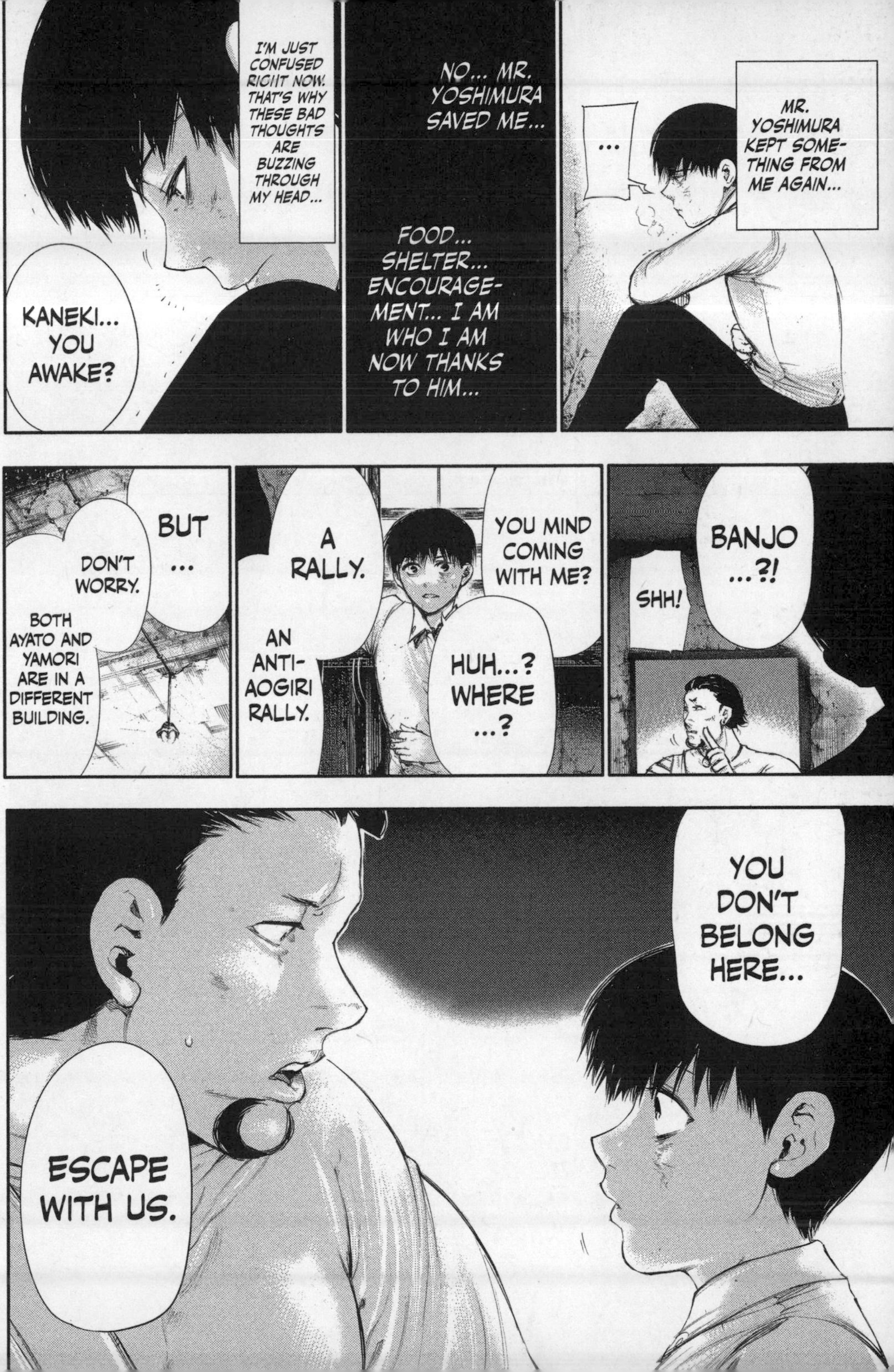
MR. YOSHIMURA KEPT SOMETHING FROM ME AGAIN...
...
NO... MR. YOSHIMURA SAVED ME...
FOOD... SHELTER... ENCOURAGEMENT... I AM WHO I AM NOW THANKS TO HIM...
I'M JUST CONFUSED RIGHT NOW. THAT'S WHY THESE BAD THOUGHTS ARE BUZZING THROUGH MY HEAD...
KANEKI... YOU AWAKE?
BANJO ...?!
SHH!
YOU MIND COMING WITH ME?
HUH...? WHERE ...?
A RALLY.
AN ANTI-AOGIRI RALLY.
BUT ...
DON'T WORRY.
BOTH AYATO AND YAMORI ARE IN A DIFFERENT BUILDING.
YOU DON'T BELONG HERE...
ESCAPE WITH US.

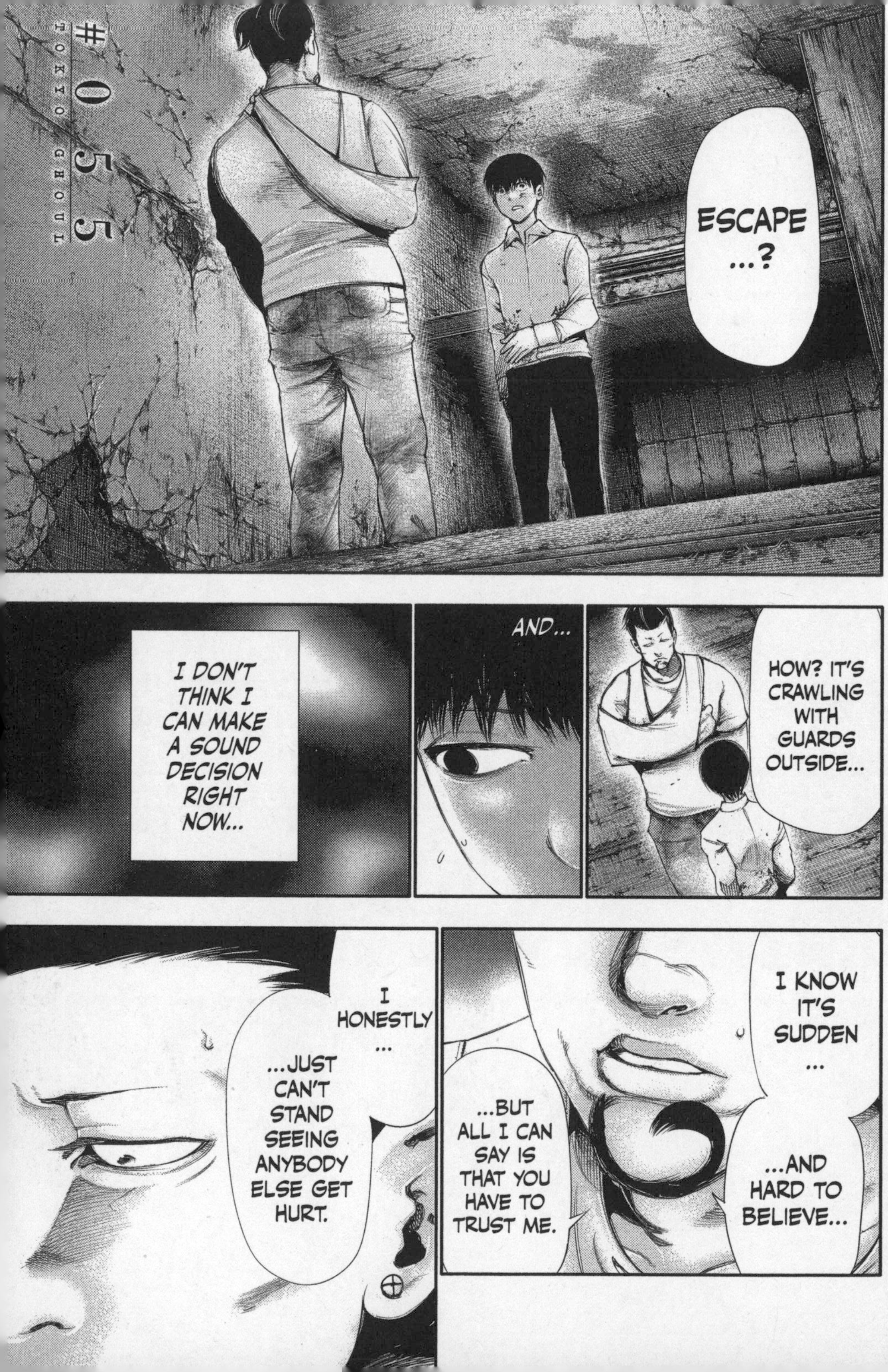
#055
TOKYO GHOUL
ESCAPE ...?
HOW? IT'S CRAWLING WITH GUARDS OUTSIDE...
AND...
I DON'T THINK I CAN MAKE A SOUND DECISION RIGHT NOW...
I KNOW IT'S SUDDEN ...
...AND HARD TO BELIEVE...
...BUT ALL I CAN SAY IS THAT YOU HAVE TO TRUST ME.
I HONESTLY ...
...JUST CAN'T STAND SEEING ANYBODY ELSE GET HURT.

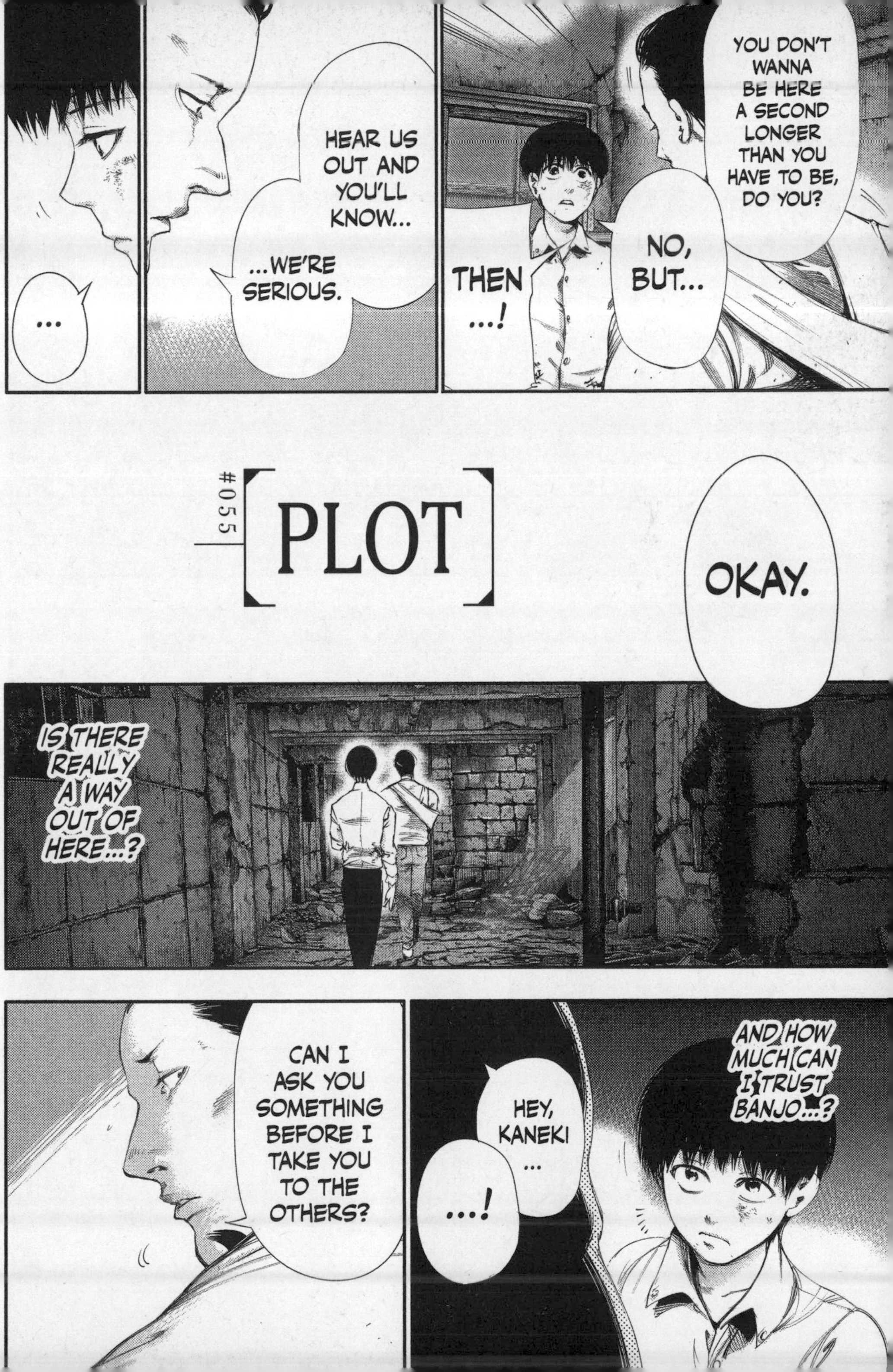
YOU DON'T WANNA BE HERE A SECOND LONGER THAN YOU HAVE TO BE, DO YOU?
NO, BUT...
THEN ...!
HEAR US OUT AND YOU'LL KNOW...
...WE'RE SERIOUS.
...
OKAY.
#055
PLOT
IS THERE REALLY A WAY OUT OF HERE...?
AND HOW MUCH CAN I TRUST BANJO...?
HEY, KANEKI ...
...!
CAN I ASK YOU SOMETHING BEFORE I TAKE YOU TO THE OTHERS?

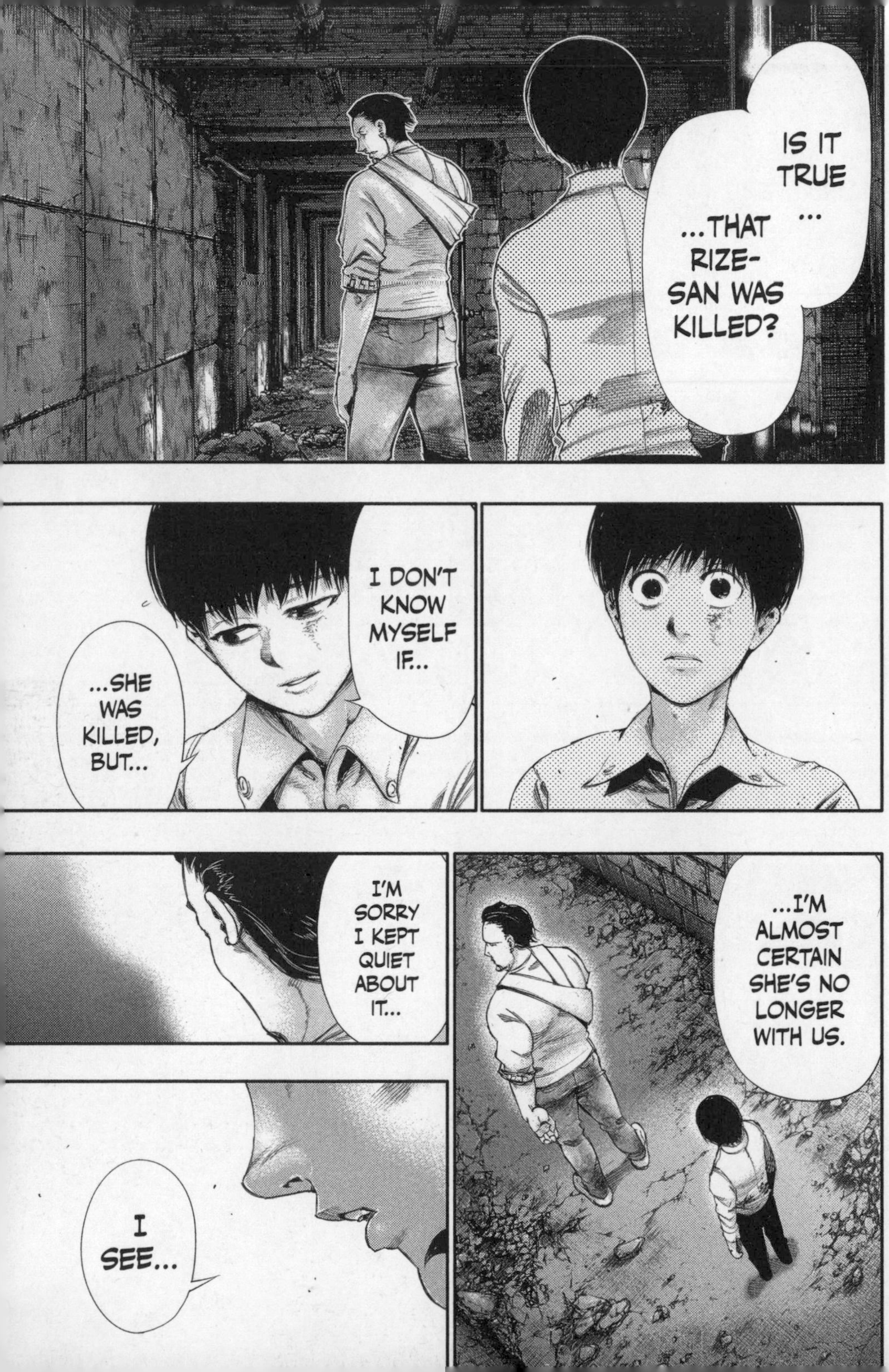
IS IT TRUE ...
...THAT RIZE-SAN WAS KILLED?
I DON'T KNOW MYSELF IF...
...SHE WAS KILLED, BUT...
...I'M ALMOST CERTAIN SHE'S NO LONGER WITH US.
I'M SORRY I KEPT QUIET ABOUT IT...
I SEE...

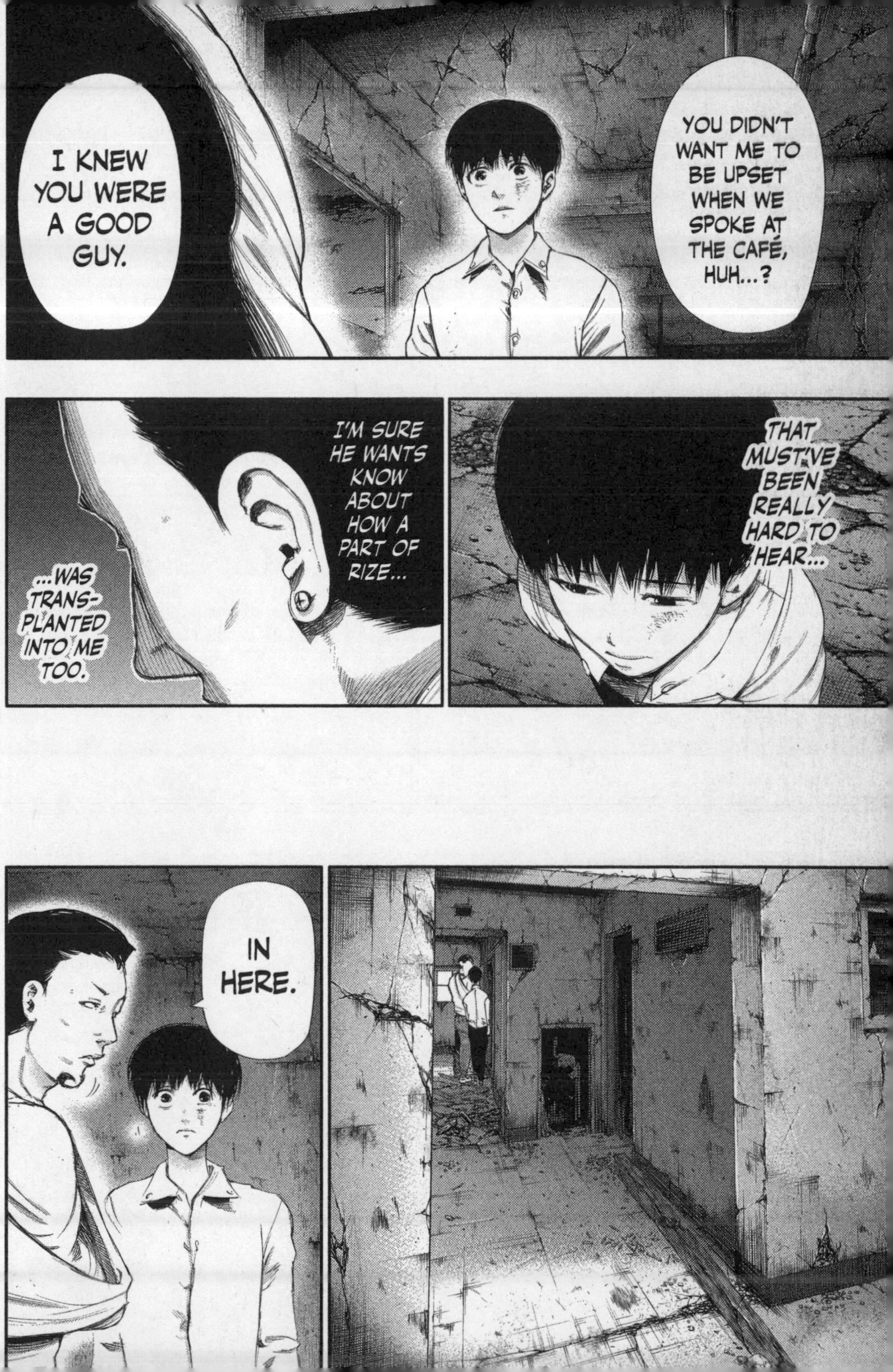
YOU DIDN'T WANT ME TO BE UPSET WHEN WE SPOKE AT THE CAFÉ, HUH...?
I KNEW YOU WERE A GOOD GUY.
THAT MUST'VE BEEN REALLY HARD TO HEAR...
I'M SURE HE WANTS KNOW ABOUT HOW A PART OF RIZE...
...WAS TRANS-PLANTED INTO ME TOO.
IN HERE.

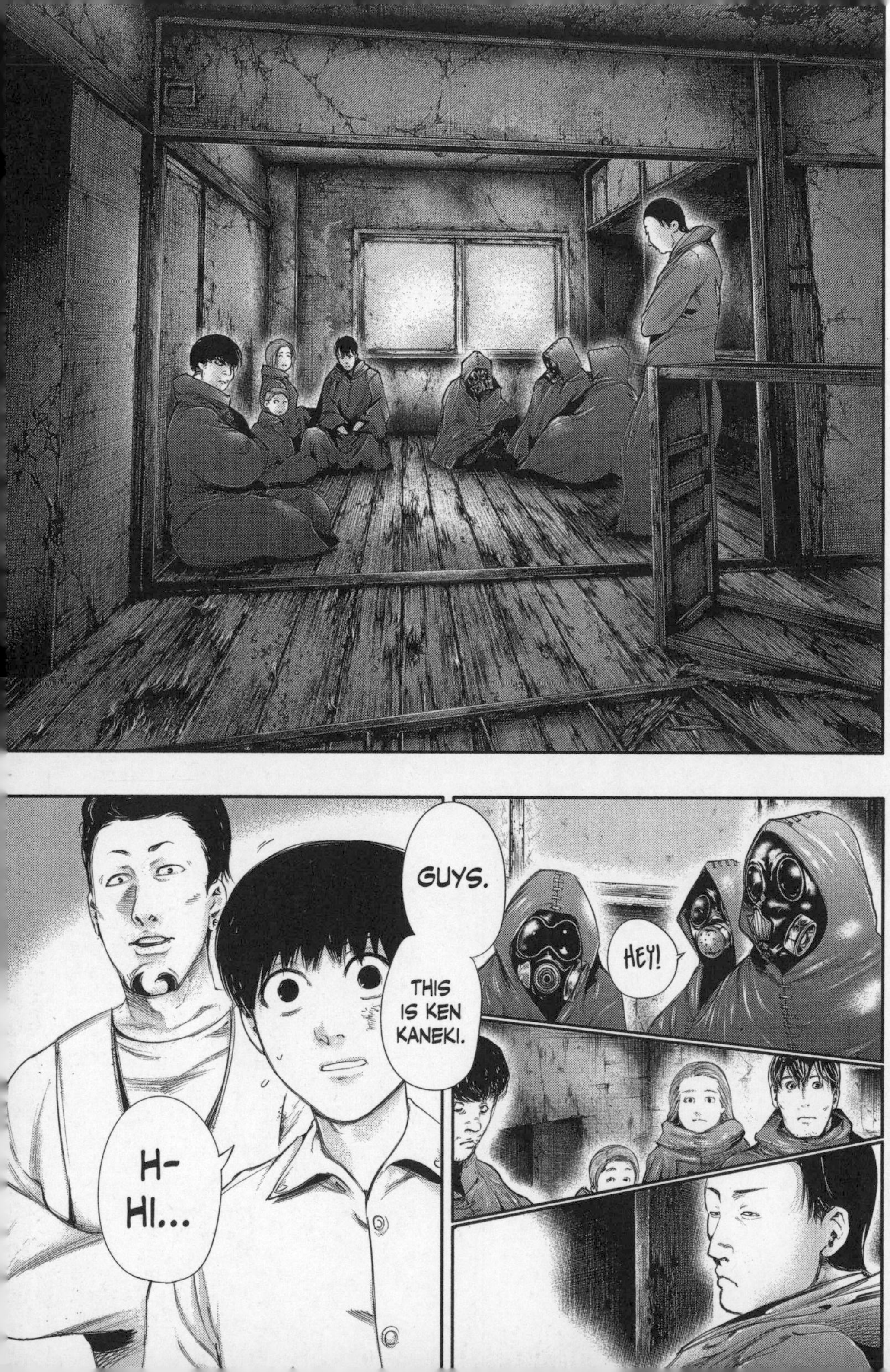
GUYS.
THIS IS KEN KANEKI.
HEY!
H-HI...

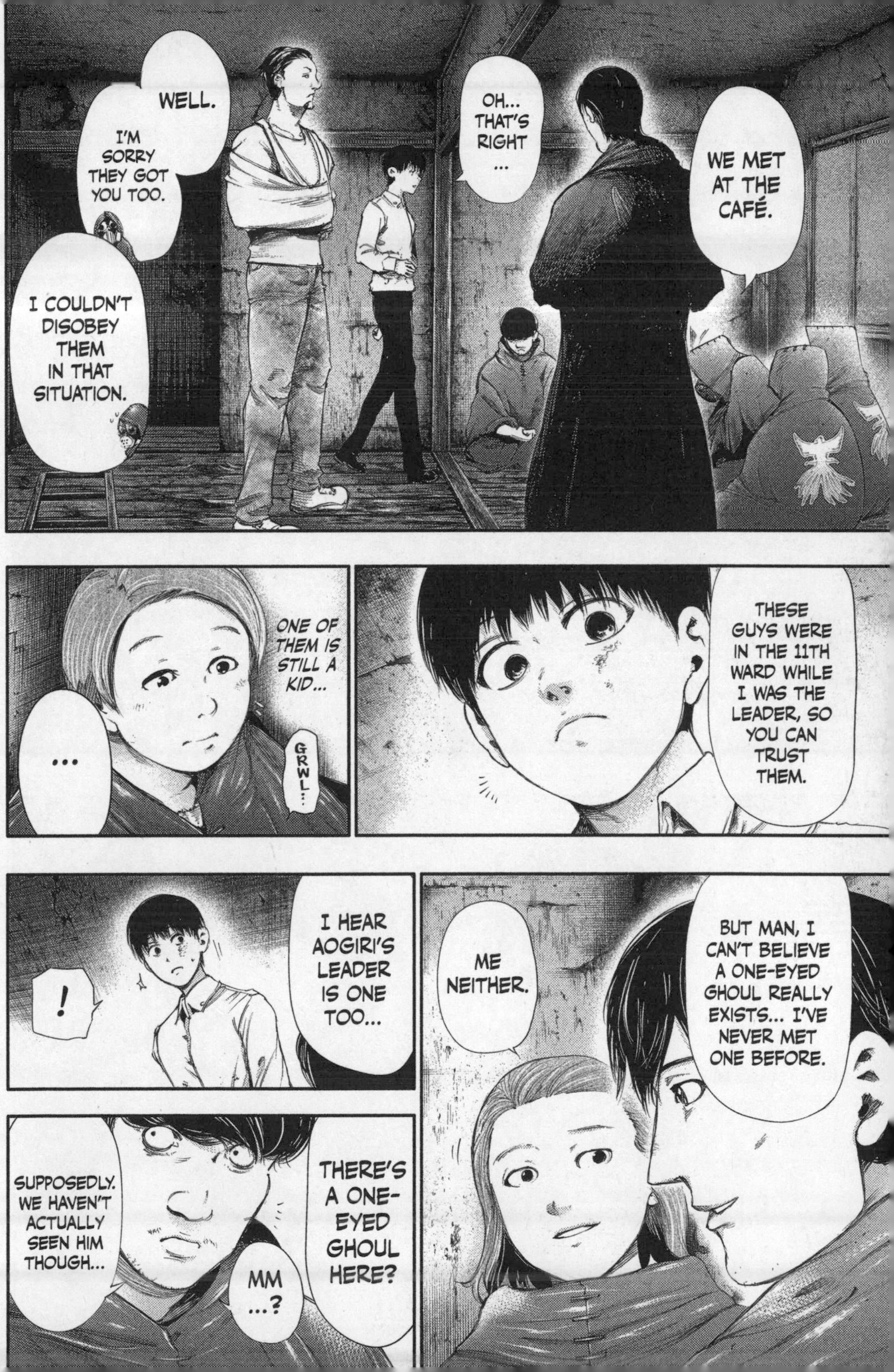
WE MET AT THE CAFÉ.
OH... THAT'S RIGHT ...
WELL.
I'M SORRY THEY GOT YOU TOO.
I COULDN'T DISOBEY THEM IN THAT SITUATION.
THESE GUYS WERE IN THE 11TH WARD WHILE I WAS THE LEADER, SO YOU CAN TRUST THEM.
ONE OF THEM IS STILL A KID...
GRWL...
...
BUT MAN, I CAN'T BELIEVE A ONE-EYED GHOUL REALLY EXISTS... I'VE NEVER MET ONE BEFORE.
ME NEITHER.
I HEAR AOGIRI'S LEADER IS ONE TOO...
!
THERE'S A ONE-EYED GHOUL HERE?
MM ...?
SUPPOSEDLY. WE HAVEN'T ACTUALLY SEEN HIM THOUGH...

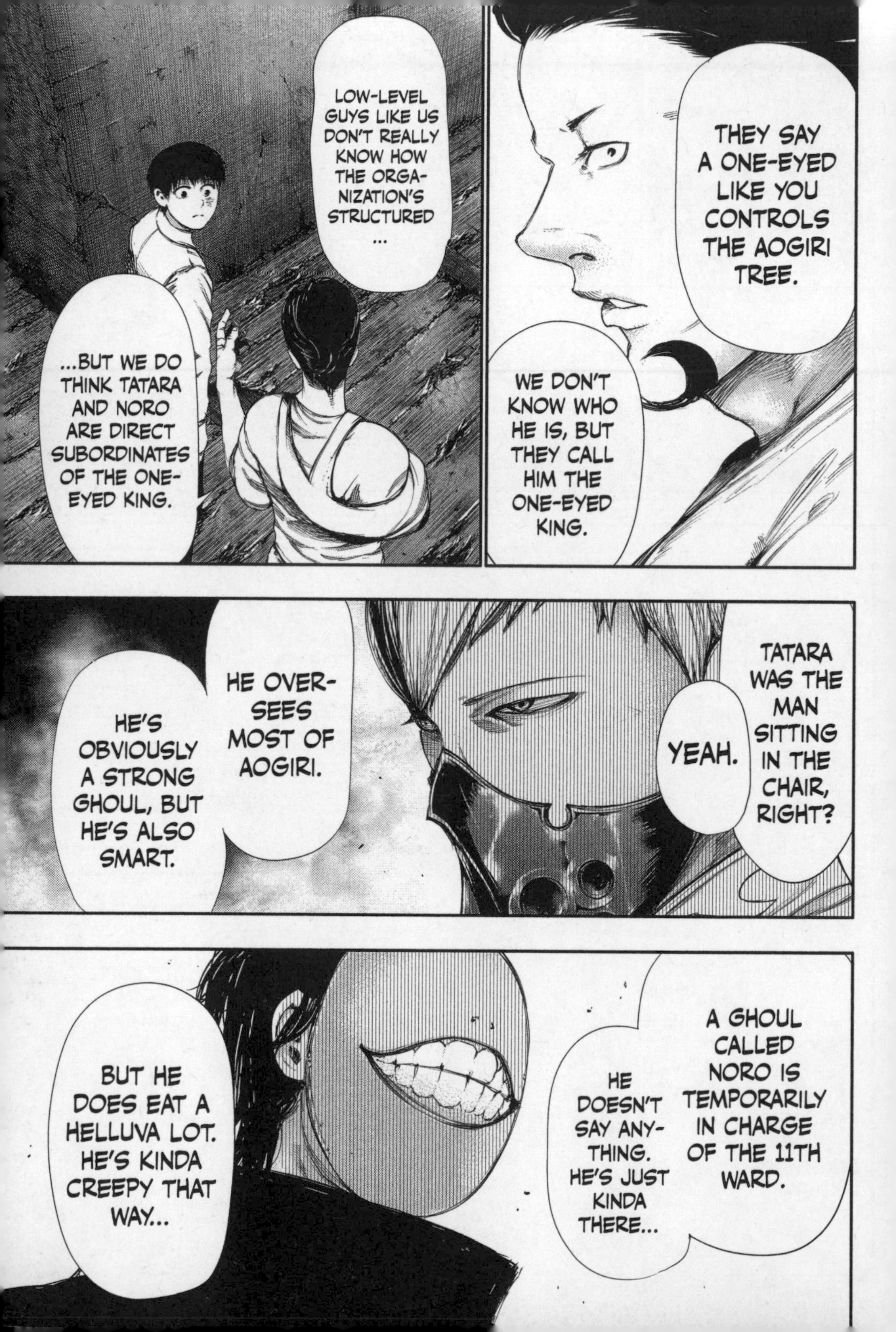
THEY SAY A ONE-EYED LIKE YOU CONTROLS THE AOGIRI TREE.
WE DON'T KNOW WHO HE IS, BUT THEY CALL HIM THE ONE-EYED KING.
LOW-LEVEL GUYS LIKE US DON'T REALLY KNOW HOW THE ORGA-NIZATION'S STRUCTURED ...
...BUT WE DO THINK TATARA AND NORO ARE DIRECT SUBORDINATES OF THE ONE-EYED KING.
TATARA WAS THE MAN SITTING IN THE CHAIR, RIGHT?
YEAH.
HE OVER-SEES MOST OF AOGIRI.
HE'S OBVIOUSLY A STRONG GHOUL, BUT HE'S ALSO SMART.
A GHOUL CALLED NORO IS TEMPORARILY IN CHARGE OF THE 11TH WARD.
HE DOESN'T SAY ANY-THING. HE'S JUST KINDA THERE...
BUT HE DOES EAT A HELLUVA LOT. HE'S KINDA CREEPY THAT WAY...

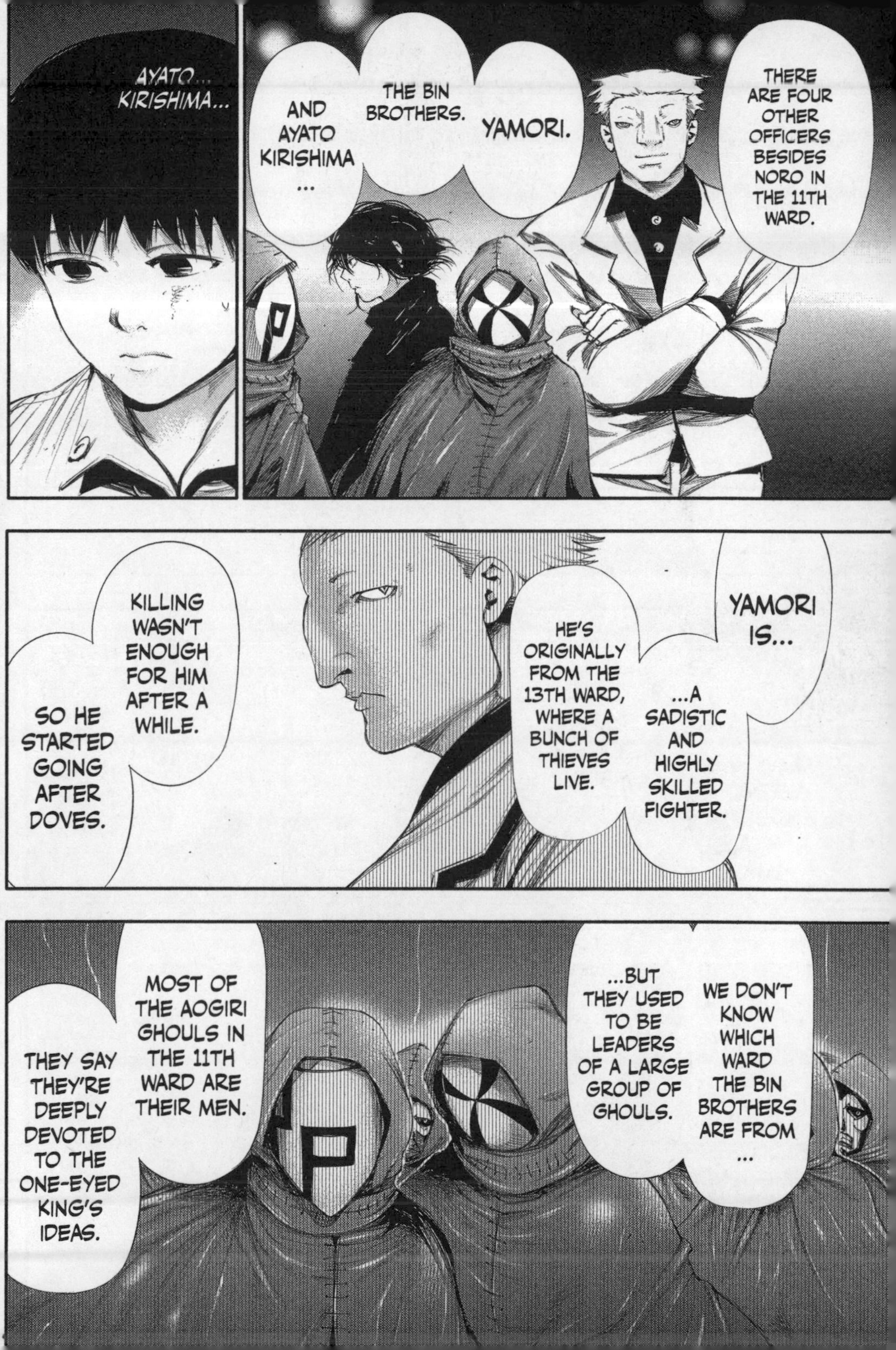
THERE ARE FOUR OTHER OFFICERS BESIDES NORO IN THE 11TH WARD.
YAMORI.
THE BIN BROTHERS.
AND AYATO KIRISHIMA ...
AYATO... KIRISHIMA...
YAMORI IS...
...A SADISTIC AND HIGHLY SKILLED FIGHTER.
HE'S ORIGINALLY FROM THE 13TH WARD, WHERE A BUNCH OF THIEVES LIVE.
KILLING WASN'T ENOUGH FOR HIM AFTER A WHILE.
SO HE STARTED GOING AFTER DOVES.
WE DON'T KNOW WHICH WARD THE BIN BROTHERS ARE FROM ...
...BUT THEY USED TO BE LEADERS OF A LARGE GROUP OF GHOULS.
MOST OF THE AOGIRI GHOULS IN THE 11TH WARD ARE THEIR MEN.
THEY SAY THEY'RE DEEPLY DEVOTED TO THE ONE-EYED KING'S IDEAS.

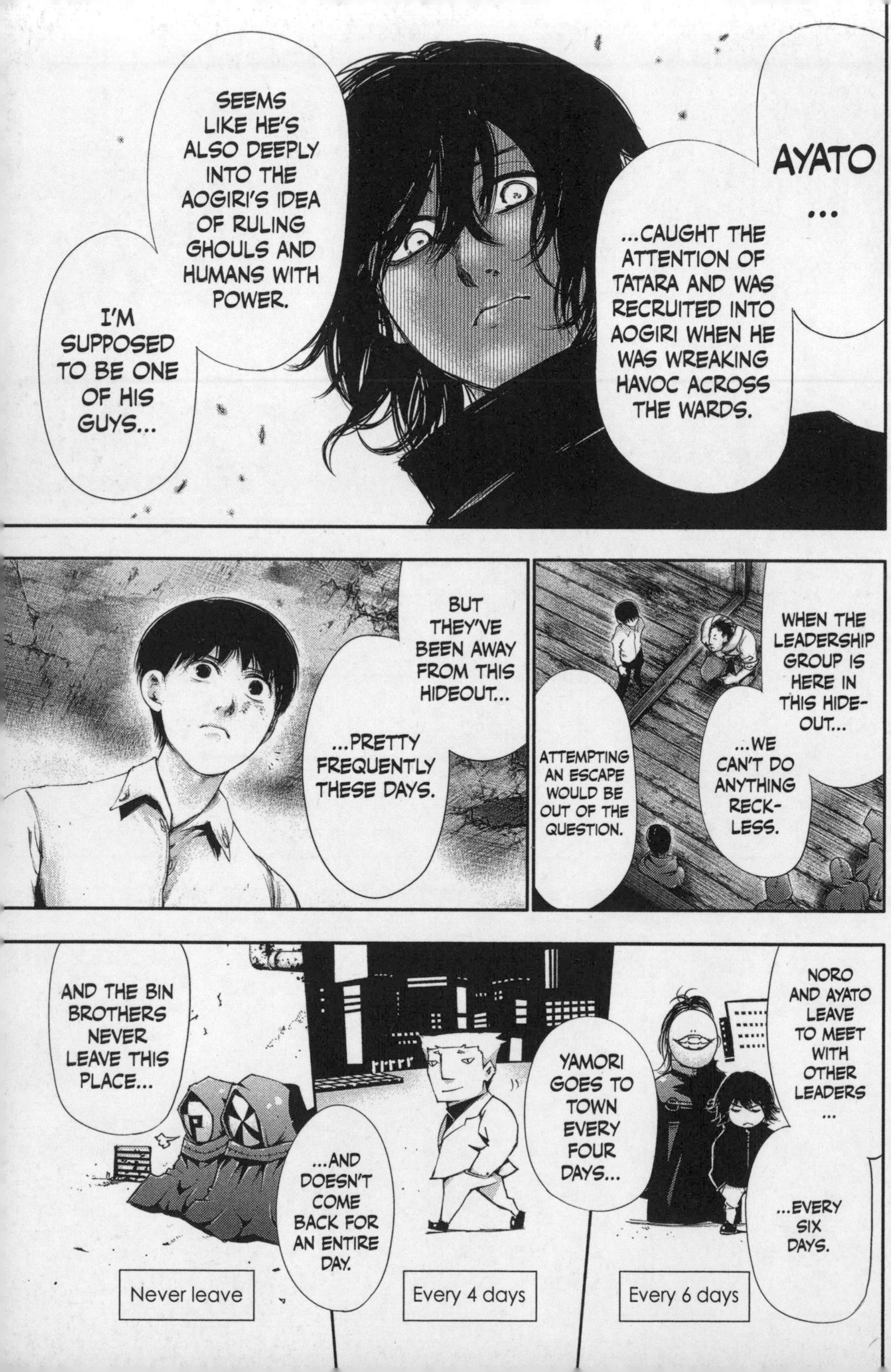
AYATO ...
...CAUGHT THE ATTENTION OF TATARA AND WAS RECRUITED INTO AOGIRI WHEN HE WAS WREAKING HAVOC ACROSS THE WARDS.
SEEMS LIKE HE'S ALSO DEEPLY INTO THE AOGIRI'S IDEA OF RULING GHOULS AND HUMANS WITH POWER.
I'M SUPPOSED TO BE ONE OF HIS GUYS...
WHEN THE LEADERSHIP GROUP IS HERE IN THIS HIDE-OUT...
...WE CAN'T DO ANYTHING RECK-LESS.
ATTEMPTING AN ESCAPE WOULD BE OUT OF THE QUESTION.
BUT THEY'VE BEEN AWAY FROM THIS HIDEOUT...
...PRETTY FREQUENTLY THESE DAYS.
NORO AND AYATO LEAVE TO MEET WITH OTHER LEADERS ...
...EVERY SIX DAYS.
Every 6 days
YAMORI GOES TO TOWN EVERY FOUR DAYS...
...AND DOESN'T COME BACK FOR AN ENTIRE DAY.
Every 4 days
AND THE BIN BROTHERS NEVER LEAVE THIS PLACE...
Never leave

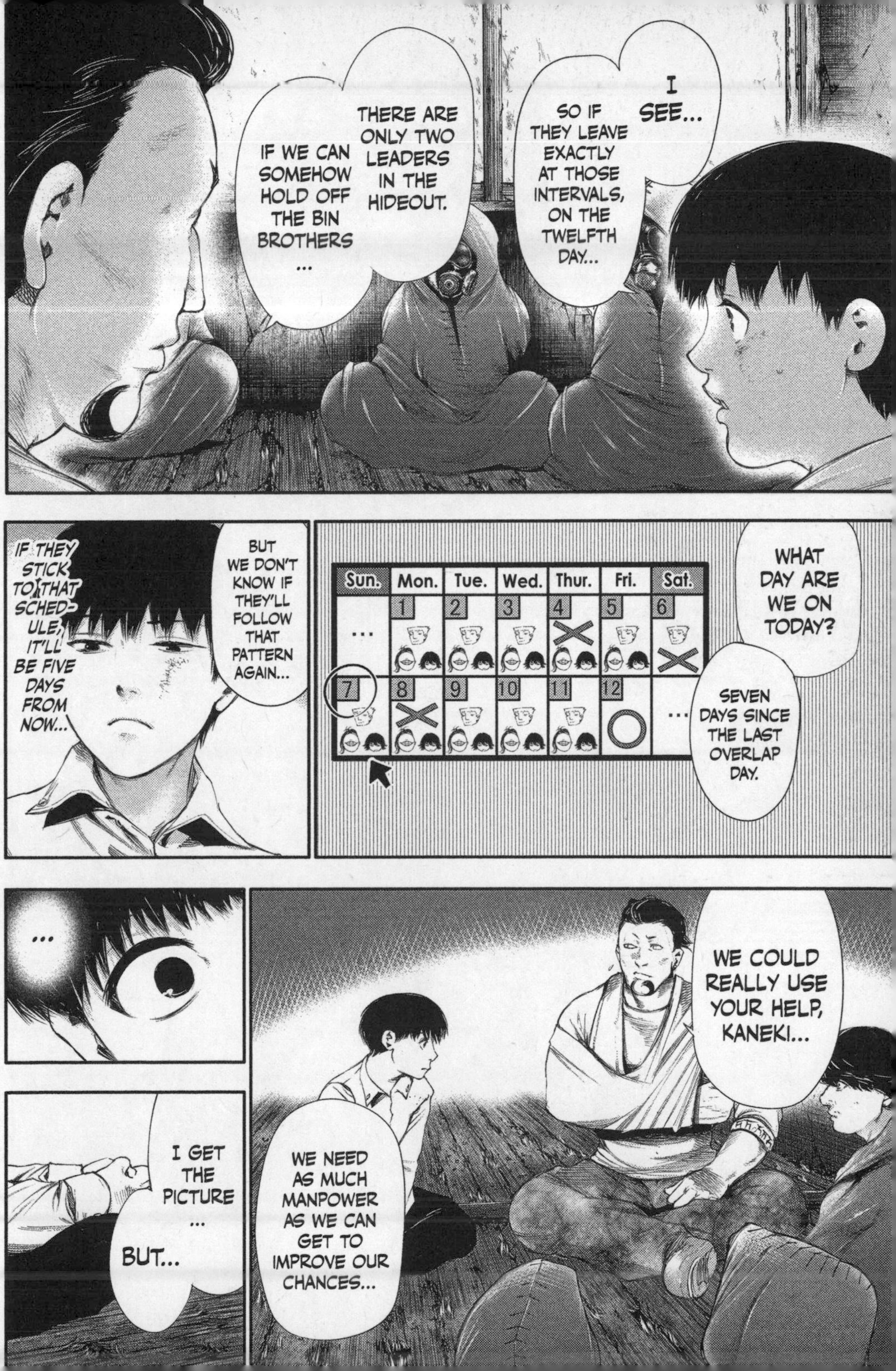
I SEE...
SO IF THEY LEAVE EXACTLY AT THOSE INTERVALS, ON THE TWELFTH DAY...
THERE ARE ONLY TWO LEADERS IN THE HIDEOUT.
IF WE CAN SOMEHOW HOLD OFF THE BIN BROTHERS ...
WHAT DAY ARE WE ON TODAY?
Sun. Mon. Tue. Wed. Thur. Fri. Sat.
1 2 3 4 5 6
7 8 9 10 11 12
SEVEN DAYS SINCE THE LAST OVERLAP DAY.
BUT WE DON'T KNOW IF THEY'LL FOLLOW THAT PATTERN AGAIN...
IF THEY STICK TO THAT SCHEDULE, IT'LL BE FIVE DAYS FROM NOW...
WE COULD REALLY USE YOUR HELP, KANEKI...
WE NEED AS MUCH MANPOWER AS WE CAN GET TO IMPROVE OUR CHANCES...
...
I GET THE PICTURE ...
BUT...

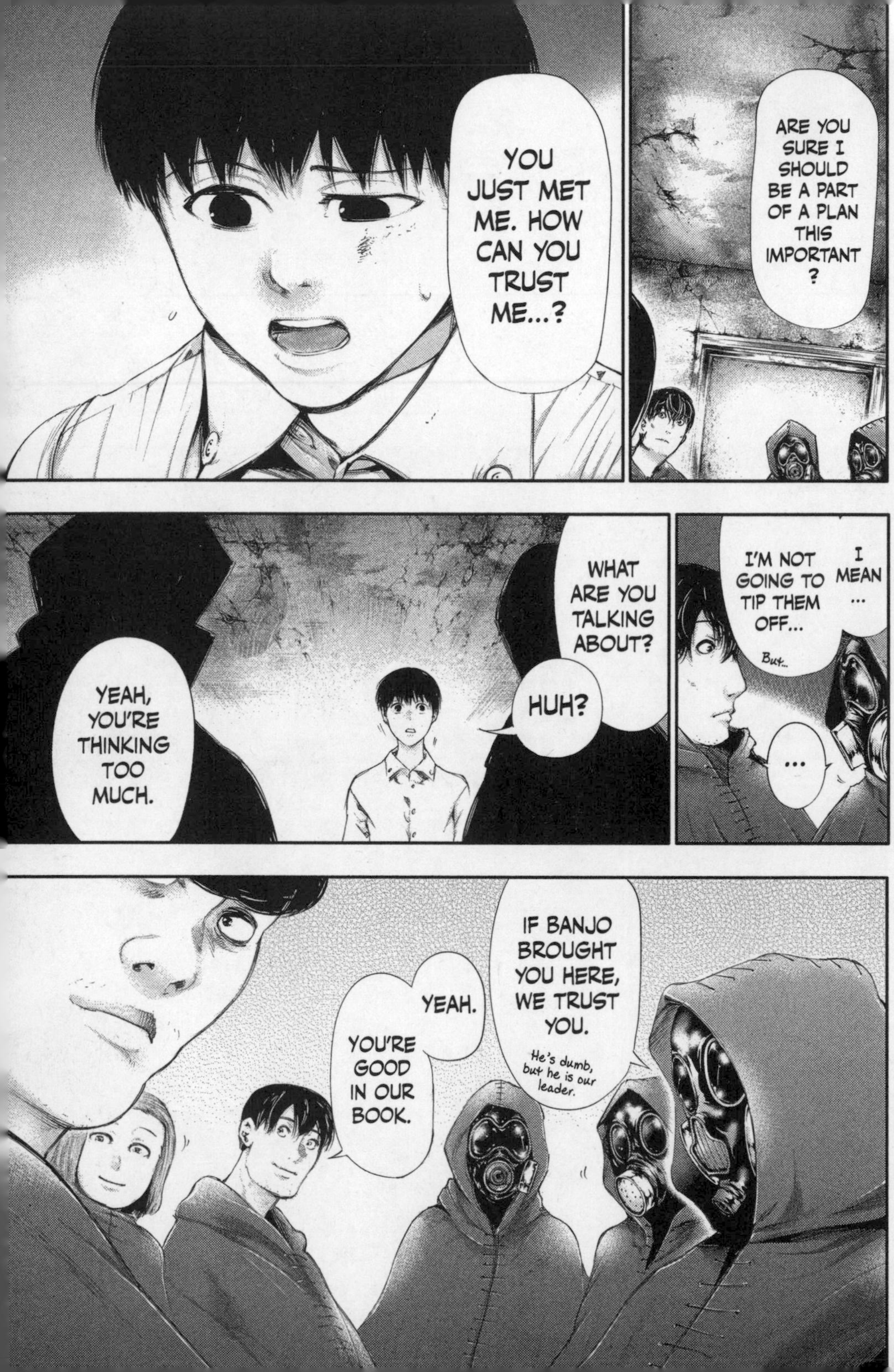
ARE YOU SURE I SHOULD BE A PART OF A PLAN THIS IMPORTANT ?
YOU JUST MET ME. HOW CAN YOU TRUST ME...?
I MEAN ...
I'M NOT GOING TO TIP THEM OFF...
But...
...
WHAT ARE YOU TALKING ABOUT?
HUH?
YEAH, YOU'RE THINKING TOO MUCH.
IF BANJO BROUGHT YOU HERE, WE TRUST YOU.
He's dumb, but he is our leader.
YEAH.
YOU'RE GOOD IN OUR BOOK.

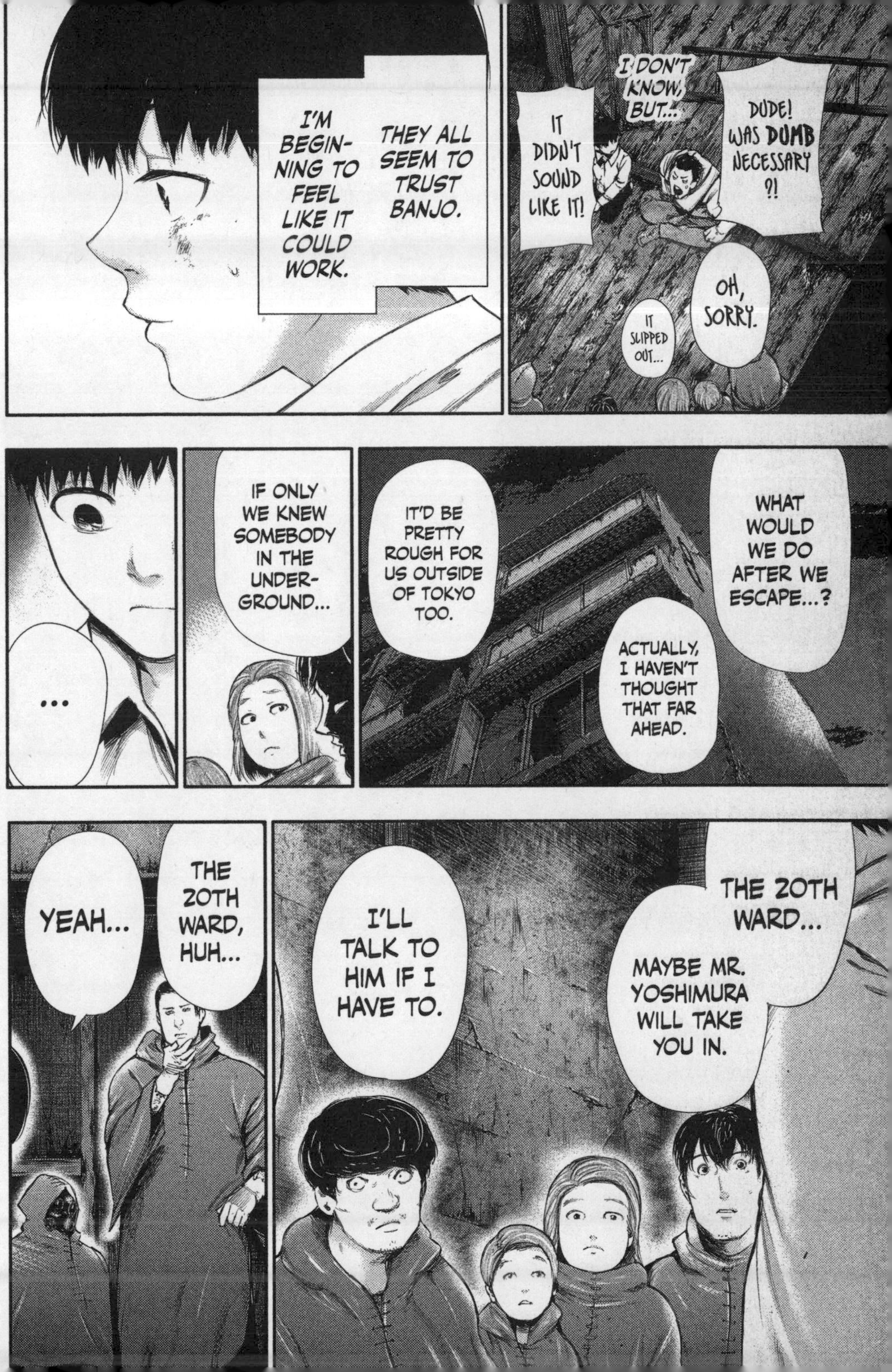
DUDE! WAS DUMB NECESSARY?!
I DON'T KNOW, BUT...
IT DIDN'T SOUND LIKE IT!
OH, SORRY.
IT SLIPPED OUT...
THEY ALL SEEM TO TRUST BANJO.
I'M BEGINNING TO FEEL LIKE IT COULD WORK.
WHAT WOULD WE DO AFTER WE ESCAPE...?
ACTUALLY, I HAVEN'T THOUGHT THAT FAR AHEAD.
IT'D BE PRETTY ROUGH FOR US OUTSIDE OF TOKYO TOO.
IF ONLY WE KNEW SOMEBODY IN THE UNDERGROUND...
...
THE 20TH WARD...
MAYBE MR. YOSHIMURA WILL TAKE YOU IN.
I'LL TALK TO HIM IF I HAVE TO.
THE 20TH WARD, HUH...
YEAH...

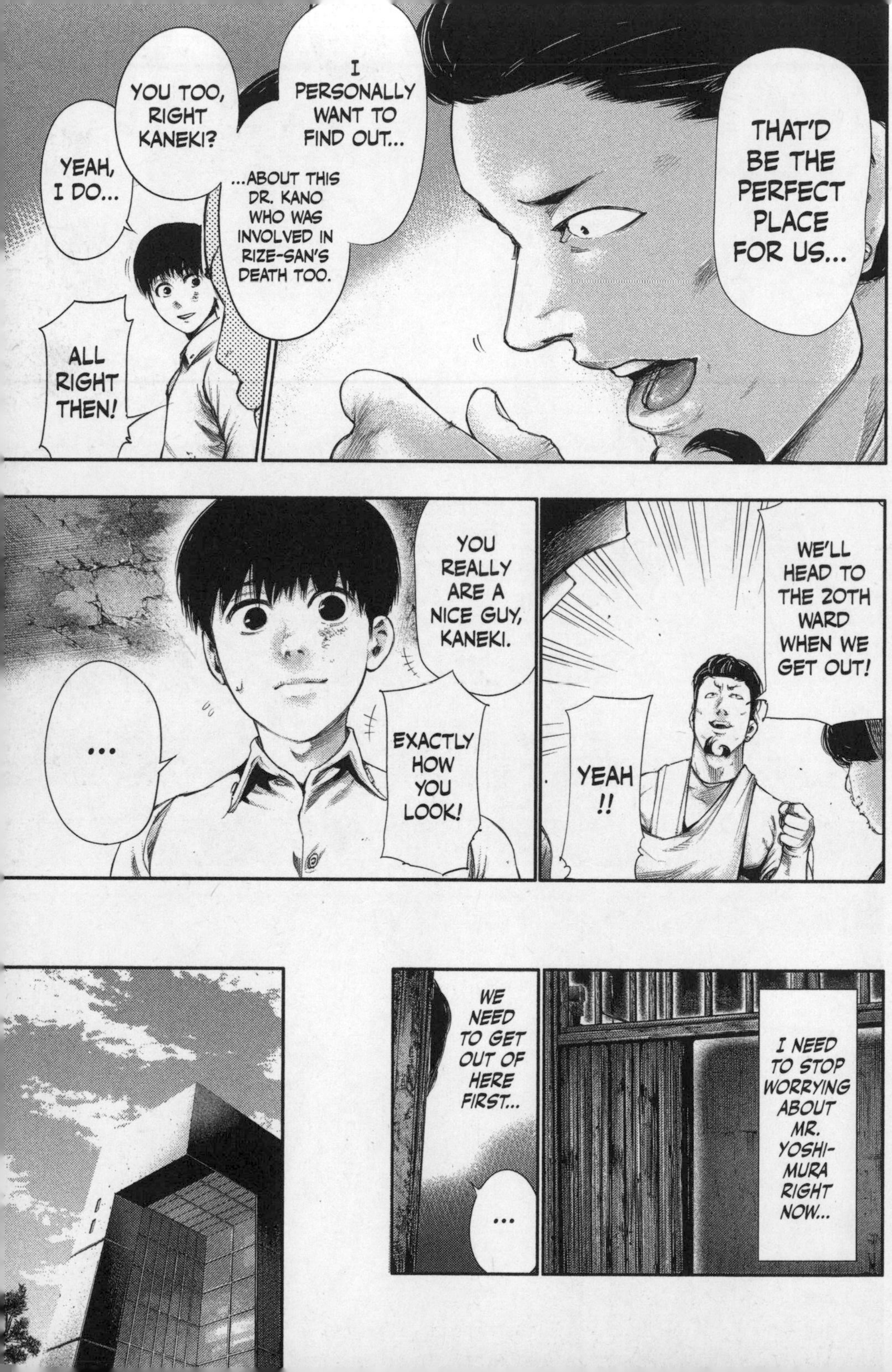
THAT'D BE THE PERFECT PLACE FOR US...
I PERSONALLY WANT TO FIND OUT...
...ABOUT THIS DR. KANO WHO WAS INVOLVED IN RIZE-SAN'S DEATH TOO.
YOU TOO, RIGHT KANEKI?
YEAH, I DO...
ALL RIGHT THEN!
WE'LL HEAD TO THE 20TH WARD WHEN WE GET OUT!
YEAH !!
YOU REALLY ARE A NICE GUY, KANEKI.
EXACTLY HOW YOU LOOK!
...
I NEED TO STOP WORRYING ABOUT MR. YOSHI-MURA RIGHT NOW...
WE NEED TO GET OUT OF HERE FIRST...
...

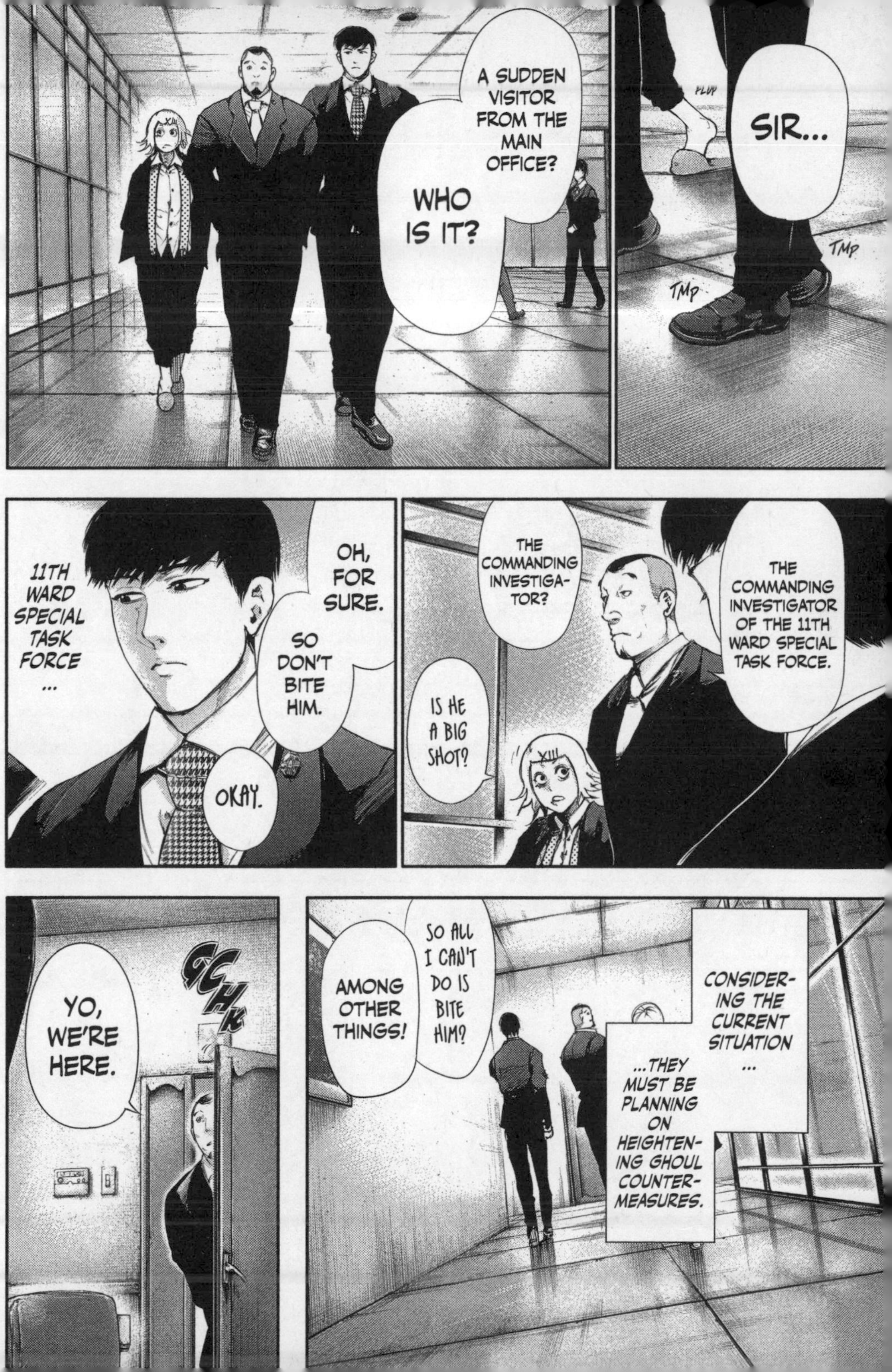

FLUP
SIR...
TMP
TMP
A SUDDEN VISITOR FROM THE MAIN OFFICE?
WHO IS IT?
THE COMMANDING INVESTIGATOR OF THE 11TH WARD SPECIAL TASK FORCE.
THE COMMANDING INVESTIGA-TOR?
IS HE A BIG SHOT?
OH, FOR SURE.
SO DON'T BITE HIM.
OKAY.
11TH WARD SPECIAL TASK FORCE ...
CONSIDER-ING THE CURRENT SITUATION ...
...THEY MUST BE PLANNING ON HEIGHTEN-ING GHOUL COUNTER-MEASURES.
SO ALL I CAN'T DO IS BITE HIM?
AMONG OTHER THINGS!
GCHK
YO, WE'RE HERE.

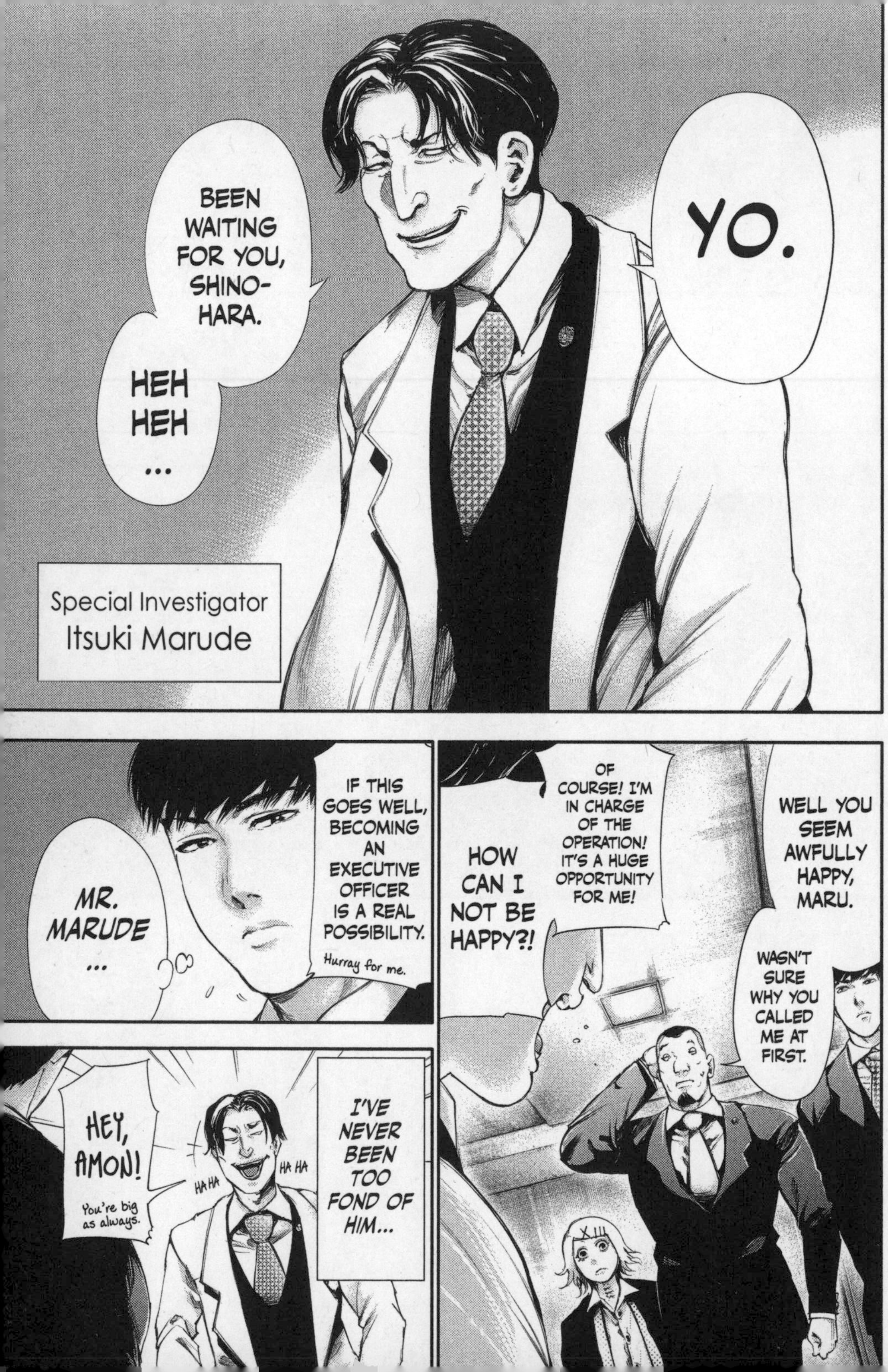
YO.
BEEN WAITING FOR YOU, SHINO-HARA.
HEH HEH ...
Special Investigator Itsuki Marude
WELL YOU SEEM AWFULLY HAPPY, MARU.
WASN'T SURE WHY YOU CALLED ME AT FIRST.
OF COURSE! I'M IN CHARGE OF THE OPERATION! IT'S A HUGE OPPORTUNITY FOR ME!
HOW CAN I NOT BE HAPPY?!
IF THIS GOES WELL, BECOMING AN EXECUTIVE OFFICER IS A REAL POSSIBILITY.
Hurray for me.
MR. MARUDE ...
I'VE NEVER BEEN TOO FOND OF HIM...
HA HA
HEY, AMON!
HA HA
You're big as always.

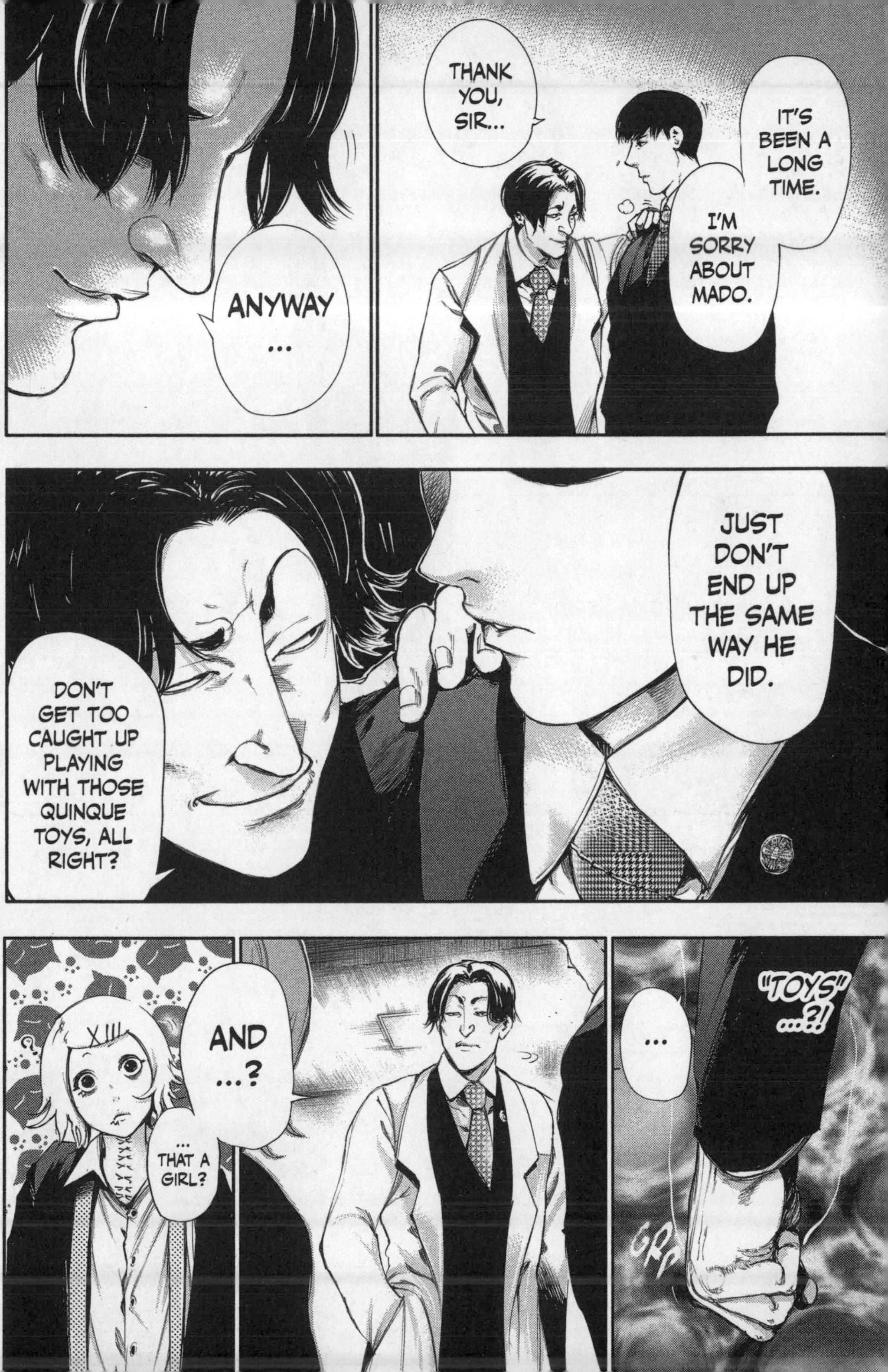
IT'S BEEN A LONG TIME.
I'M SORRY ABOUT MADO.
THANK YOU, SIR...
ANYWAY ...
JUST DON'T END UP THE SAME WAY HE DID.
DON'T GET TOO CAUGHT UP PLAYING WITH THOSE QUINQUE TOYS, ALL RIGHT?
"TOYS" ...?!
...
AND ...?
... THAT A GIRL?

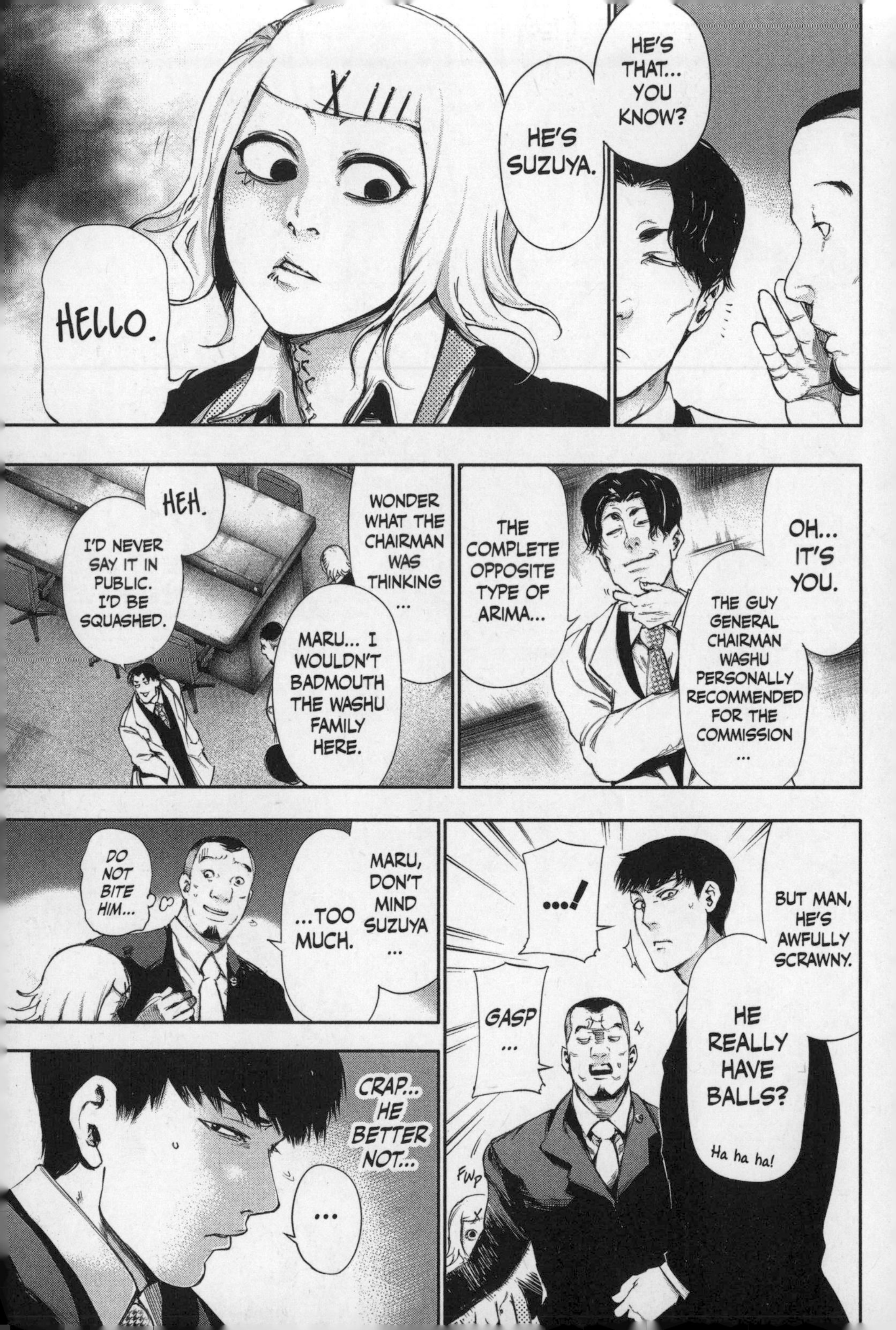
HE'S THAT... YOU KNOW?
HE'S SUZUYA.
HELLO.
OH... IT'S YOU.
THE GUY GENERAL CHAIRMAN WASHU PERSONALLY RECOMMENDED FOR THE COMMISSION...
THE COMPLETE OPPOSITE TYPE OF ARIMA...
WONDER WHAT THE CHAIRMAN WAS THINKING...
MARU... I WOULDN'T BADMOUTH THE WASHU FAMILY HERE.
HEH.
I'D NEVER SAY IT IN PUBLIC. I'D BE SQUASHED.
BUT MAN, HE'S AWFULLY SCRAWNY.
HE REALLY HAVE BALLS?
Ha ha ha!
...!
GASP...
FWP
MARU, DON'T MIND SUZUYA...
...TOO MUCH.
DO NOT BITE HIM...
CRAP... HE BETTER NOT...
...

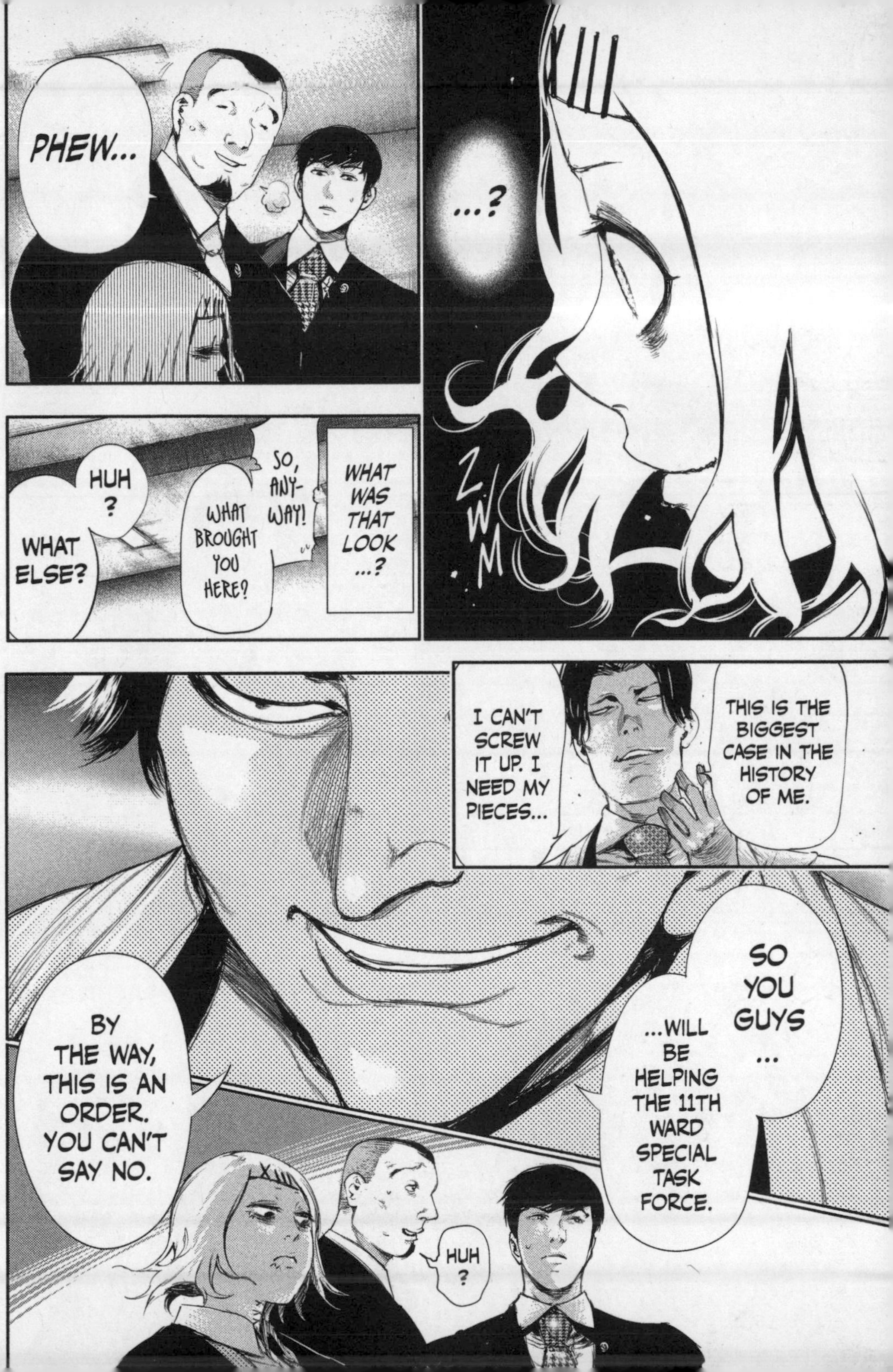
...?
ZWM
PHEW...
WHAT WAS THAT LOOK ...?
SO, ANY-WAY!
WHAT BROUGHT YOU HERE?
HUH?
WHAT ELSE?
THIS IS THE BIGGEST CASE IN THE HISTORY OF ME.
I CAN'T SCREW IT UP. I NEED MY PIECES...
SO YOU GUYS ...
...WILL BE HELPING THE 11TH WARD SPECIAL TASK FORCE.
BY THE WAY, THIS IS AN ORDER. YOU CAN'T SAY NO.
HUH?

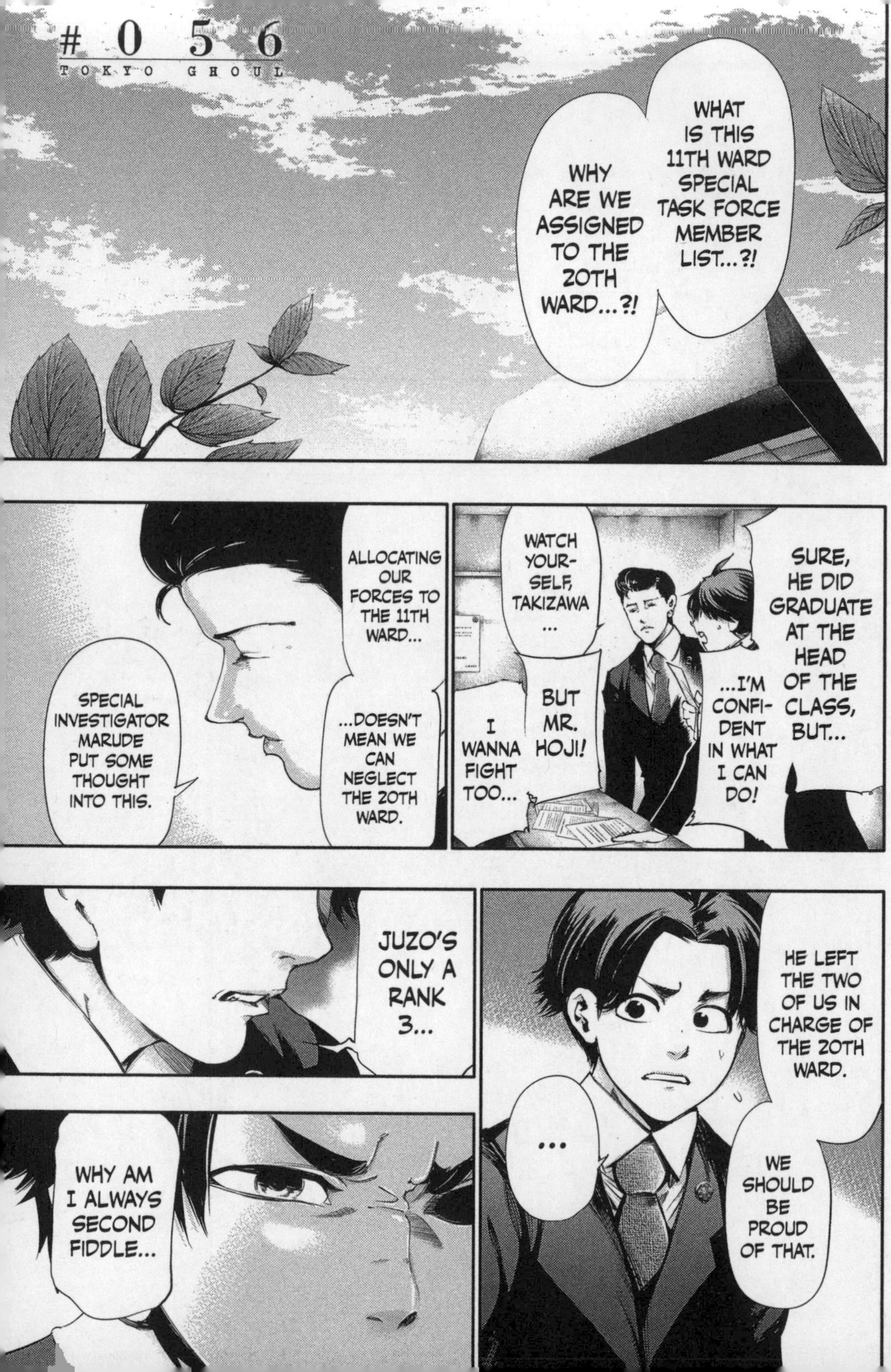
#056
TOKYO GHOUL
WHAT IS THIS 11TH WARD SPECIAL TASK FORCE MEMBER LIST...?!
WHY ARE WE ASSIGNED TO THE 20TH WARD...?!
SURE, HE DID GRADUATE AT THE HEAD OF THE CLASS, BUT...
...I'M CONFIDENT IN WHAT I CAN DO!
WATCH YOURSELF, TAKIZAWA...
BUT MR. HOJI!
I WANNA FIGHT TOO...
ALLOCATING OUR FORCES TO THE 11TH WARD...
...DOESN'T MEAN WE CAN NEGLECT THE 20TH WARD.
SPECIAL INVESTIGATOR MARUDE PUT SOME THOUGHT INTO THIS.
HE LEFT THE TWO OF US IN CHARGE OF THE 20TH WARD.
WE SHOULD BE PROUD OF THAT.
...
JUZO'S ONLY A RANK 3...
WHY AM I ALWAYS SECOND FIDDLE...

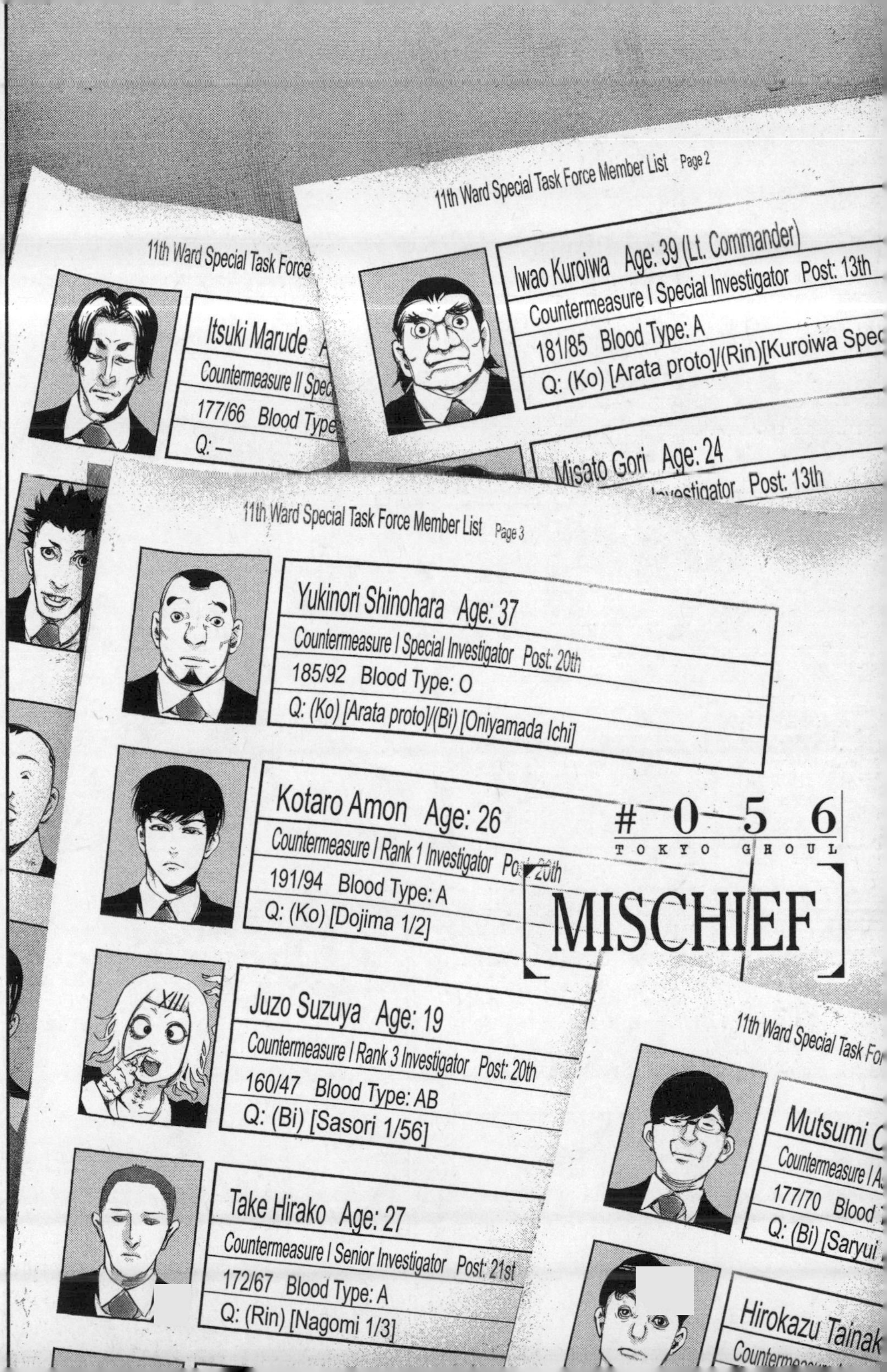
11th Ward Special Task Force Member List Page 2
Iwao Kuroiwa Age: 39 (Lt. Commander)
Countermeasure I Special Investigator Post: 13th
181/85 Blood Type: A
Q: (Ko) [Arata proto]/(Rin)[Kuroiwa Spec
Misato Gori Age: 24
Investigator Post: 13th
11th Ward Special Task Force
Itsuki Marude A
Countermeasure II Spec
177/66 Blood Type
Q: —
11th Ward Special Task Force Member List Page 3
Yukinori Shinohara Age: 37
Countermeasure I Special Investigator Post: 20th
185/92 Blood Type: O
Q: (Ko) [Arata proto]/(Bi) [Oniyamada Ichi]
Kotaro Amon Age: 26
Countermeasure I Rank 1 Investigator Post: 20th
191/94 Blood Type: A
Q: (Ko) [Dojima 1/2]
Juzo Suzuya Age: 19
Countermeasure I Rank 3 Investigator Post: 20th
160/47 Blood Type: AB
Q: (Bi) [Sasori 1/56]
Take Hirako Age: 27
Countermeasure I Senior Investigator Post: 21st
172/67 Blood Type: A
Q: (Rin) [Nagomi 1/3]
#056
TOKYO GHOUL
[MISCHIEF]
11th Ward Special Task For
Mutsumi C
Countermeasure I A
177/70 Blood
Q: (Bi) [Saryui
Hirokazu Tainak
Countermeasure

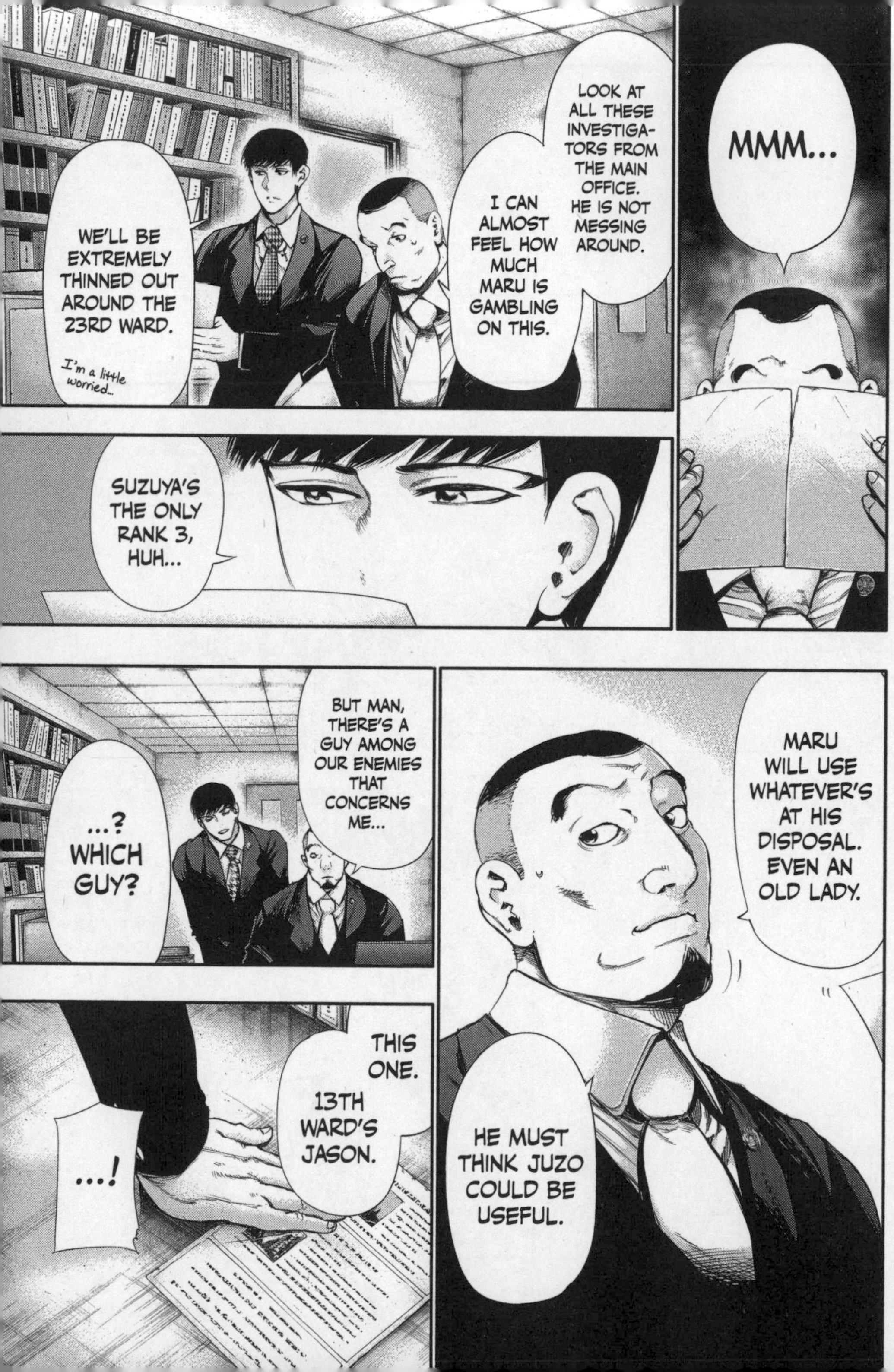
MMM...
LOOK AT ALL THESE INVESTIGA-TORS FROM THE MAIN OFFICE. HE IS NOT MESSING AROUND.
I CAN ALMOST FEEL HOW MUCH MARU IS GAMBLING ON THIS.
WE'LL BE EXTREMELY THINNED OUT AROUND THE 23RD WARD.
I'm a little worried...
SUZUYA'S THE ONLY RANK 3, HUH...
MARU WILL USE WHATEVER'S AT HIS DISPOSAL. EVEN AN OLD LADY.
HE MUST THINK JUZO COULD BE USEFUL.
BUT MAN, THERE'S A GUY AMONG OUR ENEMIES THAT CONCERNS ME...
...? WHICH GUY?
THIS ONE.
13TH WARD'S JASON.
...!

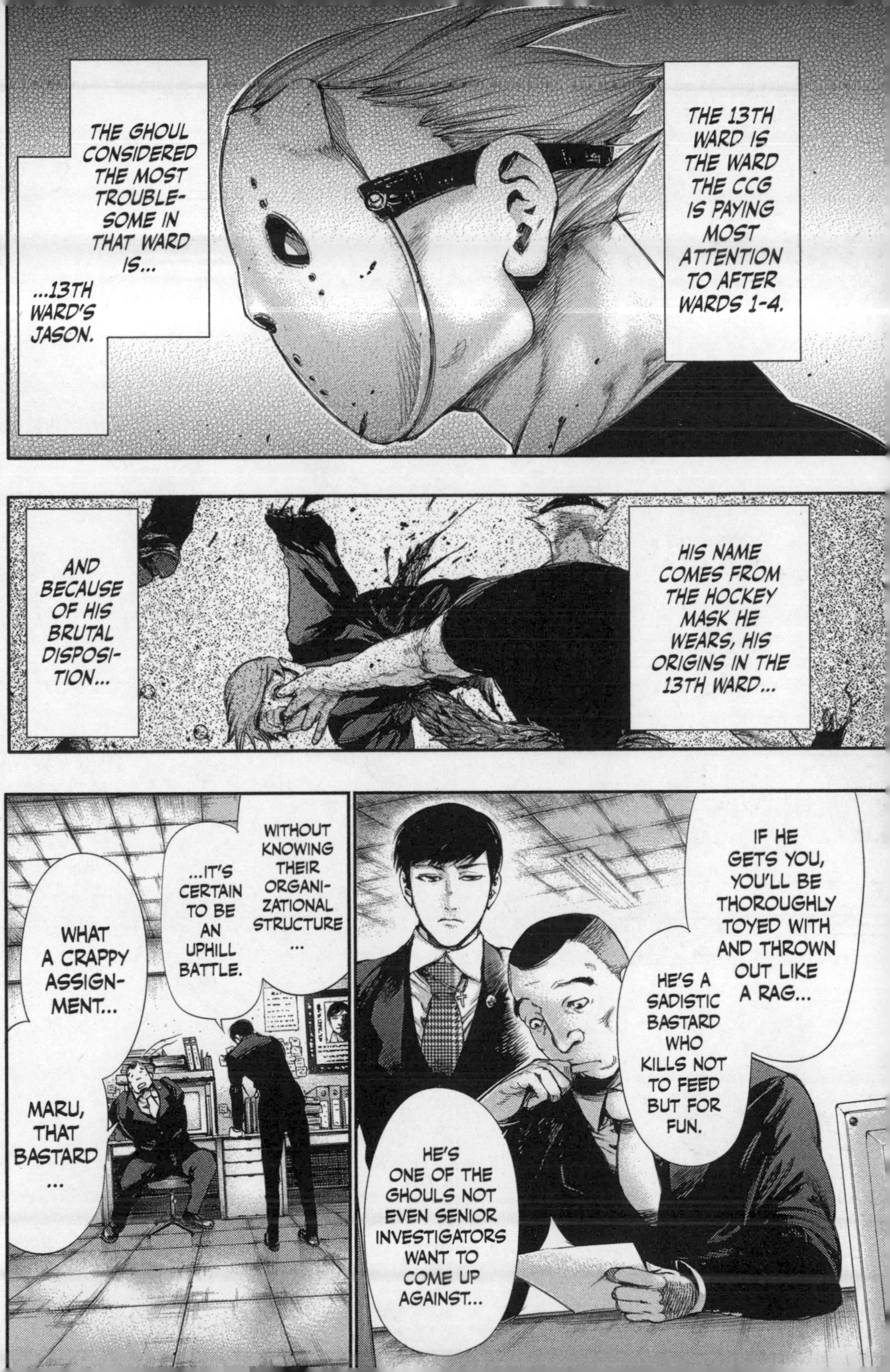
THE 13TH WARD IS THE WARD THE CCG IS PAYING MOST ATTENTION TO AFTER WARDS 1-4.
THE GHOUL CONSIDERED THE MOST TROUBLESOME IN THAT WARD IS...
...13TH WARD'S JASON.
HIS NAME COMES FROM THE HOCKEY MASK HE WEARS, HIS ORIGINS IN THE 13TH WARD...
AND BECAUSE OF HIS BRUTAL DISPOSITION...
IF HE GETS YOU, YOU'LL BE THOROUGHLY TOYED WITH AND THROWN OUT LIKE A RAG...
HE'S A SADISTIC BASTARD WHO KILLS NOT TO FEED BUT FOR FUN.
HE'S ONE OF THE GHOULS NOT EVEN SENIOR INVESTIGATORS WANT TO COME UP AGAINST...
WITHOUT KNOWING THEIR ORGANIZATIONAL STRUCTURE...
...IT'S CERTAIN TO BE AN UPHILL BATTLE.
WHAT A CRAPPY ASSIGNMENT...
MARU, THAT BASTARD...

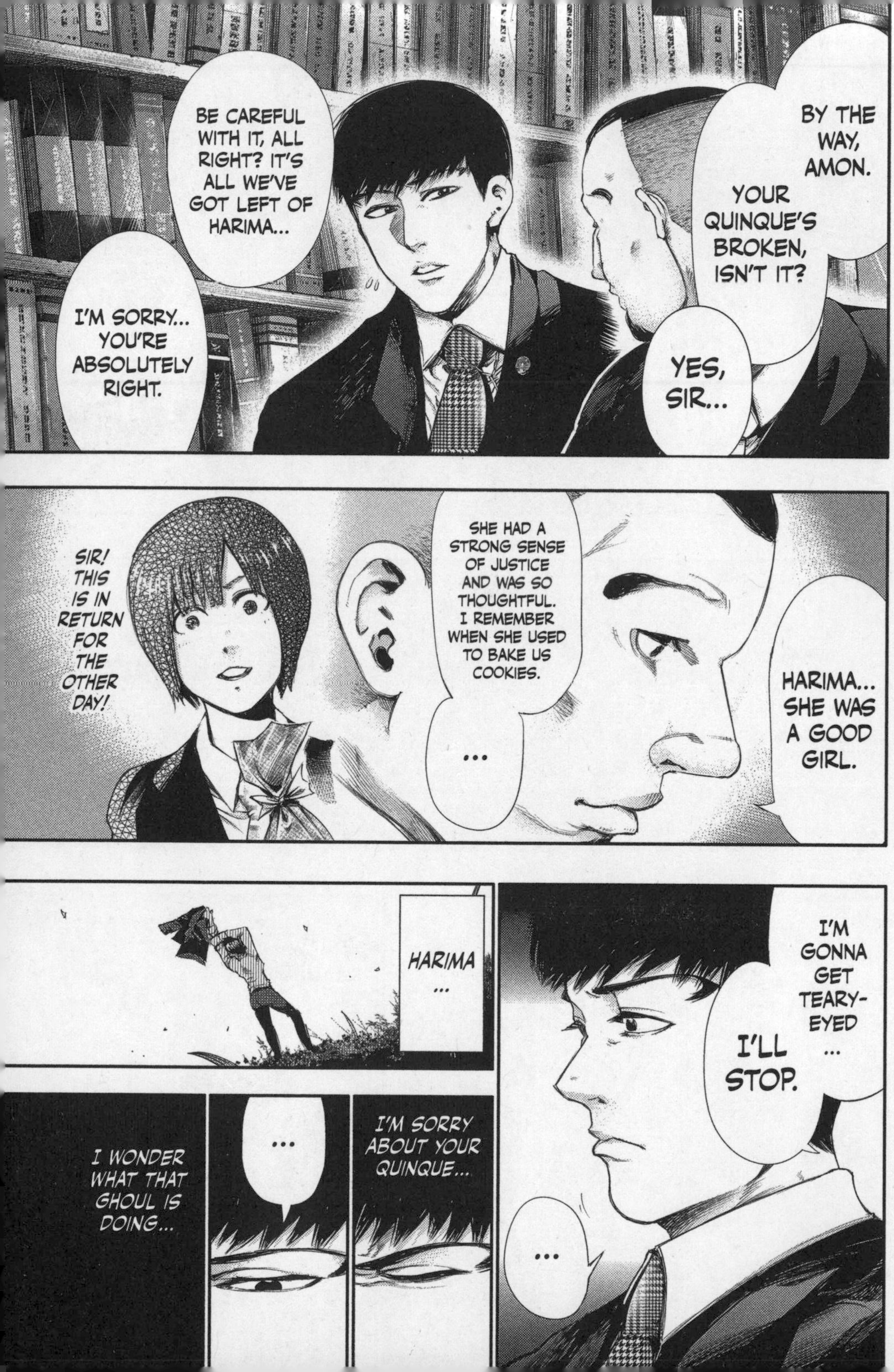
BY THE WAY, AMON.
YOUR QUINQUE'S BROKEN, ISN'T IT?
YES, SIR...
BE CAREFUL WITH IT, ALL RIGHT? IT'S ALL WE'VE GOT LEFT OF HARIMA...
I'M SORRY... YOU'RE ABSOLUTELY RIGHT.
HARIMA... SHE WAS A GOOD GIRL.
SHE HAD A STRONG SENSE OF JUSTICE AND WAS SO THOUGHTFUL. I REMEMBER WHEN SHE USED TO BAKE US COOKIES.
...
SIR! THIS IS IN RETURN FOR THE OTHER DAY!
I'M GONNA GET TEARY-EYED...
I'LL STOP.
...
HARIMA...
I'M SORRY ABOUT YOUR QUINQUE...
...
I WONDER WHAT THAT GHOUL IS DOING...

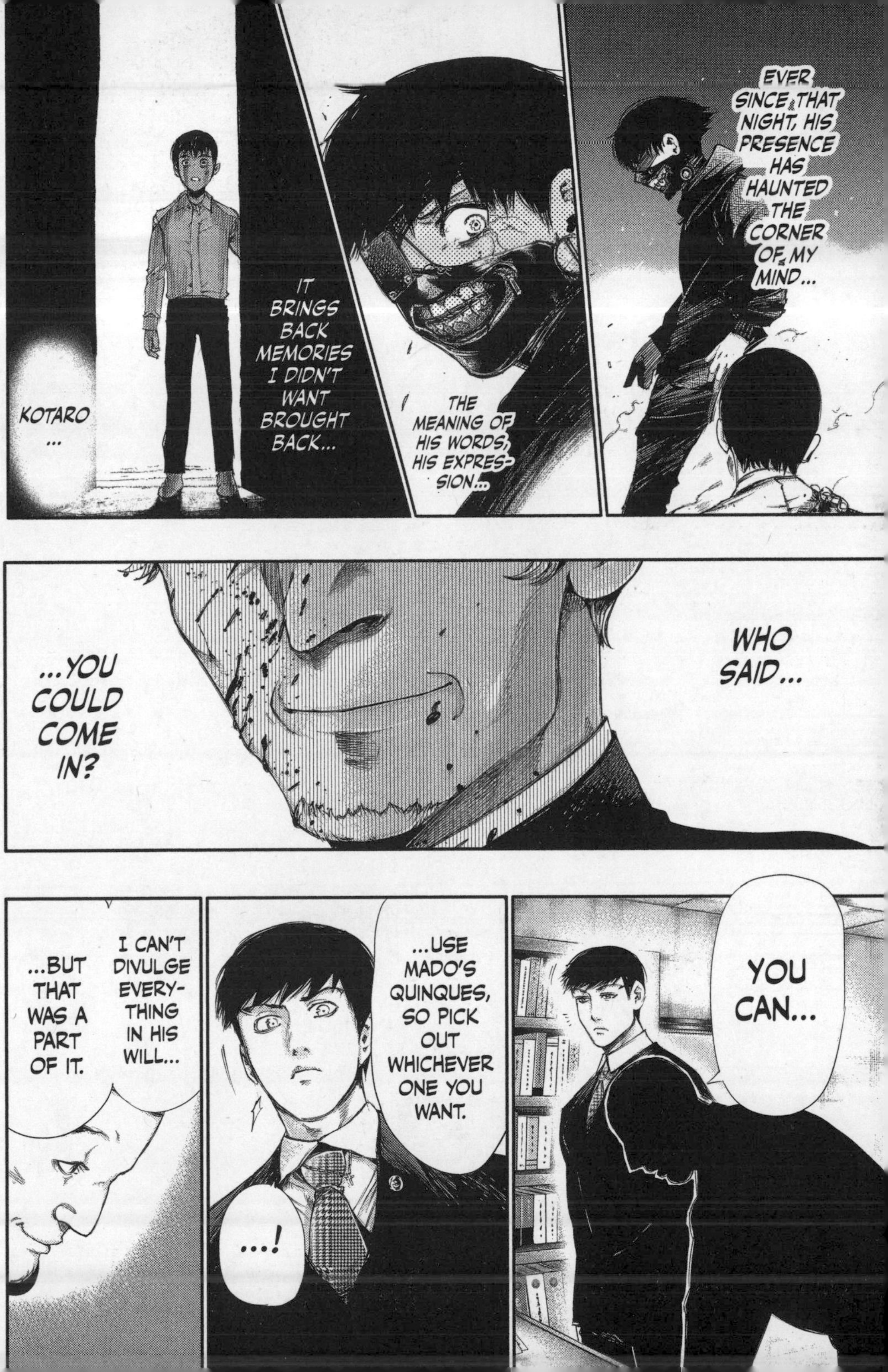
EVER SINCE THAT NIGHT, HIS PRESENCE HAS HAUNTED THE CORNER OF MY MIND...
THE MEANING OF HIS WORDS, HIS EXPRESSION...
IT BRINGS BACK MEMORIES I DIDN'T WANT BROUGHT BACK...
KOTARO ...
WHO SAID...
...YOU COULD COME IN?
YOU CAN...
...USE MADO'S QUINQUES, SO PICK OUT WHICHEVER ONE YOU WANT.
...!
I CAN'T DIVULGE EVERYTHING IN HIS WILL...
...BUT THAT WAS A PART OF IT.

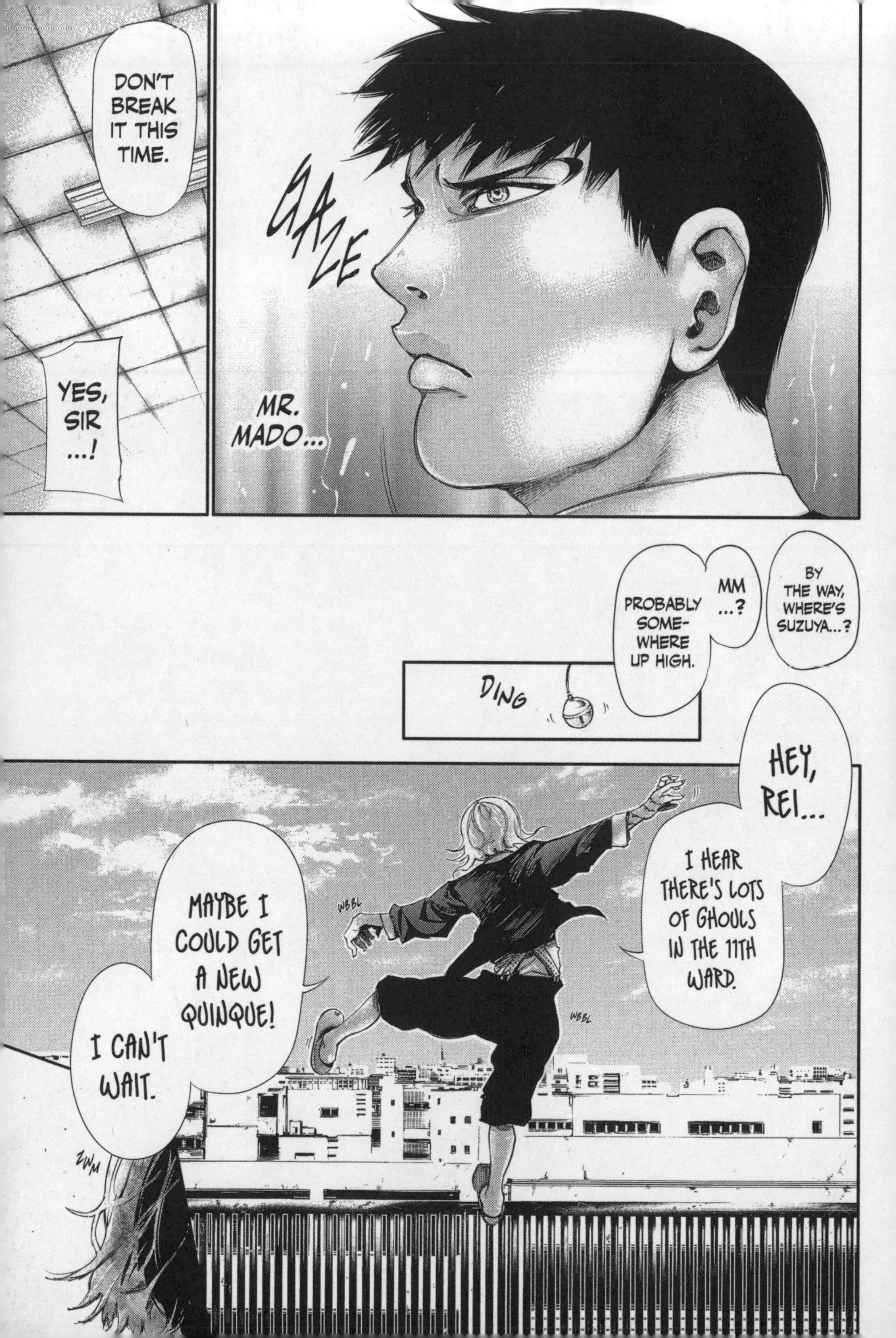
GAZE
MR. MADO...
DON'T BREAK IT THIS TIME.
YES, SIR ...!
BY THE WAY, WHERE'S SUZUYA...?
MM ...?
PROBABLY SOME-WHERE UP HIGH.
DING
HEY, REI...
I HEAR THERE'S LOTS OF GHOULS IN THE 11TH WARD.
WBBL
WBBL
MAYBE I COULD GET A NEW QUINQUE!
I CAN'T WAIT.
ZWM

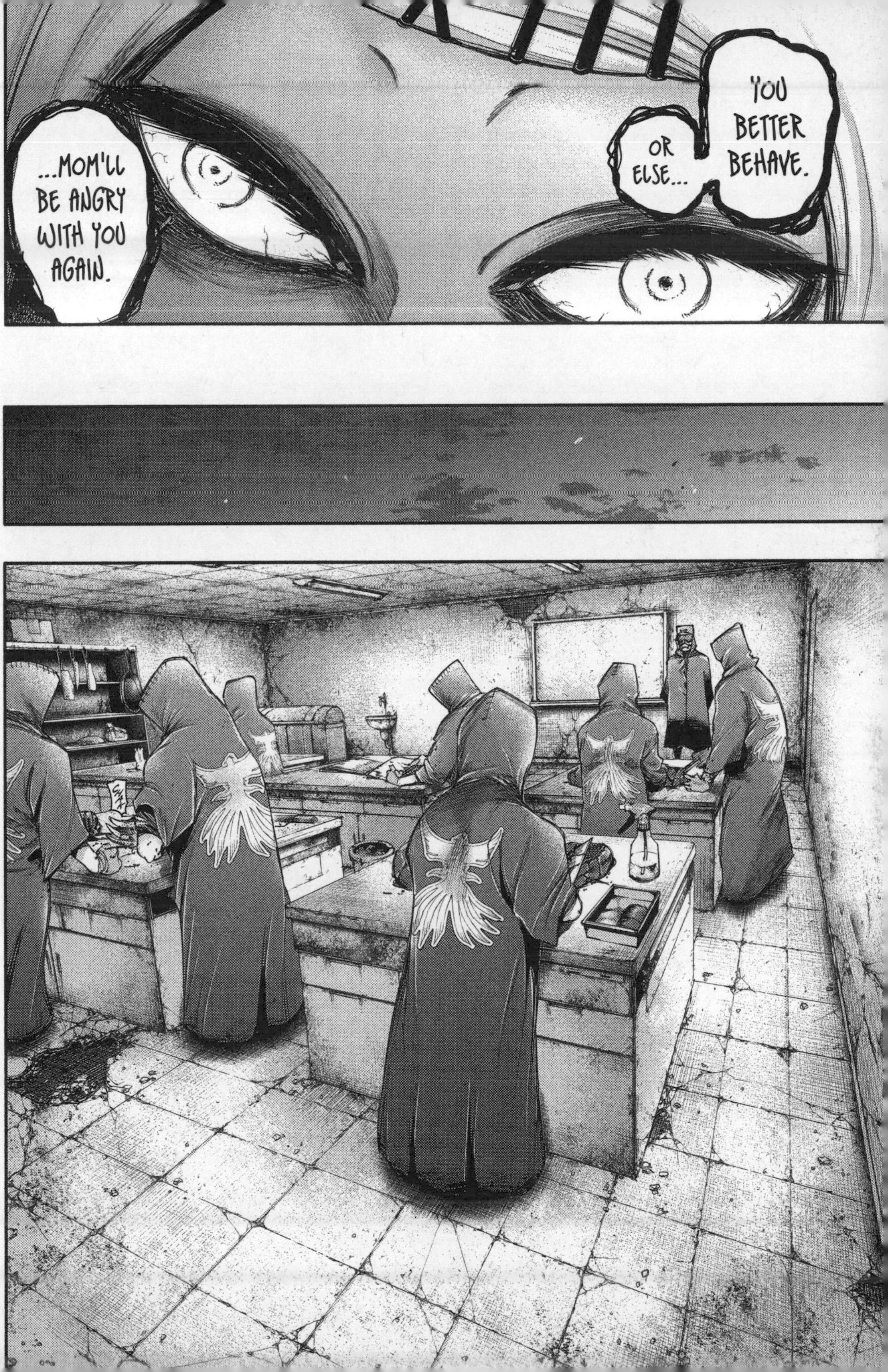
YOU BETTER BEHAVE.
OR ELSE...
...MOM'LL BE ANGRY WITH YOU AGAIN.

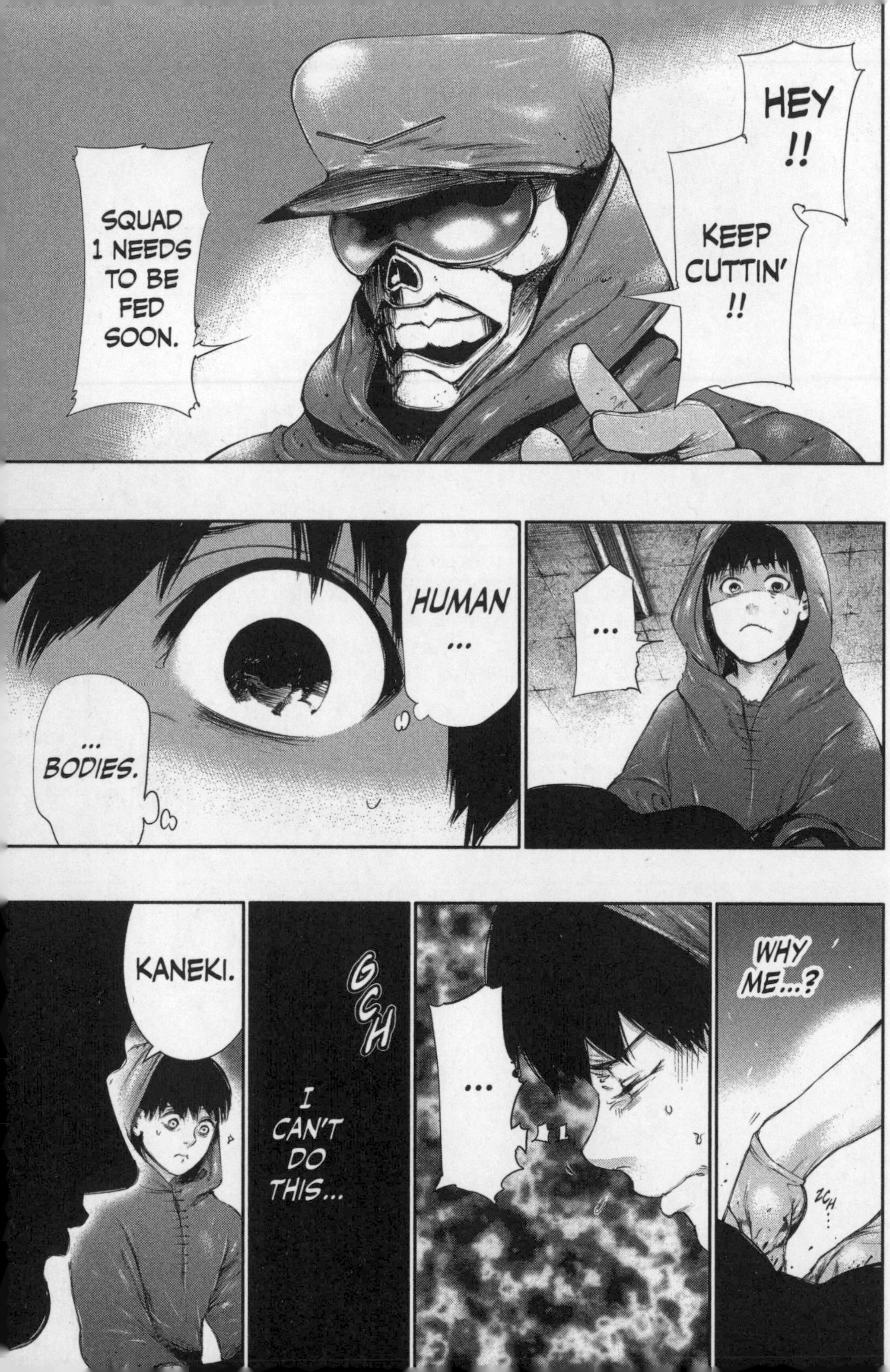
HEY !!
KEEP CUTTIN' !!
SQUAD 1 NEEDS TO BE FED SOON.
...
HUMAN ...
... BODIES.
WHY ME...?
ZCH...
...
GCH
I CAN'T DO THIS...
KANEKI.

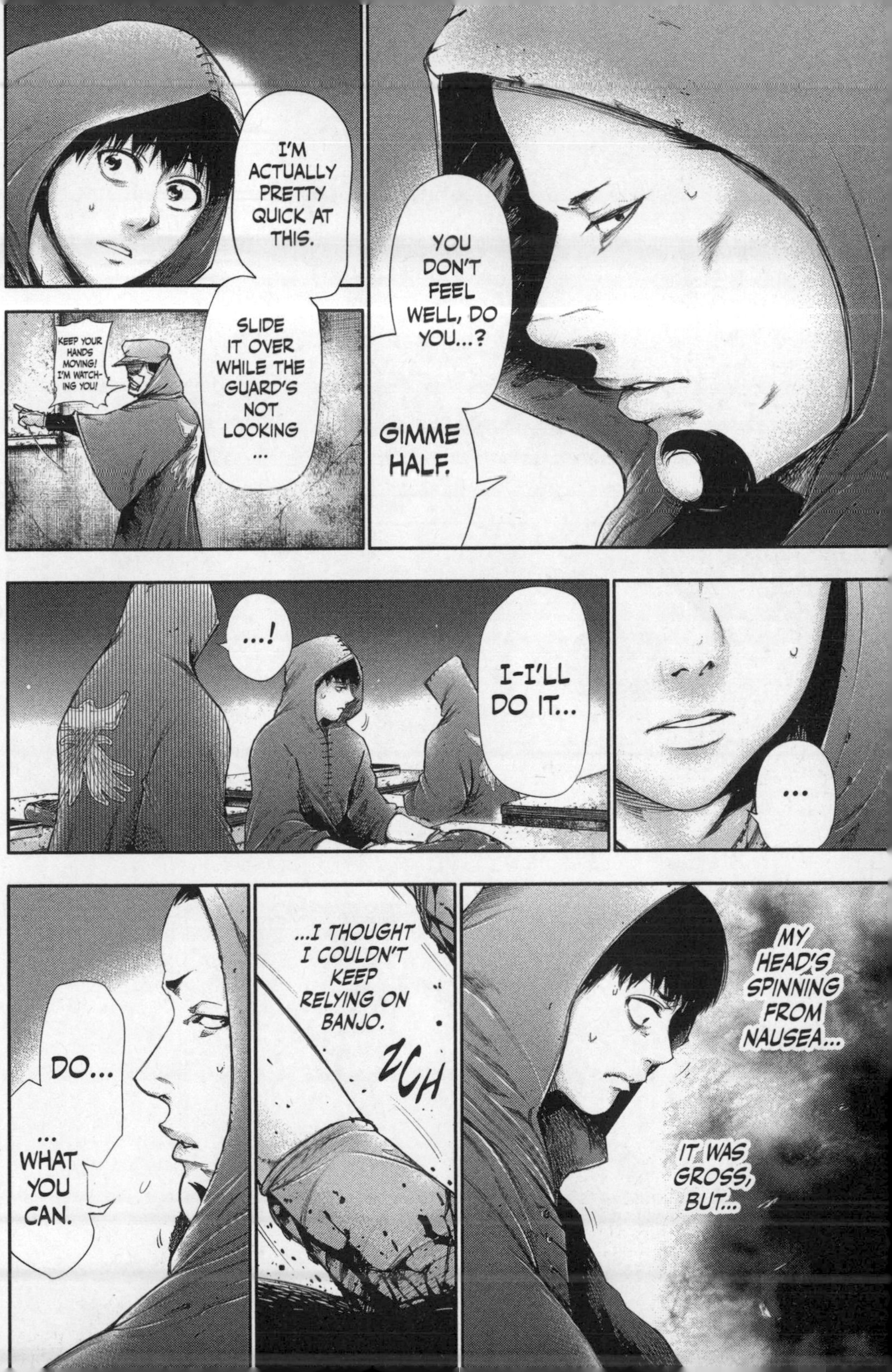
YOU DON'T FEEL WELL, DO YOU...?
GIMME HALF.
I'M ACTUALLY PRETTY QUICK AT THIS.
SLIDE IT OVER WHILE THE GUARD'S NOT LOOKING ...
KEEP YOUR HANDS MOVING! I'M WATCHING YOU!
...
I-I'LL DO IT...
...!
MY HEAD'S SPINNING FROM NAUSEA...
IT WAS GROSS, BUT...
...I THOUGHT I COULDN'T KEEP RELYING ON BANJO.
ZCH
DO...
... WHAT YOU CAN.

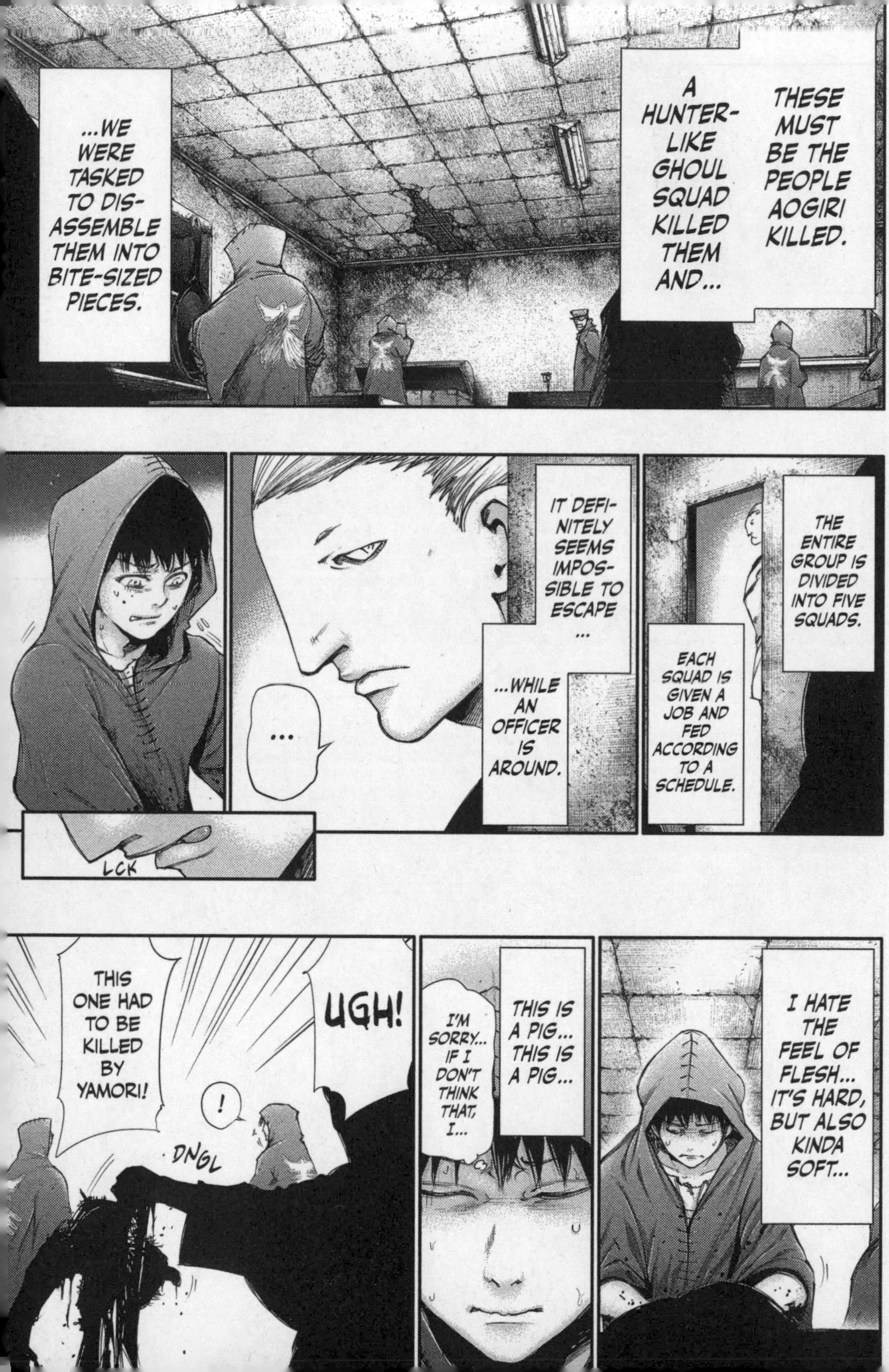
THESE MUST BE THE PEOPLE AOGIRI KILLED.
A HUNTER-LIKE GHOUL SQUAD KILLED THEM AND...
...WE WERE TASKED TO DISASSEMBLE THEM INTO BITE-SIZED PIECES.
THE ENTIRE GROUP IS DIVIDED INTO FIVE SQUADS.
EACH SQUAD IS GIVEN A JOB AND FED ACCORDING TO A SCHEDULE.
IT DEFINITELY SEEMS IMPOSSIBLE TO ESCAPE ...
...WHILE AN OFFICER IS AROUND.
...
LCK
I HATE THE FEEL OF FLESH... IT'S HARD, BUT ALSO KINDA SOFT...
THIS IS A PIG... THIS IS A PIG...
I'M SORRY... IF I DON'T THINK THAT, I...
UGH!
THIS ONE HAD TO BE KILLED BY YAMORI!
!
DNGL

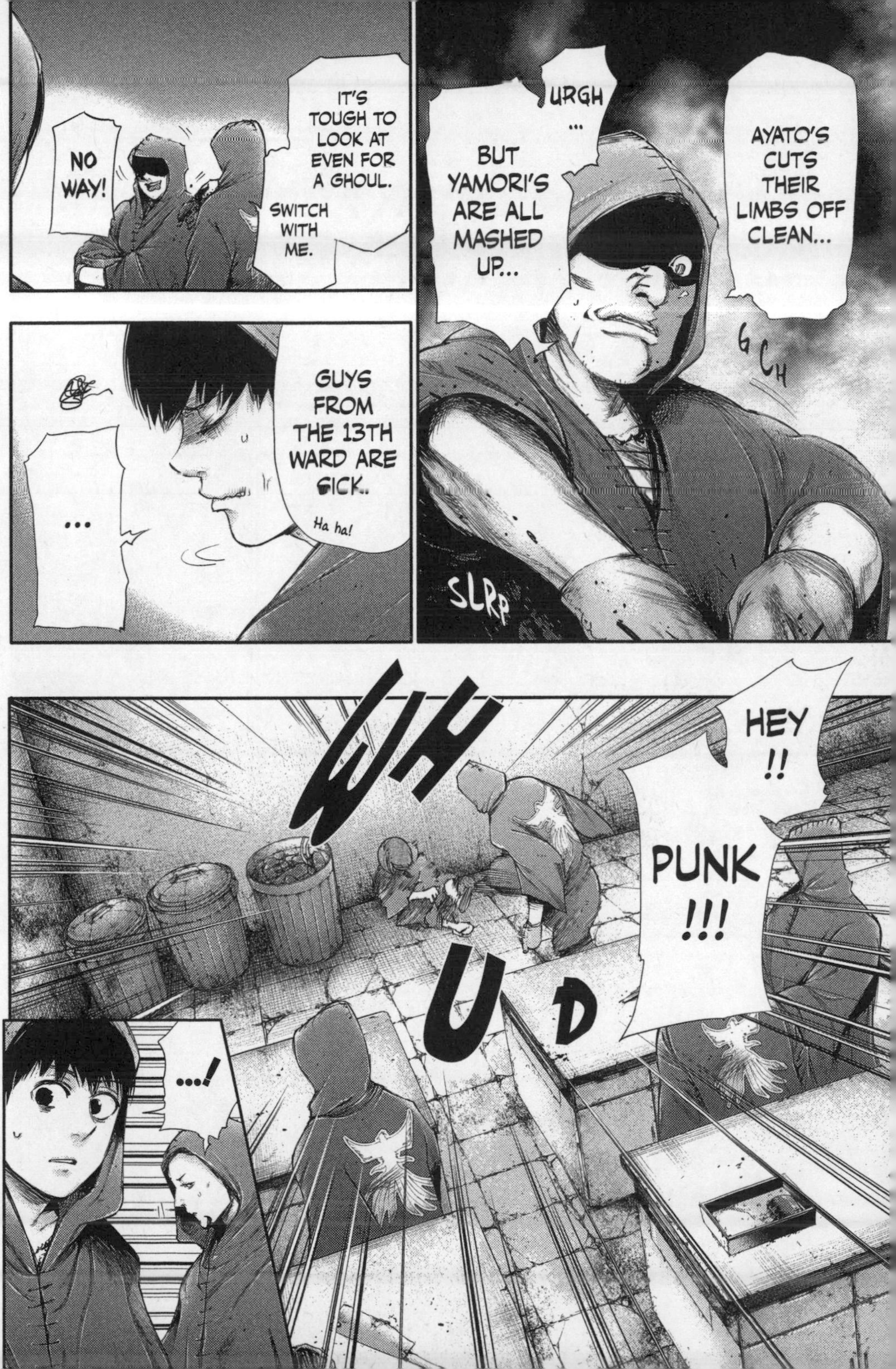
AYATO'S CUTS THEIR LIMBS OFF CLEAN...
URGH ...
BUT YAMORI'S ARE ALL MASHED UP...
GCH
SLRP
IT'S TOUGH TO LOOK AT EVEN FOR A GHOUL.
NO WAY!
SWITCH WITH ME.
GUYS FROM THE 13TH WARD ARE SICK..
Ha ha!
...
HEY !!
PUNK !!!
WHUD
...!

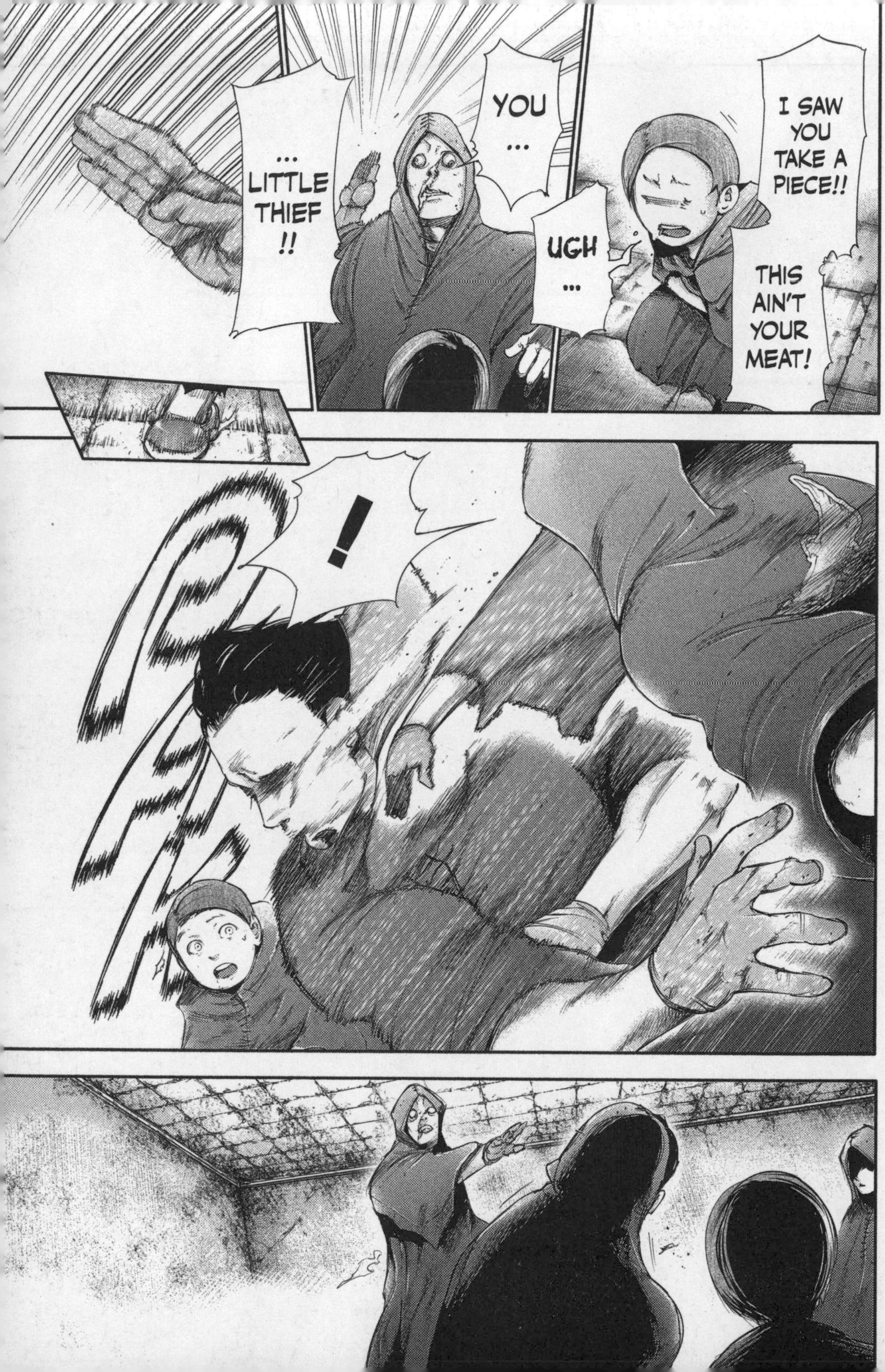
I SAW YOU TAKE A PIECE!!
THIS AIN'T YOUR MEAT!
UGH ...
YOU ...
... LITTLE THIEF !!
!

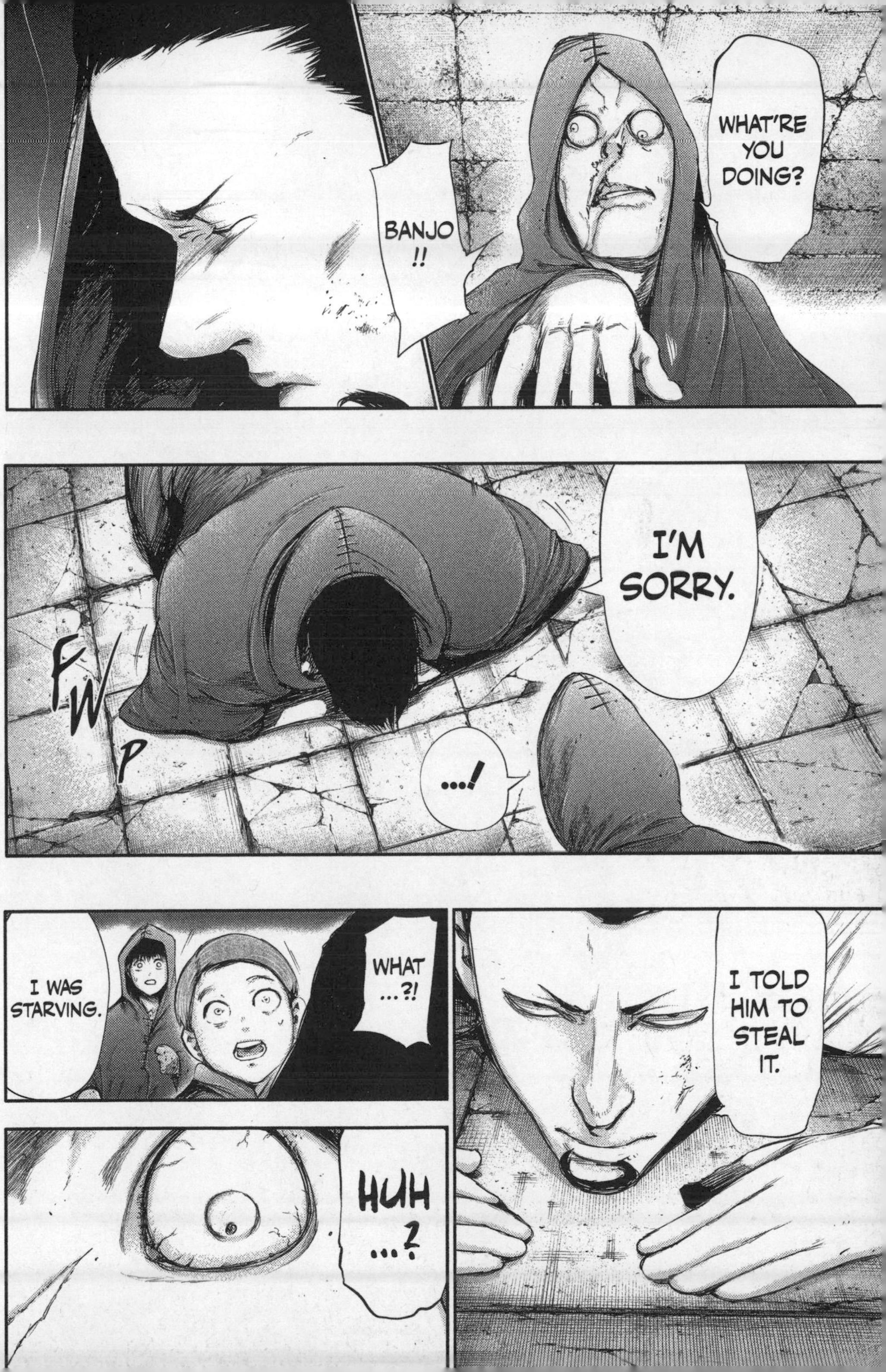
WHAT'RE YOU DOING?
BANJO !!
I'M SORRY.
...!
FWP
I TOLD HIM TO STEAL IT.
WHAT ...?!
I WAS STARVING.
HUH ...?

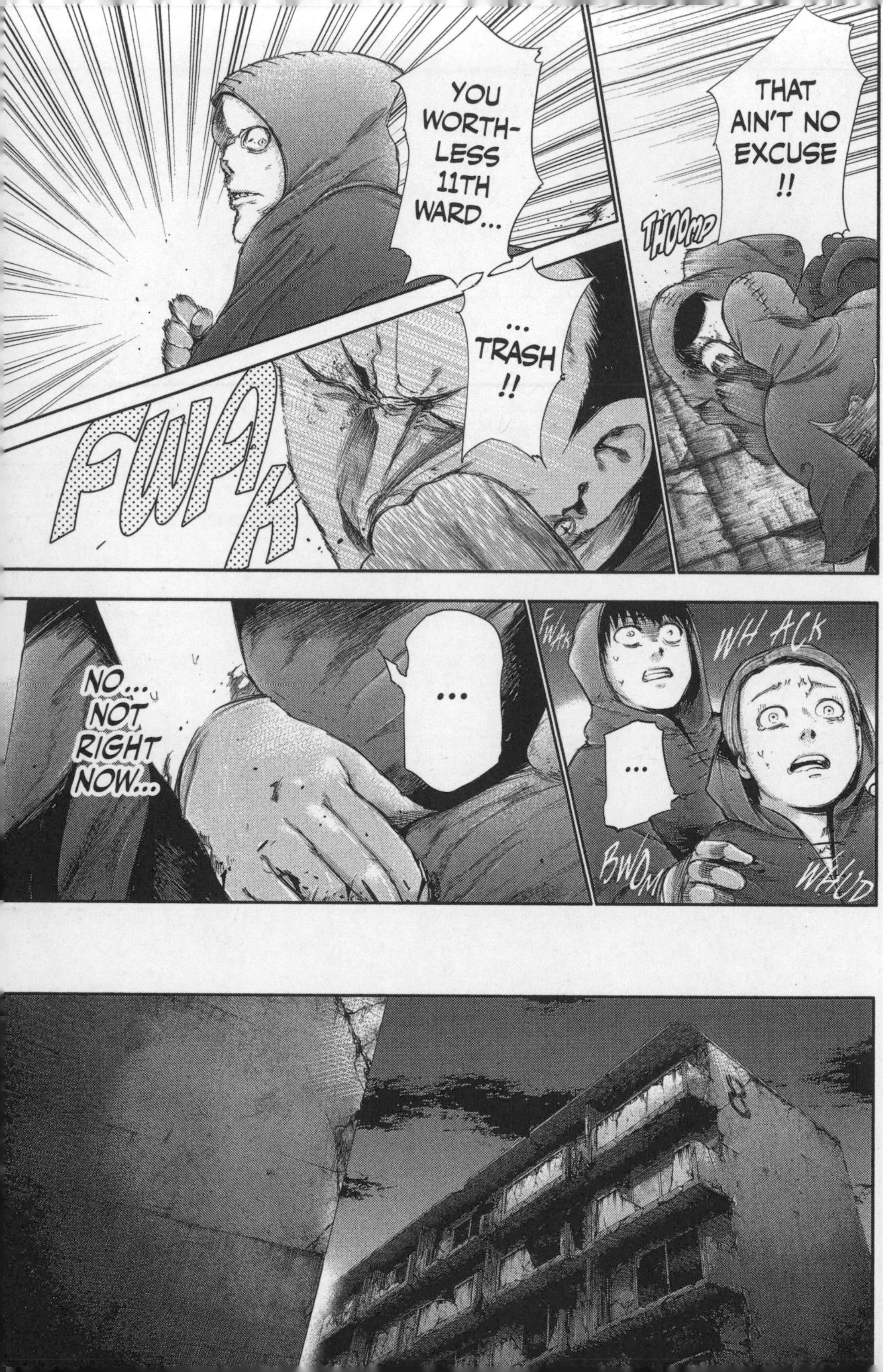
THAT AIN'T NO EXCUSE !!
THOOMP
YOU WORTH-LESS 11TH WARD...
... TRASH !!
FWAK
FWAK
WHACK
...
BWOM
WHUD
...
NO... NOT RIGHT NOW...

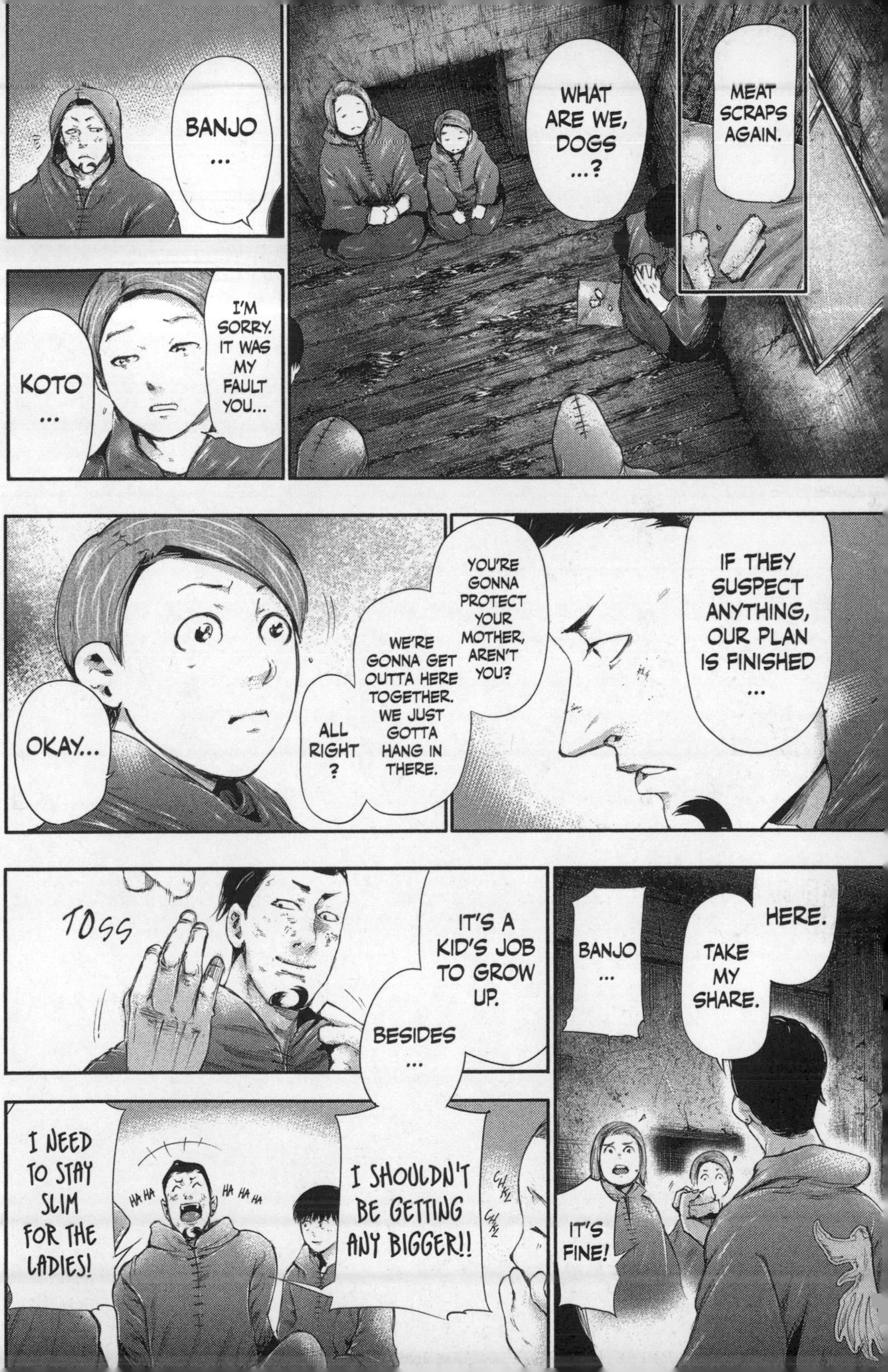
MEAT SCRAPS AGAIN.
WHAT ARE WE, DOGS ...?
BANJO ...
I'M SORRY. IT WAS MY FAULT YOU...
KOTO ...
IF THEY SUSPECT ANYTHING, OUR PLAN IS FINISHED ...
YOU'RE GONNA PROTECT YOUR MOTHER, AREN'T YOU?
WE'RE GONNA GET OUTTA HERE TOGETHER. WE JUST GOTTA HANG IN THERE.
ALL RIGHT ?
OKAY...
HERE.
TAKE MY SHARE.
BANJO ...
IT'S FINE!
CHKL
CHKL
TOSS
IT'S A KID'S JOB TO GROW UP.
BESIDES ...
I SHOULDN'T BE GETTING ANY BIGGER!!
HA HA HA
HA HA
I NEED TO STAY SLIM FOR THE LADIES!

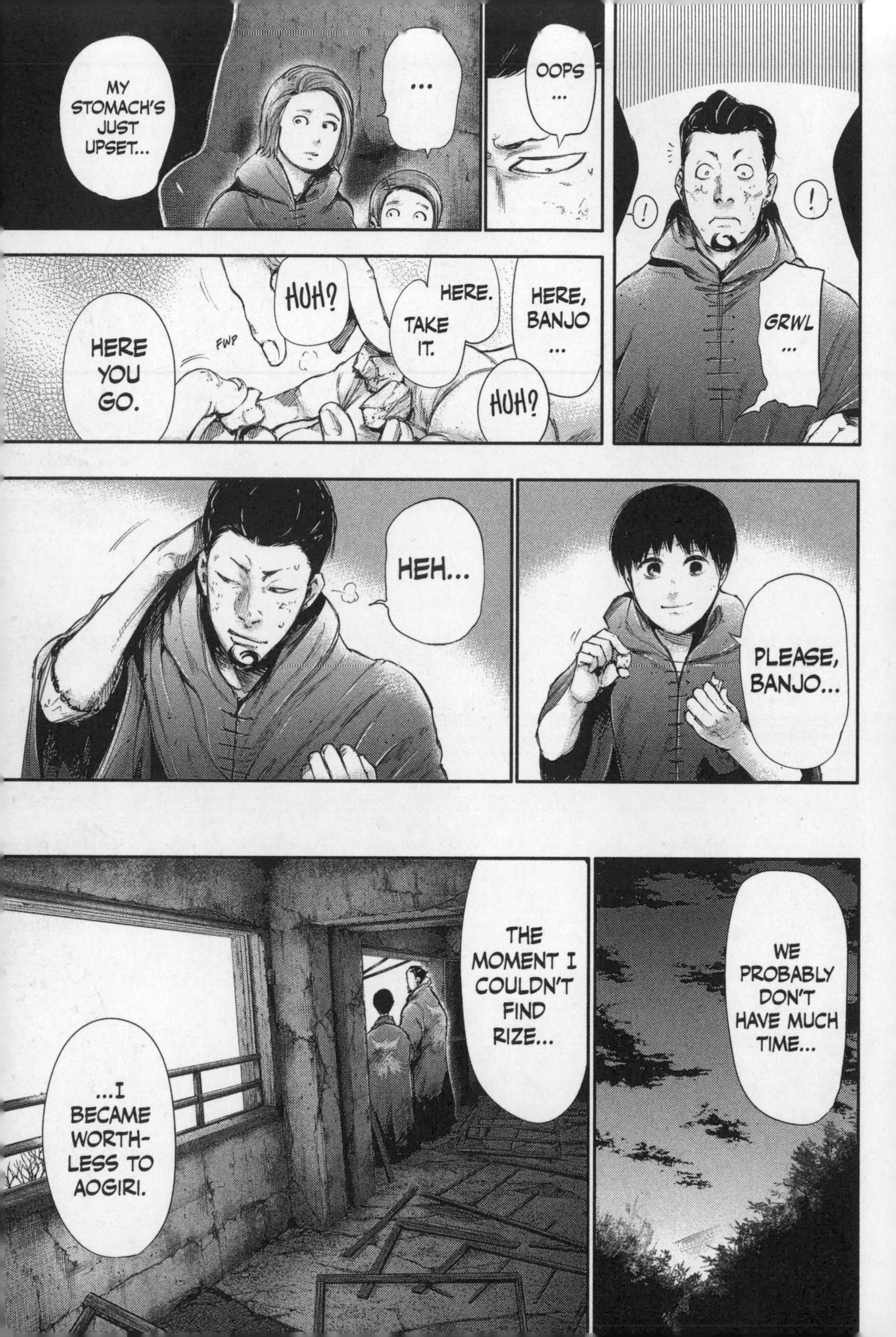
!
!
GRWL ...
OOPS ...
...
MY STOMACH'S JUST UPSET...
HERE, BANJO ...
HUH?
HERE. TAKE IT.
HUH?
FWP
HERE YOU GO.
PLEASE, BANJO...
HEH...
WE PROBABLY DON'T HAVE MUCH TIME...
THE MOMENT I COULDN'T FIND RIZE...
...I BECAME WORTH-LESS TO AOGIRI.

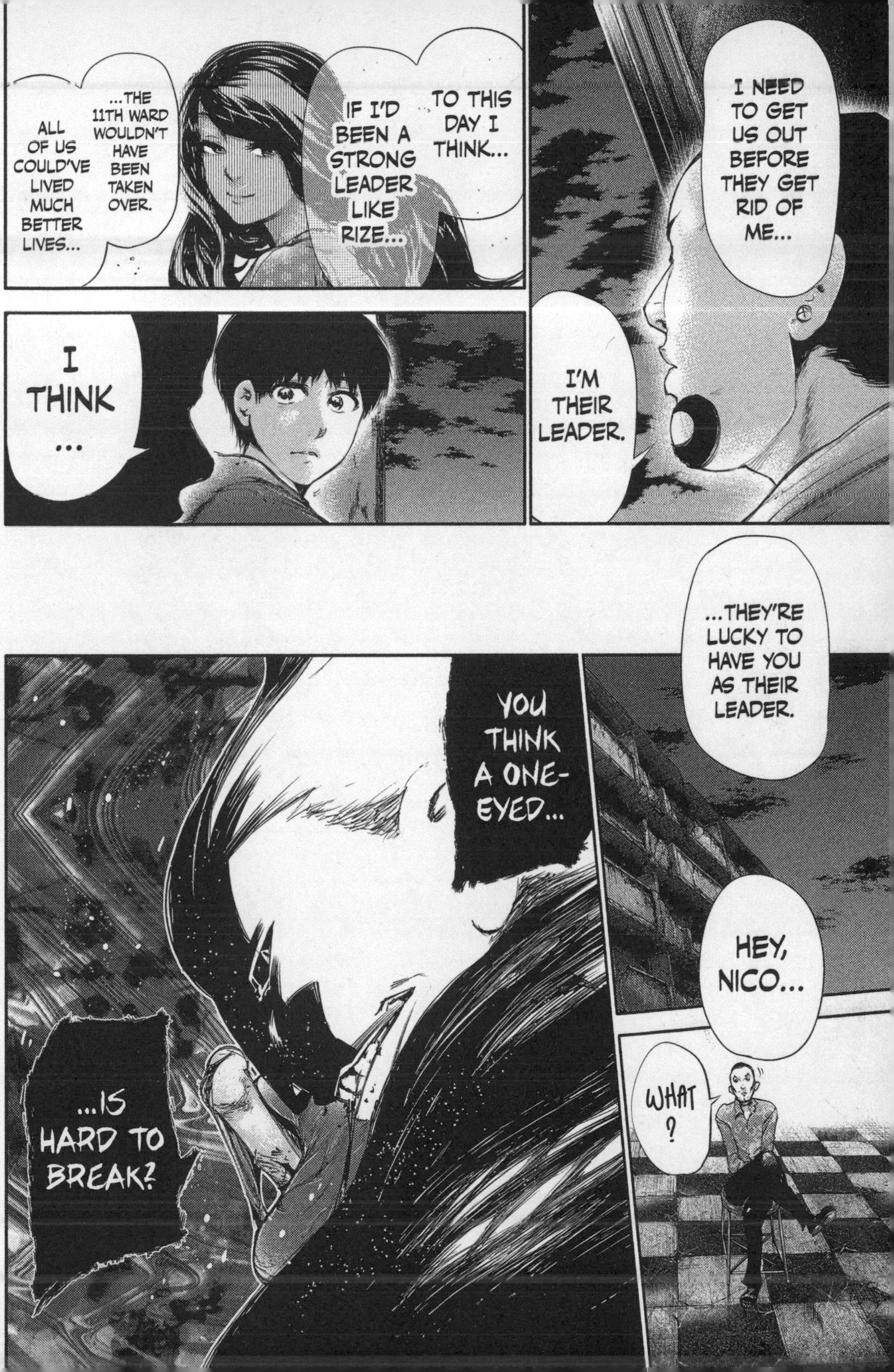
I NEED TO GET US OUT BEFORE THEY GET RID OF ME...
I'M THEIR LEADER.
TO THIS DAY I THINK...
IF I'D BEEN A STRONG LEADER LIKE RIZE...
...THE 11TH WARD WOULDN'T HAVE BEEN TAKEN OVER.
ALL OF US COULD'VE LIVED MUCH BETTER LIVES...
I THINK ...
...THEY'RE LUCKY TO HAVE YOU AS THEIR LEADER.
HEY, NICO...
WHAT ?
YOU THINK A ONE-EYED...
...IS HARD TO BREAK?

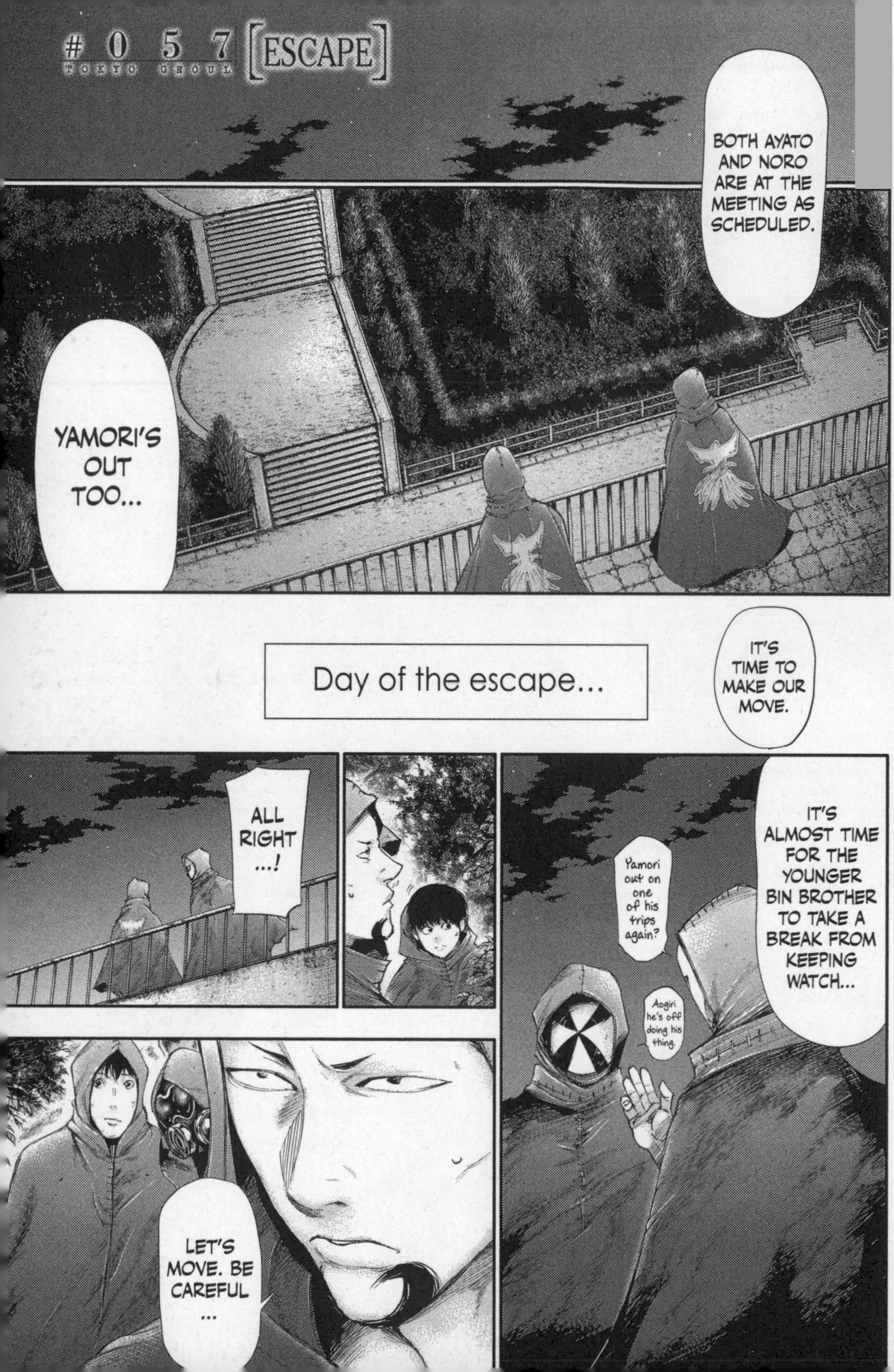
#057 [ESCAPE]
TOKYO GHOUL
BOTH AYATO AND NORO ARE AT THE MEETING AS SCHEDULED.
YAMORI'S OUT TOO...
IT'S TIME TO MAKE OUR MOVE.
Day of the escape...
IT'S ALMOST TIME FOR THE YOUNGER BIN BROTHER TO TAKE A BREAK FROM KEEPING WATCH...
Yamori out on one of his trips again?
Aogiri he's off doing his thing.
ALL RIGHT ...!
LET'S MOVE. BE CAREFUL ...

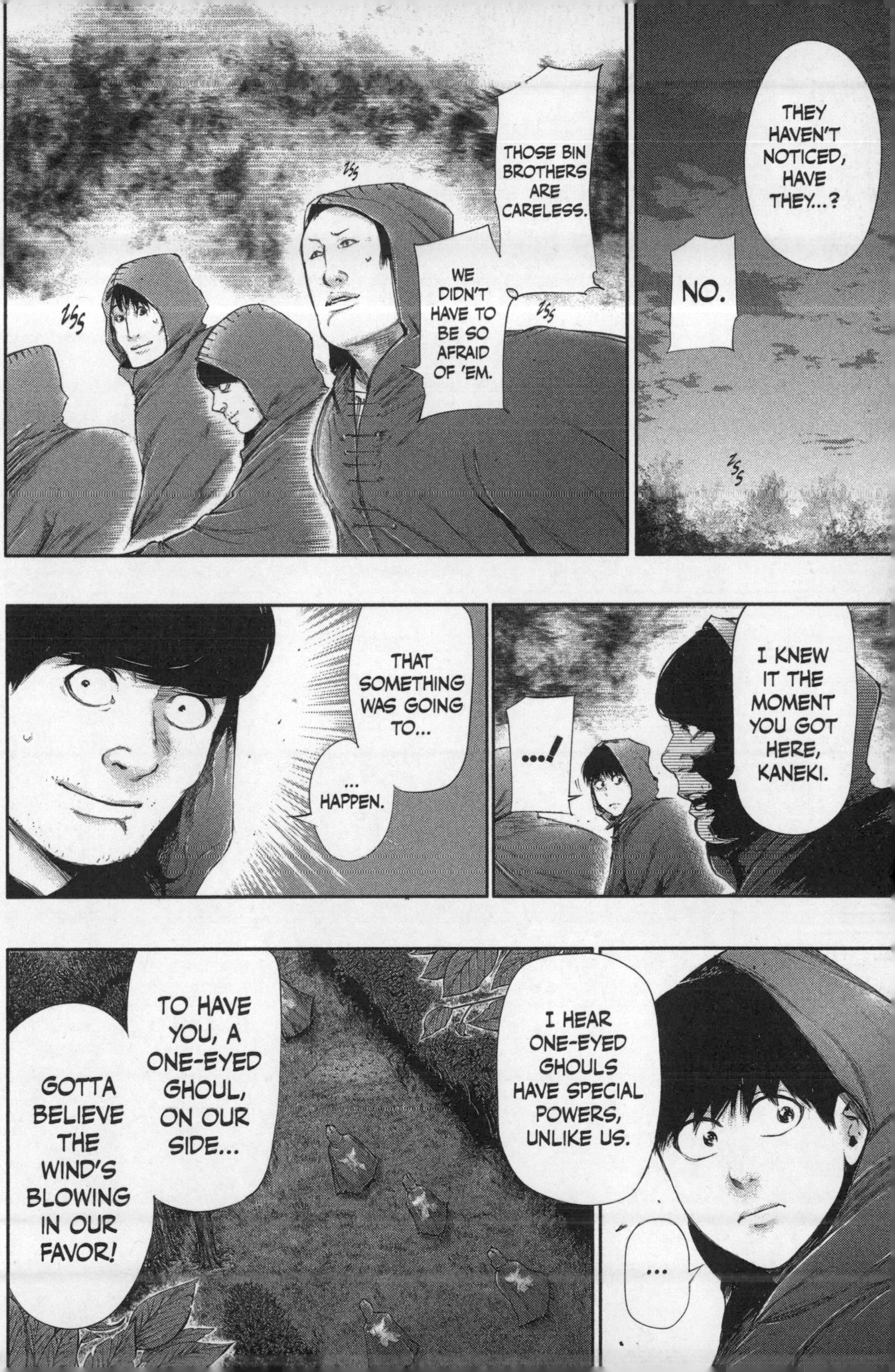
THEY HAVEN'T NOTICED, HAVE THEY...?
NO.
THOSE BIN BROTHERS ARE CARELESS.
WE DIDN'T HAVE TO BE SO AFRAID OF 'EM.
I KNEW IT THE MOMENT YOU GOT HERE, KANEKI.
...!
THAT SOMETHING WAS GOING TO...
... HAPPEN.
I HEAR ONE-EYED GHOULS HAVE SPECIAL POWERS, UNLIKE US.
...
TO HAVE YOU, A ONE-EYED GHOUL, ON OUR SIDE...
GOTTA BELIEVE THE WIND'S BLOWING IN OUR FAVOR!

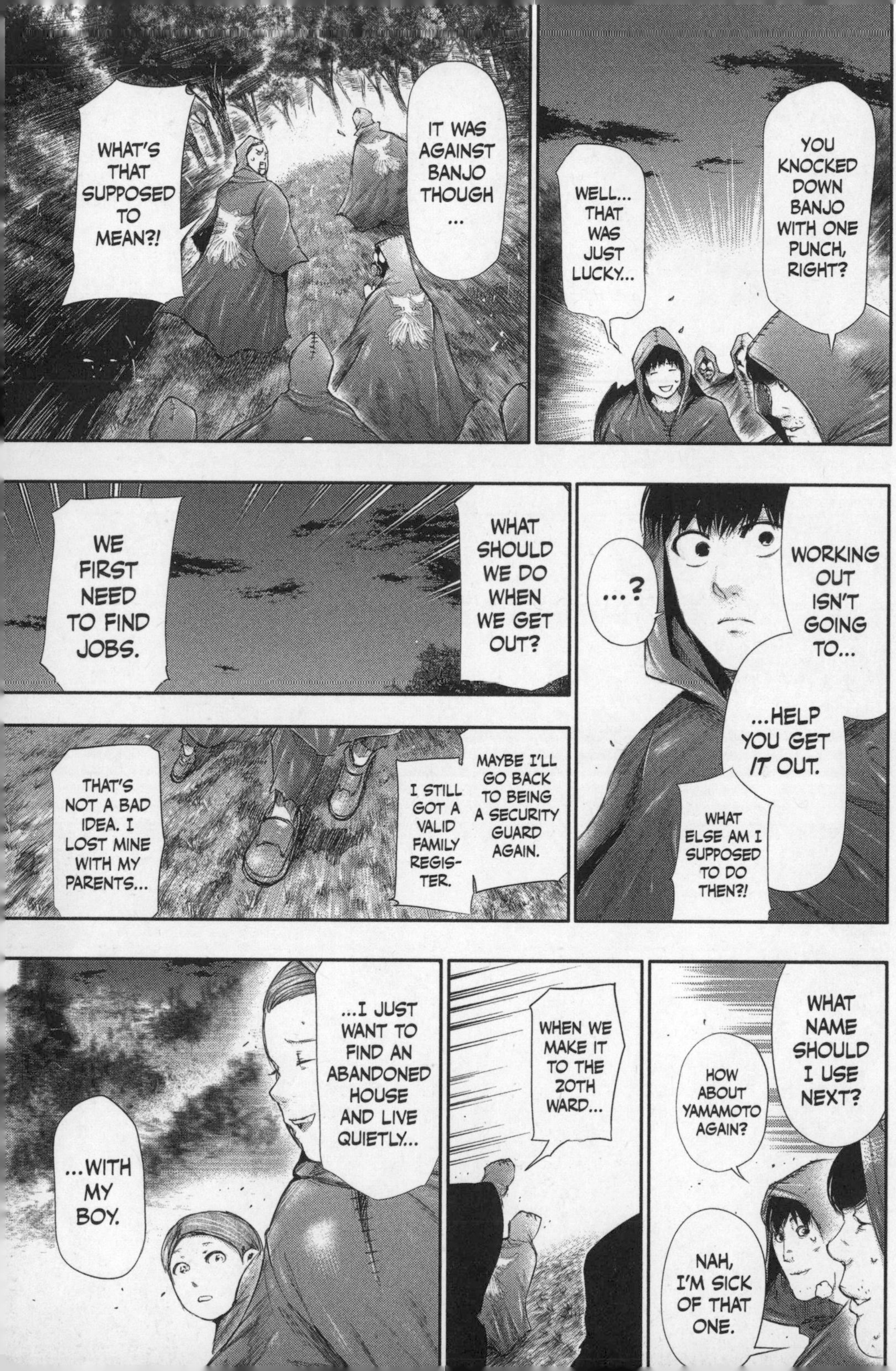
YOU KNOCKED DOWN BANJO WITH ONE PUNCH, RIGHT?
WELL... THAT WAS JUST LUCKY...
IT WAS AGAINST BANJO THOUGH...
WHAT'S THAT SUPPOSED TO MEAN?!
WORKING OUT ISN'T GOING TO...
...HELP YOU GET *IT* OUT.
WHAT ELSE AM I SUPPOSED TO DO THEN?!
...?
WHAT SHOULD WE DO WHEN WE GET OUT?
WE FIRST NEED TO FIND JOBS.
MAYBE I'LL GO BACK TO BEING A SECURITY GUARD AGAIN.
I STILL GOT A VALID FAMILY REGIS-TER.
THAT'S NOT A BAD IDEA. I LOST MINE WITH MY PARENTS...
WHAT NAME SHOULD I USE NEXT?
HOW ABOUT YAMAMOTO AGAIN?
NAH, I'M SICK OF THAT ONE.
WHEN WE MAKE IT TO THE 20TH WARD...
...I JUST WANT TO FIND AN ABANDONED HOUSE AND LIVE QUIETLY...
...WITH MY BOY.

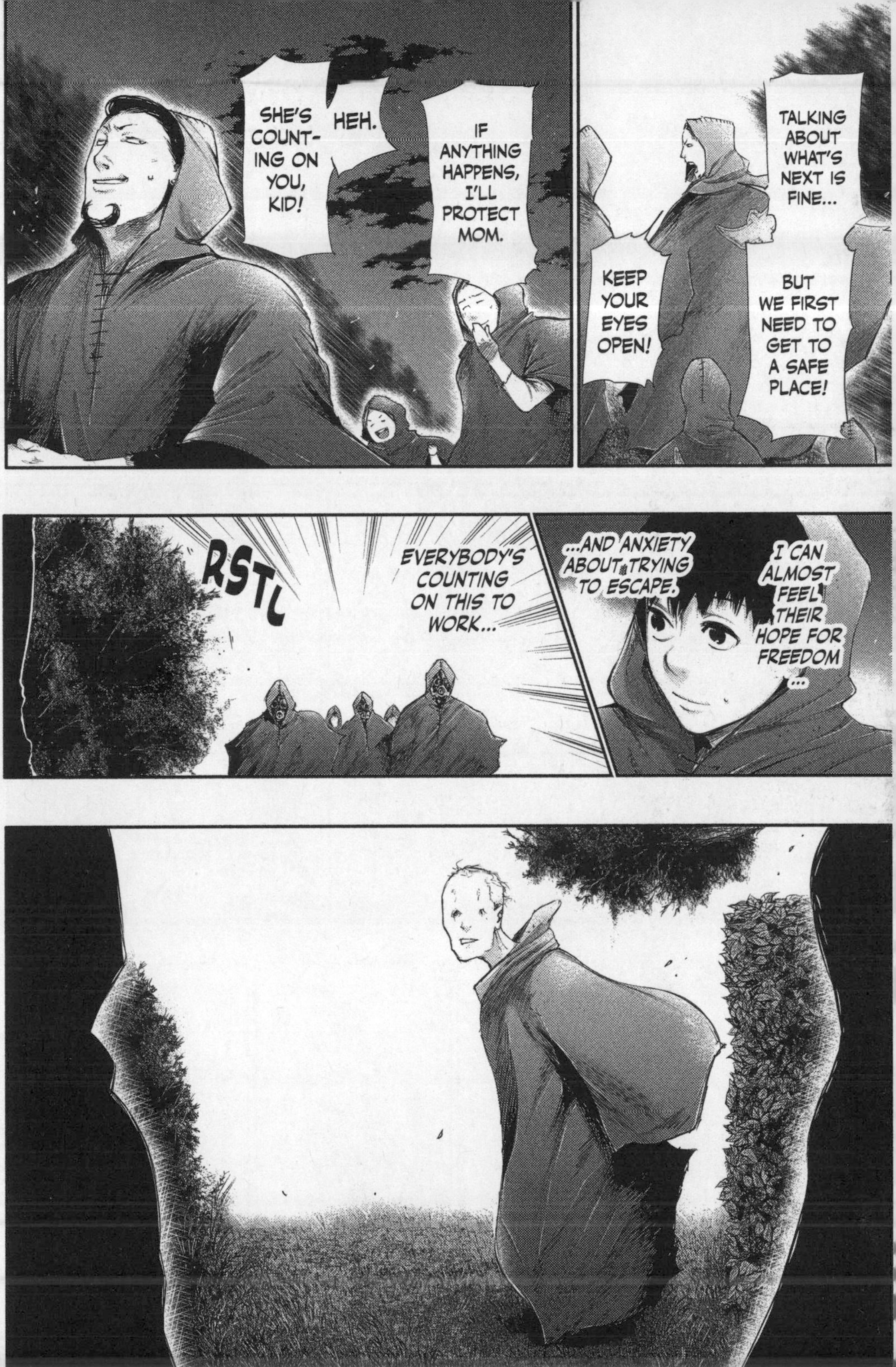
TALKING ABOUT WHAT'S NEXT IS FINE...
BUT WE FIRST NEED TO GET TO A SAFE PLACE!
KEEP YOUR EYES OPEN!
IF ANYTHING HAPPENS, I'LL PROTECT MOM.
HEH.
SHE'S COUNTING ON YOU, KID!
I CAN ALMOST FEEL THEIR HOPE FOR FREEDOM...
...AND ANXIETY ABOUT TRYING TO ESCAPE.
EVERYBODY'S COUNTING ON THIS TO WORK...
RSTL

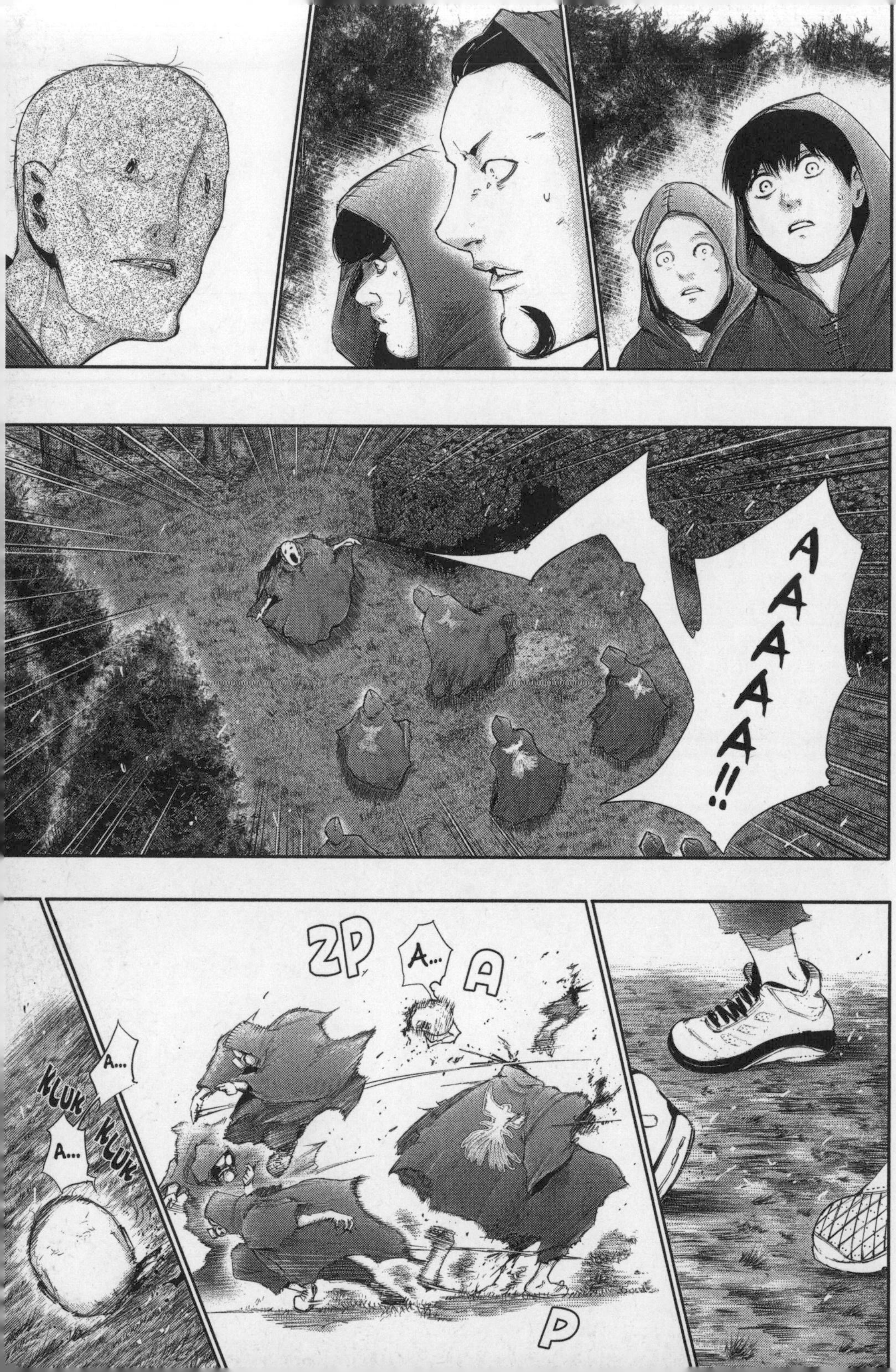
AAAAA!!
A
A...
ZP
A...
KLUK
KLUK
A...
P

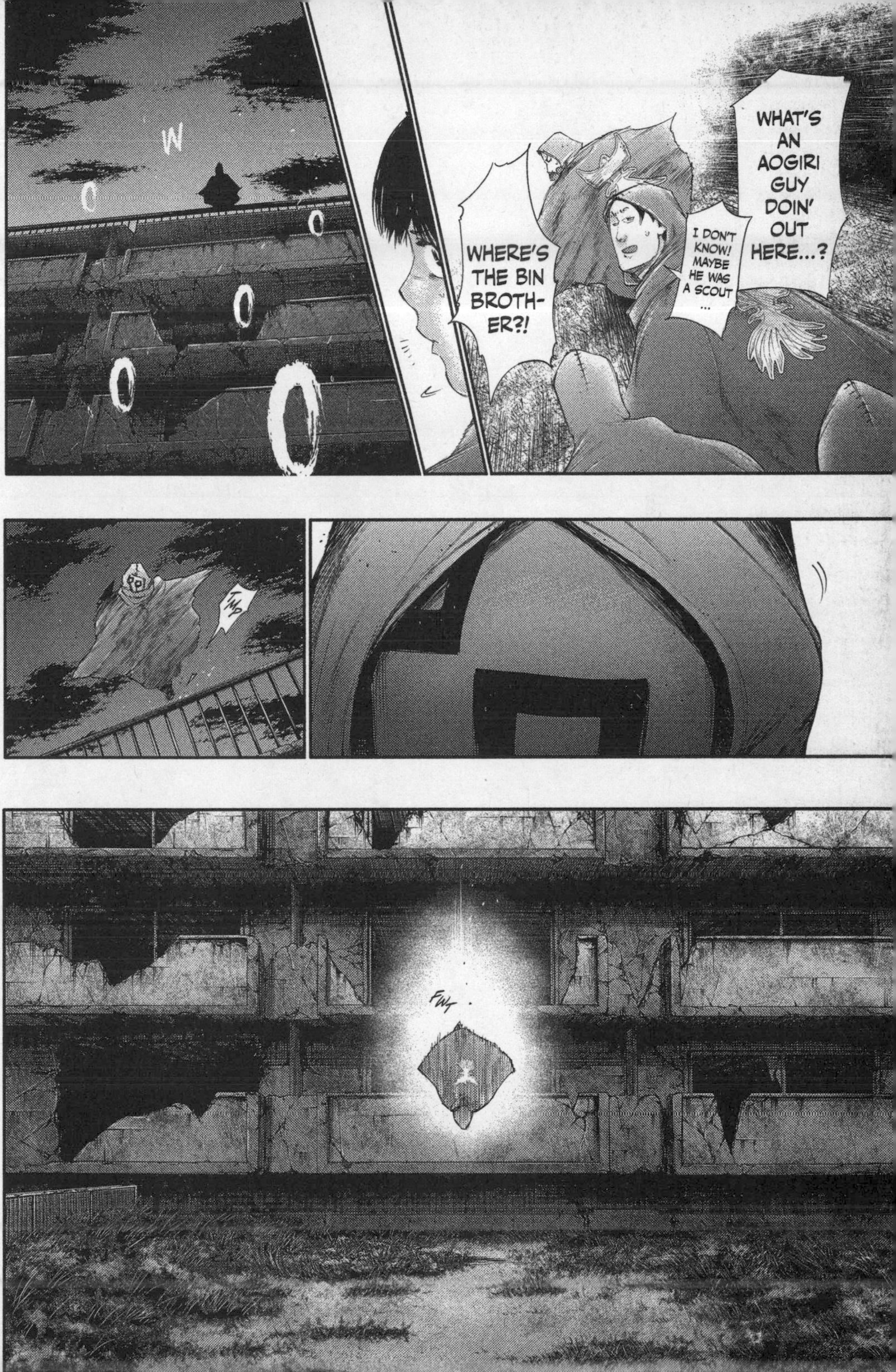
WHAT'S AN AOGIRI GUY DOIN' OUT HERE...?
I DON'T KNOW! MAYBE HE WAS A SCOUT ...
WHERE'S THE BIN BROTHER?!
WOOOOO
TMP
FWT

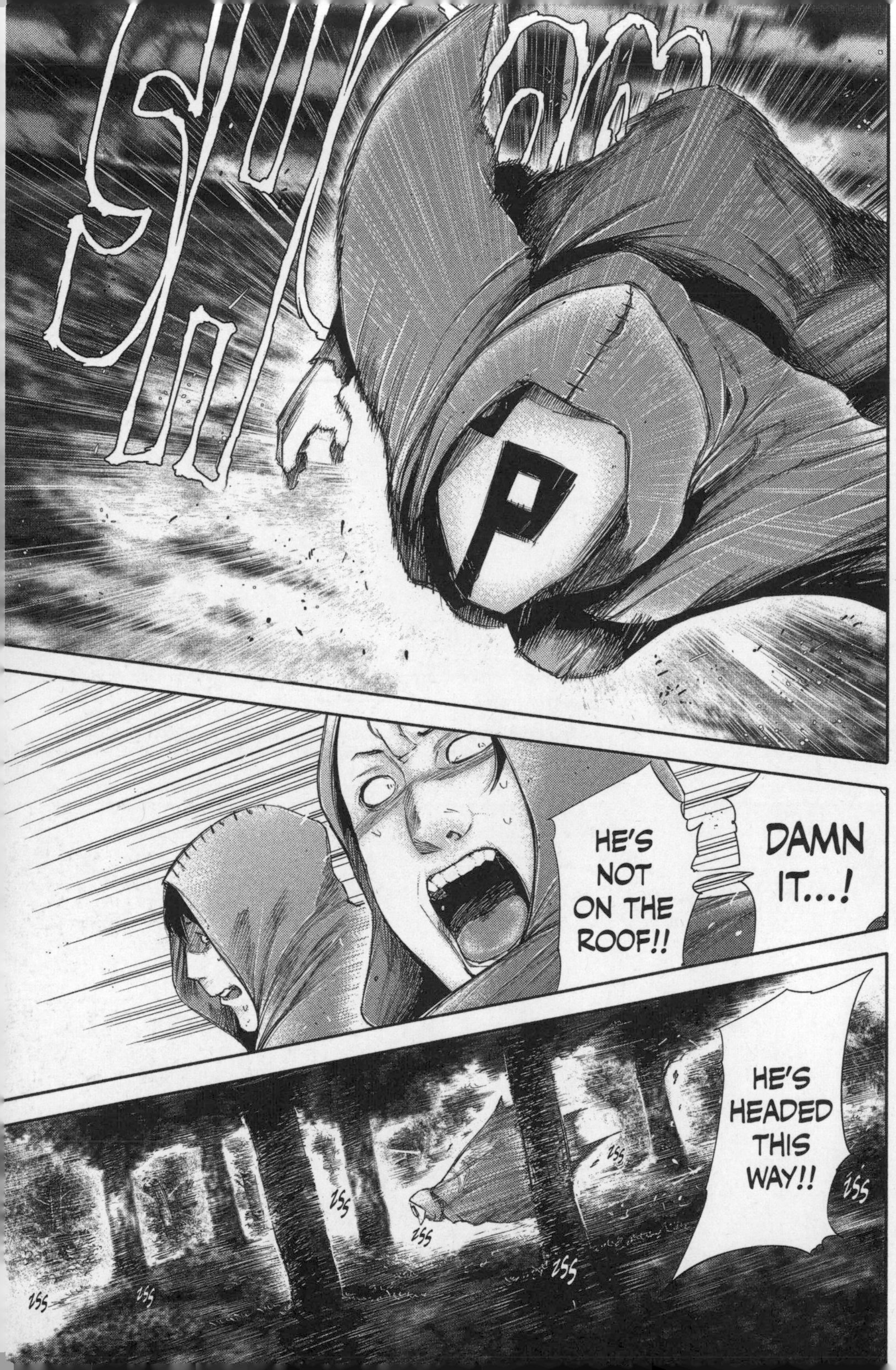
DAMN IT...!
HE'S NOT ON THE ROOF!!
HE'S HEADED THIS WAY!!
zss
zss
zss
zss
zss
zss
zss

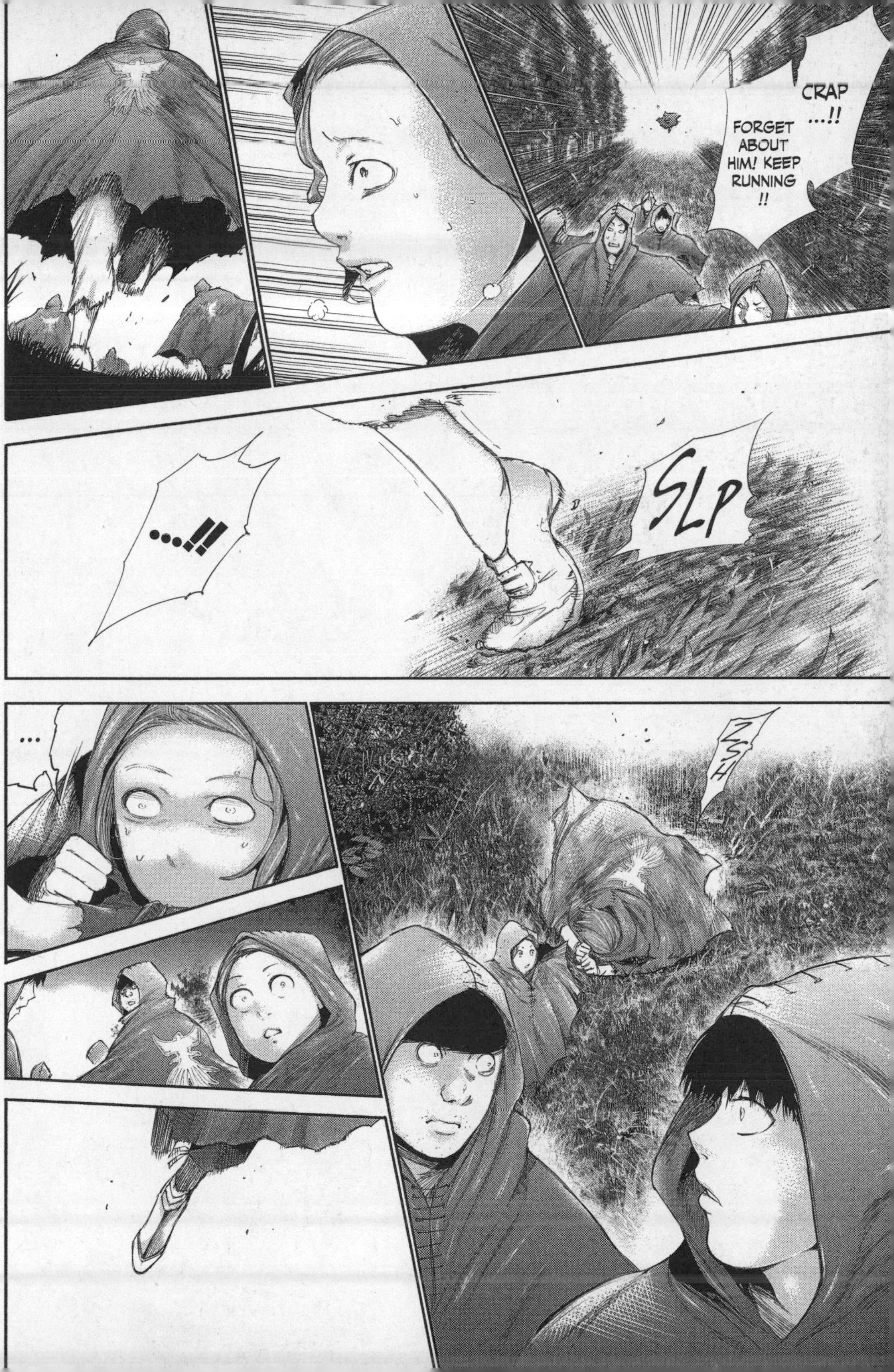
CRAP ...!!
FORGET ABOUT HIM! KEEP RUNNING !!
SLP
...!!
ZSH
...

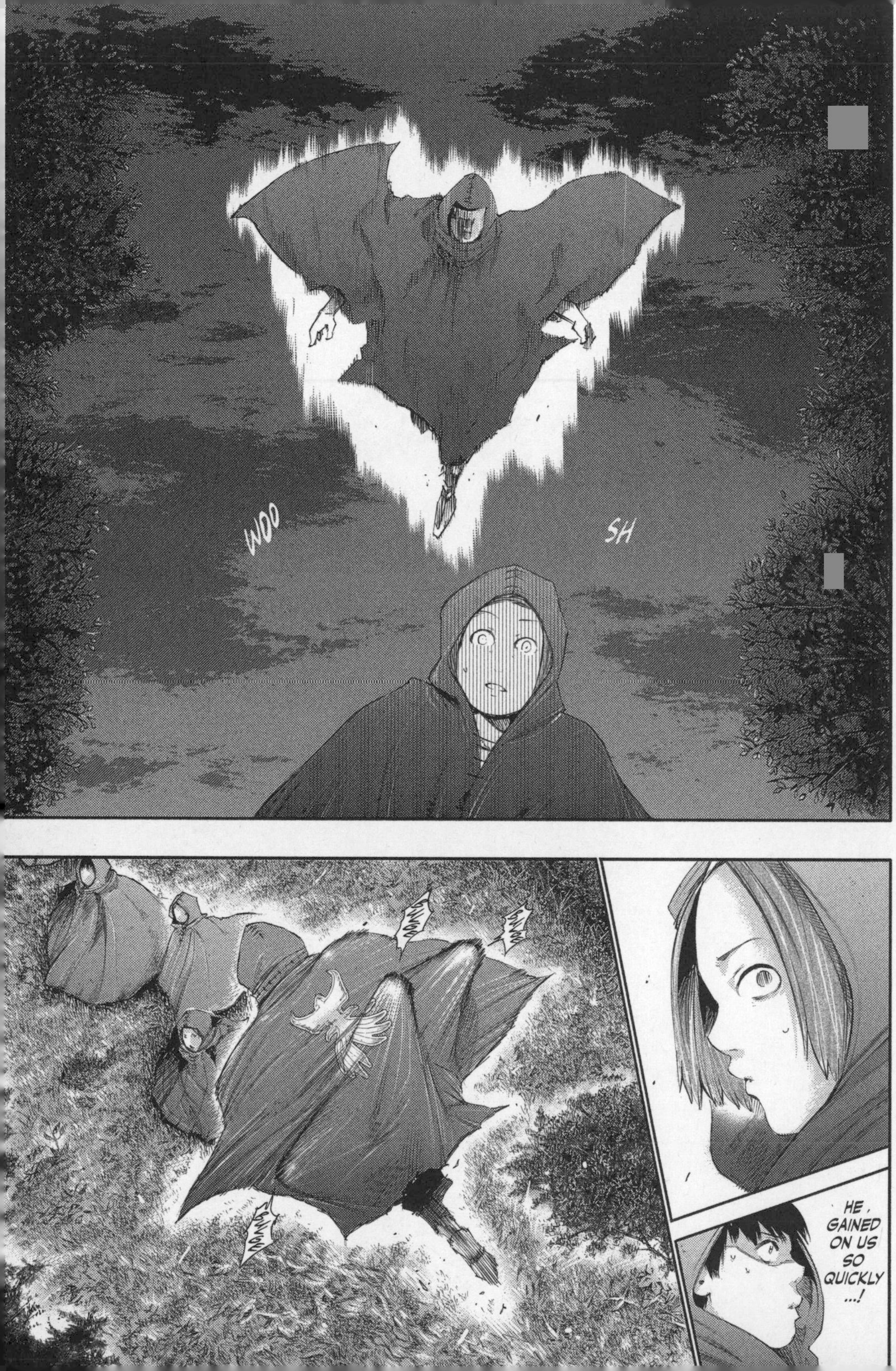
WOO
SH
HE, GAINED ON US SO QUICKLY ...!
billow
billow
billow

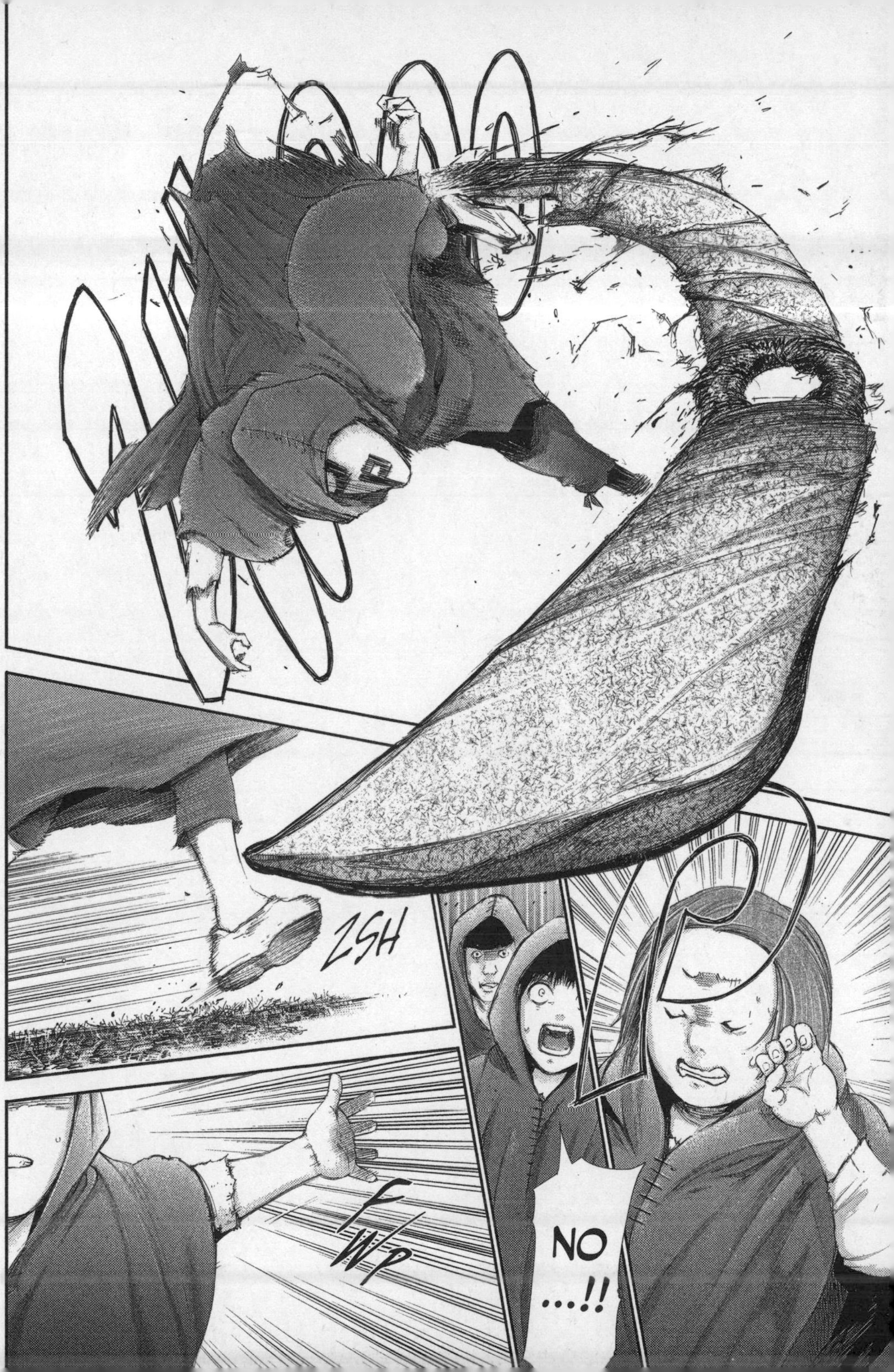
ZSH
NO
...!!
FWP

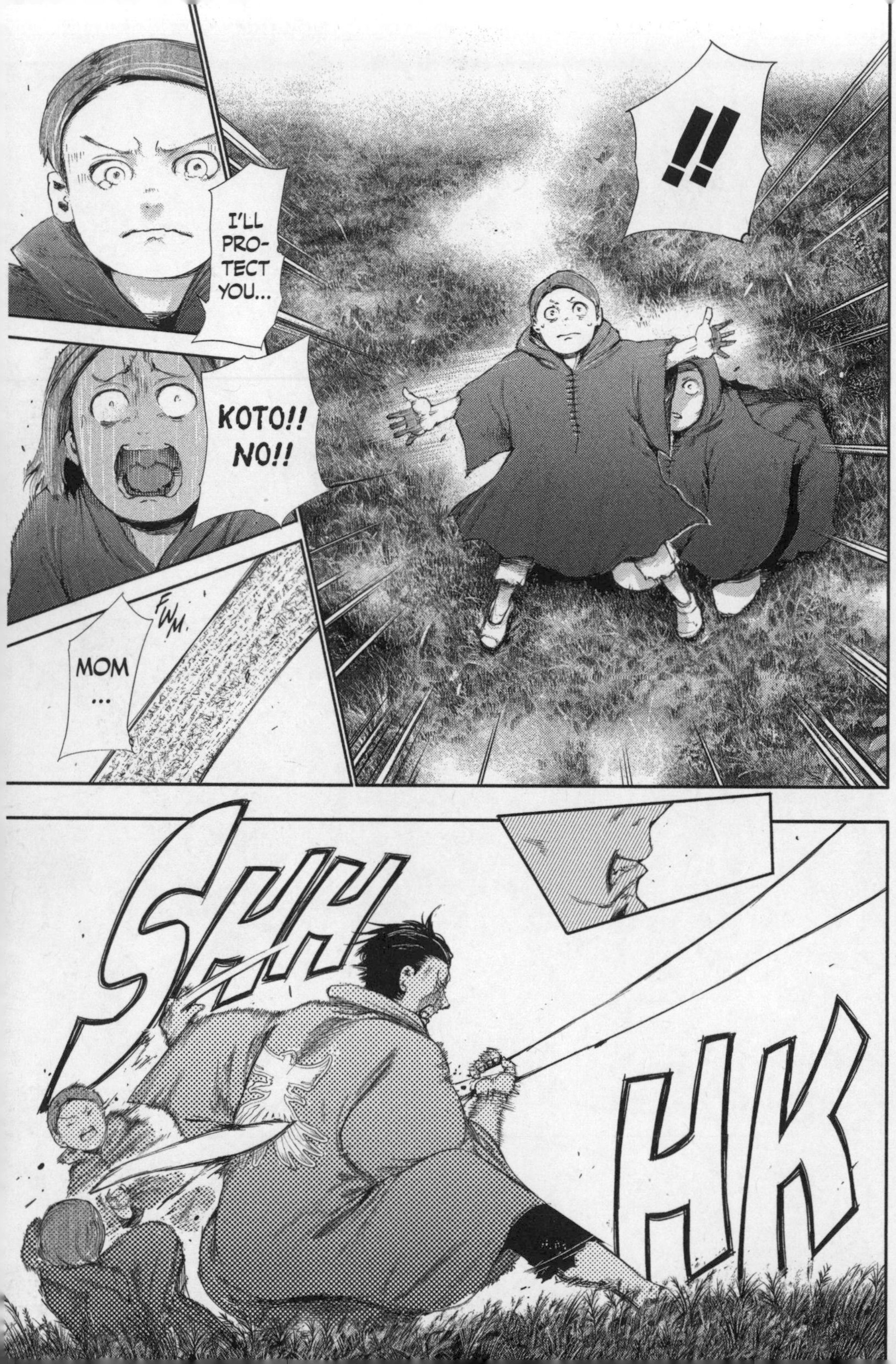
!!
I'LL PROTECT YOU...
KOTO!! NO!!
FWM
MOM ...
SHH
HK

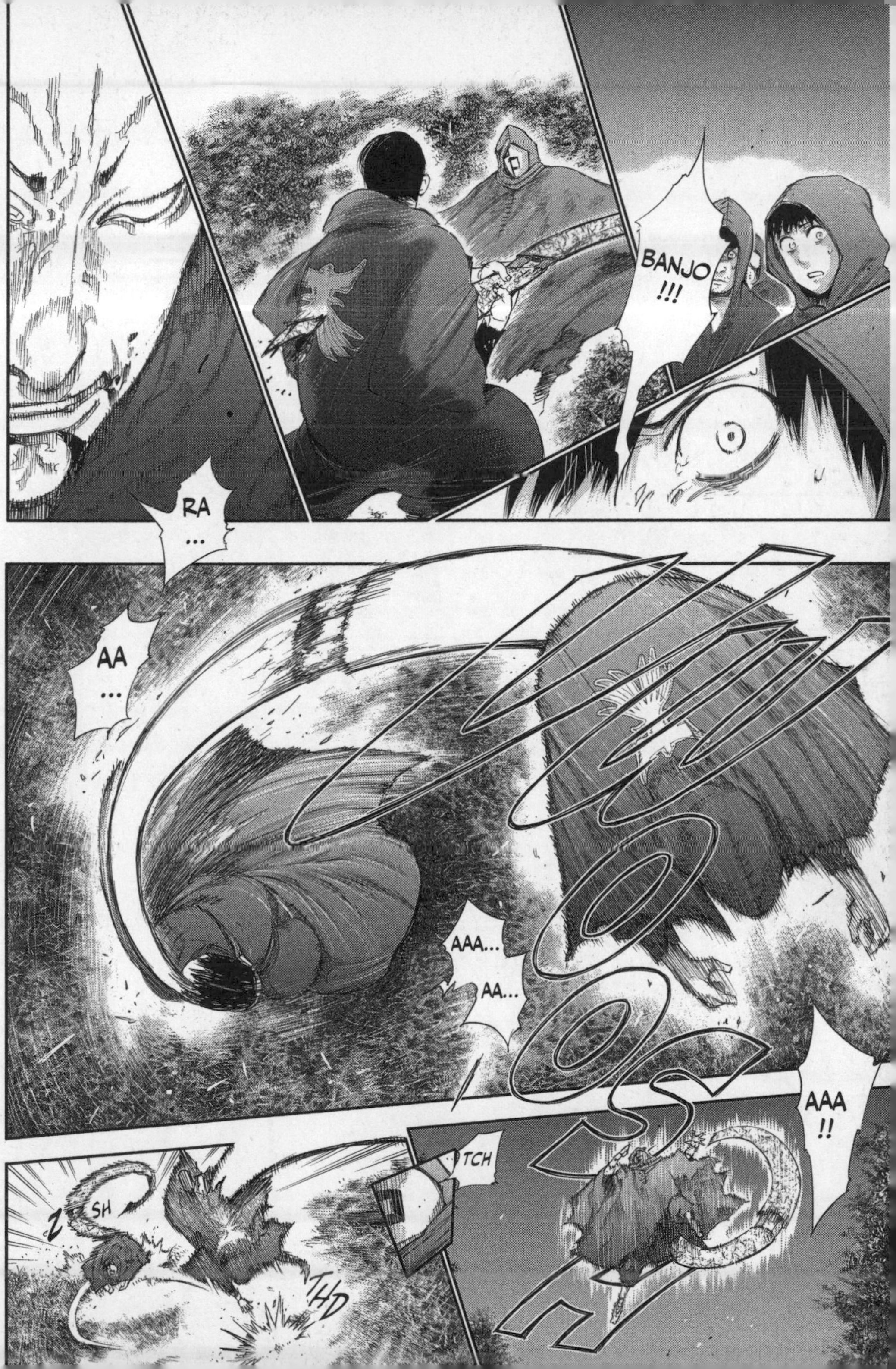
BANJO !!!
RA ...
AA ...
AAA...
AA...
AAA !!
TCH
Z
SH
THD

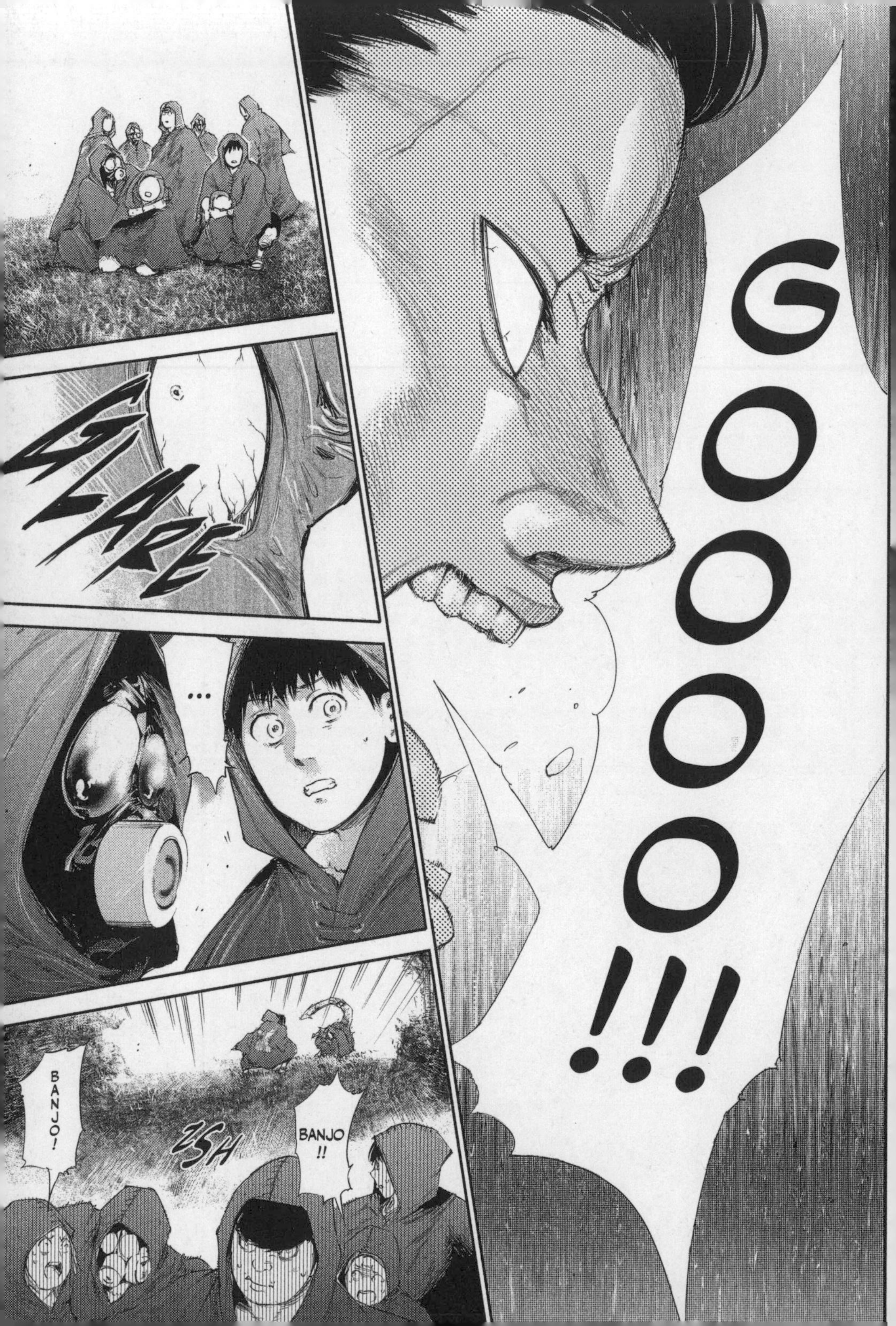
GOOOOO!!!
GLARE
...
BANJO !!
ZSH
BANJO!

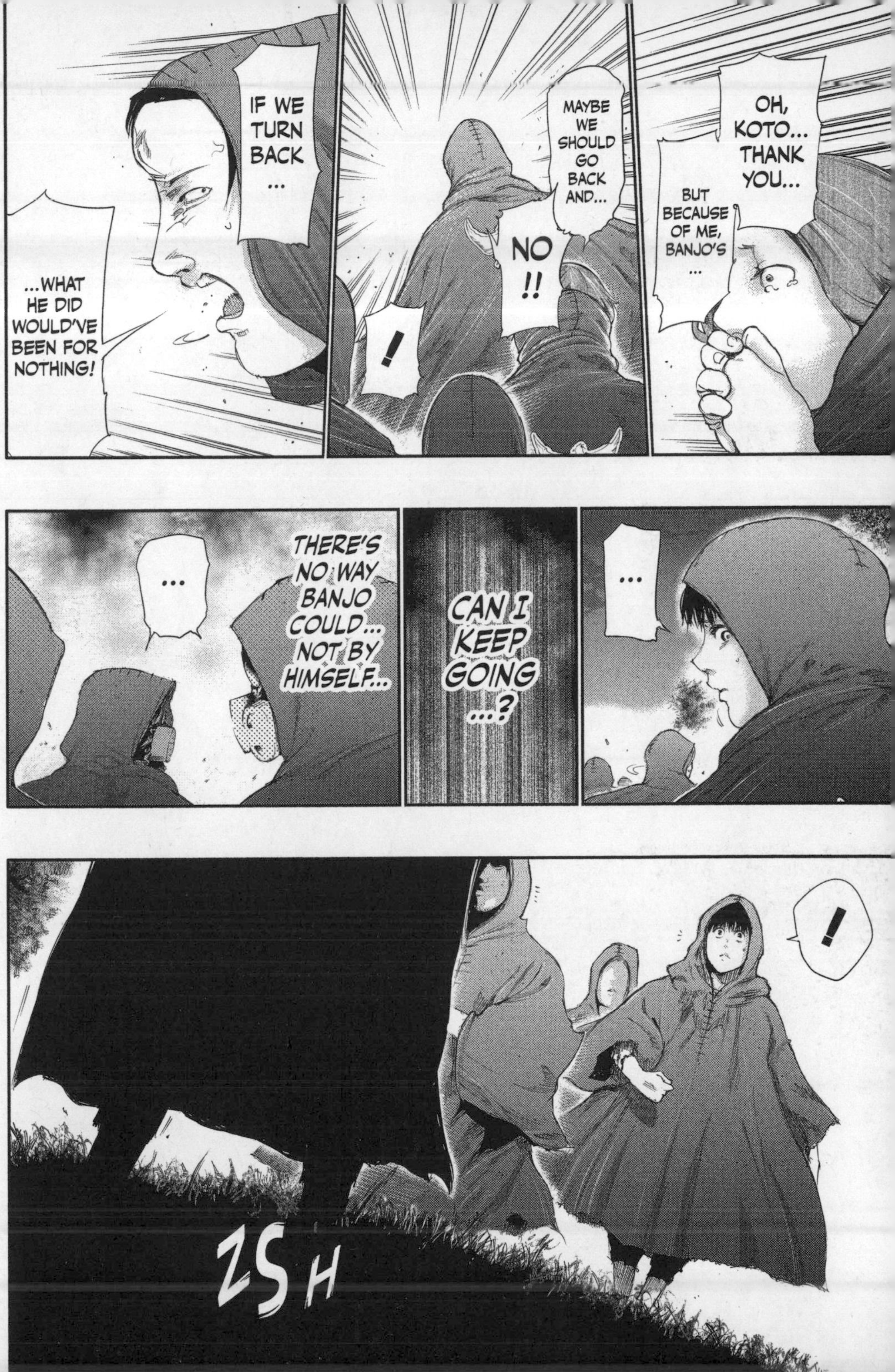
OH, KOTO... THANK YOU...
BUT BECAUSE OF ME, BANJO'S ...
MAYBE WE SHOULD GO BACK AND...
NO !!
!
IF WE TURN BACK ...
...WHAT HE DID WOULD'VE BEEN FOR NOTHING!
...
CAN I KEEP GOING ...?
THERE'S NO WAY BANJO COULD... NOT BY HIMSELF...
...
!
ZSH

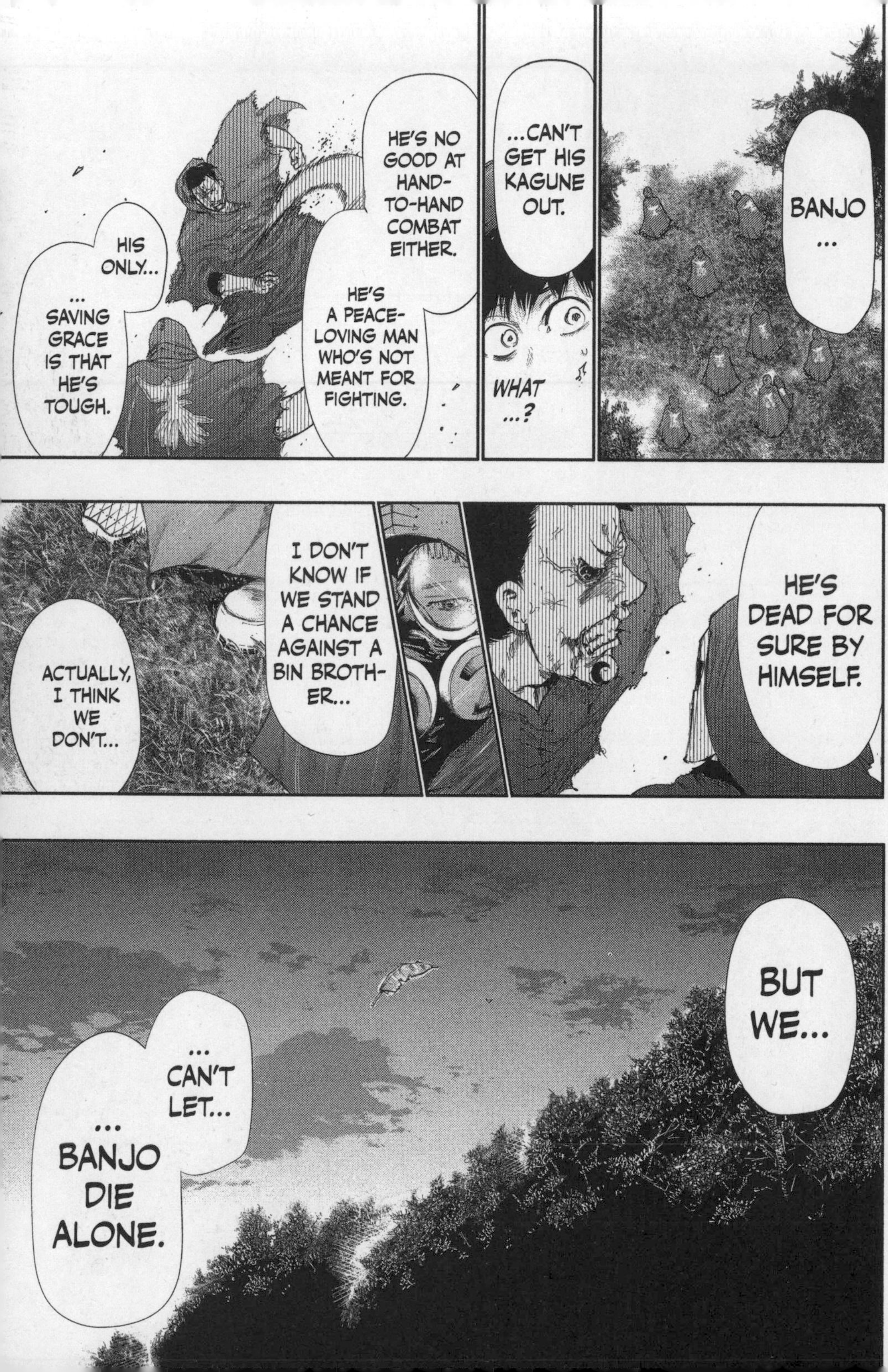
BANJO ...
...CAN'T GET HIS KAGUNE OUT.
WHAT ...?
HE'S NO GOOD AT HAND-TO-HAND COMBAT EITHER.
HE'S A PEACE-LOVING MAN WHO'S NOT MEANT FOR FIGHTING.
HIS ONLY...
... SAVING GRACE IS THAT HE'S TOUGH.
HE'S DEAD FOR SURE BY HIMSELF.
I DON'T KNOW IF WE STAND A CHANCE AGAINST A BIN BROTH-ER...
ACTUALLY, I THINK WE DON'T...
BUT WE...
... CAN'T LET...
... BANJO DIE ALONE.

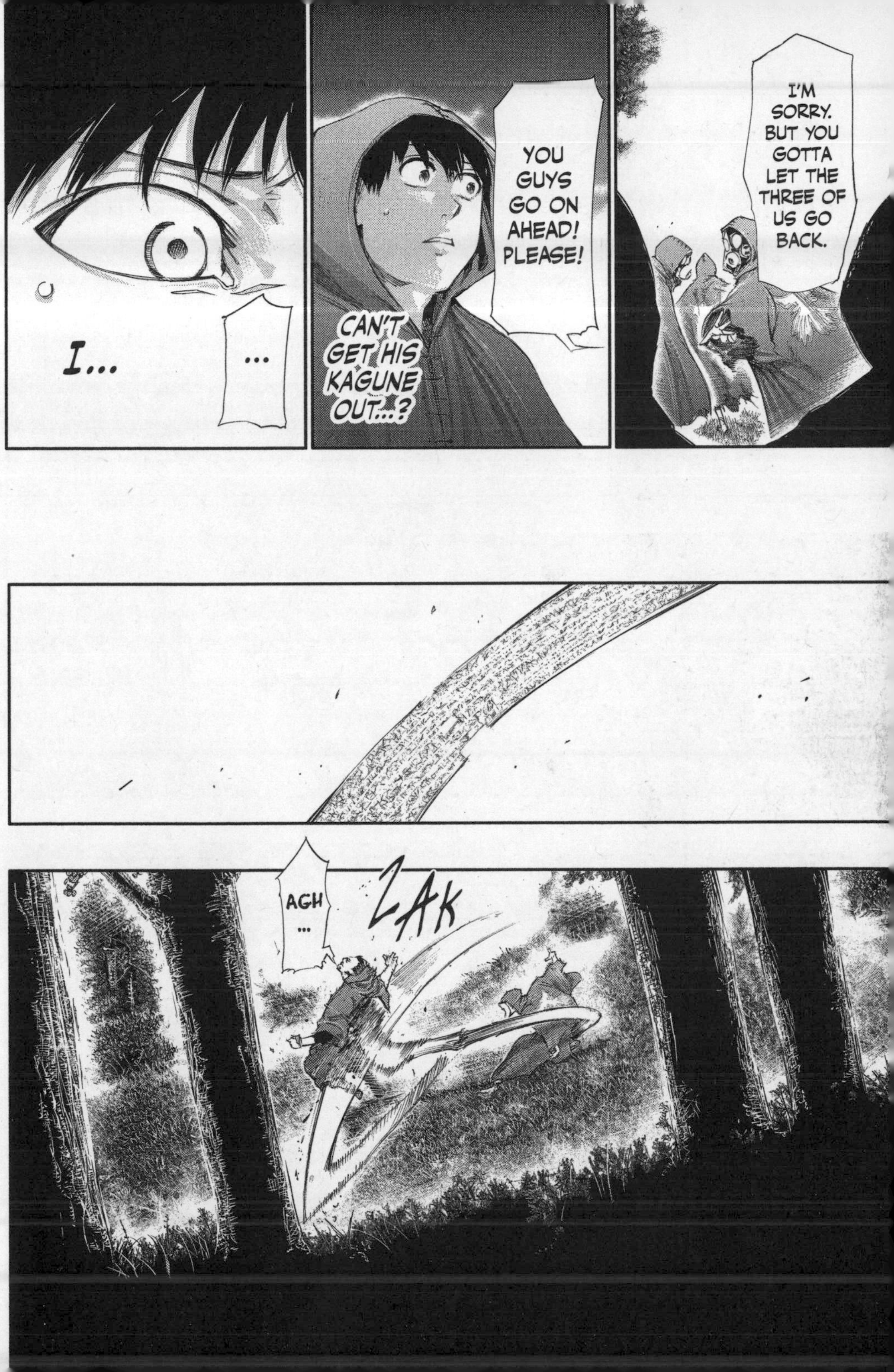
I'M SORRY. BUT YOU GOTTA LET THE THREE OF US GO BACK.
YOU GUYS GO ON AHEAD! PLEASE!
CAN'T GET HIS KAGUNE OUT...?
...
I...
ZAK
AGH ...

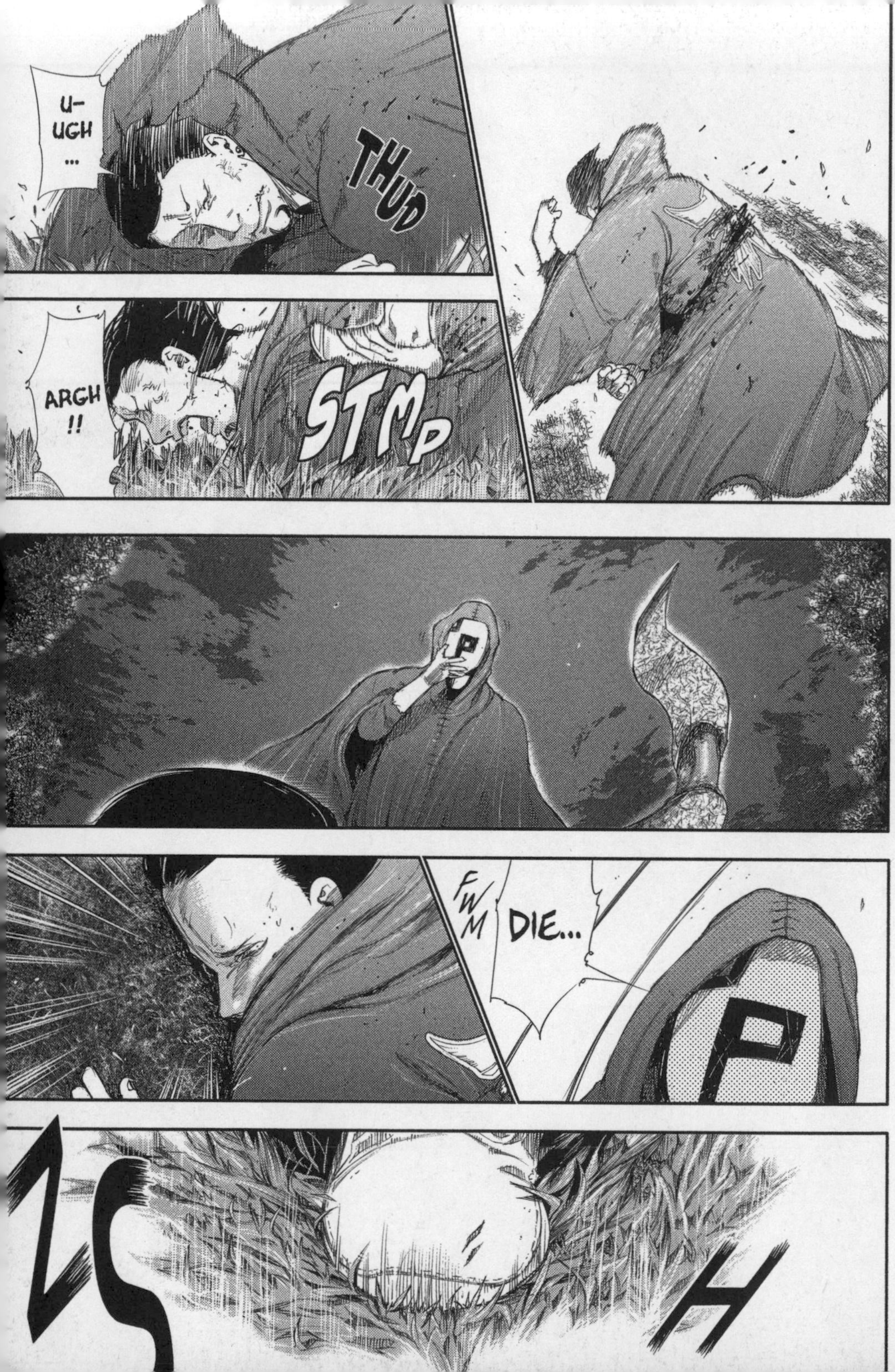

U-UGH ...
THUD
ARGH !!
STMP
FWM
DIE...
ZSH

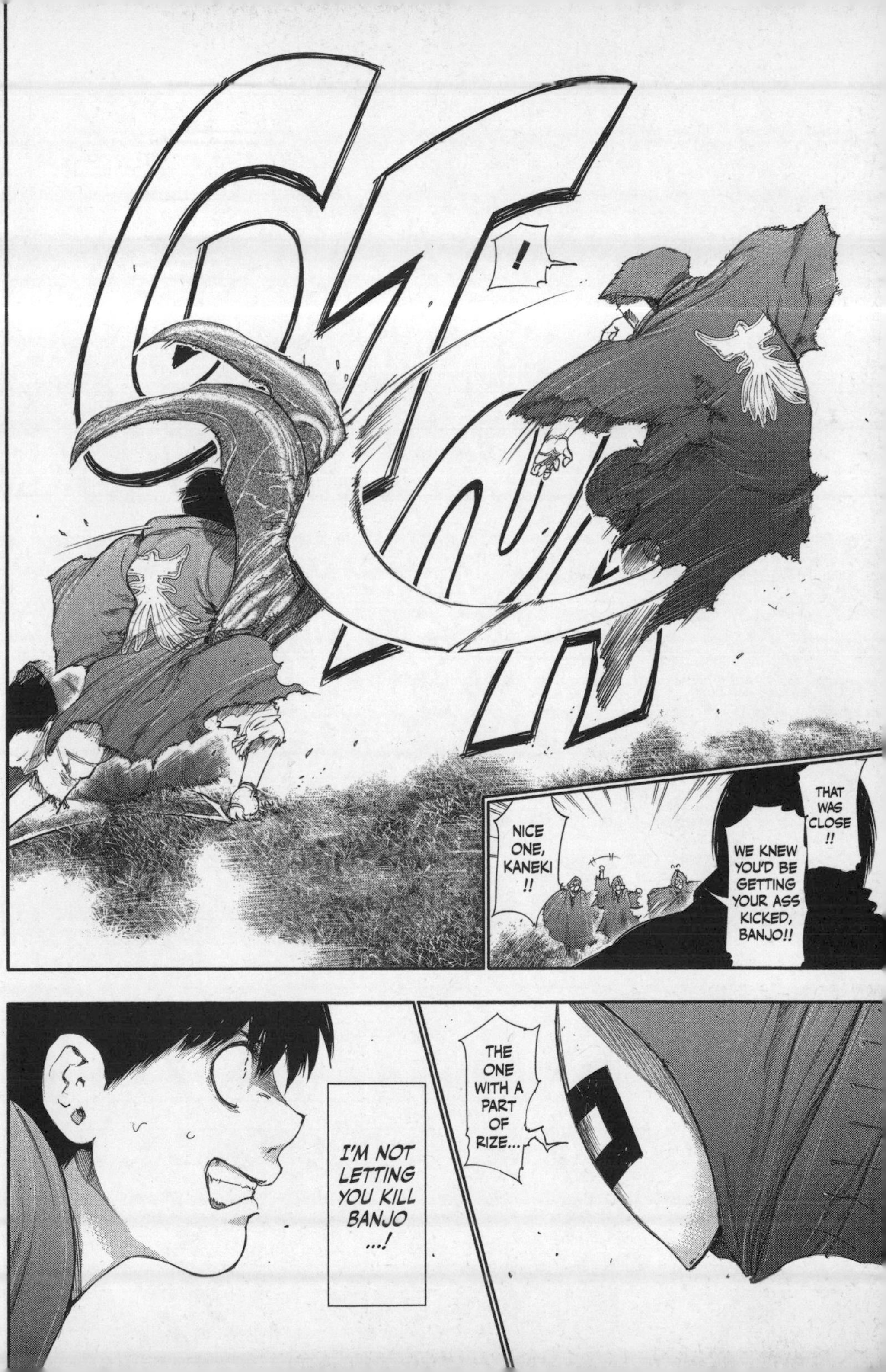
!
THAT WAS CLOSE!!
WE KNEW YOU'D BE GETTING YOUR ASS KICKED, BANJO!!
NICE ONE, KANEKI!!
THE ONE WITH A PART OF RIZE...
I'M NOT LETTING YOU KILL BANJO ...!

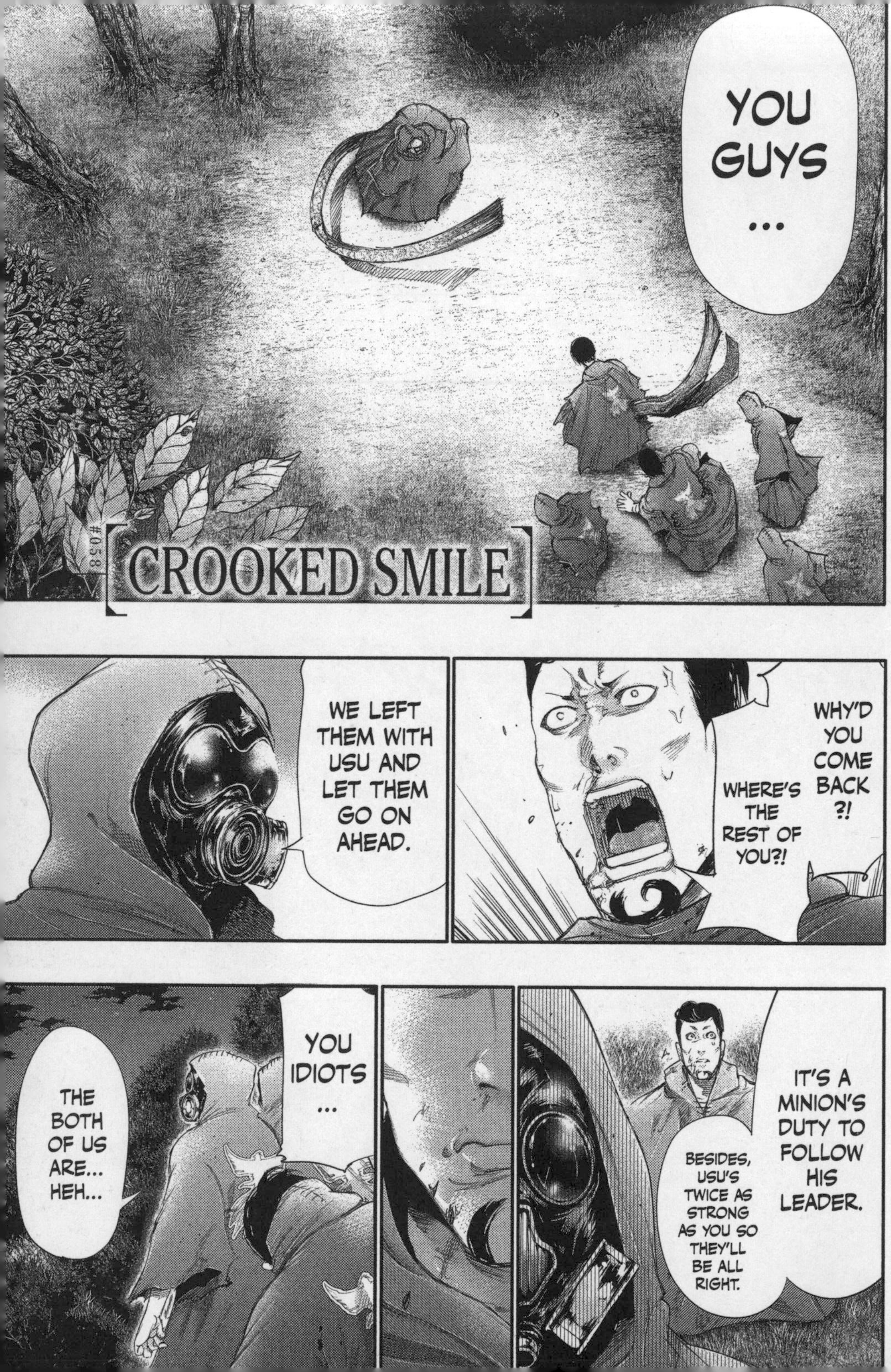
YOU GUYS ...
#058
CROOKED SMILE
WHY'D YOU COME BACK?!
WHERE'S THE REST OF YOU?!
WE LEFT THEM WITH USU AND LET THEM GO ON AHEAD.
IT'S A MINION'S DUTY TO FOLLOW HIS LEADER.
BESIDES, USU'S TWICE AS STRONG AS YOU SO THEY'LL BE ALL RIGHT.
YOU IDIOTS ...
THE BOTH OF US ARE... HEH...

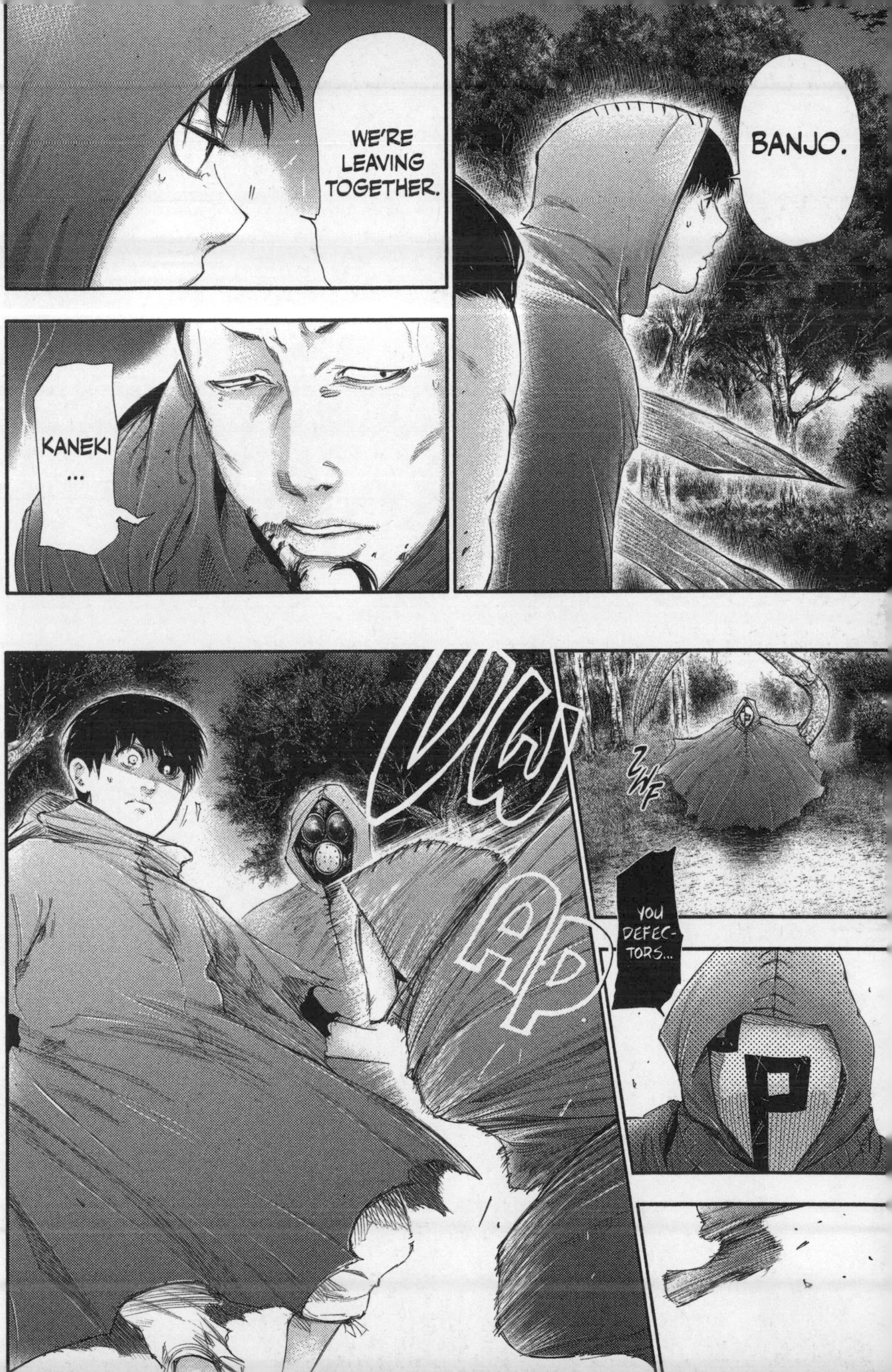
BANJO.
WE'RE LEAVING TOGETHER.
KANEKI ...
ZWF
YOU DEFECTORS...
WAP

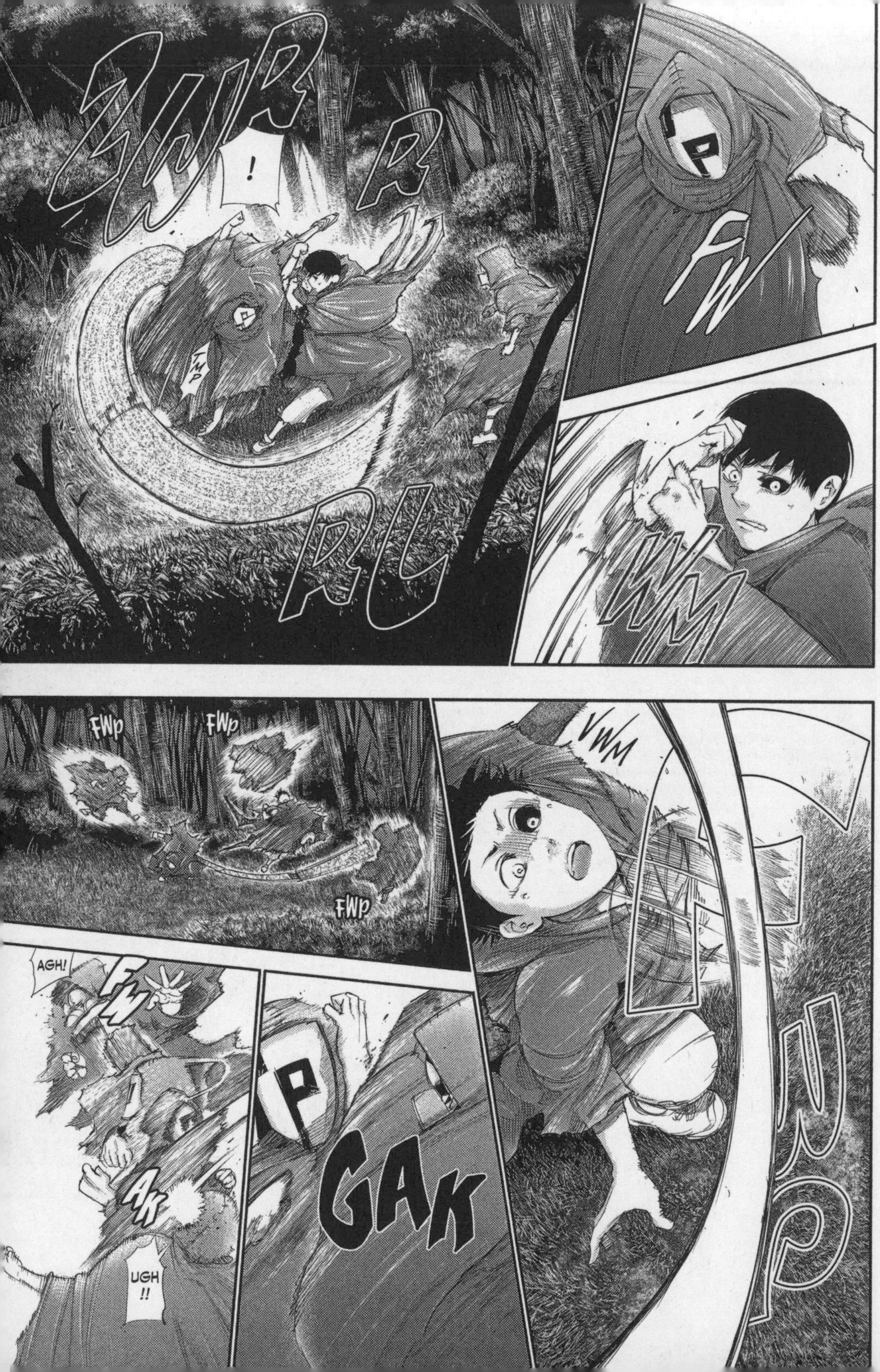
FW
WM
ZWR
!
RR
TMP
RRL
VWM
WRRP
FWp
FWp
FWp
P
GAK
AGH!
FW
!
AK
UGH !!

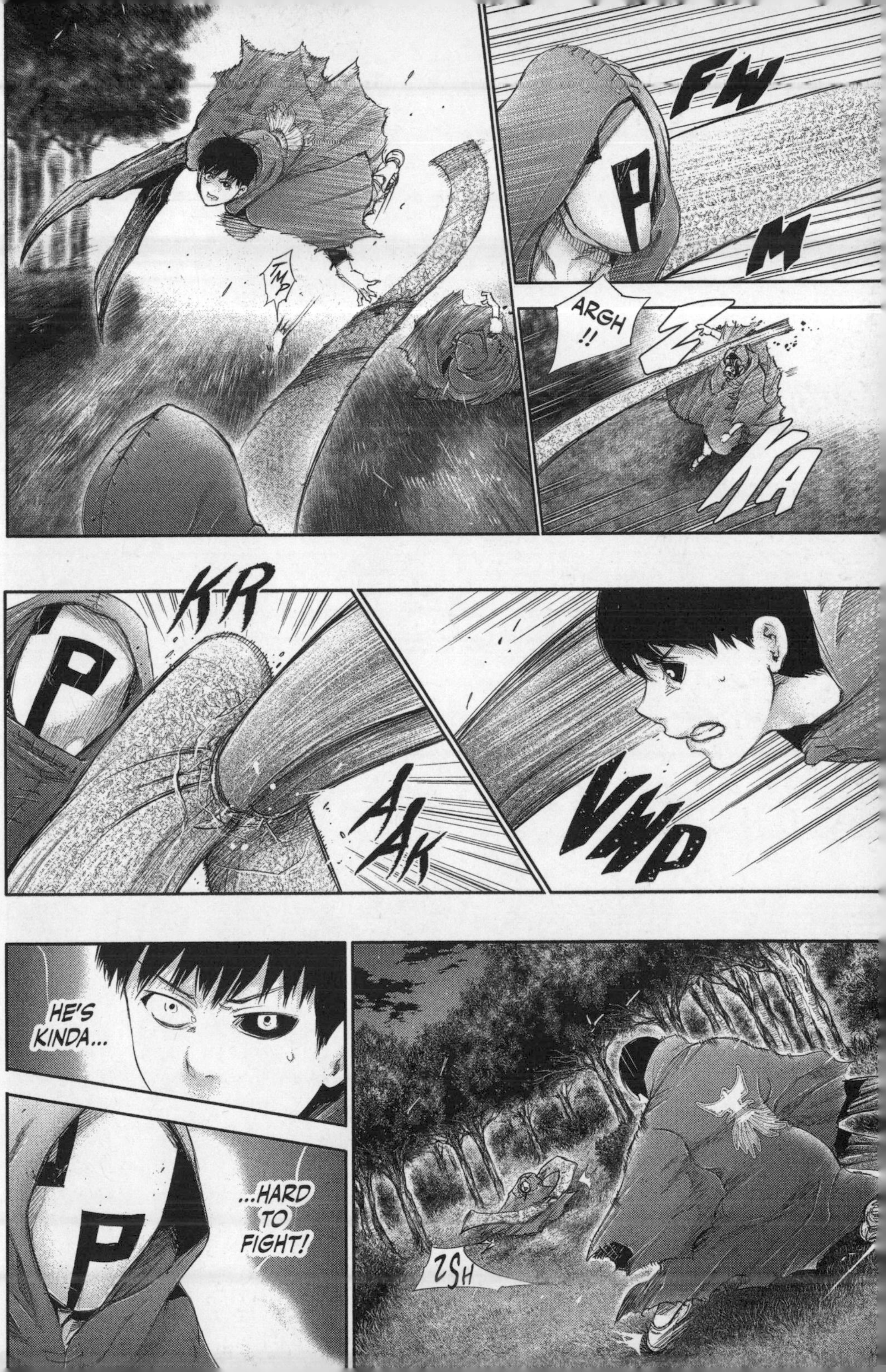
FW
M
ARGH!!
KA
TMP
VWP
KR
AAK
ZSH
HE'S KINDA...
...HARD TO FIGHT!

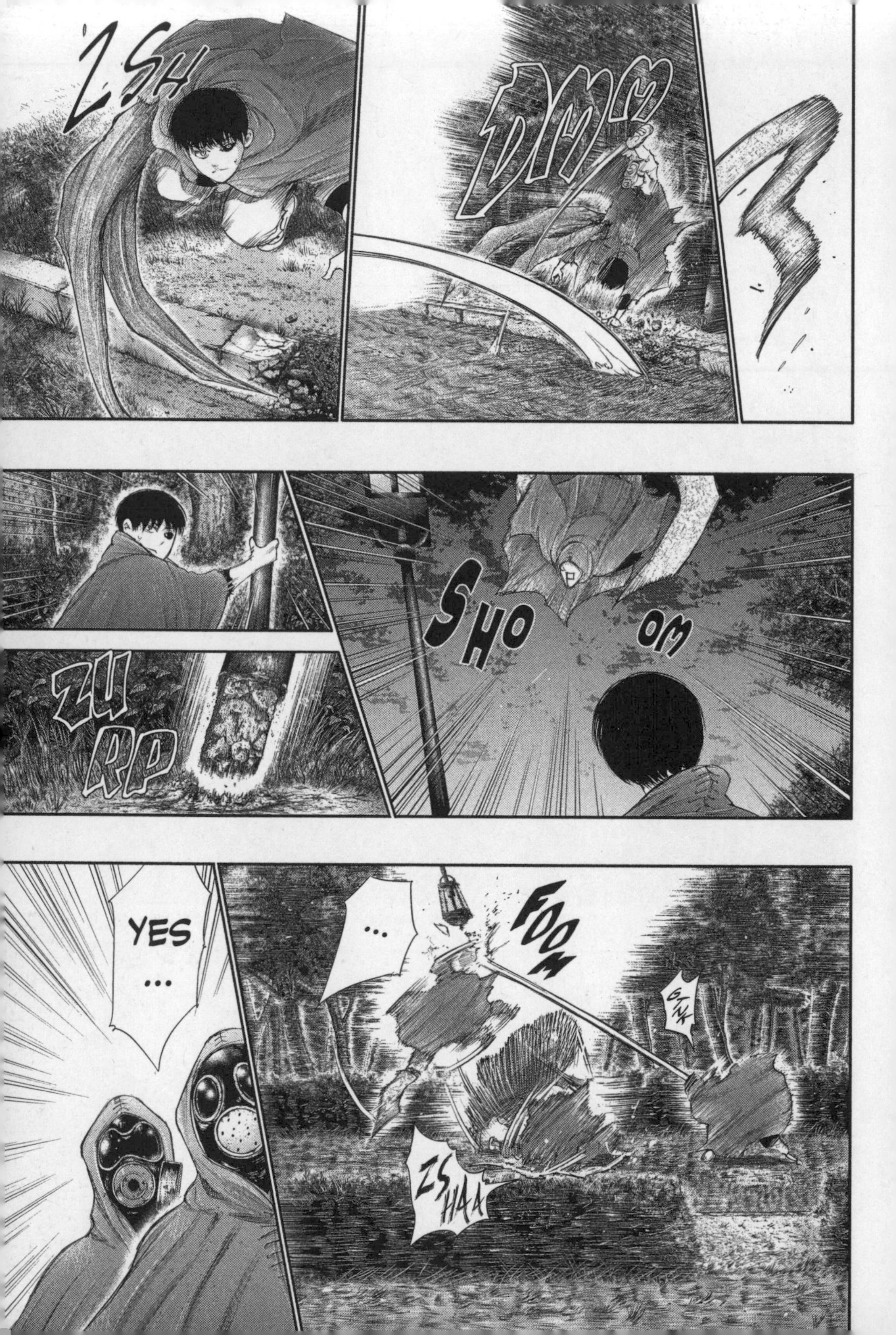
DMM
ZSH
SHO OM
ZURP
...
FOOM
GINK
ZSHAA
YES ...

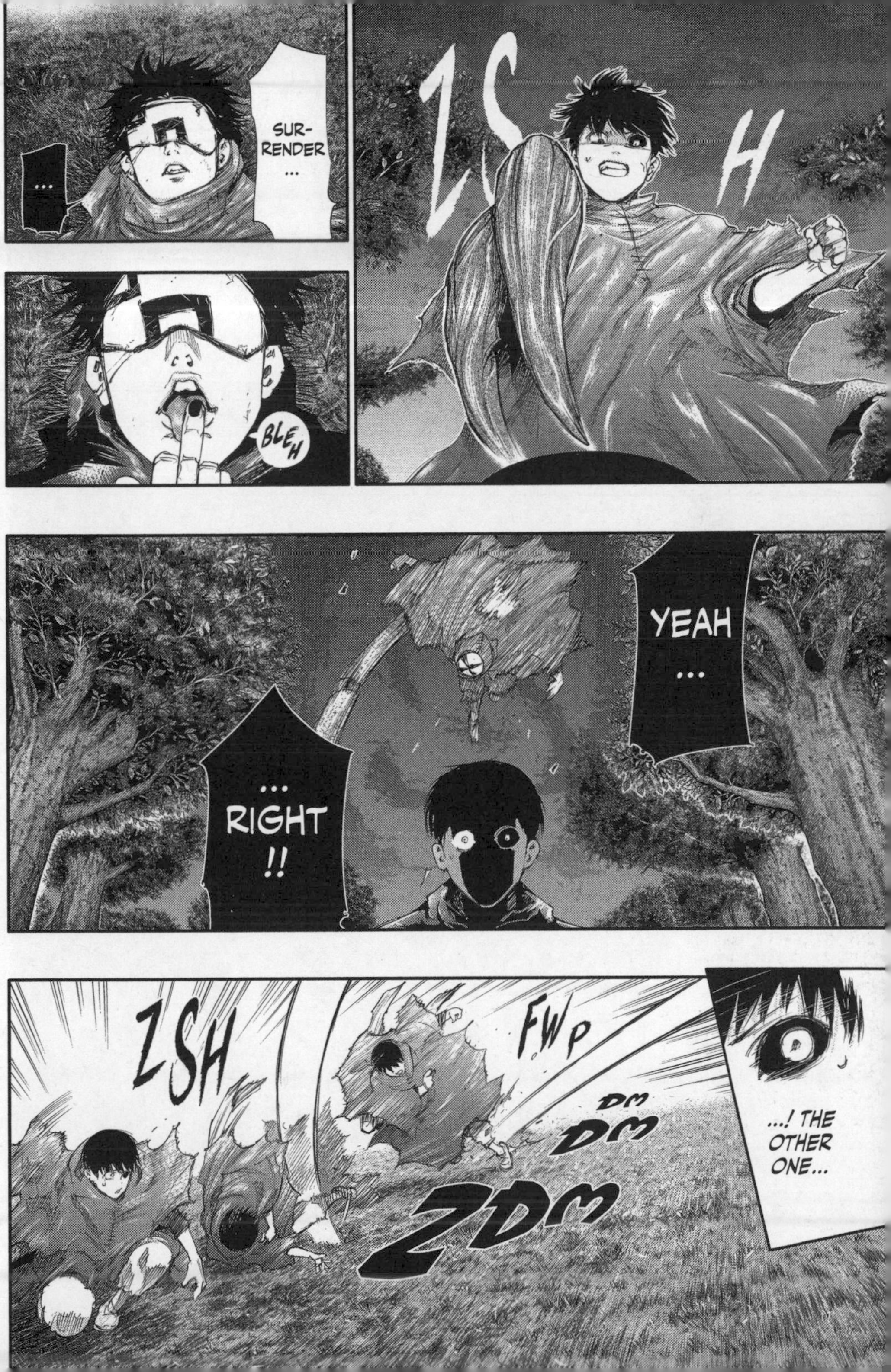
ZSH
SUR-RENDER ...
...
BLEH
YEAH ...
... RIGHT !!
...! THE OTHER ONE...
FWP
ZSH
DM DM
ZDM

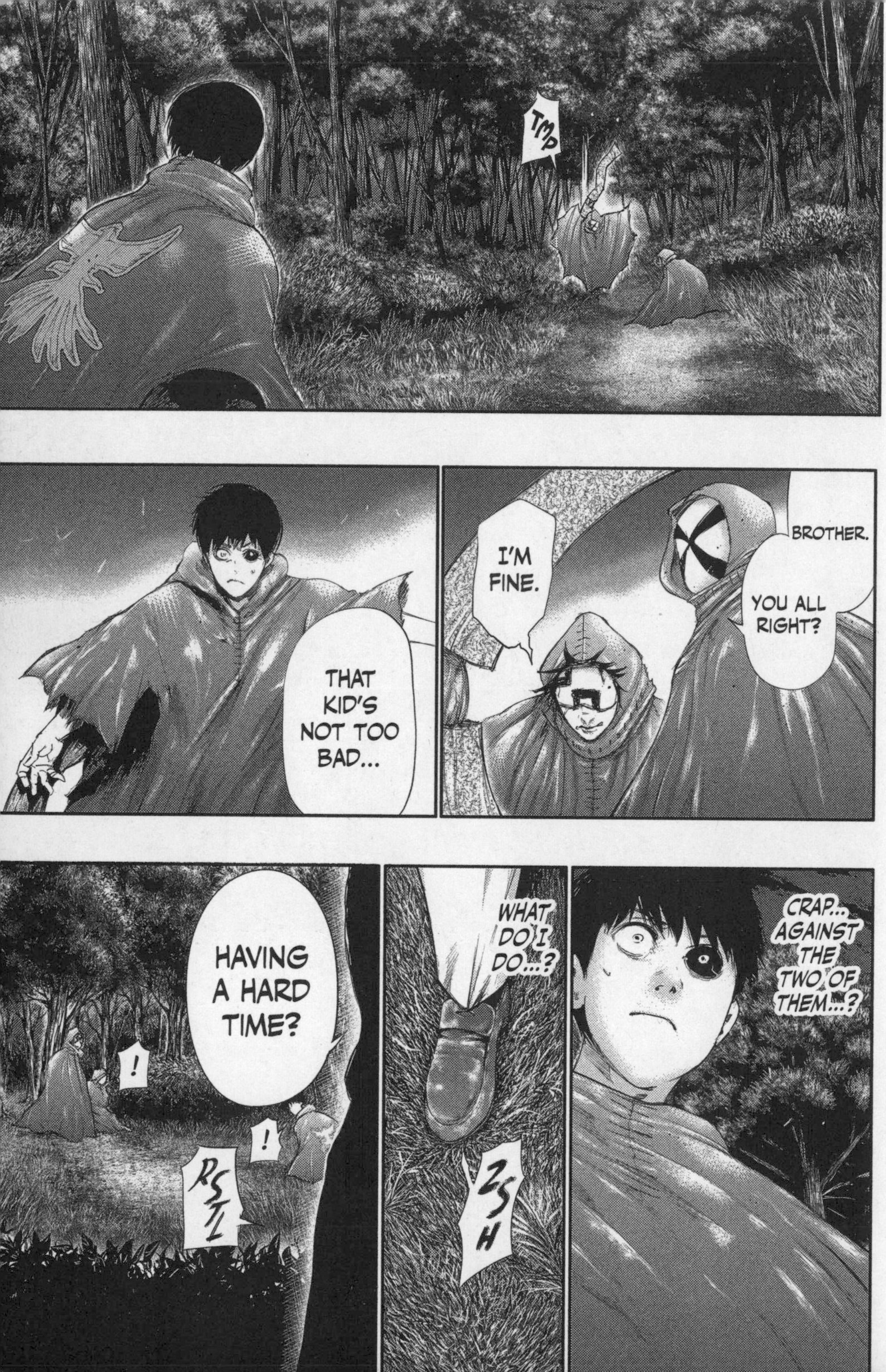
TMP
BROTHER.
YOU ALL RIGHT?
I'M FINE.
THAT KID'S NOT TOO BAD...
CRAP... AGAINST THE TWO OF THEM...?
WHAT DO I DO...?
ZSH
HAVING A HARD TIME?
!
!
RSTL

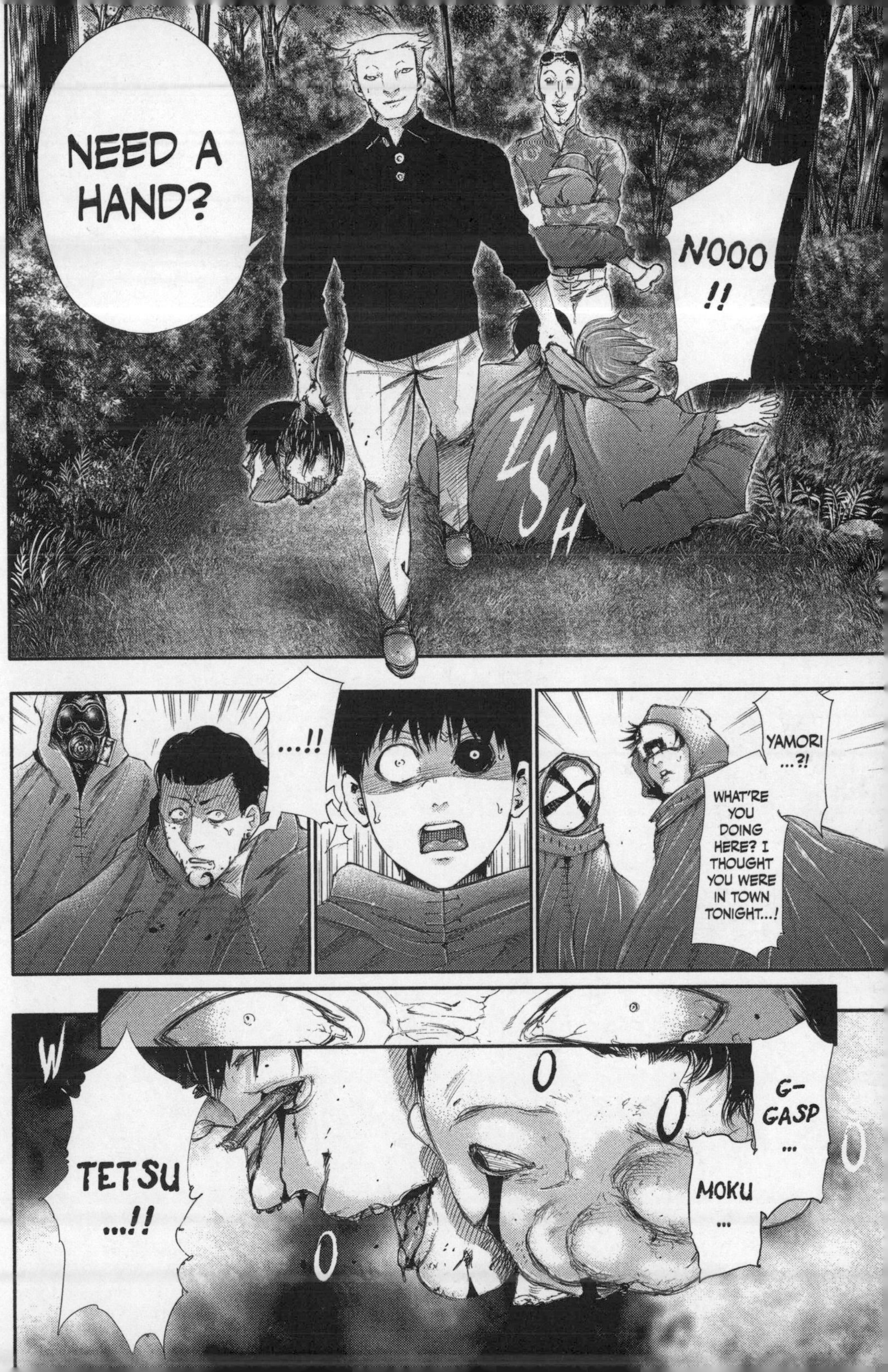
NOOO !!
NEED A HAND?
ZSH
YAMORI ...?!
WHAT'RE YOU DOING HERE? I THOUGHT YOU WERE IN TOWN TONIGHT...!
...!!
G-GASP ...
MOKU ...
OOOO
TETSU ...!!
W

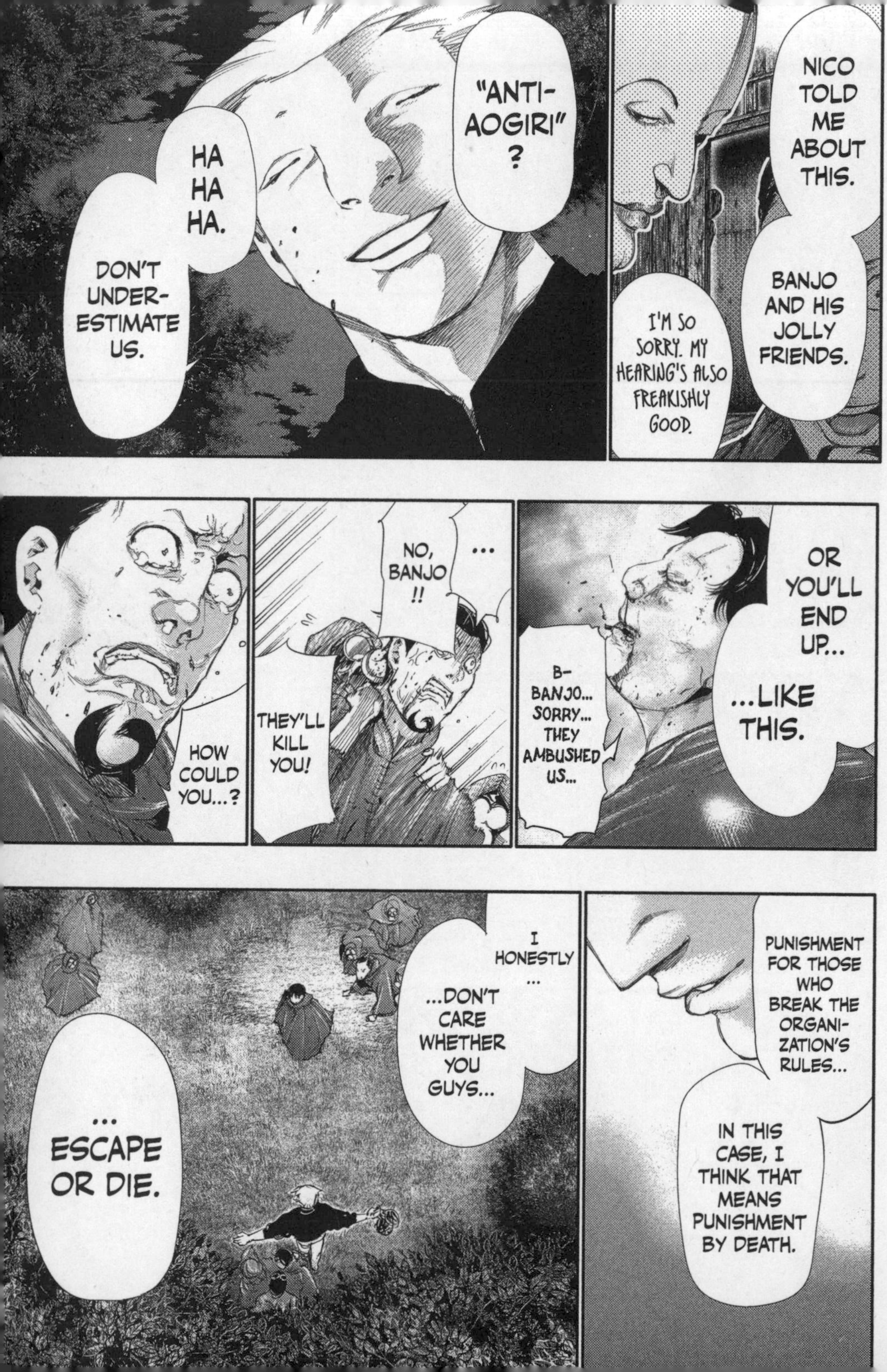
NICO TOLD ME ABOUT THIS.
BANJO AND HIS JOLLY FRIENDS.
I'M SO SORRY. MY HEARING'S ALSO FREAKISHLY GOOD.
"ANTI-AOGIRI"?
HA HA HA.
DON'T UNDER-ESTIMATE US.
OR YOU'LL END UP...
...LIKE THIS.
B-BANJO... SORRY... THEY AMBUSHED US...
...
NO, BANJO!!
THEY'LL KILL YOU!
HOW COULD YOU...?
PUNISHMENT FOR THOSE WHO BREAK THE ORGANIZATION'S RULES...
IN THIS CASE, I THINK THAT MEANS PUNISHMENT BY DEATH.
I HONESTLY...
...DON'T CARE WHETHER YOU GUYS...
...ESCAPE OR DIE.

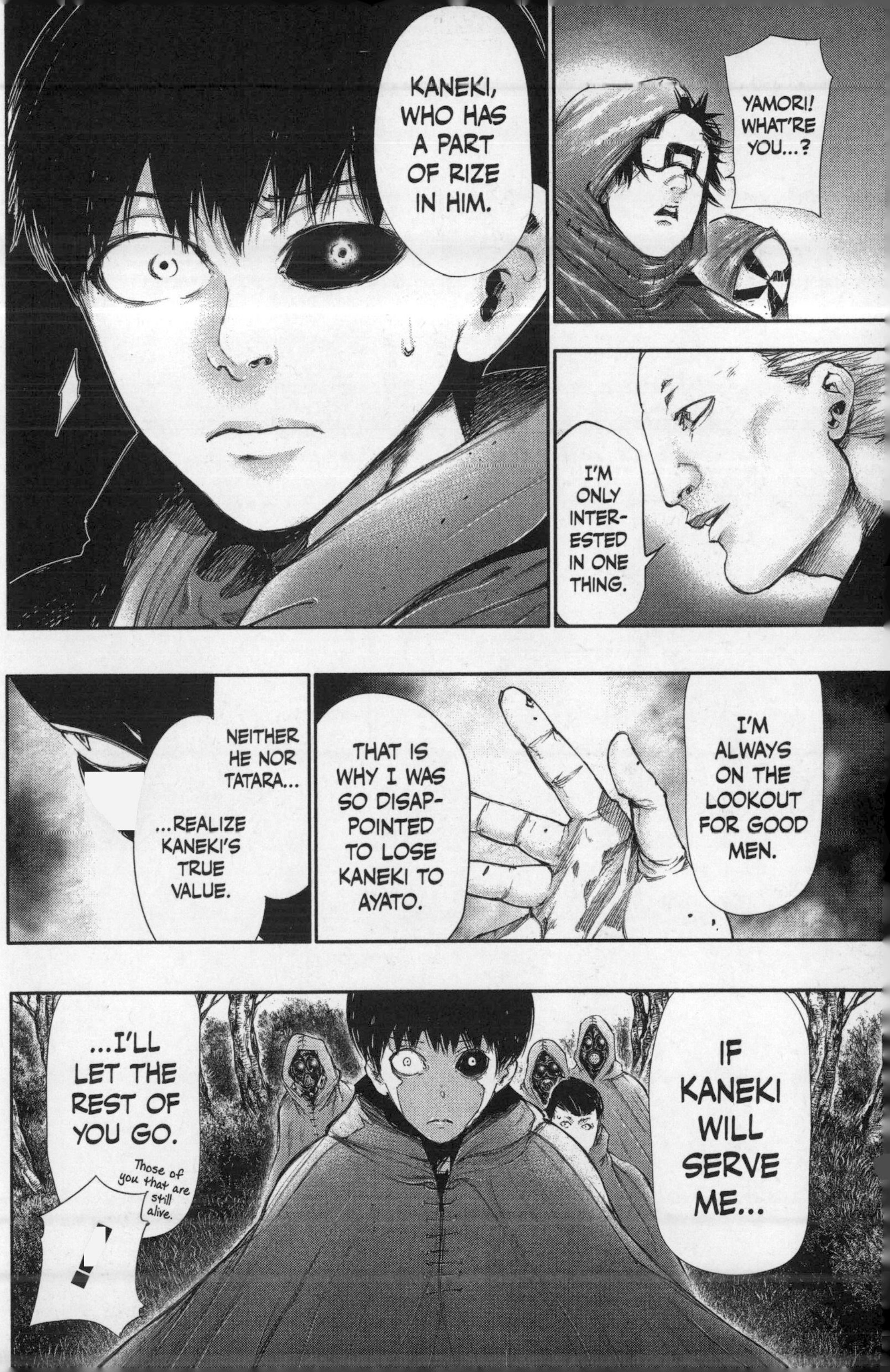
YAMORI! WHAT'RE YOU...?
I'M ONLY INTERESTED IN ONE THING.
KANEKI, WHO HAS A PART OF RIZE IN HIM.
I'M ALWAYS ON THE LOOKOUT FOR GOOD MEN.
THAT IS WHY I WAS SO DISAPPOINTED TO LOSE KANEKI TO AYATO.
NEITHER HE NOR TATARA...
...REALIZE KANEKI'S TRUE VALUE.
IF KANEKI WILL SERVE ME...
...I'LL LET THE REST OF YOU GO.
Those of you that are still alive.

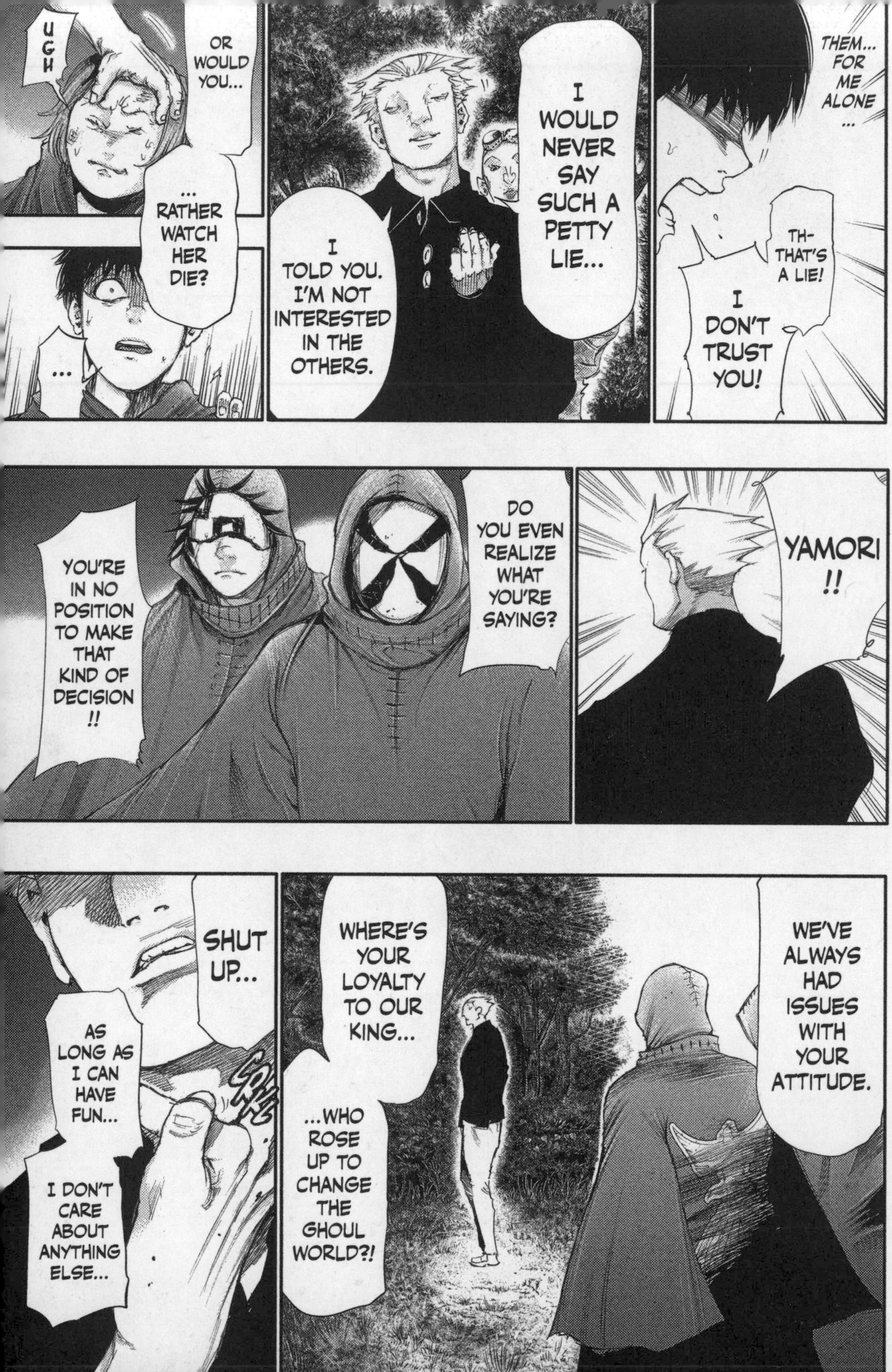
THEM... FOR ME ALONE ...
TH-THAT'S A LIE!
I DON'T TRUST YOU!
I WOULD NEVER SAY SUCH A PETTY LIE...
I TOLD YOU. I'M NOT INTERESTED IN THE OTHERS.
OR WOULD YOU...
UGH
...RATHER WATCH HER DIE?
...
YAMORI !!
DO YOU EVEN REALIZE WHAT YOU'RE SAYING?
YOU'RE IN NO POSITION TO MAKE THAT KIND OF DECISION !!
WE'VE ALWAYS HAD ISSUES WITH YOUR ATTITUDE.
WHERE'S YOUR LOYALTY TO OUR KING...
...WHO ROSE UP TO CHANGE THE GHOUL WORLD?!
SHUT UP...
AS LONG AS I CAN HAVE FUN...
I DON'T CARE ABOUT ANYTHING ELSE...

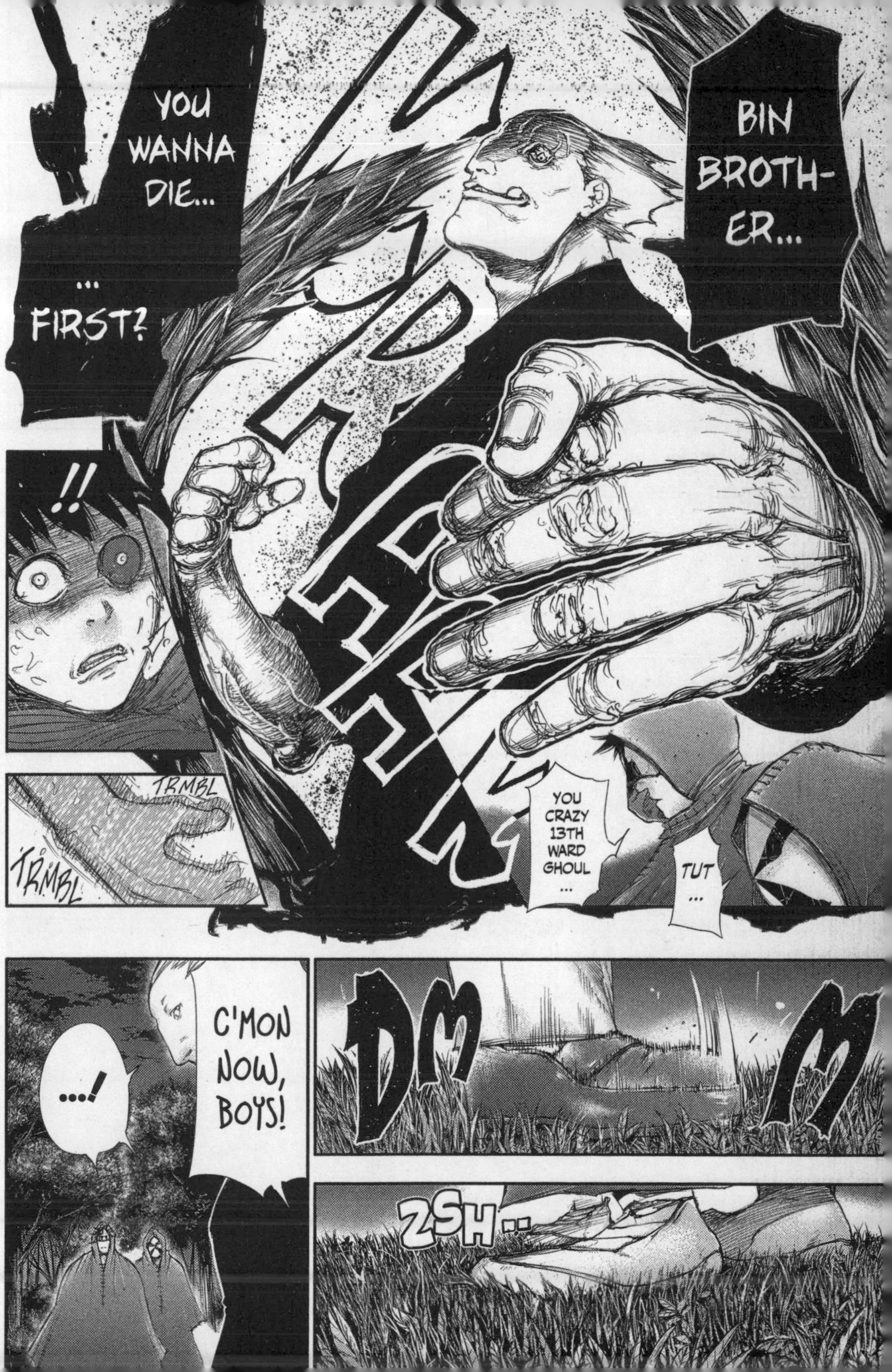
BIN BROTHER-ER...
YOU WANNA DIE...
...FIRST?
YOU CRAZY 13TH WARD GHOUL...
TUT...
!!
TRMBL
TRMBL
DM
M
ZSH..
C'MON NOW, BOYS!
...!

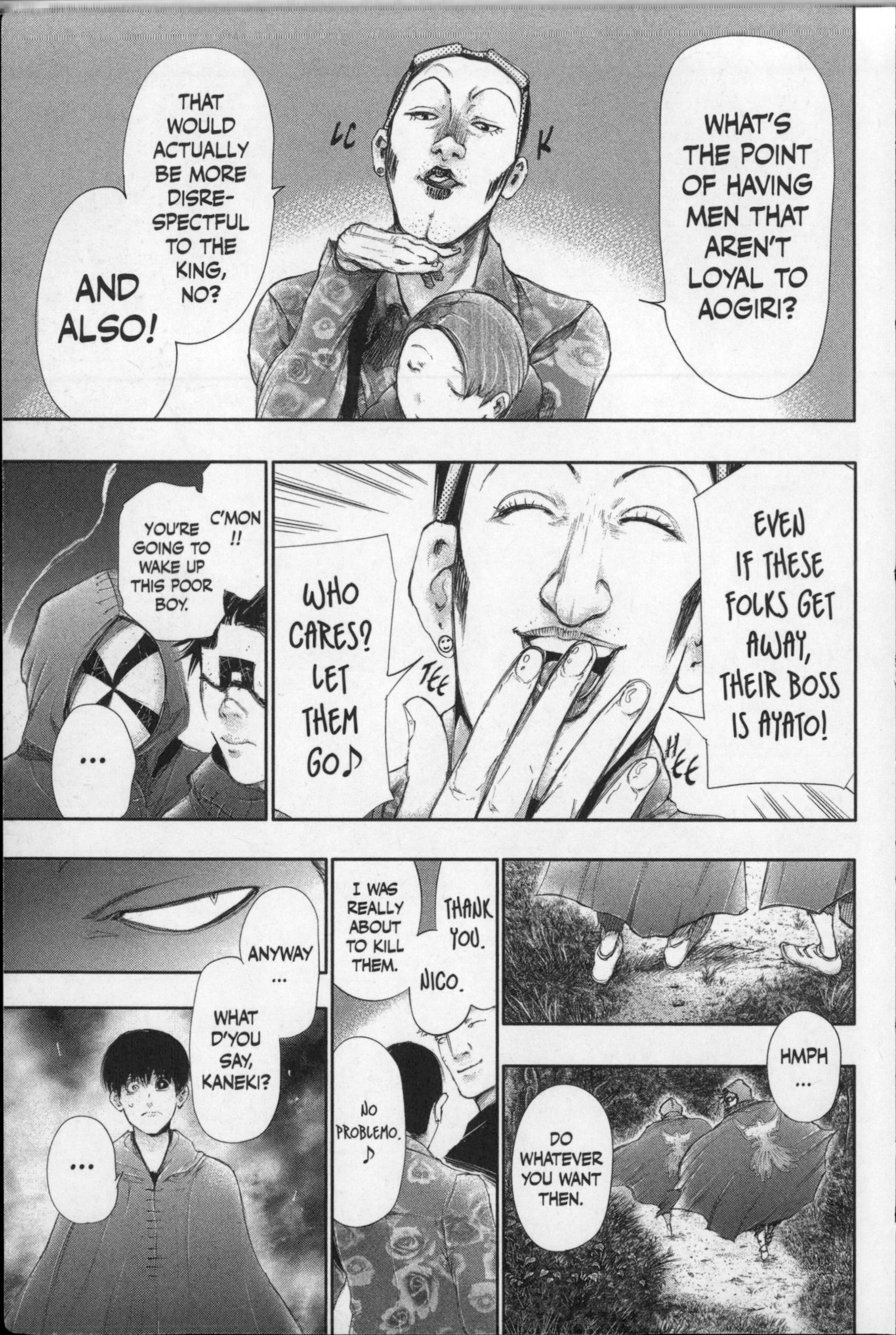
WHAT'S THE POINT OF HAVING MEN THAT AREN'T LOYAL TO AOGIRI?
THAT WOULD ACTUALLY BE MORE DISRE-SPECTFUL TO THE KING, NO?
AND ALSO!
EVEN IF THESE FOLKS GET AWAY, THEIR BOSS IS AYATO!
HEE
TEE
WHO CARES? LET THEM GO♪
C'MON !!
YOU'RE GOING TO WAKE UP THIS POOR BOY.
...
HMPH ...
DO WHATEVER YOU WANT THEN.
THANK YOU.
I WAS REALLY ABOUT TO KILL THEM.
NICO.
NO PROBLEMO. ♪
ANYWAY ...
WHAT D'YOU SAY, KANEKI?
...

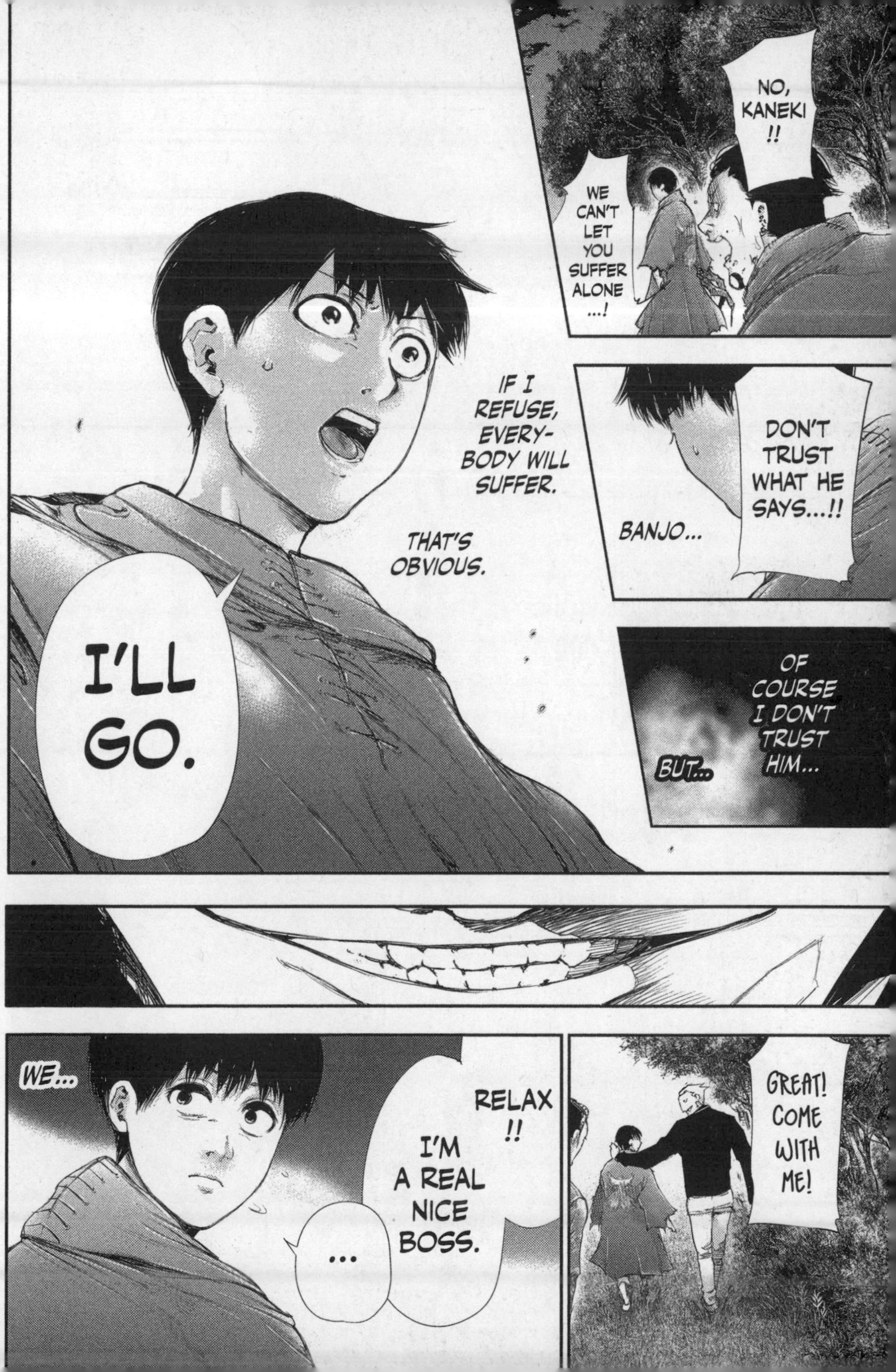
NO, KANEKI !!
WE CAN'T LET YOU SUFFER ALONE ...!
DON'T TRUST WHAT HE SAYS...!!
BANJO...
OF COURSE I DON'T TRUST HIM...
BUT...
IF I REFUSE, EVERY-BODY WILL SUFFER.
THAT'S OBVIOUS.
I'LL GO.
GREAT! COME WITH ME!
RELAX !!
I'M A REAL NICE BOSS.
...
WE...

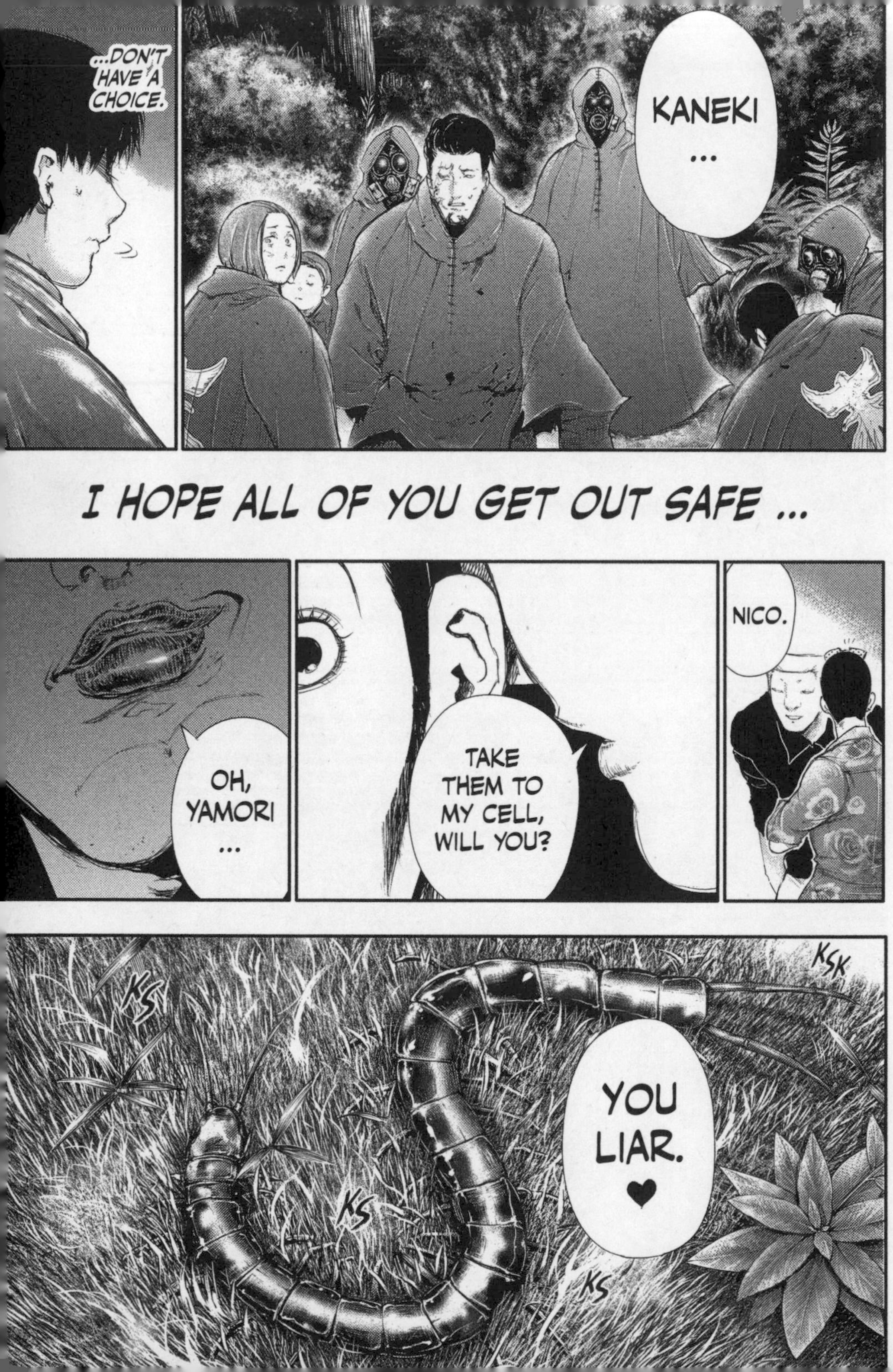
KANEKI ...
...DON'T HAVE A CHOICE.
I HOPE ALL OF YOU GET OUT SAFE ...
NICO.
TAKE THEM TO MY CELL, WILL YOU?
OH, YAMORI ...
KSK
YOU LIAR. ♥
KS
KS
KS

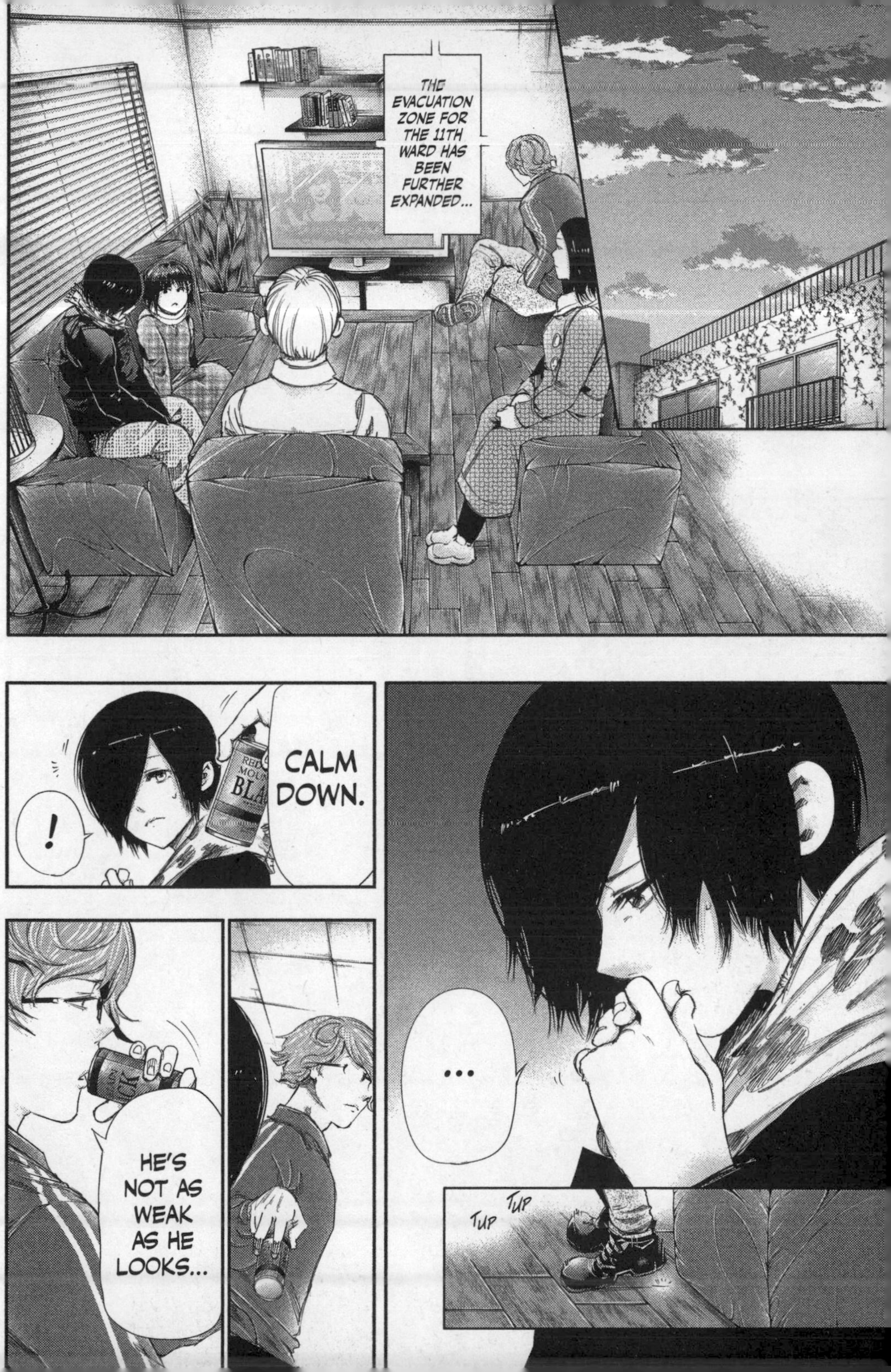
THE EVACUATION ZONE FOR THE 11TH WARD HAS BEEN FURTHER EXPANDED...
...
TUP TUP
CALM DOWN.
!
HE'S NOT AS WEAK AS HE LOOKS...

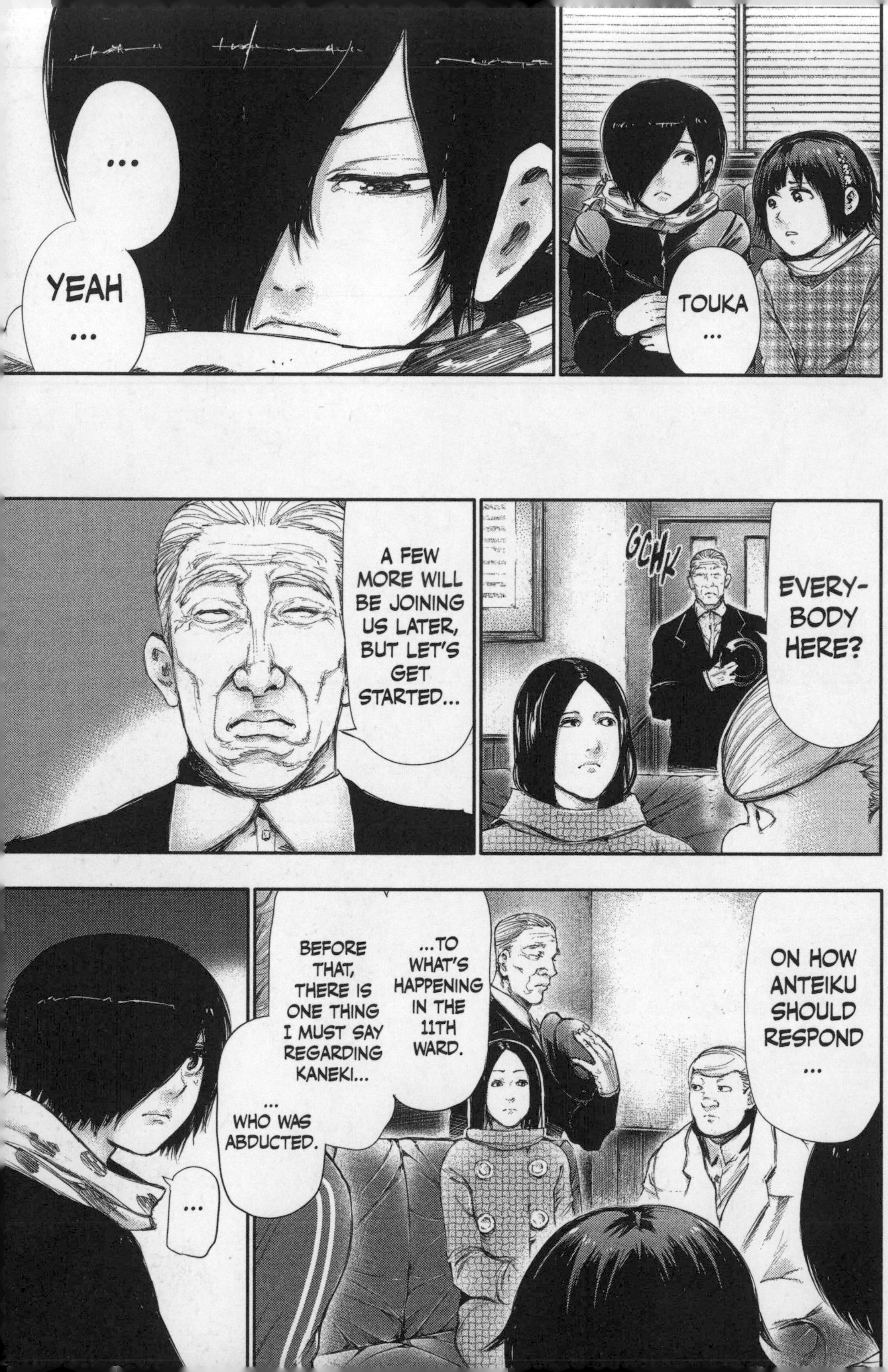
TOUKA ...
...
YEAH ...
GCHK
EVERY-BODY HERE?
A FEW MORE WILL BE JOINING US LATER, BUT LET'S GET STARTED...
ON HOW ANTEIKU SHOULD RESPOND ...
...TO WHAT'S HAPPENING IN THE 11TH WARD.
BEFORE THAT, THERE IS ONE THING I MUST SAY REGARDING KANEKI...
... WHO WAS ABDUCTED.
...

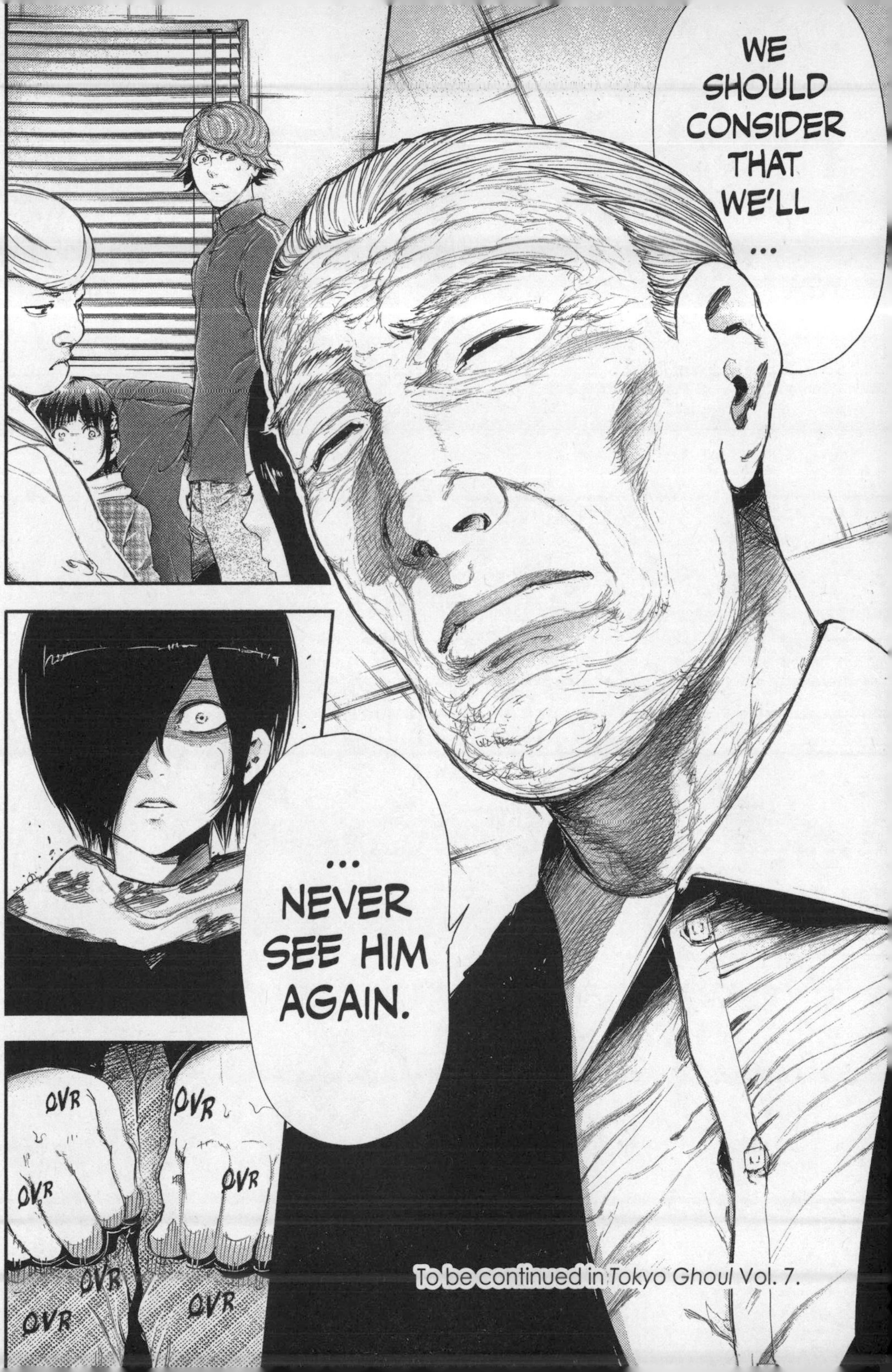
WE SHOULD CONSIDER THAT WE'LL ...
... NEVER SEE HIM AGAIN.
QVR
QVR
QVR
QVR
QVR
QVR
QVR
To be continued in *Tokyo Ghoul* Vol. 7.

# Tokyo Ghoul

## Sui Ishida

Staff eda Mizuki Ide
Ryuji Miyamoto Matsuzaki

Help Hirose-san

Thanks Ririnra-san

Design Hideaki Shimada (L.S.D.)

Cover Miyuki Takaoka (POCKET)

Editor Jumpei Matsuo

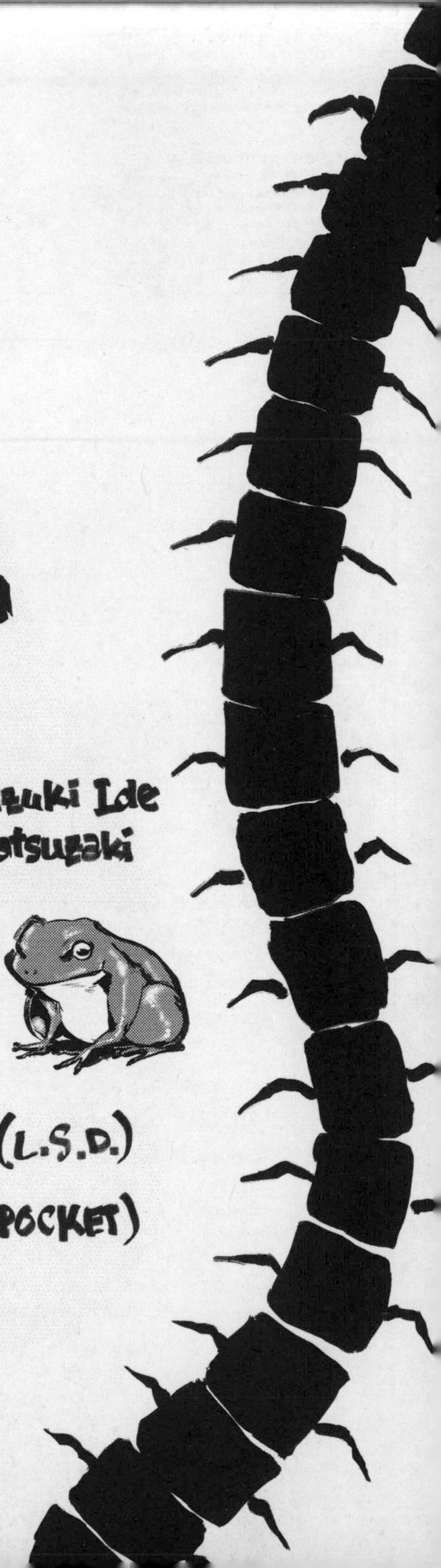

# Mr. Shinohara's SPECIAL LECTURE

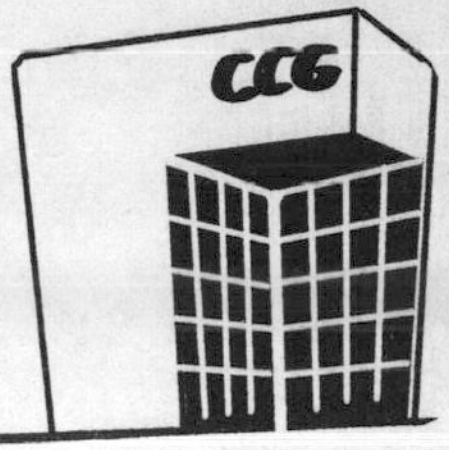
CCG

**Ghoul Investigator and (CCG) Bureau Investigator**

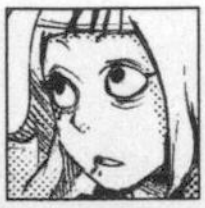

Sir, I was wondering...

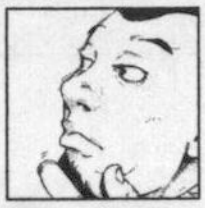

Mm?

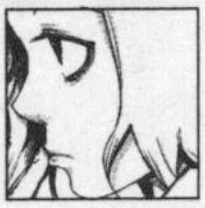

Is everybody at CCG graduates of the Academy?

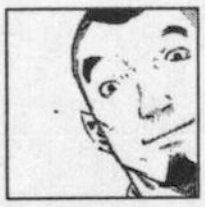

Not everybody…

Amon and Seido, Hoji, me and Mado, and Maru too are all Academy graduates.

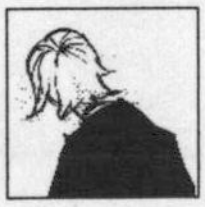

I feel left out...

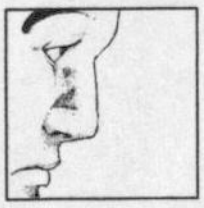

There are non-Academy graduates too. They were trained at a place called the Ghoul Countermeasure Training Center. They are CCG Bureau Investigators. The guy who partnered with Amon and investigated the Rabbit was a Bureau Investigator of the 20th Ward.

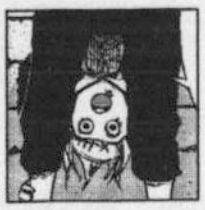

This man? →

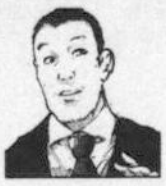

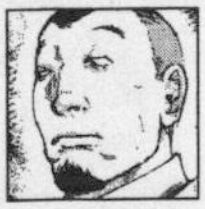

That guy. The CCG is made up of Ghoul Investigators, or Academy graduates that investigate and capture Ghouls, and Bureau Investigators, or Ghoul Countermeasure Training Center graduates that do administrative work and assist Ghoul Investigators.

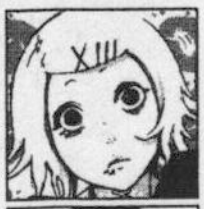

Ghoul Investigators and Bureau Investigators... But do Bureau people enjoy only assisting? Don't they want to get crazy like Ghoul Investigators?

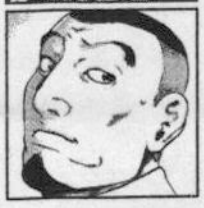

Not everybody is like you.
You risk your life daily on this job. It's hard both physically and emotionally.
Bureau work can be fulfilling too. And it's stable.

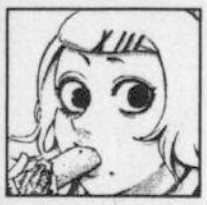

What's the difference between Ghoul Investigators and Bureau Investigators?

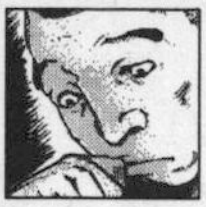

Let's see… Small things here and there. The biggest difference is probably Quinques. Quinques are special weapons given only to Ghoul Investigators. Big ones take a long time to master and they have to be the right match for you.

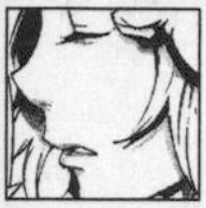

Nobody taught me.

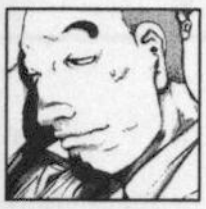

Well, yours is a small Quinque…Oh yeah, the starting ranks are different too. Academy graduates start off as Rank 2 Investigators. Bureau Investigators start off as Rank 3 Investigators.

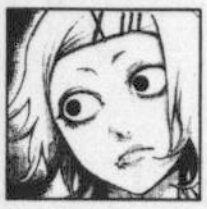

So there's a one-rank difference from the get-go?

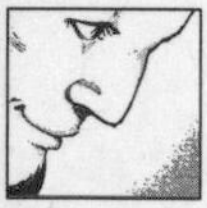

Exactly. There's also a difference in the speed of promotions too. Ghoul Investigators are required to learn how to handle a Quinque as well as in-depth knowledge of Ghoul physiology and psychology. They are anti-Ghoul specialists. For that, they get promoted faster.

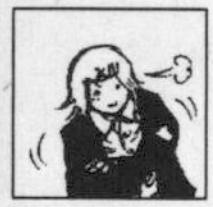

Ooh, a chance to get rich.

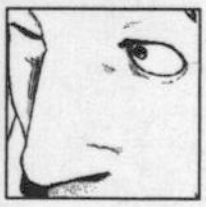

We don't have much time to spend it though. Another difference is where we're stationed after graduating. Bureau Investigators are directly assigned to CCG Branch Offices, but Ghoul Investigators are only assigned to the Main Office, the 1st Ward. We conduct investigations in each ward as an Investigator assigned to 1st Ward.

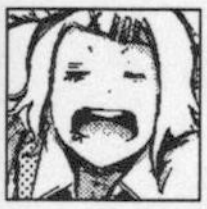

Hmm... So Ghoul Investigators get to go all over the place. Sounds fun.

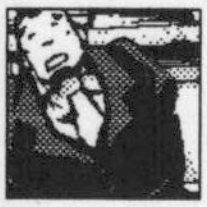

That's your only response to everything I just said?

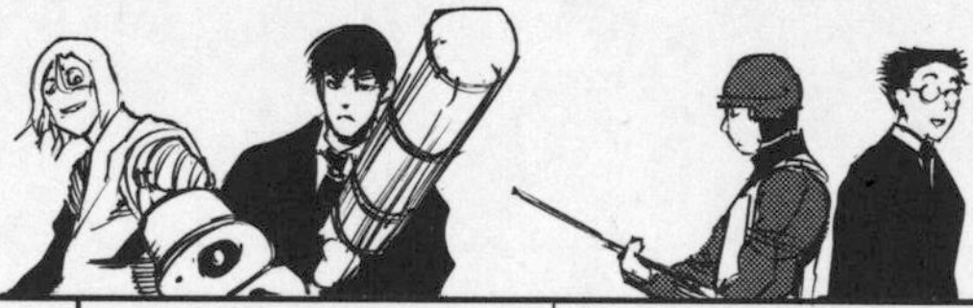

| | GHOUL INVESTIGATORS | CCG BUREAU INVESTIGATORS |
|---|---|---|
| Training | (Academy)<br>Ghoul Investigator training | Ghoul Countermeasure |
| Equipment | Quinque/Various small arms | Handguns/Rifle (firing Q Bullets) |
| Training Duration | 2 Years | 1 Year |
| Starting Rank | Rank 2 Investigator | Rank 3 Investigator |
| Post-Grad Station | 1st Ward (Main Office),<br>24th Ward (*Posted at 1st Ward, Investigate all wards) | Wards 2-23 |

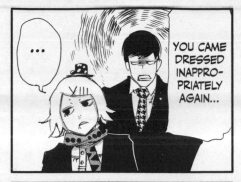

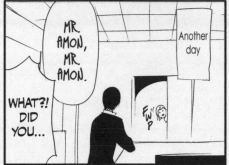

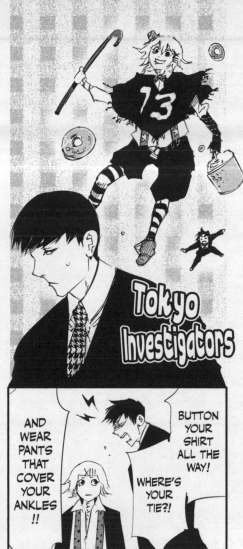

Tokyo Investigators
13
BUTTON YOUR SHIRT ALL THE WAY!
WHERE'S YOUR TIE?!
AND WEAR PANTS THAT COVER YOUR ANKLES!!
XIII
The next day
YOU ...!!
MORNING.
DR OOP
YOU CAME DRESSED INAPPROPRIATELY AGAIN...
...
XIII
Another day
MR. AMON, MR. AMON.
WHAT?! DID YOU...
FWP
I BOUGHT THE LATEST DONUTS FROM DONUT MEISTER.
YOU WANT SOME?
XIII
Donut 3 Meister
WE'LL TALK ABOUT YOUR ATTIRE LATER...
THIS IS GOOD.

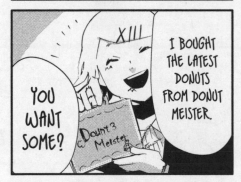

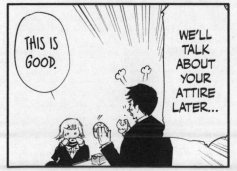

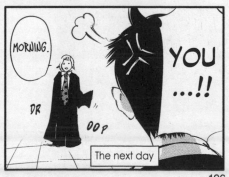

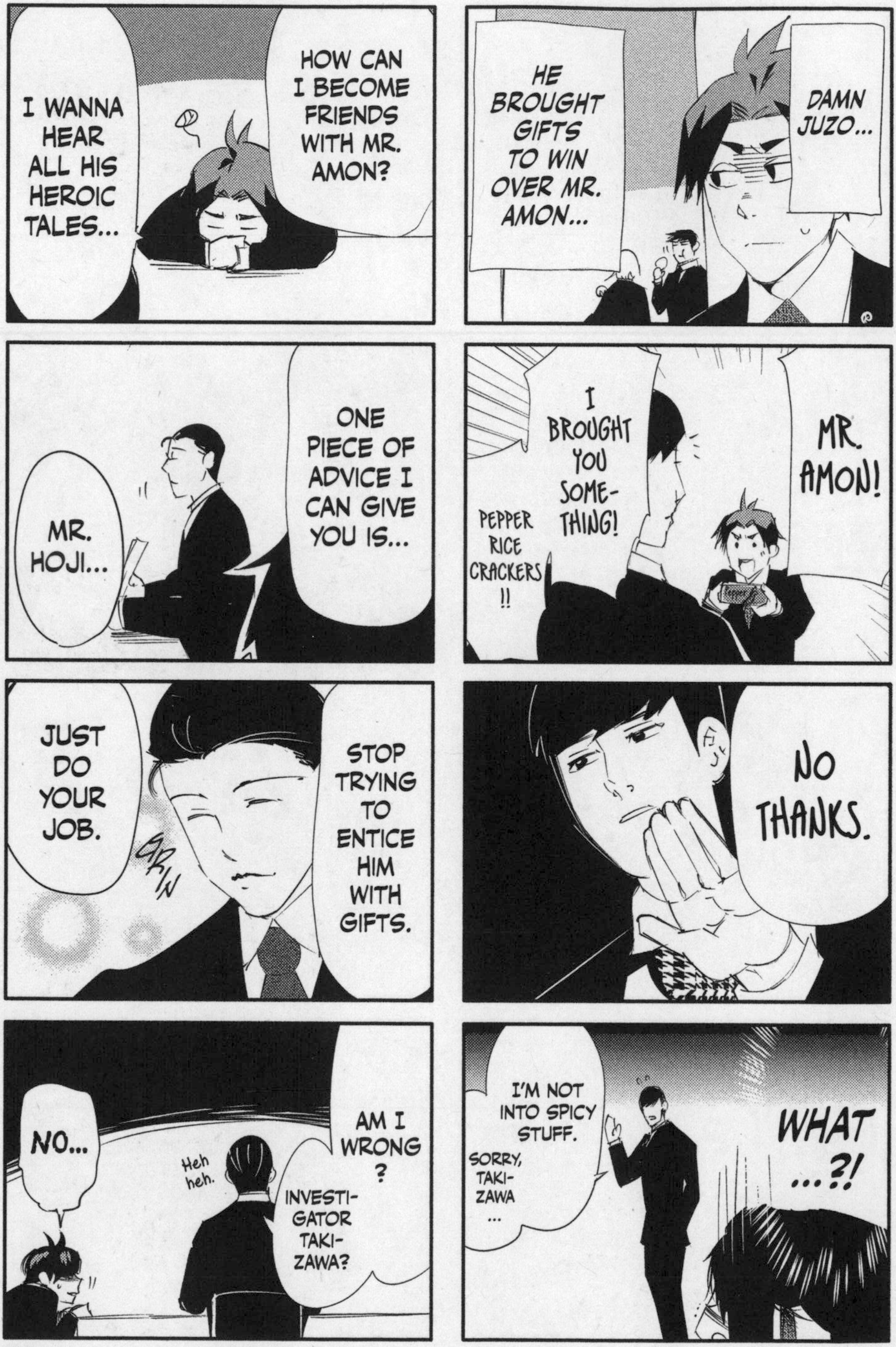
DAMN JUZO...
HE BROUGHT GIFTS TO WIN OVER MR. AMON...
HOW CAN I BECOME FRIENDS WITH MR. AMON?
I WANNA HEAR ALL HIS HEROIC TALES...
MR. AMON!
I BROUGHT YOU SOMETHING!
PEPPER RICE CRACKERS !!
ONE PIECE OF ADVICE I CAN GIVE YOU IS...
MR. HOJI...
NO THANKS.
STOP TRYING TO ENTICE HIM WITH GIFTS.
JUST DO YOUR JOB.
GRIN
WHAT ...?!
I'M NOT INTO SPICY STUFF.
SORRY, TAKIZAWA ...
AM I WRONG ?
INVESTIGATOR TAKIZAWA?
Heh heh.
NO...

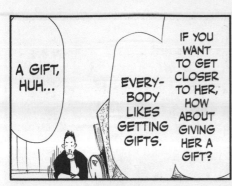

I fight with my built up body. 10% body fat percentage.
2% fight winning percentage.
A 25-year-old who hates pain and insects.
That's who I am. Nice to meet you.
My name is Kazuichi Banjo.
I'm the former leader of 11th Ward Ghouls
I can't even get my kagune out.
IF YOU WANT TO GET CLOSER TO HER, HOW ABOUT GIVING HER A GIFT?
EVERYBODY LIKES GETTING GIFTS.
A GIFT, HUH...
BUT, WOULDN'T IT BE WEIRD IF I ASKED HER MYSELF...?
IT WON'T BE MUCH OF A SURPRISE ...
SO YOU WANT ME TO ASK WHAT SHE WANTS.
YOU'RE SUCH A WUSS.
JIRO ...
HOW LIKELY IS IT THAT RIZE HAS ANY FEELINGS FOR ME...?
LET'S SEE...
RIZE-SAN.
RIZE-SAN.
CAN I ASK YOU SOMETHING...?
I'D SAY IT'S INFINITELY LOWER THAN THE CHANCES OF YOU...
... MAKING HER ANGRY AND GETTING YOUR ASS BEAT.
Ahaha!
...
SHE SAID...
...ANY INTERNAL ORGAN.
OKAY, THANKS ...
SHE'S A GHOUL... I'M A GHOUL TOO...

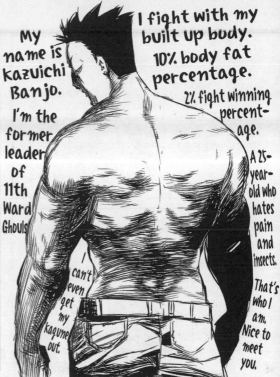

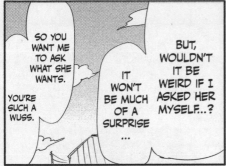

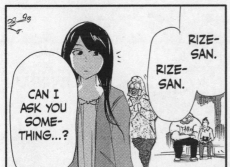

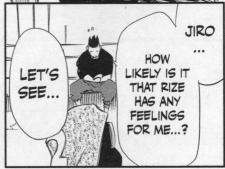

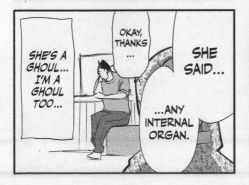

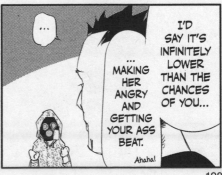

WOMEN LIKE AGGRESSIVE MEN!
ICHIMI.
SANTE... ALL RIGHT.
RIZE!
WHAT A COINCIDENCE!
YEAH.
WHAT A SURPRISE!
HOW ABOUT SOME COFFEE TO GO WITH YOUR BOOK?
You like coffee, don't you?
...
HEY, WHAT'RE YOU READING?! CAN I READ IT TOO?! ALTHOUGH I CAN BARELY READ!
WHAT'S WRONG, BANJO?
SHE SAID I WAS ANNOYING.

...
HE'S BEEN LIKE THAT EVER SINCE RIZE-SAN LEFT THE 11TH WARD.
HE SHOULD'VE TOLD HER HOW MUCH HE LIKES HER THEN.
BANJO.
HOW ABOUT WRITING HER A LETTER?
AND SEND IT TO THAT COFFEE SHOP IN THE 20TH WARD...
YOU SAYING THAT KNOWING I'VE NEVER GONE TO SCHOOL...?
I can only write my name.
!
Banj



Volume 7 will be out in June.

Hope you pick up a copy.

TOKYO GHOUL

THIS IS THE LAST PAGE

TOKYO GHOUL READS RIGHT TO LEFT

# TOKYO GHOUL
東京喰種

VOLUME 6
VIZ Signature Edition

Story and art by
**SUI ISHIDA**


First published in Japan in 2011 by
SHUEISHA Inc., Tokyo.
English translation rights arranged by
SHUEISHA Inc.

TRANSLATION. Joe Yamazaki

TOUCH-UP ART AND LETTERING. Vanessa Satone

DESIGN. Fawn Lau

EDITOR. Joel Enos



Printed in the U.S.A.

Published by VIZ Media, LLC
P.O. Box 77010
San Francisco, CA 94107

10 9 8 7 6 5 4 3 2 1
First printing, April 2016

viz media
www.viz.com

RATED T+ FOR OLDER TEEN

**PARENTAL ADVISORY**
TOKYO GHOUL is rated T+ for Older Teen and is recommended for ages 16 and up. This volume contains violence and gore.
ratings.viz.com

VIZ SIGNATURE